INSIDE RURAL IRELAND

INSIDE RURAL IRELAND

POWER AND CHANGE SINCE INDEPENDENCE

edited by

TOMÁS FINN AND TONY VARLEY

UNIVERSITY COLLEGE DUBLIN PRESS
PREAS CHOLÁISTE OLLSCOILE BHAILE ÁTHA CLIATH
2024

First published 2024
by University College Dublin Press
UCD Humanities Institute, Room H103,
Belfield,
Dublin 4

www.ucdpress.ie

ISBN 978-17-3-90863-67

CIP data available from the British Library

Typeset in Dublin by Gough Typesetting Limited
Text design by Lyn Davies
Printed in England on acid-free paper by
CPI Antony Rowe, Chippenham, Wiltshire

In Memory of Tom Fitzgerald and Diarmuid Ó Cearbhaill

Contents

THE CONTEMPORARY COUNTRYSIDE

Biographies

Tomás Finn is a Lecturer in History at the University of Galway and is currently a member of the Social Sciences Research Centre at the University of Galway. He has published a book and articles on the role of intellectuals and the influence of ideas in the modernisation of Ireland. His monograph *Tuairim, Intellectual Debate and Policy formulation: Rethinking Ireland, 1954-75* was published by Manchester University Press in 2012.

Tony Varley is a former Senior Lecturer in Political Science and Sociology and is now a member of the Social Sciences Research Centre at the University of Galway. He has co-edited *A Living Countryside? The Politics of Sustainable Development in Rural Ireland* (Ashgate, 2009), *Integration through Subordination: The Politics of Agricultural Modernisation in Industrial Europe* (Brepols, 2013), and *Land Questions in Modern Ireland* (Manchester University Press, 2013).

Anne Byrne is Professor Emerita, School of Political Science and Sociology, University of Galway. Located in the sociology of the Irish family, previous publications concern gender and identity, singleness and stigma, family secrets, gender issues in family farming and agriculture, and the historiography of the Harvard-Irish social anthropological mission to Ireland in the 1930s. Current book projects concern the visit of Virginia Woolf and Leonard Woolf to Ireland in 1934 and the epistolary friendships of Nancy Nolan and Leonard Woolf (1943-1969).

Anne Cassidy has a Bachelor of Arts in History and Sociological and Political Studies and a Masters in Community Development, both from the University of Galway. Her PhD (University of Galway) focused on the impact of belonging to the farming community on young university students and their role in the succession process in Irish farming. She has been working with Galway Rural Development since 2018 and is the Senior Manager for the Social Inclusion Community Activation Programme (SICAP).

Mary Cawley, Senior Lecturer Emerita, School of Geography, Archaeology and Irish Studies, is Adjunct-Professor, Social-Economic Marine Research Unit (SEMRU), College of Business, Public Policy and Law, University of Galway. Mary has special research interests in rural societal change and development. Her sole and joint publications on population themes are in edited collections and journals, including *Irish Geography, Journal of Ethnic and Migration Studies, Journal of Rural Studies, Population, Space and Place* and *Sociologia Ruralis*.

Caitriona Clear is a former Senior Lecturer in History in the University of Galway. Her research interests include many aspects of nineteenth and twentieth-century social and cultural history. Caitriona's last book was *Women's Voices in Ireland: Women's Magazines in the 1950s and 60s* (Bloomsbury Publishing, 2016) and she is a contributor to the *Cambridge History of Ireland* Vol. IV (2018).

Mary E. Daly is Professor Emeritus in Modern Irish History at University College Dublin. She is a member (and former President), of the Royal Irish Academy and the Academia Europaea. A graduate of University College Dublin and Oxford University, she was awarded honorary doctorates by the National University of Ireland and Queen's University Belfast and she is an Honorary Fellow of the Royal College of Physicians of Ireland. Recent publications include *Sixties Ireland: Reshaping the Economy, State and Society* (Cambridge University Press, 2016); *The Social History of Modern Ireland,* (co-edited with Eugenio Biagini (Cambridge University Press, 2017) and *The Battle to Control Female Fertility in Modern Ireland* (Cambridge University Press, 2023).

Eoin Devereux is Professor and Co-Director of the Centre for the Study of Popular Music and Popular Culture at the University of Limerick and Adjunct Professor in Contemporary Culture at the University of Jyvaskyla, Finland. Widely published on music and media, his most recent book (co-edited with Martin J. Power) is *Always Different, Always The Same: Critical Essays on The Fall* (Rowman and Littlefield, 2023). A creative writer, his work has been published and broadcast in numerous settings including *The Irish Times* and RTÉ Radio 1.

Bryan Fanning is Professor of Migration and Social Policy at University College Dublin. He has published extensively on migration, social change in Ireland and on Irish intellectual history. His previous books include *Quest for a Modern Ireland: The Battle of Ideas 1912–1986* (Irish Academic Press, 2012), *Histories of the Irish Future* (Bloomsbury Publishing, 2014), *Diverse Republic* (University College Dublin Press, 2021) and *Public Morality and the Culture Wars: The Triple Divide* (Emerald Publishing, 2023).

Maria Feeney holds a doctorate in sociology and has held numerous teaching and research positions at Maynooth University, Froebel College of Education, Dublin City University and the Church of Ireland Centre, Dublin City University. She has co-authored two books *Church, State and Social Science in Ireland: Knowledge Institutions and the Rebalancing of Power, 1937–73* (Manchester University Press 2016) with Peter Murray and *Come & C Growing in the Image & Likeness of God. A Review of the Discipleship Project* and *Five Marks of Mission in the United Dioceses of Dublin and Glendalough* (SPELL Training and Development 2019) with David Tuohy.

Peter Murray is a member of the Maynooth University Social Science Institute (MUSSI). He has contributed to a wide variety of historical and social science journals as well as to a substantial number of edited collections. His book *Facilitating the Future? US Aid, European Integration and Irish Industrial Viability, 1948-73* was published by UCD Press in 2009 and he is the co-author (with Maria Feeney) of *Church State and Social Science in Ireland: Knowledge Institutions and the Rebalancing of Power, 1937-73* which was published in 2016 by Manchester University Press.

Mícheál Ó Fathartaigh is an historian of modern Ireland who is a specialist in agricultural and rural history. He is a member of the Social Sciences Research Centre at the University of Galway and a research fellow at the Archives of Rural History in Bern. To date, he has published four books, two of which concern agricultural and rural history: *Irish Agriculture Nationalised: The Dairy Disposal Company and the Making of the Modern Irish Dairy Industry* (Institute of Public Administration, 2014) and *Developing Rural Ireland: A History of the Irish Agricultural Advisory Services* (Wordwell Books, 2021).

Gearóid Ó Tuathaigh is Professor Emeritus in History at the University of Galway. His academic publications – in Irish and English – relate mainly to modern Irish history and they include essays on land and society in nineteenth and twentieth century Ireland. Recently publications, as editor and contributor, include *The GAA & Revolution in Ireland 1913–1923* (Collins Press, 2015) and *An Piarsach agus 1916: Briathar, Beart agus Oidhreacht* (Cló Iar-Chonnacht Teo, 2016).

Tanya Watson received her PhD from the School of Political Science and Sociology at the University of Galway. She has contributed to several collaborative publications that draw from field research on farm women's lives. These include 'Older Rural Women, Work and Retirement' (with, Nata Duvvury and Áine Ní Léime) in *Rural Gerontology: Towards Critical Perspectives on Rural Ageing* (Routledge, 2020), and 'Finding "Room to Manoeuvre": Gender, Agency and the Family Farm' (with Anne Byrne, Nata Duvvury, and Áine Macken-Walsh) in *Feminisms and Ruralities* (Lexington Books, 2014).

Acknowledgements

This collection of essays has had its origins in a conference held in what is now the University of Galway in June 2018 to mark the acquisition by the James Hardiman library of the archive of Muintir na Tíre, a still-active Irish rural renewal movement that began life in 1931. The conference, which took 'rural Ireland in the twentieth century' as its theme, was convened by a committee in the university that had Caitriona Clear, John Cox, Monica Crump, Tomás Finn, Áine Macken-Walsh, Niall McSweeney and Tony Varley as its members. Among those present at the 2018 conference was the late Tom Fitzgerald, Muintir na Tíre's chief administrator for many decades and someone who more than anyone was responsible for the donation of the archive to the university. Over a long stretch of years Tom had maintained a very close friendship with the late Diarmuid Ó Cearbhaill, a former Dean of the Faculty of Commerce and Statutory Lecturer in Economics in the university and a person with a long-time research interest in Muintir na Tíre. This friendship was crucial in Tom Fitzgerald's decision to look to Galway as a home for the archive that he had carefully safeguarded in Muintir na Tíre's national office, and elsewhere in Tipperary Town, for many decades.

The preliminary work of surveying the Muintir archive, and in making arrangements for its transfer from Tipperary to Galway, was left in the expert hands of the archivist Kieran Hoare of the James Hardiman Library. By the time of the 2018 conference in Galway Fiona Kearney had – at once skilfully and expeditiously – completed the cataloguing of the archive. As well as expressing our heartfelt thanks to Fiona and Kieran, we would like to thank sincerely Professor Chris Curtin, then Vice-President for Innovation and Performance in the university, for his efforts in securing funding to cover the cost of cataloguing the Muintir papers.

Our warmest thanks go to the staff of the Archives and Special Collections department of the James Hardiman Library – Marie Boran, Catriona Cannon, Geraldine Curtin, Margo Donohoe, Jacqueline Finnerty, Kieran Hoare, Barry Houlihan and Aisling Keane – for their much-appreciated advice and assistance during the period when the book was being prepared for publication. A special word of thanks must also go to Caitriona Clear for her dedicated efforts in organising the 2018 conference and for her advice during the early stages of the editing process. We must also thank UCD Press's two readers for their insightful and helpful comments; as well as Peter Moser for his contribution to the 2018 conference and subsequent advice. Much of the actual editing of the book was completed in the Research Room of the University's Social Science Research Centre, and the encouragement and technical assistance of Mike Hynes of the Centre is very much appreciated. Last, but by no means least, the financial assistance towards this publication received from the university's publication fund is gratefully acknowledged.

Abbreviations

ACOT	An Chomhairle Oiliúna Talmhaíochta
AOH	Ancient Order of Hibernians
CAP	Common Agricultural Policy
CDB	Congested Districts Board
CDC	Central Development Committee
CDT	County Development Team
Clann	Clann na Talmhan
CVO	Commission on Vocational Organisation
DAFM	Department of Agriculture, Food and the Marine
DATI	Department of Agriculture and Technical Instruction
DFA	Department of Foreign Affairs
DDA	Dublin Diocesan Archives
DT	Department of the Taoiseach
EDI	Equality, Diversity and Inclusivity
EEC	European Economic Community
EPA	Environmental Protection Agency
EU	European Union
FDI	Foreign Direct Investment
FHM	Farm Home Management
GCC	Galway County Council
GDA	Galway Diocesan Archives
ICA	Irish Countrywomen's Association
ICMSA	Irish Creamery Milk Suppliers' Association
IDA	Industrial Development Authority
IFF	Irish Farmers' Federation
IFS	Irish Free State
IFU	Irish Farmers' Union
IGGA	Irish Grain Growers' Association
Muintir	Muintir na Tíre
NAI	National Archives of Ireland
NCP	National Centre Party
NFA	National Farmers' Association
NFRL	National Farmers' and Ratepayers' League
OEEC	Organisation for European Economic Co-operation
REPS	Rural Environmental Protection Scheme
RFRA	Roscommon Farmers' and Ratepayers' Association
SEA	Socio-Economic Advisor
TD	Teachta Dála
UCC	University College Cork

List of Illustrations

P134_14_271
COVER IMAGE Fr Hayes attending a Rural Week seminar in Cork with other delegates, August 1943 [Muintir na Tíre Collection, P134/15/271].

P134_15_273
Delegates at Rural Week, held at St. Patrick's College, Thurles, August 1962 [Muintir na Tíre Collection, P134/14/273].

P134_15_261
Delegates enjoying an outdoor seminar at Rural Week, held at St. Maccartan's seminary, Monaghan, August 1947 [Muintir na Tíre Collection, P134/15/261].

P134_15_124
Fr Hayes addressing delegates at Rural Week, held in Mungret College, Limerick. Pictured (l to r) Fr McMahon, Rector of Mungret College; P. J. Meghen; Fr Hayes; Most Rev. Patrick O'Neill, Bishop of Limerick; Minister Keyes T.D.; Dr. McKevitt Maynooth, August 1949 [Muintir na Tíre Collection, P134/15/124].

P134_15_092
Some of the walkers on Wexford's first sponsored charity walk for Muintir, August 1973 [Muintir na Tíre Collection, P134/15/92].

P134_15_247
Fr Hayes pictured with Archbishop Cushing and friends at the Archbishop's house in Boston (l to r) Mr. J. Bergin, Boston; Rev. J. Bergin, C.C., Thurles; Very Rev. M. J. Houlihan, St. Patrick's Seminary; Mrs. J. Bergin, Boston; Mr. Joseph Shields, Irish Consul; Fr Hayes; Archbishop Cushing; Paul Tierney, President, Boston AOH; Dr. James Russell and Mrs. Russell. December 1949 [Muintir na Tíre Collection, P134/15/247].

P134_15_289
Meeting of Muintir supporters and staff. Included in the photograph are William Looby, Muintir HQ staff; Fr Joe Bergin; W. F. Roe, Chairman ESB; Fr Hayes; Seamus O'Farrell, Editor of *The Landmark*; Paddy Carey, Dublin Muintir Guild and Tom Fitzgerald, Muintir HQ Staff. *c.*1950 [Muintir na Tíre Collection, P134/15/289].

P134_15_085
Fr Hayes in the Dorothy Quincy Suite, John Handcock Hall, Boston, Massachusetts, at a reception held in his honour by Archbishop Richard J. Cushing. Also in the picture are Dr. & Mrs. Russell, Bansha, Co. Tipperary, Dr. and Mrs. Russell, Slaterstown, Massachusetts, Mr. & Mrs. Paul Tierney (John Handcock Auditor), Mr. & Mrs. Bergin, Rev. Joseph Bergin, M. Frances Fox (an admirer of Mr. de Valera, and also a John Hancock associate. 1949) [Muintir na Tíre Collection, P134/15/85].

P134_15_081

The photograph depicts one of the UNESCO instructors at ENIR, Yaoundé. The aim is to develop a new type of rural teacher, who would help in the community and on the land, as well as in the classroom. February 1971 [Muintir na Tíre Collection, P134/15/81.]

P134_15_082

The photograph depicts growing and harvesting crops as part of the teacher's training. The methods they learned were passed on to the communities where they worked. February 1971 [Muintir na Tíre Collection, P134/15/82].

P134_15_056

Fr Raymond Browne, National Chairman and Andy Roche, National PRO, meeting Senator Ted Kennedy in Washington. June 1965 [Muintir na Tíre Collection, P134/15/56].

P134_15_030

Photograph of promotion stand of the Cork County Federation featuring two women members of the federation. 1971 [Muintir na Tíre Collection, P134/15/30].

P134_15_010

Rural Week, Virginia, Co Cavan. The photo includes the Most Rev. P. Lyons, Bishop of Kilmore, Fr Hayes, Lord ffrench, Vice-President, Prof A. A. O'Rahilly, UCC, Rev. Dr. C. Lucey, Maynooth and Rev. Dr Comey. August 1940 [Muintir na Tíre Collection, P134/15/10.]

P134_14_618

Advert from "Rural Ireland", *c*.1950 [Muintir na Tíre Collection, P134/15/618].

P134_14_616

Delegates at a social event during Rural Week, held at Westport, 1972 [Muintir na Tíre Collection, P134/15/616].

P134_14_615

Liam Maher, Fr Hayes, Frank Lyddy and Fr Morris, *c*.1953 [Muintir na Tire Collection, P134/15/615].

P134_14_614

Muintir na Tire Hall, Murroe, Co. Limerick, *c*.1950 [Muintir na Tíre Collection, P134/15/614].

P134_14_607

Fr Hayes meeting Pope Pius XI in the Vatican. 1953 [Muintir na Tíre Collection, P134/15/607].

P134_14_603

Fr Hayes with Éamon de Valera and others attending a Rural Week, Knockbeg College, Co. Carlow, August 1948 [Muintir na Tíre Collection, P134/15/603].

P134_14_290

Fr Hayes, National Chairman of Muintir na Tíre with Éamon de Valera and a group of priests, with Mr. Martin Madden of Cappawhite, Co. Tipperary, *c.*1950 [Muintir na Tíre Collection, P134/15/290].

P134_14_220

Fr Hayes, Fr Bergin, Archdeacon Nolan and Fr Kelly with a group of Muintir supporters in Tipperary town. 1930s [Muintir na Tíre Collection, P134/15/220].

All images reproduced courtesy of the James Hardiman Library Archives, University of Galway.

INTRODUCTION

Inside and Outside Rural Ireland:
The Politics of Change since 1922

Tony Varley and Tomás Finn

'Change there is in the rural community and change their will and must be. But it is both possible and desirable so to direct and effect such change as to succeed in maintaining a genuine rural life and predominantly rural values'.[1]

'The death of rural Ireland', the historian Mary E. Daly observes in her essay in this book, 'has been foretold on countless occasions over the past century'. A series of modernising economic and social changes in recent decades – changes she regards as overwhelmingly for the better – is viewed as proving these gloomy predictions emphatically false, though further change is inevitable given that the Irish countryside 'must evolve in order to survive'.[2] The turnaround in rural Ireland's economic and social fortunes since the 1960s Professor Daly mainly attributes to the countryside's radically changed relationships with the wider national (and increasingly globalised and urban-centred) economy, with the Irish state, and with what became the European Union (EU) in 1993.

For Mary Daly the Irish state's emergence in recent times as a crucial modernising economic and socioeconomic force contrasts starkly with its failure to become such a force throughout most of the pre-1960s post-independence years.[3] The export-led industrialisation drive of the 1960s critically reliant on foreign direct investment, along with the targeted small town rural industrialisation policy the IDA pursued for a spell in the 1970s, are deemed to have been highly advantageous to rural Ireland. Besides its central role in stimulating the new economy, the Irish state has further asserted itself as a major modernising socioeconomic and social force, as is well illustrated by the free second-level public education introduced in 1967 and the subsequent rolling out of the third-level regional technical colleges.

Broadly speaking Mary Daly views the opening up of European markets to Irish farmers as of enormous benefit to Irish agriculture and to rural Ireland as a whole. There may have been much early alarm among small farmers that Ireland's EEC membership would threaten their survival on the land, but as time passed these fears are viewed as being substantially allayed by such ameliorating supports as the Rural Environmental Protection Scheme (REPS). Mary Daly has charted the vital contribution of Irish and European gender equality legislation to loosening the grip of patriarchal power in Irish society.[4]

Anchored in the political economy tradition, a distinctly less optimistic body of history and social science writing would concur with modernisation writers in viewing change inside the Irish countryside as driven fundamentally by forces outside it. A characteristic desire of writers within the critical political economy approach is their insistence on locating post-independence Ireland among those smaller countries whose dependence 'economically and politically on big and powerful ones' generally implies 'that the decisive causes of their politics lie outside their own boundaries'.[5] Much of Ireland's economic and political dependence can be linked historically to it being a colonised country;[6] and to the continuing power being exerted by external market forces. Even after the attainment of political independence in 1922–3 Irish export agriculture still depended crucially on the English 'cheap food' market;[7] and it was (mostly unskilled or semi-skilled) labour markets in industrial England and North America that young Irish rural emigrants would depend heavily on for employment throughout much of the last century.[8] In its turn, the form of the export-led industrialisation occurring since the 1960s has been seen as 'dependent' in the sense of being shaped and reshaped by waves of global economic restructuring and as prone to periodic crises as well as being accompanied by high levels of relative inequality.[9]

Where contemporary rural Ireland is concerned the process of restructuring has been considered sufficiently uneven in its impacts to have had 'different outcomes in different spaces or localities, and different effects on the different social groups within these localities'.[10] Rather than concentrate on the places and groups that have done best under these waves of restructuring change, the focus of a recent Irish strand of critical political economy social science research has fallen on those rural places and those groups that have lagged behind and found themselves at risk of structural (or persisting) poverty and its associated relative economic and social powerlessness. Much of the relevant social science research since the 1960s has thus pointed to the sharp numerical contraction of farmers and to the accelerating economic and social marginalisation of the western smallholders and small-scale fishermen in particular.[11] And a feature of much of this research – in keeping with its critical political economy orientation – has highlighted the part the Irish state and the EEC/EU have played in at once maintaining and challenging the prevailing patterns of land- and sea-based economic inequalities.[12]

Claims for the primacy of external forces (including the state) in generating rural change – as advanced by writers working within both the modernisation and political economy traditions – prompt us to ask whether Irish rural dwellers in general are best regarded as more the *subjects* than the *agents* of rural change since 1922. Here our modernisation and critical political economy interpretive frameworks present us with two very diverging possibilities. The optimistic starting point of much classical modernisation writing is that ordinary members of society can use their power as agents (both as individuals and as collective actors or collectivities) to avail of – and so benefit from – the new opportunities that broadly benign external modernising forces bring along with them. By contrast, much political economy writing would suggest that during times of significant change the experience of many relatively disadvantaged persons in society is one of finding themselves at the mercy of hostile external forces that can exert dominating power over them. How well these people can mobilise themselves as agents (both individually and collectively) to resist the negative effects of the hostile external forces at play becomes a pressing question for many writers within the critical political economy tradition.[13]

At the very least to focus on the power of external forces (however differently interpreted) is to raise the question of how rural people themselves – and those claiming to speak for them and to act on their behalf – have responded to the external forces perceived to be at work in generating rural changes at different times. And here the reality that the Irish countryside has been home historically to relatively powerful as well as relatively powerless groups raises the possibility that the agents of rural change can be very much internal as well as external in their provenance. Several of the contributors to this book explore this possibility by considering how groups of farmers, members of the Catholic clergy, and organised local communities in particular have fared in their efforts at promoting or resisting certain distinctive forms of rural change. Other contributors turn their attention to how much certain relatively powerless groups in rural society – in particular farm women and paid farmworkers – have been able to negotiate the circumstances of their own day-to-day relative powerlessness to their own advantage.

As much as change in rural Ireland has been interpreted differently by writers within the modernisation and political economy traditions, the manner they each accord primacy to external forces raises the further question of how central a part the southern state has played – not just as an external force in its own right but one that has recently built dynamic collaborative relationships with powerful global economic actors – in promoting certain forms of economic and social change. Certainly the impetus for efforts at promoting change in the twentieth-century Irish countryside has regularly come from above in the form of different state interventions and the pursuit of public policies designed to stimulate new forms of economic and social activity.[14] For this reason several of our contributors choose to scrutinise the actions (and inactions) of the post-independence southern state as a potential force capable of driving rural change at different junctures.

STATE INTERVENTIONS AND RURAL PLANNING

That not all Irish rural areas are the same and that not all classes of farmers are equally well-off comes across strikingly in this book's first section that looks in large part at state interventions and rural planning with particular reference to certain facets of 'the western question' in the 1920s and again in the 1960s. Rural Ireland's most pronounced expressions of spatial and socioeconomic inequality have historically been found in the west (especially in the seaboard counties) where 'congested' smallholders and smallholder-fishermen farming poor agricultural land had long existed in dense concentrations. In response to such conditions the Congested Districts Board of Ireland (CDB) was launched in 1891 to relieve land 'congestion' and associated rural poverty.[15]

Besides considering the CDB's general orientation to the needs of the congested districts (greatly expanded in 1909), its land reform efforts, and the circumstances of its demise in 1923, Gearóid Ó Tuathaigh's main concern in Chapter 2 is to compare the CDB's developmental approach to tackling the social and economic disadvantages of the poorest western areas – areas where Irish was still very much the vernacular in many places – with the approach that came to replace it under native rule. To this end the recommendations of the Commission of the Gaeltacht (appointed in 1925), and what subsequently became of them, are examined in considerable detail. As things turned out successive governments chose either to ignore or to implement 'fitfully' the Commission's main recommendations.

Of more long-term and enduring significance was the way two minority reservations to the Commission's main report published in 1926 – in their proposals relating to organisational structures and industrialisation – came to prefigure later Gaeltacht-centred state interventions. When the long-run survival prospects of the Gaeltacht areas are considered, a number of lessons can be learned retrospectively from the fateful decision to abolish the CDB in 1923, to abandon its novel area-based developmental approach, and to replace it with what turned out to be a set of well-meaning but ultimately rather disjointed and sometimes ineffectual Gaeltacht-centred state interventions in the early post-independence decades.[16]

In the early 1960s state elites turned anew to address the developmental challenges of the rural west, a region that continued to be marked by heavy out-migration and population loss. An Interdepartmental Committee on the Problems of Small Western Farms recommended in 1962 the creation of new western jobs in the manufacturing industry, in tourism, forestry, and fishing as well as the building of a more productive agriculture on economically viable farms. The following year the County Development Team (CDT) system – another of the Committee's recommendations – began functioning to promote economic development in 13 designated western counties. Alongside these state initiatives there appeared a new western protest movement built around the Charlestown Committee in Mayo. Leading activists (including Father James McDyer of Glencolumbkille) of what became known popularly as the Save the West campaign were fearful that the increasing trend in state planning was favouring a rapidly urbanising and industrialising society in which the decline of western smallholder communities could only be expected to accelerate. The main projects the Charlestown Committee pursued, the tactics it relied on, and how it got on are among the topics Peter Murray and Maria Feeney discuss in Chapter 3. The Committee's pilot areas scheme – designed to trial new ways of making western small-scale agriculture more economically viable – was accepted, though not its demand to be granted a steering role in the scheme's actual implementation. A significant concession to the Committee came in 1965–6 when changes were made to the social welfare code that were to the advantage of western smallholders. And after Charles Haughey became Minister for Agriculture in 1964 his department took on 'a new western regional focus'. Murray and Feeney view the various concessions made to the Charlestown Committee – concessions that can be linked to local fears within the ruling Fianna Fáil Party that its western electoral support base was under serious threat – as sufficient to placate 'the more reconcilable elements of the Charlestown Committee support base'.

The fact that two prominent members of the Charlestown Committee (Father Raymond Browne of Roscommon and Seán McEvoy of Mayo) were also Muintir na Tíre (People of the Countryside) activists illustrates how this heavily Munster-centred rural defence movement had made some inroads into the western province of Connacht by the 1960s. Yet, in contrast to the western protest movement Murray and Feeney present Muintir's national organisation as anxious, in the 1960s, to build collaborative partnership-type relationships with the state that would enable it (once officially recognised and adequately resourced) to address – via 'community development' and rural sociology – some perceived-to-be neglected dimensions of the planning exercise recently outlined in the Second Programme for Economic Expansion. The Taoiseach Seán Lemass was sympathetic to Muintir's 'plan' for Irish community development submitted to the government in late 1964, but senior civil servants (particularly those in the Department of Agriculture) were by no means convinced. Apart from the concession of a small annual grant to strengthen its organisation, Muintir's hopes for building an ambitious partnership with the Irish state were therefore to be disappointed, an outcome Murray and Feeney view as throwing the movement into a 'state of deep crisis' by the early 1970s.

CLERICAL POWER AND RURAL CIVIL SOCIETY

The Catholic clergy have been identified as another powerful group in early post-independence Ireland, but what can be said of the bases of clerical power? As members of a self-proclaimed universal church, the clergy's power can be regarded as external; simultaneously clerical power can be considered internal insofar as the clergy could command the loyalty and obedience of the Catholic laity in various ways. Seemingly much of the infrastructure of the clergy's power in rural Ireland was built up in the nineteenth century on the back of tighter central church control, an ambitious church-building programme, the deployment of an ever-larger contingent of clergy (both male and female) across the country, and an impressive rise in popular devotionalism.[17] In the rural context Catholicism's popular power has been seen as critically dependent on how well its teachings and ritual practices appealed to certain classes and population groups, especially to the rising 'commercially oriented farmer class' and to Irish women (mothers especially).[18] Some years ago Eugene Hynes suggested that the church's message to the economically and socially subordinate elements of rural society – to submit themselves to authority and to discipline their wants and impulses (especially in matters relating to sexuality) – proved effective by virtue of fitting well with the material interests of an increasingly powerful highly property-conscious tenant-farmer class.[19]

Both historically, and in the more contemporary period, a capacity to lead the way in agrarian and community activism presents us with another identifiable source of clerical power in the Irish countryside.[20] Accordingly, the second section of our book explores the power of clerical agency in civil society with specific reference to Muintir na Tíre, a still extant rural renewal movement that first appeared in 1931. Two chapters in this section devote themselves to facets of the activist and leadership career of Muintir's founder Father (later Canon) John M. Hayes; and a third chapter explores how Muintir as a movement fared after the death of its founder in 1957 by comparing it with the urban-centred Tuairim movement (1954–75).

Framing his discussion around some key insights of yet another strand of the critical political economy approach – the critical community development literature – Eoin Devereux seeks to put the leadership of Father Hayes firmly under a searching spotlight. Lacking solid organisational skills didn't stop the Tipperary priest from asserting himself as a charismatic yet pragmatic leader, unafraid to take risks in post-civil war Ireland. Under his guidance Muintir achieved much at local parish level, and its founder was central to the movement's ability to forge effective working relationships with different arms of the state, as can be seen for instance in its central involvement in the post-war rural electrification campaign, the Parish Plan for Agriculture, and in a range of other educational and training schemes. While Father Hayes had some progressive ideas concerning local development, Eoin Devereux also considers him to have had an overly idealised view of rural life that hampered his ability to deal effectively with some of the big challenges confronting rural Ireland in his time. In the end Devereux deems conflict between certain rural classes, and between Muintir and other interest groups, as proving to be insurmountable obstacles to progress. Father Hayes's failure to come to terms with power differences between propertied and non-propertied classes is viewed as indicative of his (and Muintir's) underlying social conservatism.

Even though Muintir's chief concern was to stem perceived rural decline and to 'save' rural Ireland, organising farmers (and restoring Irish agriculture to prosperity) was a central concern it shared with a number of other farmers' movements appearing in the 1930s. Comparing Father Hayes's approach to organising Irish agriculture with that of the main leaders of the National Farmers' and Ratepayers' League/National Centre Party (1932–3) and of Clann na Talmhan (Family of the Land) (1938/9–1965) provides Tony Varley with his topic in Chapter 5. In comparing the activist careers of his three main leaders, Varley pays attention to their analyses of the interwar agrarian crisis, their views on how Irish farmers might best organise themselves, the tactics they used (especially in their dealings with the state), and how much their relations with the governing party and other relevant considerations impacted on how well they fared in their efforts to organise agriculture and cultivate vocational or class solidarity among those who worked the land.

At first glance a comparison of Muintir na Tíre (1937–) and Tuairim (1954–75) – the subject of Tomás Finn's chapter – might appear to be chiefly an exercise in tracing the many differences between the two movements. How, after all, might a movement founded by a Catholic priest, built around the Catholic parishes, heavily dependent on clerical support, and whose *raison d'être* by the early 1960s had become the protection of rural Ireland via 'community development' be anything but strikingly different from the solidly urban-based and liberal-leaning Tuairim? Tuairim's fundamental aim – in contrast to Muintir's rural regeneration project – was to help generate an intellectual climate that would aid the Irish people (and its ruling elites) in coming to terms with the many social, cultural, economic and political challenges facing a rapidly urbanising and industrialising society. At the same time both movements were committed to asserting themselves as instruments of change in post-war Ireland at a time when the nature of change itself was shifting radically (compared to what had gone before) and its pace had notably speeded up. As far as organisational matters were concerned, both movements experienced somewhat comparable difficulties in attempting to stay alive and to remain relevant and vibrant over the longer run. More than anything perhaps, both movements found themselves with little alternative but to build strategic relations with leading ruling politicians – and with powerful members of the Catholic hierarchy – if they were to make progress in advancing their respective projects. It is these relations that Finn's chapter explores especially with a view to shedding light on the wider politics rural and urban-based civil society groups found themselves obliged to engage in when interacting with two major power blocs in early post-war Irish society – the Catholic bishops and the Irish state's ruling politicians. Unlike Tuairim, however, Muintir did succeed in overcoming many obstacles so as to stay alive as a movement to the present day.

INTELLECTUALS, RURAL IDYLLS AND GRITTY REALITIES

In spite of – or perhaps just as much on account of – Ireland's long history of colonial conquest and land confiscations, subsistence crises and persisting rural poverty,[21] as well as bouts of prolonged agrarian disorder,[22] there has been a lengthy intellectual tradition in Ireland of producing idealised images of rural life. By way of explicating the phenomenon Gearóid Ó Tuathaigh observes perceptively how:

> This general sentiment – the identification of the land and rural society as a privileged habitat for 'authentic' living, close to nature and to God, bonded in feeling and in values – was bound to be especially strong in Ireland with its emotive history of land dispossession.[23]

Certainly expressions of the view that life on the land was, or could be, purer (in the sense of more morally and socially preferable and superior) than life in the city were common by the early years of the last century. In many ways, Charles J. Kickham's novel *Knocknagow, or the Homes of Tipperary* – published in book form in 1873 – contributed much to introducing a set of themes to be worked and re-worked in later normative idealisations (and glorifications) of Irish rural life.[24] Nationalists, the Catholic clergy, co-operative movement activists as well as an assortment of artists and fiction writers – typically urban-based – all played their part in articulating conceptions of a socially and culturally powerful rural Ireland.[25]

Of course, idealised images of rural life could always be faulted for drawing a veil over a profusion of dissonant realities, particularly perhaps when idylls were located in the remote west where the forces making for economic and social decline were especially vigorous.[26] Even ethnographic accounts – Arensberg and Kimball's classic study of interwar rural Clare is the prime example – have been accused of falling into the trap of idealising western small farm life by blurring (or even collapsing entirely) the boundary between normative assertions of how the world should be and objective descriptions of the way things actually are. 'The problem with "real" communities', as Peter Gibbon pointed out in his trenchant critique of the American ethnographers,

> is that they are never actually observed – they are always (coincidentally) going out of existence. It is disputable whether the 'real' Ireland of the nativists, revivalists and Arensberg and Kimball ever existed *anywhere* in Ireland, in fact. But it is certain it never existed as it was depicted in County Clare in 1931–4.[27]

Guided by a critical political economy perspective, Gibbon's alternative account of early 1930s rural Clare claims to find class divisions and tensions between big and small farmers, as well as widespread family discord, where the American ethnographers are taken as having recorded only class and family harmony.[28] What led Arensberg and Kimball so astray in Gibbon's view was the fatal reliance on an idealising structural-functionalism as the conceptual underpinning of their ethnographic work. One central question the case of functionalist-influenced ethnography raises is whether rural idylls are typically generated outside the countryside and chiefly reflect romanticising urban sensibilities. It is relevant here to recall Alice Curtayne's observation in 1940:

The romantic and sentimental lovers of the land are beyond classification. They have one thing positively in common. None of them derive their livelihood from the land. Few of them even live on it....[29]

In the writings of the two sets of intellectuals discussed in our book's third section, idealised images of rural life are either conspicuous by their absence (as in the novels Caitriona Clear deals with) or are viewed as under serious threat in light of perceived accelerating rural decline (as Bryan Fanning suggests was substantially true of the stance taken by Professor Jeremiah Newman and his like-minded (mainly) clerical contributors to the Maynooth-produced *Christus Rex* journal). Far from idealising or celebrating rural society or spending time imagining past or future rural idylls, the novelists Caitriona Clear examines in Chapter 7 – popular in their day but now largely forgotten – saw their task as presenting their readers with up-close fictional portrayals of the mundane realities of rural life in the 1940s and 50s.[30] Written with an eye to definite readerships, the popular, widely-read (and therefore not as a rule banned) novels she dissects had much to say about how ordinary rural folk sought to navigate everyday life within a familiar range of social settings. In the course of exploring how the social and economic pressures of rural life were impinging on the lives of their fictionalised characters, Clear's novelists were by times attentive to class, gender, and spatial differences and tensions as well as to the power Catholic priests were capable of wielding over their parishioners and local community life. By and large the novelists' fictional characters are eager – with the notable exception of jazz – to embrace the contemporary modern world. They tend, for instance, to regularly visit the city, to be conversant with international affairs, and to have developed up-to-date tastes in clothes and in house furnishings. Why the prevailing modernising sensibilities were keen to reject idealisations of Irish rural life Caitriona Clear relates to a still too-close widespread familiarity with 'the half-doors, water-barrels, flour-bags, chamber-pots, pig-killings, and tea-dinners of mid-century rural life'.

To the fore in some of the essays published in *Christus Rex* – the journal of Catholic sociology founded in 1947 and edited between 1954 and 1970 by the Maynooth professor of sociology and later Bishop of Limerick, Jeremiah Newman – were the anxieties of Catholic (mainly clerical) intellectuals in the 1950s and 60s born of a growing fear that rural Ireland had entered a period of deepening crisis that was throwing its future (and that of Irish Catholicism) into serious doubt. Stoking such anxieties, as Bryan Fanning points out in Chapter 8, was a belief that popular Catholicism's power in Ireland had become critically dependent historically on a viable and vibrant rural economy and society. Not content to sit back and watch the calamity of a treasured traditional countryside losing its battle to survive, the challenge was to understand the nature and dimensions of the rural malaise with a view to deciding what sort of effective remedial action was required – from both above and below – to stem the threat of decline and decay. A new and less vulnerable balance would need to be struck between the forces of traditionalism and modernity. Such was the background to *The Limerick Rural Survey* published by Muintir na Tíre in 1964. This work, edited by Jeremiah Newman and heavily influenced by a contemporary Dutch school of rural sociology, contained Newman's elaboration of 'rural centrality' as a new and alternative approach to rural planning. *The Limerick Rural Survey* also contained the partly Dutch-trained Patrick McNabb's two cogent chapters on post-war rural life in east Limerick. The case made for rural community development in the pages of *Christus Rex*, and in the local- and national-level efforts of Muintir more generally, may have been entwined in Fanning's view with a conservative Catholic critique of urban modernity but it still succeeded in making a highly distinctive contribution to debates about Ireland's (and the countryside's) future.

Certain developments in recent Dutch rural sociology may have made a big impression on Jeremiah Newman, but by no means was he the first leading figure within Muintir to draw on continental rural development experience. Three decades earlier Father Hayes had looked to the Belgian Boerenbond as a model of sorts for his relatively short-lived co-operatively organised movement of agricultural producers that materialised as Muintir na Tíre Limited in 1931. Nor was John Hayes the first would-be Irish rural reformer to look to continental Europe for inspiration. As far back as the 1890s Horace Plunkett, the founder of the Irish co-operative movement, had striven (along with T. P. Gill) to learn from what they took to be continental best practice in making their case for what eventually emerged as Ireland's Department of Agricultural and Technical Instruction (DATI) in 1899.[31] Transnational influence proved to be a two-way street for Plunkett and Hayes as – later on in their careers – their rural development efforts in Ireland attracted levels of attention abroad, especially in North America.[32]

FARM WOMEN, THE STATE, AND NEGOTIATING RELATIVE POWERLESSNESS

Along with farm labourers – whose already much depleted numbers fell off sharply with rural electrification and the post–1945 wave of tractor-based farm mechanisation[33] – farm women stand out as another very numerous relatively powerless group in the post-independence decades. But how uniform was this relative powerlessness? And how did it impact on what individual and collective agency farm women were able to exercise? If it is accepted that women belong to dominant and subordinate classes in society,[34] then we would expect to find significant differences between the relative powerlessness and capacity for agency of farm women in big farm households (typically employing one or more 'domestic servants' in the early decades of the last century) and those in small farm households wholly reliant on family labour.

Prolonged economic depression during the interwar years, along with the power of Catholic and nationalist thinking that woman's true calling was domestic rather than civic or public,[35] made for an external climate hostile to notions of gender equality.[36] Within such a climate a whole series of interwar state policies can be read as attempting either to exclude women or to severely restrict their involvement in key segments of public life.[37] To go by much of the early ethnographic research, patriarchy was also deeply embedded internally in the farm households. Recurring themes in the ethnographic studies were the subordination of women to patriarchal authority and the manner a myriad of patriarchal practices had become enshrined institutionally in everyday life within the farm households. Against such a backdrop the first four decades of native rule were to witness an enormous shedding of female labour on Irish farms. Altogether 'there were 72 per cent fewer domestic servants in Ireland in 1961 than in 1926, and 65 per cent fewer women working in agriculture...'.[38]

This dramatic change and the outflow of women from the land it occasioned, along with the external and internal power being exerted by ideas and practices hostile to notions of gender equality, provide a central feature of the background to Anne Byrne's and Tanya Watson's review in Chapter 9 of anthropological and sociological studies of Irish farm women stretching back to the 1930s. Their discussion focuses primarily on the private sphere of the household and on the structural position, as well as the living and working conditions, of Irish farm women. Of the ethnographic studies surveyed by Byrne and Watson only Patrick McNabb's east Limerick in the late 1950s is taken as featuring farms with hired (and sometimes live-in) labour.

The fundamental and long-enduring patriarchal principles structuring gender inequality identified in Byrne's and Watson's review of the ethnographic literature revolve around two normative expectations: that land ownership should be in male hands and that its transmission across the generations should see it pass patrilineally from father to son. If we leave aside household-based poultry-keeping and butter-making,[39] land ownership and the control of production agriculture tended to be intimately tied together in early twentieth-century Ireland. Married farm women – as two young Harvard-based anthropologists observed them in early 1930s small farm Clare – had to contend with a social order strongly inclined to exclude them from owning land, from mainstream productive activity on the farm, and a social order that heavily restricted their involvement in civic and public life.[40] For young mothers a daily round of recurring housework, childcare, and unpaid farm work made for lives of almost endless drudgery. Yet, by virtue of having responsibility for the running of their own households, farmers' wives were not entirely without autonomy in the domestic sphere where their labour was commonly regarded as critical to small farm survival.[41] In the situation they found themselves in, it was motherhood more than anything that gave married farm women most of their social standing and agency.[42]

Much of the ethnographic evidence dating from the 1950s and 60s – as found in the writings of Patrick McNabb, Ethna Viney, John C. Messenger, and Hugh Brody in particular – documents the extent to which young single farm women were more likely to emigrate than to marry and become a farmer's wife and a rural mother. Change was in the air in the 1970s when Damian Hannan's and Louise Katsiaouni's survey research revealed that some farmers' wives, influenced by prestigious urban reference groups, were actively renegotiating spousal power relations by embracing the ideal of joint decision-making.

A striking shortcoming of the post-independence ethnographic research – in Anne Byrne's and Tanya Watson's view – was its lack of an explicit feminist theoretical framework capable of focusing more explicitly on the constraining effects of patriarchal expectations and practices on women's power of agency. Where the early ethnographic literature fell short was in its failure to challenge (and so help delegitimatise) the prevailing patriarchal order in which men felt entitled to own, inherit, and work land, thus routinely excluding women from the occupational category of farmer. Only with the research of Patricia O'Hara and Sally Shortall in the 1980s and 90s – inspired as it was by a conscious feminist desire to advance the ideal of securing greater gender equality on the land – do Byrne and Watson see this crippling deficiency beginning to be identified and addressed.[43]

While accepting that male landownership constituted a central pillar of patriarchal power in Irish farming, Mícheál Ó Fathartaigh's and Anne Cassidy's discussion in Chapter 10 nonetheless maintains that women's control of household-based poultry-keeping and butter-making did empower them to significantly challenge the patriarchal order on Irish farms early in the last century. Such challenge is viewed as owing much to the early state-employed agricultural instructresses who advised the women household-based poultry-keepers and butter-makers as to how to organise their production and marketing practices along more rational and commercial lines. Seemingly it was women from strong farmer households who took the lead in encouraging poor farm women to involve themselves in the poultry economy in early twentieth-century County Galway. The so-called egg money is viewed as leaving farm women more economically independent as individuals within their households while concurrently increasing their economic and social importance to the well-being of their families.[44] What transpired as the decades passed was that patriarchal power reasserted itself as first butter-making and then poultry-keeping underwent restructuring that saw them coming substantially under the control of men.

In line with the official view gathering strength in the 1960s that farm modernisation needed to occur in the home as well as on the farm – and reflecting the rising power of the discipline of home economics – the poultry-keeping and butter-making instructresses began to be retrained as Farm Home Management (FHM) advisors from 1962. Typically the FHM advisors worked on a one-to-one basis with individual farm women in the home, advising them on a wide spectrum of home improvements. No less than the early poultry instructresses decades earlier, the FHM advisors tended – as living standards rose across the country from the 1960s – to get a broadly receptive hearing from home improvement-minded farm women. Their work also brought them into contact with community development groups offering educational programmes, and with other organised rural interests seeking advice and state assistance.

Despite their impressive record of achievement, the pioneering FHM advisors found themselves being rebranded as Socio-Economic Advisors (SEAs) in 1984. Once retrained, the remit of the new SEAs extended to offering technical advice on a range of enterprise and financial management issues that included farm accounts and capital taxation matters. Above all, the SEAs were tasked with the challenge of dealing with the many intractable difficulties associated with delayed farm succession on Irish farms. Not without considerable irony the SEAs, in their efforts to remove the blockages viewed as frustrating the efficient transmission of farmland from father to son, regularly found themselves attempting to sort out the various difficulties thrown up by patrilineal succession in particular cases.

Another consequential change discussed in Chapter 10 involved the removal in the mid-1980s of the long-existing convention that prevented women advisors being allocated the same roles as their male colleagues within the advisory service's division of labour. For all its early promise to achieve gender parity – by integrating women into the advisory service on an equal footing to men – this initiative has fallen far short of early optimistic expectations. Today the women advisors constitute but a small minority of the full complement of advisors, and they have yet to be integrated across the full span of the service's advisory roles on anything like equal terms.

THE CONTEMPORARY COUNTRYSIDE

Discussed in the book's final section are certain connections between power and change in the most recent decades. The tendency to idealise the countryside by 'ordinary' people in everyday life surfaces prominently in Mary Cawley's discussion of migration from, and return to, rural Ireland in recent times. Based on the narratives of 42 returnees interviewed in 2013, the migration histories of Cawley's returnees extend from the 1950s onwards. In spite of social differences among them, certain common themes emerge from their accounts of the experience of leaving and returning to rural Ireland. Reasons for outmigration and return tended to be framed strongly around two well-recognised tropes that are often discussed separately in the literature – the perceived negative realities of rural life and the contrasting recollections of an idyllic countryside. The general reasons for migration given by Cawley's returnees referred to shortages of employment and career opportunities, to personal aspirations, and to a desire for independence and travel. Still, as emigrants in overseas cities many of her returnees recalled having idyllic memories of the Irish countryside they had left behind. Among those of working age returning to Ireland was facilitated critically by improved employment opportunities, but closeness to family also counted for much. Parents in particular rated very highly the perceived advantages of the Irish countryside as a place to bring up young children. Upon returning to rural Ireland there was a tendency for some gritty realities of daily life to make their presence felt, notably in perceived poor service provision, inefficiencies, and in a lack of privacy. Many returnees adapted to the challenges they encountered on returning but some of them actually migrated again, relying on links established while overseas to facilitate another leaving. One of Mary Cawley's essay's policy-relevant conclusions is that 'local communities and planning authorities have roles to play in protecting the character of small villages and towns so that they are attractive to returnees whose presence will, in turn, contribute to improved service demand and supply'.

Mary Daly's impressively wide-ranging survey of emerging patterns of rural change in present-day rural Ireland documents the many ways in which reports of the demise of rural Ireland over the years have been proven false by developments since the 1960s. Over the past five decades the population of rural Ireland has risen significantly, and the countryside has experienced a plethora of major, largely positive, changes. Agriculture may remain the dominant economic activity, but many of those living in the rural areas no longer work on the land. A key factor in this transformation – one encouraged by the ending of the marriage bar on married women in state employment in 1973 – has been the growth in the numbers of rural women in paid work outside farming. Other consequential and related developments have seen the emergence of a more diversified economy, the steep rise in the proportion of farmers' children participating in third-level education, and the much improved roads network. Not all boats, however, are viewed as being lifted by the rising tide. While the population in the countryside has risen, small rural towns are finding themselves increasingly being bypassed as centres of economic and social activity. The close relationship between transformation and displacement needs also to be kept in mind when considering the prospects for family farming. Family farms may have survived much longer than the doomsayers had predicted, but now there are indications that some fundamental changes are well under way. Alongside the substantial growth in part-time farming, tenant-farmers have begun to re-appear in recent times even if land-renting has yet to result 'in the re-emergence of an identifiable landlord class'. And the ever-deepening climate crisis is seen – in view of Ireland's heavily pastoral agriculture – as presenting contemporary rural Ireland with 'a potentially existential challenge'. Linked in part to the climate emergency, environmental policies aimed at discouraging one-off housing can be expected to be equally (if not more) contentious as time passes. This is especially so given the manner rural Ireland's long-established dispersed settlement pattern has 'played a critical role in sustaining the rural population and rural communities'.[45]

THE SHIFTING CONTOURS OF RURAL POWER

By the late twentieth century Ireland was being regarded as '...one of the most "globalised" economies in the world, with high levels of investment, trade, migration and financial flows'.[46] And with globalisation's onward march, rural Ireland's present and near-term future came progressively to be more determined by powerful external pressures and forces. But where did all this leave the collective power of internal collective actors to shape the patterns of rural change? This question we will now briefly explore by considering how well farmers and the Catholic clergy – groups widely viewed as possessing considerable internal power in rural Ireland at the time of independence – have fared since 1922 in using collective action to maintain their standing as relatively powerful interests. At the opposite end of the internal rural power distribution, farm women in the deeply patriarchal Irish society of 1922 stood out as a relatively powerless group. How women have fared since independence in the farm households, and in using collective action to combat their relative powerlessness, can therefore also serve to illuminate the changing contours of power in the Irish countryside.

In view of the ongoing transfer of land ownership from landlord to tenant and the redistribution of economic and social power this implied,[47] cases have been made for regarding big or strong farmers,[48] 'sturdy smallholders',[49] and farmers in general as dominant economic and political classes in the early post-independence decades.[50] But how did these different farmer classes get on in influencing the policy stances of the main nationalist political parties in the early post-independence decades? The main pro-Treaty parties (Cumann na nGaedheal and Fine Gael) have frequently been particularly identified with big farmer interests and the early Fianna Fáil Party with the interests of smallholders.[51] Whatever about their political influence, the post-war slump and the ongoing market difficulties left the market power of all farmer classes much reduced in the interwar years. Such market weakness helped inspire a number of attempts at organising farmers independently,[52] some of which gravitated to the electoral sphere before ending in failure and seeing themselves substantially absorbed by either the Cumann na nGaedheal or Fine Gael parties.[53]

Between 1944 and 1955 a new wave of professedly 'non-political' farmer interest groups – composed of Macra na Feirme, the Irish Creamery Milk Suppliers' Association (ICMSA), and the National Farmers' Association (NFA) in the main – appeared on the scene. Shortly after its appearance in 1955 some government recognition of the NFA was secured and joint 'annual reviews' were instituted in 1958.[54] Even if relations between the NFA and the state

> were formalized in 1964, with the government agreeing to consult the NFA on all agricultural matters, the remainder of the 1960s was a decade of increased farmer militancy as farmers protested at what they perceived as their increasingly disadvantageous situation.[55]

Membership of the European Community gave Irish farmers access to the Common Agricultural Policy and cleared the way for the forging of significantly stronger ties between the leading farming groups and the Irish state, ties that added to their power to organise and represent farming interests.[56] What is also evident is that the influence organised Irish farmers could exert as interest groups (within the IFA most prominently) increased dramatically as the numbers engaged in farming continued to fall. Between 1926 and 1981 Irish farmers practically halved in number, 'relatives assisting' declined by 90 per cent, and paid farm workers shrunk by 85 per cent.[57]

But was the organised farmers' greater influence in the recent period used to maintain and extend class differences among Irish farmers? Ethel Crowley's exploration of the changes occurring in the relative power of big and small farmers in our own time suggests that the underlying play of external and internal pressures at work was continuing to advantage the larger more highly commercial farmers while simultaneously weakening the less intensive small producers, sometimes to the point of pushing them out of farming altogether.[58] The larger farmers are seen as being able to depend on the IFA to represent their interests;[59] and to have their economic and political power routinely shored up by European Union and Irish state policies.[60]

In the face of multiple perceived crisis conditions – born of fresh price-cost squeezes, policy moves to bring about a lower carbon agriculture, to restore biodiversity and improve water quality, along with the ongoing degradation of rural services – some Irish farmers by mid-2023 were privately questioning the wisdom of relying solely on the mainstream political parties (and, by implication, on their long-established interest groups as well) to represent and defend their interests effectively. With the recent electoral advance of the BBB – Farmer-Citizen movement in the Netherlands – fresh in their memory, a poll of 1,982 Irish farmers in the late summer of 2023 found 72 per cent of them (74 per cent of dairy farmers) saying they would 'be likely' to give their first-preference votes to a new farmers' party should one appear by the time of the next general election.[61]

Along with farmers, the Catholic clergy were widely regarded as members of a powerful group in the early 1920s Irish countryside, but how well have they retained their internal power in the rural communities over the past century? At the time of the Free State's inception in 1922–3 the Catholic Church in Ireland has been viewed as 'more secure and more confident than at any previous time; it had little to fear from rival churches and enjoyed close links with the state'.[62] As much as 93 per cent of the southern Irish population was recorded as Catholic in the 1926 census (as against 69 per cent in the 2022 census); and in the 1920s there were 'over 13,000 clergy and religious' in the country.[63] The Church's controlling influence on Irish society may have reached historic new heights in the early post-independence decades,[64] but such power was apparently accompanied by considerable anxiety among top church leaders that Catholic Ireland was under attack from alien external cultural and social forces. The bishops' fear was that '…the traditional standards of their people were under unprecedented pressure. New mass media – the cinema, the radio, and above all the English sensational newspapers…were bringing unfamiliar values to the attention of their flocks'.[65] 'Despite legislation and moral protectionism', Daithí Ó Corráin can describe this period as 'a time of vigilance and fortress Catholicism'.[66]

Besides its pervasive presence in swathes of everyday life, what controlling power the pre-1960s Catholic Church in Ireland possessed was most strongly rooted in the institutional spheres of education, health, and social welfare. Taking as their model Muintir na Tíre's 1937 vocationalist communitarian approach to reorganising local interests in the Catholic parishes, Father John Hayes and Bishop Michael Browne of Galway were particularly keen to see Catholic influence expand into the sphere of rural civil society. In the event, the refusal of leading figures of the ruling party to commit the state to backing and resourcing this vision – as set forth in detail in the Commission on Vocational Organisation Report of 1944 – delivered a crushing blow to the communitarian project of Catholic rural vocationalism in Ireland. And, with Catholic influence waning steadily from the late 1960s as the forces of external secular modernity progressively grew in power and penetrated to the point of dominating Ireland, significantly stiffer challenges for any would-be attempts at building a Catholic (or even a Christian) civil society in rural Ireland lay ahead. Over time the dramatic decline in new recruits to the priesthood was bound to weaken the Catholic clergy's presence and influence in the rural parishes. A recent survey revealed that the complement of priests ministering in Ireland's 26 dioceses in 2022 had fallen to 2,116, and that a third of these men were aged over 60.[67] Between 1937 and 1973 all of Muintir na Tíre's national presidents had been Catholic clergymen, yet all the subsequent presidents – with the exception of Father John Stapleton (1976–80) – have been lay persons.[68] This is not to say that individual Catholic priests didn't still continue to possess the power to play a vital leadership role in Muintir at a local level. Chris Eipper's ethnographic study of Bantry published in 1986 observes, for instance, how:

> The Bantry guild of Muintir was successful because it had the active support of the town's business influentials and because it made good use of the politicians – but it was a priest who gave the organization its unity, drive and focus.[69]

Has the relative powerlessness of women charted by Anne Byrne's and Tanya Watson's ethnographers undergone change in rural Ireland in the more recent period? Much revealing light on this question is shed by Patricia O'Hara's pioneering fieldwork research of the 1990s. Accepting that family farming can regularly be oppressive for women, O'Hara nonetheless views power relations between men and women as in principle best regarded as a matter of negotiation. When the spectrum of actual negotiations is explored empirically the world of Irish family farming in the 1990s was throwing up different patterns that saw some women accepting certain versions of the patriarchal order – to the point of becoming active accomplices in their maintenance and reproduction – while others were conspicuous for consciously rejecting and actively resisting them. Those most likely to put up with and accommodate themselves to the patriarchal order O'Hara categorises as women 'farm helpers' and 'farm homemakers'. Those most likely to reject and resist the long-established status quo she categorises as women 'working for the family farm' and 'farm women in paid work'. The social and material circumstances of farm women 'working for the farm' and 'in paid work' were what was leaving them in a strong position to negotiate the patriarchal order along more equalitarian lines. Such negotiation is viewed as being not just to their own advantage but to that of their households and family farms. Patricia O'Hara concludes her discussion of Irish farm women in the 1990s with this observation:

> Most importantly of all, feminist theory needs to pay a great deal more attention to what it has heretofore largely neglected and what this study has shown to be the core of women's influence

– their power as mothers. In this, the emphasis should be not just on motherhood as a socially constructed role, but on mothers as critical actors in the process of social reproduction.[70]

A class-related continuity here with the 1950s and 60s ethnographies is the tendency among O'Hara's women to see no future for their daughters in marrying into small farms. The desire instead was to see their daughters sufficiently well-educated to improve their chances in urban labour markets. Over time this desire was bound to undermine the reproduction of the traditional patriarchal order (such as it still is) within the small farmer class.[71]

What can be said of rural women's capacities and abilities to use collective action either to accommodate themselves to patriarchal domination or to resist it passively or actively? It can be easily argued that the economic and social power that landownership conferred on men on the farm also provided them with the means to carve out a dominant position for themselves in agriculture-related civic and public life. Late in the last century, for instance, there were 'four women and 72 men on the national committee of the main farming organisation, the Irish Farmers' Association (IFA), and no men on the IFA's family-farm committee'.[72] And although Irish country women may long have had their own national network in the Irish Countrywomen's Association (ICA), some writers have viewed the ICA as historically slow to advocate anything resembling genuine feminist change.[73] Writing of Irish women's changing circumstances and worldviews in recent decades, Linda Connolly and Tina O'Toole observe how

> ...the tensions that arose between rural women leaders, whose aspirations were originally shaped and formed in a vastly different period and political climate, and new urban-based feminist organisations, which were mobilising in a more radical period of political protest and activism, reflect the transformation of Irish women's lives by 1970.[74]

Some historians, however, see more to the early ICA than its critics would allow. With around 2,000 members in 1940 the ICA, in Caitriona Clear's view, 'did not call itself "feminist"' yet still 'stated clearly that one of its aims was to prepare women for public life, and it was loudly lobbying for better working conditions for women on farms as early as 1938'.[75] From its beginnings as the United Irishwomen in 1910 Diarmuid Ferriter presents the ICA as a forward-looking force.[76] In the economically depressed 1950s he views the association breaking new ground as:

> It expanded its educational facilities of a practical and theoretical nature, it succeeded in obtaining a grant-in-aid from the government, it successfully lobbied funds from abroad, it employed full-time organisers to tour the country in an attempt to increase membership, and encourage women's participation in rural trade, education and social activities. Once again it became comfortable in its confidence to achieve practical results. It learned how to project itself and in the process became a highly professional organisation.[77]

Patrick McNabb's study of east Limerick in 1959–60 characterised the ICA's local 'social significance' as '...not so much its educational value as the fact that for the first time, women [had] the opportunity to assume an institutionalised role outside the home'. What the ICA was providing local women with was 'a platform from which to air their opinions in public and a group to support them'. And as the ICA's membership in the rural districts was increasing, McNabb's expectation was that 'women in the region will have a greater influence in community affairs'.[78] McNabb also records a definite class dimension to the ICA's membership when he notes how the women with farm labourer class backgrounds he interviewed '...had no direct experience of the Countrywomen's Association but said they would not join because the farmers' wives would look down on them'.[79]

The women Patricia O'Hara categorises as the 'farm homemakers', and who are subject to considerable patriarchal domination, are more likely than members of her other categories 'to be involved in organisations such as the ICA, which they see as a way of getting out of the house and relieving the boredom and autonomy of housework. It is also a way of creating a personal involvement away from home'.[80] Ethel Crowley's discussion of a 'much underestimated' ICA in the early twenty-first century has this to say:

> Perhaps it is an example of a type of 'indigenous feminism' that is attractive to ordinary women and does not necessarily follow the well-trodden path of Western liberal feminism. It is quite likely that its role has been and continues to be at least as important as that of female representation in government in women's everyday lives.[81]

As much as patriarchal power may, in practice, have always been subject to some ongoing negotiation within farm households and to have been contested as well to some degree by the collective action of the ICA, it has only been in recent decades that patriarchal power has experienced a widespread and more sustained challenge. This challenge gathered momentum from the 1960s as the normative ideal of gender equality made its way in the wider society, a new women's movement appeared in Ireland, and (especially among the young) both Catholicism and patriarchal nationalism began to lose more and more of their influence. For their part farm women became better educated, began to acquire greater social and economic independence via off-farm employment, and the co-management of family farms became an option for some of them. Minor change to the long-standing pattern of male land ownership has even begun to occur though it is obvious – with women accounting for a mere 13.4 per cent of farm holders (a little over 18,000 in number) in 2020 as compared with 12.4 per cent of farm holders (or 17,345 in total) in 2010 – that the pace of change here in eroding this vital linchpin of patriarchal power in Irish family farming remains stubbornly slow.[82] A telling point made in a very recent discussion of the succession issue was that 'women are still one step removed from the farm succession planning process'.[83]

Yet another notable development in the early years of the new millennium saw the Irish state's commitment to promoting greater gender equality in Irish society leading to attempts to make women more central to family farming. Within a changing policy climate, and drawing much of its popular energy from a rising feminist consciousness in society at large, some recent sociological research has shown how farm co-management agreements in the form of 'joint farming ventures' (first appearing in 2002) have begun to contribute to a loosening of traditional gender divisions in productive and reproductive work on some farms, to more women expressly identifying themselves as farmers, and to enabling some women to resist patriarchal controls more actively.[84]

When viewed in the broad, recent experience continues to illustrate the power of external forces – whether economic, social, cultural, political, or technological in character

– to shape and reshape the contexts in which farm women as individuals and as collective actors find themselves as they seek to live their lives in rural Ireland. Some of this external power continues to underpin the patriarchal order (particularly where land ownership is concerned) while more of it has created new opportunities for certain farm women to challenge patriarchal expectations and practices in the domestic domain and beyond. In certain vital respects, the external power emanating from outside the Irish countryside is more sympathetic today to the advancement of rural women – and to the projects of challenging patriarchy in agriculture in its many forms – than it is to the plight of those farmers and members of the Catholic clergy who nowadays find themselves coping with the challenges of increasing relative powerlessness.

STATE INTERVENTIONS AND RURAL PLANNING

Shifting the Goalposts: Changing Narratives of Western Regeneration in the 1920s

Gearóid Ó Tuathaigh

Whatever political considerations may have been paramount at the time of its establishment in 1891, the Congested Districts Board was the first state agency dedicated to addressing the specific economic and social problems of extensive districts in the western counties of Ireland. In essence, the Congested Districts Board (CDB) was a development board, focused on tackling economic retardation, depressed living standards and, at regular intervals, subsistence crises in counties mainly on the Atlantic rim of the island. 'Congestion' in this context referred not to consistently heavy or dense population pressure throughout the entire region, but rather to the dangerous pressure of population on poor land.

While the problems and challenges with which the CDB was grappling survived the establishment of Saorstát Éireann in 1922, the Board itself did not. Many of its schemes and programmes were distributed among the various departments established by the new government. However, the new government did move promptly to investigate – and committed itself to improving – the condition of particular communities within the western counties, namely the remaining Irish-speaking or Gaeltacht communities. Among the declared 'national aims' of the new Irish Free State government was the revival of Irish as a general vernacular (i.e. the reversal of its long-term abandonment). Central to this objective was arresting the continuing vernacular shift – from Irish to English – in the communities in which Irish was still a strong, if not always a dominant, vernacular. In 1925 the government appointed a Gaeltacht Commission charged with investigating the circumstances of these base-communities of Irish-speakers and with recommending measures by which they might be fortified as Irish-speaking communities. Such recommendations for the stabilisation of a linguistic community would, it was universally accepted, encompass proposals for purposeful economic and social interventions by the state.

How precisely did it happen, then, that a dedicated agency (the CDB), with a brief for targeted intervention in the welfare of a broad community defined by precise criteria of economic and social disadvantage, was abolished in 1923, with the new government focusing its attention on the predicament of a sub-set of that disadvantaged community, now defined by cultural-linguistic criteria. That is the question considered in this essay.

The CDB and western congestion

Under the Directive Principles of Social Policy, the 1937 Bunreacht na hÉireann included the following statement (Article 45, 2, v):

> The State shall in particular direct its policy towards ensuring: that there may be established on the land in economic security as many families as in the circumstances shall be practicable.

The Bunreacht came into effect on 29 December 1937. A month earlier, in County Tipperary, the first branch was established of a newly reconfigured organisation, Muintir na Tíre, dedicated to raising the standard of living across all aspects of Irish rural life, with an emphasis on local improvement through the participation of the people themselves in the welfare of their communities. This vision of rural community development, based on the parish, on 'neighbourliness, self-help and self-reliance', chimed well with the social objective enshrined in the constitutional injunction.[1]

The body of Catholic social thought that informed both the founders of Muintir na Tíre and the Principles of Social Policy set out in de Valera's 1937 Constitution, has been the subject of scholarly examination and analysis for some time; its origins identified as deriving from papal encyclicals (notably, *Rerum Novarum*, 1891 and *Quadragesimo Anno*, 1931), a suspicion of the over-mighty state, advocacy of varieties of vocationalism, and anxiety at unchecked urbanisation and social atomisation. These strands of Catholic social thought were present in the shaping of social policy in several states with a substantial Catholic population, from the later nineteenth to the middle of the twentieth century.[2]

However, in the case of Ireland, in addition to mainstream Catholic social thought, there was also a powerful indigenous source sustaining this vision of a contented, densely settled and family-centred rural society. Firmly embedded in Irish nationalist rhetoric was a powerful set of 'restorative' motifs, based on popular historical consciousness of dispossession. The notion that, from the seventeenth century, the structure of land ownership was, in a fundamental sense, based on conquest, injustice and spoliation and that any version of Irish 'freedom' must encompass the undoing of this aspect of the conquest, was long an integral element of the received nationalist historical narrative. The toppling of Irish landlordism (Davitt's 'fall of feudalism') would, in this narrative of liberation, involve restoring the descendants of the disposed to their rightful place of dignity on the land of Ireland. The extent to which, by the later nineteenth century, this restoration myth was taken literally, as distinct from providing an enabling myth for popular mobilisation, is impossible to calculate. But Fintan Lalor's credo of 1848 was echoed in the rallying slogans of the early phase of the land war: 'keep a firm grip on your homesteads', 'the land for the people'.[3]

Of course, the actual outcome of the successive phases of the land agitation – that is, the precise terms of the Land Acts from 1881 to 1909 – was the creation, through land purchase schemes funded by Treasury advances, of a highly dispersed ownership of farms by people who were previously tenants of these same farms. Thus, the hierarchy of the rural society at sub-landlord level was largely consolidated. This left a substantial portion of rural dwellers with an unsatisfied craving for land or for an enlarged holding of land. The acquisition and redistribution of landlord estates and, indeed of large farms or ranches, was advocated (including 'advocacy' involving direct action) by leaders of later phases of land agitation, notably by the United Irish League (UIL) and by leading activists of the 'ranch war'.[4] At the bottom of the social pyramid of Irish rural society, the landless labourers and the cottiers reaped no direct relief or benefit from the principal land purchase schemes sanctioned by the Land Acts. There was, it is true, direct government intervention related to improved dwellings for labourers, but such interventions did not pertain to the question of land ownership.[5]

A particularly acute version of the problem of an insatiable thirst for land among smallholders and landless men, was the predicament of the so-called 'congests'; that is, occupants of small holdings of poor land, holdings that were simply not adequate for the support of a family in even the most frugal comfort. The heavy concentration of such congestion in parts of counties west of a line from Loch Foyle to west Cork led the government in 1891 to establish the Congested Districts Board. Initially covering some 3.6 million acres, with a population of 550,000, the CDB, with modest funds voted directly by parliament, supported a variety of projects and activities – in infrastructure, education and training, improved husbandry and fishing, arts and crafts, marketing – directed towards raising living standards and relieving congestion through a programme of what may be described as regional economic and social development.[6]

It is true that many of the early functions and areas of activity of the CDB – relating, for example, to home industries, education and training, improved husbandry and stock management, fisheries, crafts and native textiles – were transferred or reallocated to the Department of Agriculture and Technical Instruction (DATI) in the years following its establishment in 1899. Indeed, from 1896 – and certainly from 1903 – the main work of the CDB was increasingly concerned with acquiring, managing and redistributing land. Moreover, coinciding with this redirection of policy and priorities, the western territory over which the CDB had jurisdiction was expanded so that its remit extended by 1911 over more than a third of the total acreage of the island, with approximately a quarter of the population.[7] Arguably this gave it a slightly less 'congested western' focus. It also secured for the CDB a larger budget – needed for land acquisition and redistribution, though still less than the Board and its clients would have considered justified or necessary. Demand for land redistribution always outran supply.

Whatever disappointment or impatience may have been felt by those seeking land distributed by the CDB or the Land Commission, the abrupt suspension of land purchase and distribution by the state, caused by the outbreak of war in 1914, inevitably triggered sporadic episodes of agitation and direct action. This posed a challenge to the revolutionary leadership of Sinn Féin, which emerged as the dominant political force in the secessionist Dáil following the general election of December 1918. Committed to asserting its authority as the legitimate government of the country, the government of Dáil Éireann was determined to show that it was respectful of the rights and interests of all sections of the community: this emphatically included property rights. The 'people's struggle for freedom' would not be weakened or undermined by divisive class conflict or the freelance 'settlement' of land hunger through land seizure and redistribution in different localities. The Sinn Féin courts would adjudicate on disputes regarding access to land and, where necessary, the Volunteers would enforce the decisions of the courts. Almost invariably, such interventions by the republican counter-state proved protective of existing property rights.[8]

There was nothing new, therefore, in the firmly conservative stand taken by the new Free State government of the early 1920s in dealing with any attempts by local groups to act outside the law, in attempting forceful land occupation and redistribution. Significantly, Kevin O'Higgins's much-quoted description of the Free State ministers, as 'the most conservative revolutionaries that ever put through a successful revolution...', was uttered during a Dáil exchange on the government's resistance to illegal land agitation.[9] The 1923 Land Act is generally acknowledged as a landmark in the history of Irish land legislation and, in particular, in the history of the fledgling Irish Free State (IFS). It consolidated the series of Land Acts and related schemes, notably in land purchase, that had been enacted in the final decades of the Union.[10]

The problem of 'congests' featured prominently in Minister Patrick Hogan's declaration of policy objectives for the 1923 Land Act. The various forms of land 'agitation' (seizures, running off cattle, intimidation) during the revolutionary years, with the first half of 1920 and later the civil war period being especially disturbed, gave urgency to the enactment of a new, consolidating Land Act, enjoying the authority of Dáil Éireann.

The terms of the 1923 act relating to the core issue of land purchase were of high political sensitivity. They needed to meet key, and often competing, demands. The British government needed reassurance that what was being done was 'fair' and not expropriation, as the British Treasury would have to advance the monies and be satisfied with the terms of repayment. Additionally, the terms would attempt to meet the hopes (for some, certainly, the expectations) of a land-hungry constituency, for most of whom the fruits of the struggle for 'freedom' would have to mean the right to comfortably live in their own country; in effect, to have a holding of land sufficient to enable them to rear a family in reasonable comfort.

Other pressures included the strong anti-grazier rhetoric of earlier, including more recent, agitations, and demands for the break-up of large grazing farms, whether promoted as part of a final push against old landlordism or against über-strong grazier farmers. The radical demand was to till more soil and retain population, not bleed away the struggling elements through emigration. Finally, there was the predicament of the landless men; those who were simply agricultural or general labourers, without a holding. Given the competing claims and complex legal context from which the 1923 Act emerged, it was hardly surprising that its impact failed to meet all expectations.

For many, the acquisition and redistribution of land during the 1920s was too slow and too limited, beset as it was by bureaucratic and legal snares. A major complication, in political and in broadly equitable terms, was the realisation that congests were not, in fact, confined to the areas in the western counties that had been so designated by the CDB. There were 'congests' – quite numerous, in fact – in other, including many prosperous, counties. These local congests – and their entitlements – had to be taken into account when the government and the Land Commission were responding to the claims of potential 'migrant' congests; that is, those that might be considered for transfer from the west. Furthermore, relocating substantial farmers from the poorer west in order to enable progress to be made on reducing congestion in the western counties, required finding in the east and south, alternative farms – as valuable as those they were surrendering, if not more so – for these farmers, whenever or wherever suitable land could be acquired by the Land Commission.

There was the further crunch issue of cost, upon which the Department of Finance was constantly – aggressively at times, depending on the relevant minister – vigilant. For example, migrant congests being moved from the west to the east – even to the east of the same county or province – had to be assisted in relocation (for example, provided with house, stock, equipment), whereas 'local' congests, simply being allocated an extra portion of land, incurred no such costs. The Department of Finance's preference in these circumstances isn't hard to understand.[11]

The acceleration of acquisition and redistribution of land by the Land Commission reached its high point in the first five years of Fianna Fáil in office (1932–7), when the Land Act of 1933 gave extra powers to the Land Commission, seeking to close many of the loopholes through which landowners whose estates seemed liable for acquisition and redistribution had contrived to delay or to frustrate such acquisition. But, after an initial spurt, Fianna Fáil-driven land redistribution slackened. Stubborn realities intervened. There was not an infinite supply of land for acquisition and redistribution. Neither was there an infinite supply of credit: indeed, with the 'economic war' of 1932–8, there was considerable hardship throughout the entire farming community. Furthermore, there was the continuous urging of the Department officials, that giving parcels of land to landless men, who had neither the capital nor, in many instances, the capacity to work these holdings so as to secure for settlers a reasonable living, was not a sensible policy. Certainly, it would do nothing to improve agricultural output or productivity, to say nothing of profitability, in strictly economic terms. And, while de Valera remained tied to the rhetoric of facilitating the maximum number of contented families living in modest comfort on 'the land of Ireland', an increasing number of his ministers, both in Finance and in Agriculture/Lands, were increasingly unconvinced by the zealous commitment to sub-division that had been the Fianna Fáil cry in its first radical decade, 1927–37. Moreover, even 'sound' rural TDs like Seán Moylan (notably as Minister for Lands in 1943) were opposed to men getting land who could not or would not use it; some, leaving it idle, others leasing it back to those from whom it was acquired for redistribution.[12]

One critical aspect of the debates on the CDB, the wider issue of congests, the viability of holdings and land redistribution generally, was the highly sensitive issue of emigration; specifically, whether the relief of chronic congestion would require state-assisted emigration. In the post-Famine decades, as Irish population decline became an embedded feature of socio-economic change, commentators were increasingly denouncing heavy emigration as signifying a failure of effective government. Such a verdict was not confined to ardent nationalist commentators. In 1852 John Stuart Mill had declared that: 'When the inhabitants of a country quit the country *en masse* because the government will not make it a place fit for them to live in, the government is judged and condemned'.[13]

After J. H. Tuke's significant scheme of assisted emigration from western districts in the 1880s, Irish nationalist opposition to emigration as a solution to western poverty hardened. Tuke himself remained committed to assisted emigration, at least as one element of the solution to western 'congestion'.[14] But the rise in the rate of voluntary emigration from the west in the 1880s, together with the dominant rhetoric of the land war in its decisive early phase, resulted in emigration being denounced by most nationalists as baleful evidence of British misrule in Ireland, the emptying out of the lifeblood of the country; and this at precisely the time that the demand for Home Rule for Ireland had gathered what seemed irreversible momentum.

In truth, the strictly economic prescription for the relief of congestion and of poverty in the western districts – which might well require emigration – had to contend with a powerful, historically-rooted, current in Irish nationalist rhetoric that emphasised the historic right of Irish people to remain and enjoy a comfortable living in their own land. The emotional charge of the land war slogans drew on this deep longing. The economic ideas of Parnell, in his vision for a prosperous Home Rule Ireland, declared that Ireland was generally underpopulated, but 'overpopulated in spots'; he was adamant, however, that the labour that would be required for a self-governing Ireland increasing its industrial activity should not be siphoned off through emigration.[15] The more extreme version of the ideal of settling as many families on the land as could be accomplished in comfort was proclaimed by successive agrarian radicals, from Davitt's early advocacy of land nationalisation to the abrasive anti-grazier rhetoric of the likes of Lawrence Ginnell.[16]

What all of this points to, therefore, is that the objective of settling as many families as possible on the land of Ireland – enunciated as the 'social ideal' by successive nationalist leaders since Parnell – had to contend with a land settlement, brought about by the state-funded land purchase schemes (1880–1909), that created a rural society of peasant occupier-owners, but that confirmed the existing, hierarchical social structure of the countryside. So far as the poorer peasants of the congested districts were concerned, this posed a stark choice: if they were to have any future, let alone one that promised a decent living, the choice lay between migration or drastic redistribution of land. The latter option was canvassed repeatedly by champions of the struggling smallholders, right up to the 1960s: but the Land Commission, for all its best efforts, repeatedly failed to satisfy the hopes and the needs of the claimants.[17]

Not surprisingly, emigration became the default option for thousands of the disappointed, the impatient and the desperate. This was the case in the generation before the establishment of the Irish Free State (the decades of the Land Acts and the operations of the CDB). It remained so in the decades after the establishment of native government. The figures for the western counties (and the CDB area as a whole) told their own story.[18] But the wider phenomenon of the 'flight from the land' in the state as a whole prompted questions not only regarding the viability of agricultural holdings (their size and the quality of land) for rearing a family in tolerable comfort, but also about a range of quality of life issues that seemed to militate against the attractions of rural society for the rising generation.[19] It is within this larger context of anxieties about continuing emigration and disenchantment with the quality of rural life that the founding of Muintir na Tíre can best be understood.

The 1923 Land Act – whatever its merits or shortcomings – did not include the continuation of the CDB or any alternative structure dedicated to promoting region-specific development. Mary Daly has emphasised the high degree of continuity between the old DATI and the Department of Agriculture of the new IFS – in terms of its personnel, functions, and official mind. In particular, the new Department was determined to exercise central control over all aspects of rural development. It certainly did not countenance any other bodies, with rival or complementary ambitions, interfering in its exclusive domain. Such centralising determination sealed the fate of the CDB.[20]

While the first Saorstát governments declined to formally recognise the special character and distinct socio-economic needs of any particular region or community in the state (as the CDB had done), or, *a fortiori*, to establish any dedicated new structures for dealing with such needs, there was one exceptional and problematic community that posed a particular challenge to this official view. The formal commitment of the new government to the revival of the long-declining Irish language as a general vernacular demanded that urgent action be taken to arrest the further decline of the Gaeltacht or Irish-speaking communities, dispersed, overwhelmingly, in the western districts of several counties of the Atlantic seaboard.[21]

THE GAELTACHT COMMISSION, 1925–6

In 1925 the new Saorstát government appointed a special Commission to enquire as to what districts could be plausibly regarded as Irish-speaking districts (Gaeltacht) and to make recommendations on what actions should be taken to ensure their continued survival as such.[22] In his letter of appointment to the Commission, W. T. Cosgrave (President of the Executive Council) acknowledged that the socio-economic problems of the Gaeltacht communities constituted a serious impediment to their continued survival and he emphasised that such problems must be addressed by the Commission:

> These districts are known to coincide more or less with areas of rural Ireland which present an economic problem of the greatest difficulty and complexity. The language problem and the economic problem are in close relation to each other, and your Commission is asked to consider both together.[23]

As it happened, the membership of the Commission was dominated by ardent language revivalists. The Commission was chaired by Risteard Ó Maolcatha, recently a senior government minister, with a formidable reputation as a military leader in the War of Independence and on the pro-Treaty side of the Civil War: he was a strong supporter of the Irish language. Of the other 11 members, the only one with expertise in an area concerned with socio-economic disadvantage was L. C. Moriarty, who had held senior office in the CDB and who by the mid-1920s was Secretary of the Department of Fisheries in the IFS government.[24] Between April and October 1925 the commissioners visited areas in Counties Donegal, Galway, Mayo, Clare, Cork, Kerry, Waterford and Louth. Evidence from witnesses was also taken in Dublin. Some 100 witnesses gave public evidence and others made written submissions. The co-operation of teachers, priests and gardaí was crucial to the work of the Commission.

Of course, it was axiomatic that for Irish-speaking communities to survive and prosper as Gaeltachtaí, they must first survive as viable communities, in essentially social and economic terms. Many of the witnesses who made submissions to the Commission, orally or in writing, expressed their anxiety with regard to the economic and social deficits that threatened the continuing viability of the Gaeltacht communities as living communities, irrespective of language.

When the Commission finally reported in mid-1926, its main recommendations (there were 82 in all), related to language competence and behaviour, notably aimed at ensuring that Irish would be the medium in all transactions between the state apparatus and its public officials and the Irish-speaking communities of the Gaeltacht.[25] There was particular emphasis on those government departments – Lands, Agriculture, Fisheries, Social Welfare, Education and Justice (teachers, Gardaí, inspectors of all kinds) – with high levels of direct communication with the Gaeltacht communities.

On the economic front, the Commission's recommendations concentrated on land, fisheries and limited home crafts: there is very little in the Report that is specific to any new initiatives in industrialisation as such. Apart from predictable and highly laudable proposals for the provision of educational and training facilities relevant to the exploitation of the natural resources and craft skills of the areas, and for a system of grants and aids in agricultural development, the most controversial and significant recommendation of the Commission was that relating to the basic problem of heavy population pressure on generally very poor land (notably in Counties Donegal, Mayo and Galway). The Commission favoured the break-up of 'all grasslands in the Western counties' and recommended radical land redistribution. Where state-sponsored population transfer was judged advisable, it was proposed that English-speaking groups should be the groups to be transferred out of the Gaeltacht areas. But even with this, the Commission conceded that congestion in western Donegal, Erris in County Mayo and in Connemara in County Galway was so chronic that migration of Irish-speakers from these areas was inevitable. Here it proposed planned migration of 'homogenous communities' (i.e. colonies) and their resettlement, preferably in other parts of Donegal, Mayo and Galway, or alternatively in Counties Sligo, Roscommon, Wicklow, Kildare and Meath. In effect, this meant planned Gaeltacht colonies transplanted to land which could support a community in tolerable comfort.[26]

The size and social composition of the proposed colony – critical for its sustained viability as a distinct Irish-speaking community – was clearly a core issue for several witnesses. Thus, for example, Dr Bartley Ó Beirne, dispensary doctor for County Galway, recommended that 'a number of families' be moved from na hOileáin in Connemara (the poorest districts, in his view) to east Galway:

> I would migrate them in 100 families, taking their own teachers and priests with them, and I would have the villages close together. For the first few years the Government should give them all the help they could, in line of supplying them with farm tools and equipment. They are only accustomed to the spade; they know nothing of plough or harrow, and the East Galway land would be new to them. They should also have Irish instructors. I would place them close to the railway line, my idea that people from Dublin, students and others, would often come down there. That would encourage them and create an interest in the language.[27]

Alasdar Mac Cába, another advocate of internal migration, claimed that:

> I would be in favour of a community large enough to be self-contained. I would say no less than fifty families. I would say about thirty or forty farmers would do, and the remainder would be employed on supply services or meeting their wants in the nature of shops and interests.

With an average size of circa 20 acres per family, this would amount to about 800 acres in all for the colony. Again, Mac Cába was concerned with the continuing viability of the colony as an Irish-speaking community:

...the ideal organisation to aim at in such a settlement would be: the migrants to be settled in reasonably-sized villages with their own schools, churches, co-operative stores, creameries and shops, if possible, where only Irish-speaking clergymen, teachers, shopmen, managers etc., would be employed. Voluntary help could, without doubt, be secured for the building of places of entertainment, such as picture houses, theatres and recreation halls, in which Irish alone would be used.[28]

Mac Cába also hoped the colony would be settled near a railway line, to facilitate visitors coming to learn or improve their Irish in the colony.

The final recommendation of the Commission was: 'That a special Commission be set up charged with the duty of seeing that all Departments carry out, in detail, the Government's policy with regard to the language in the Gaeltacht'.[29] In effect, this would be an oversight body, with no executive or administrative powers or competence and no budget for meaningful intervention.

Among the minority reservations to the Commission's main Report, two that merit further comment are those of the Donegal priest, Father Seaghan Mac Cuinneagáin and that of Mr L. C. Moriarty. Father Mac Cuinneagáin contended that 'there should be no general effort to transfer any large percentage of the inhabitants of the Gaeltacht, either as self-contained colonies or as scattered units to districts totally different to their own'. Such transfers would mean they would be lost to the Gaeltacht. He urged that the proposed Parish Committees should have certain administrative powers: a merely advisory role would bring no practical benefits. But, crucially, in order to address effectively the socio-economic as well as linguistic predicament of the Gaeltacht, he declared that it would be 'absolutely necessary' to 'set up a permanent commission or Bord for the Gaeltacht...as a practical solution to the problems confronting the Gaeltacht, and to preserve it in every phase of its existence...'.[30] Mac Cuinneagáin outlined the competence of the proposed Commission:

The functions in general of this proposed Commission should be to see and insist that the recommendations of the Gaeltacht Commission are carried out in the spirit and in the letter; therefore it should have an active and directive voice in the activities of the various Governmental departments functioning in the Gaeltacht, the general plans and schemes of which departments should, in so far as language policy etc are concerned, be first submitted to this Commission for approval or amendment in these matters... In particular, this Commission should have, besides, in relation to all industries in the Gaeltacht (including Fishing), full powers to develop the industrial life of the Gaeltacht in every respect, by setting up new industries, reviving, fostering and extending existing industries, opening up markets at home and abroad for the sale of Gaeltacht products, securing transit facilities, etc. etc.

The Donegal priest further insisted that the Commission must have control of funds voted by the Dáil for these purposes:

The provision of funds for the purposes of this Commission should present no difficulty... The funds of the late Congested Districts Board originally voted by the English Parliament to solve the economic problem of the Congested Districts, should now be made available for a similar purpose in the Gaeltacht which is practically coterminous with the original Congested Districts and can surely lay claim, with all justice, to these funds as its own.[31]

Significantly, Mr L. C. Moriarty – a veteran CDB senior official, now head of the Department of Fisheries – also added a personal statement:

> The economic development of the Gaeltacht is, to my mind, a National duty. The establishment of the Congested Districts Board in 1891 was virtually an act of reparation by the British Government of the day. The process of improving the standard of living in the Irish Speaking Districts, which was being carried on if somewhat slowly, at all events surely, by that Board has, in my opinion, been slowed down since that Board was abolished.

Accordingly, Moriarty favoured the establishment of a Permanent Commission, to be endowed by an annual grant-in-aid: 'to be devoted to the industrial development of the Gaeltacht'. He explained that:

> Departments of State administering the affairs of the whole country cannot be expected to give that close and constant attention to the conditions and needs of the Gaeltacht which is required. A merely advisory body acting in the interests of the Gaeltacht might find itself powerless to accomplish its object so far as economic development of the district is concerned, unless it was endowed with the financial power to enable its development schemes to be carried out.[32]

The official government response to the Report did not come until 1929. When it did, it did not promise or presage any urgent action. In the decades that followed, some of the Commission's recommendations were, fitfully and generally inadequately, implemented, but with limited impact. The proposal to establish a special Commission – even one confined to an oversight role – was given short shrift. Equally firm was the rejection of the migration proposal, as W. T. Cosgrave stated:

> The extensive migration schemes proposed by the [Gaeltacht] Commission do not commend themselves to us. There is only a limited amount of land available for distribution in the country... Any scheme of wholesale migration to lands which could only be rendered available by a second migration of the present occupiers is, to our minds, unthinkable.[33]

CONCLUSIONS

The strain of Jeffersonian democracy that found support in Ireland in the first four decades of the new Irish state, combined tenets of contemporary Catholic social teaching on the family and social stability with a deep-rooted nationalist myth of 'freedom', propagated as a popular liberation project encompassing the restoration of the land to 'the people' of Ireland. '[Ireland] would...be the home of a people living the life that God desires that man should live' – the too easily parodied social ideal invoked in de Valera's 1943 St Patrick's Day radio address to the Irish diaspora – was the pithy lyrical version of an idealisation of what might nowadays be described as sustainable rural living that enjoyed a wide currency at the time.[34] The interventions of the CDB in the generation before 1914 were directed at the economic improvement and social amelioration of living conditions of specific western districts with distinct socio-economic profiles and problems. However, the early decades of the new state would see a fragile and cash-strapped state step back from any coherent, structured approach to region-specific socio-economic development, trusting instead targeted assistance for increasing agricultural productivity and efficiency, thereby raising the living standards of the rural community as a whole.[35]

The radical rhetoric of Fianna Fáil, as it commenced what would prove to be long interludes of power from 1932, suggested that the *menu peuple* would have their hour (or at least some practical measure of government favour); and the early years of Fianna Fáil in office did indeed see increased activity in land acquisition and distribution by the Land Commission, though the resulting increase in the actual size of the smaller holdings benefitting from this activity did not ensure their future viability. However, the hugely disruptive impact on Irish agriculture and on farmers' incomes of the 'economic war' of the 1930s was unlikely to staunch the flight from the land, even if the wider economic depression of the 1930s checked for a time the volume of emigration out of independent Ireland.[36]

The 'scourge' of emigration, in fact, constitutes the dominant canvas against which the successive efforts of organisations and individual crusades (of which Muintir na Tíre is the outstanding example) to 'save' rural Ireland from depopulation and social anaemia must be considered. Ideology – Catholic social teaching or Jeffersonian idealism – requires close examination and has undeniable relevance for an understanding of the currents of ideas within which public policy initiatives for rural development were devised and implemented. But staunching the haemorrhage of emigration was the remorseless political imperative. In its final Report, the Commission on Emigration and Other Population Problems, 1948–54 (its very title a clear marker of national anxiety) explicitly addressed the core issue:

> We believe that measures to bring about economic development should be considered from the demographic as well as from the purely economic standpoint; a primary aim should be to encourage the development of agricultural, industrial and other resources along lines which, though necessarily in harmony with, are not wholly governed by economic considerations but take due account of the wider consideration of providing the basis for more employment and more families.[37]

Such initiatives as were undertaken by the state in addressing the national demographic crisis, rural depopulation in particular, did not extend to formal structural responses to regional differentiation in economic or social disadvantage. Thus, while the Gaeltacht Commission in 1926 recommended targeted supports based on language use within dedicated geographical areas, so far as formal structures were concerned it would be the mid-1950s before a dedicated Department of the Gaeltacht and a dedicated development agency (Gaeltarra Éireann) would be established, to give some degree of coherence to such supports as the state was providing.

In truth, the Gaeltacht case-study offers a particular, if hitherto neglected, illustration of the larger issue of the tension between, on the one hand, an essentially sociological view of the new state's mission of national renewal – in respect of halting 'involuntary' emigration and settling as many families as possible in satisfactory comfort on the land; and, on the other, an essentially liberal view of economic development, which stressed productivity, efficient use of the land as an economic resource, and an acceptance of the inevitability of migration – to towns and cities, at home or abroad, where employment could be secured by Irish men and women exercising their choice as free agents.

In a sense, therefore, the Underdeveloped Areas Act of 1952 and the tardy establishment a few years later of Gaeltacht boundaries, of a Department of the Gaeltacht and, additionally, of Gaeltarra Éireann, may be seen as belated acknowledgements of geographically-specific communities of special need; that is, communities needing a range of targeted stimuli for their overall development, perhaps their very survival. These belated initiatives also indicate an acceptance that migration of 'congests' and further land division would not be sufficient, in fact would not be the appropriate way any longer, for improving the economic prospects or for slowing the outflow from the 'designated congested areas' of the west. In the case of the Gaeltacht 'package' of initiatives of the 1950s, though it stopped short of establishing a Gaeltacht Authority, it at least acknowledged that the socio-economic developmental needs and the language-stabilisation missions would have to involve some level of integration; this was what later would be attempted, albeit with limited powers and competences, with the establishment of Údarás na Gaeltachta in 1980.

Devising the formula and policy measures – and committing the resources – for reconciling the economic objectives and the social ideal in the highly dispersed enclaves of Irish-speaking communities in independent Ireland would be the challenge to which successive governments fitfully responded in the decades after 1922. But the Gaeltacht case-study was also a version of the same essential challenge that lay at the core of the wider question to which Muintir na Tíre sought to provide an answer: what kind of society should or would characterise 'rural Ireland'; and what measures might the state adopt to ensure that a contented rural society remained the foundation of a prosperous and contented Irish society.

The Rural Dimension of State Planning: Ireland in the 1960s

Peter Murray and Maria Feeney

In the 1950s Ireland fell behind as most of western Europe boomed economically. Irish per capita income lagged behind the western European average by a widening margin. As many other countries experienced full employment and rising living standards, Ireland exhibited surging emigration and apparently inexorable population decline. Underlying this dismal profile was the prevalence of low productivity in both agriculture and industry, a policy continuity in which innovation was paralysed by fears that 'any change would lead to an even greater loss of employment' and a large degree of detachment from the European institutional developments that were helping to foster an environment of strong economic expansion.[1]

A formal Irish link to European economic reshaping was provided by the state's membership of the Organisation for European Economic Co-operation (OEEC). Initially a requirement for participating in the European Recovery Programme (to give the Marshall Plan its official title), this membership continued after the 1951 cessation of Ireland's US aid and continued to associate Ireland (somewhat tenuously) with broader moves towards removing trade restrictions and attaining the convertibility of currencies that facilitated trade expansion. By 1957 six OEEC member states had negotiated the Treaty of Rome, prompting what ultimately proved abortive moves to explore the possibility of setting up a free trade area that would encompass both the customs union of the European Economic Community (EEC) and the Organisation's 12 other member states. What struck OEEC experts examining Ireland's position in relation to this project was a unique absence of any overall state plan to stimulate economic growth.[2] Recently appointed Secretary of the Department of Finance at a remarkably young age, T. K. Whitaker had enlisted the aid of a small group of Irish civil service colleagues to begin addressing this lacuna. The fruits of their labour became publicly available in November 1958 with the publication of a White Paper on economic expansion. The period of Irish economic planning had been inaugurated.

This planning period would last for approximately 15 years and would produce a series of three government programmes for economic expansion and (in the case of the Third Programme) social development. For roughly the first half of this period state planning was generally credited with producing modest but sustained growth in place of 1950s stagnation. Then, as Whitaker put it, 'we achieved a steady growth rate, a fairly stable price level, rising employment and a reasonable balance in our external payments'.[3] During the second half of the period, however, planning exercises that had grown more complex and more ambitious found themselves driven off course within more turbulent and less stable external and internal economic environments.[4] Finally, after Seán Lemass had been succeeded as Taoiseach by Jack Lynch in late 1966, a retreat into generality and vagueness preceded the ending in the early 1970s of Irish governmental reliance on target-driven plans.[5]

The planning period in general is one in which Ireland's economic and social bases shifted decisively towards industrialisation and urbanisation. But the planners did not merely preside over the shrinking of rural Ireland: during the planning years a significant reshaping of the rural areas took place. Planning attracted both opposition and support from social movements that proclaimed themselves to be defenders of rural Ireland's interests and welfare. The period left an enduring legacy in terms of a changed mix of determinants of the Irish rural population's life chances. Planning-fostered changes, government interaction with rural opponents or supporters of the planning enterprise, and planning's transformative influence on rural Ireland are discussed in turn in this chapter.

RURAL INITIATIVES AND STATE PLANNING

The initial focal point for planning initiatives relating to rural Ireland was 'how to deal with the small (mainly western) farms and to ensure reasonable standards of income for those who live on them'. Seán Lemass, the Taoiseach, identified this early in 1961 as 'the main, if not indeed the only question arising in national economic policy to which we have not yet found a satisfactory answer'.[6] The issue was already the subject of correspondence between the Secretaries of the Departments of Finance and Agriculture;[7] and a convergence of ministerial and civil service concerns led to the establishment in March 1961 of an Inter-Departmental Committee on the Problems of Small Western Farms.[8]

Published in March 1962, and actively followed up by Lemass,[9] the Committee's Report set in motion a policy shift that had by the end of the decade installed non-farm sources of employment in industry, tourism, forestry and fishing alongside 'more intensive farming in economic units' as the key components of rural development. County Development Teams (CDTs) had been established in 13 western counties that operated in tandem with the Finance-chaired Central Development Committee (CDC) whose role was to co-ordinate the activities of all the economic departments and state agencies concerned in the development of the west. From 1967 the CDTs and the CDC could draw upon a Special Regional Development Fund for project finance. Initially through its Small Industries Programme, and subsequently through its Regional Plans and network of Regional Offices, the Industrial Development Authority (IDA) loomed ever larger on this scene as industrial decentralisation accompanied the decimation of the previously protected manufacturing base and a greatly increased inflow of foreign direct investment.[10] However, land consolidation was 'minimal' with 'small-scale landholders, by and large, holding on to their land'.[11]

Education was not one of the departments represented on the Inter-Departmental Committee but the 1962 Report contained two suggestions relating to its field. These were, first, that 'a rural bias should be given to the general education of pupils in rural schools' and, second, that 'the facilities available at the Vocational Schools should be brought within reach of all children in remote areas by organising transport or extending scholarship schemes'.[12] The sustained push for follow-up on the Report by Lemass was to provide a context within which a much further-reaching initiative was shaped, one that responded to wider internal and external forces pushing for educational change in Ireland.[13] On the grounds that, whether it was embodied in religious congregations or lay people, private enterprise had failed to supply adequate secondary schooling in remote locations and that families with children would not stay in places without educational opportunities, a proposal for a 'Comprehensive Post-Primary Education Pilot Scheme related to Small Farm areas' was brought forward in January 1963. This envisaged state initiative to ensure the provision of 'larger [school] units which could cover a much wider programme (with special reference to the teaching of Science and modern continental languages)' coupled with a subsidised system of pupil transport.[14] Despite considerable watering down of what was originally envisaged in the course of discussions with bishops,[15] state-established schools would for the first time provide academic secondary education, breaking out of the confines of an understanding with the Catholic Church hierarchy dating back to the establishment of the Vocational Education system in the early 1930s.

RURAL HOSTILITY TO PLANNING: THE CHARLESTOWN COMMITTEE

During the period immediately following the Inter-Departmental Committee Report's appearance a movement in opposition to government policy emerged in the west in the form of the Charlestown Committee. Centred in Mayo, this movement derived its inspiration from community efforts to regenerate the Glencolumbkille area of west Donegal led by its parish priest, Father James McDyer.[16] To save the west in Father McDyer's view two things were essential – 'local cooperation and adequate capital for development'. The government was in favour of local cooperation provided it was subject to official direction of a kind Father McDyer and his followers viewed with great suspicion. As the Inter-Departmental Committee was being set up Minister for Finance James Ryan deprecated 'any "solution" which involved heavier subsidisation of uneconomic production and a consequent increase in taxation adversely affecting the real growing points of the economy'. It was Father McDyer's view that 'if you are a foreign industrialist and you are looking for adequate capital, you will get it without any trouble but if you are a small farmer it's a different matter'.[17]

The relationship between state officialdom and voluntary organisations was raised soon after the CDTs were set up. Membership of the teams was confined to officials whose position, it was argued (especially by the Department of Agriculture), would be invidious were representation to be broadened. A 'right of audience' for voluntary organisations was the extent of the concession made to advocates of their full inclusion. The issue emerged again at the level of the CDC during the Summer of 1964 following Government acceptance of a Charlestown Committee proposal that pilot areas be chosen for intensive support in order to generate a wider demonstration effect throughout the west of Ireland.[18] The Charlestown Committee was rebuffed when it sought direct involvement in running the pilot area programme as

Officials are no better equipped in matters concerning Community Development than ourselves and we also feel that these good Officials might either be subjected to undesirable pressures by the respective County Committees [of Agriculture] in the choice of areas, or on the other hand might follow the line of least resistance and choose areas where the land would be good and the effort involved in promotion would be simple.[19]

Official implementation of the pilot areas proposal was subsequently accompanied by the dissociation from the initiative of the voluntary group with which it had originated.[20]

In the Autumn of 1964 the Charlestown Committee mounted a broader attack on government policy by publishing Broadsheet No.1 which, highlighting some of the Second Programme's projections, alleged that a policy of land clearances was under way – 'the truth is industry, banking, big business have taken over the State. They speak through policy-making Civil Service cadres, who preserve the appearance of democratic government by using Ministers as their public relations officers'.[21] The government response,[22] which took the form of changes in social welfare schemes, influenced policy relating to small western farms in two main ways. First, in tandem with the 1965 Land Act, the manner in which means-testing for the Old Age Pension was carried out changed to encourage the transfer of land from the inactive old to the active young. But, as Damian Hannan and Patrick Commins note, 'special pension schemes to induce elderly farmers to retire, and release the use or ownership of their land to other farmers, did not prove attractive to the targeted population'.[23] Second, the Report of the Inter-Departmental Committee suggested that 'the basis of qualification for unemployment assistance should be reviewed in so far as smallholders are concerned to remove the present disincentive effect' whilst also appreciating 'the difficulties of devising a system which would not have unfortunate side effects'.[24]

Lemass was initially inclined to dwell on the difficulties inherent in such a change. When he met a deputation from the Charlestown Committee in July 1963 the most he could offer was the possibility of 'suspending means assessments for, say, three years so that a small farmer at present qualifying for Unemployment Assistance would be assured of a continuation of payments for a certain number of years despite increases in income from vegetable growing or other productive activity'.[25] But the new assistance scheme for western smallholders enacted in 1965 went a great deal further than this and ran along the lines advocated in many speeches from Charlestown Committee platforms. Means were henceforth to be calculated by reference to the rateable valuation of the land with £20 per annum of income imputed for each £1 valuation of the land exclusive of the valuation of the buildings. As the Department of Social Welfare put it, 'under the liberalising effects of the new method' small farmers should now 'be able to take full advantage of the many schemes that have been devised for the benefit of the Western areas' without imperilling their Unemployment Assistance payments.[26] The following year the Employment Period Orders that had, since the 1930s, been used to restrict payment of Unemployment Assistance to small farmers to certain months of the year were abolished and it became a year-round source of smallholder income.[27]

Government initiatives specific to small landholders contrasted with the absence of moves to address the chronically under-developed state of Ireland's wider social welfare provision. From the outset, a key tenet of the planning enterprise held that high taxation was 'one of the greatest impediments to economic progress because of its adverse effects on saving and enterprise'.[28] 'Steady growth in real national income' would, when well established, allow improved social services to be provided alongside stabilised or reduced taxation. For the present, available resources needed to be devoted to providing productive employment rather than making improvements in social welfare – 'the national candle cannot be burned at both ends'.[29]

The positive economic growth performance achieved under the First Programme ensured that the allocation of a sizeable share in the new prosperity to higher social spending was being actively canvassed in the years preceding the 1965 general election.[30] The Minister for Social Welfare from 1961, Kevin Boland, argued that a fundamental reform of basically inadequate rates needed to be undertaken but could not secure the government support he needed to bring this about. In correspondence with Cabinet colleagues during the run-up to the 1965 general election, he pursued the line that increased social welfare spending was a matter of both social justice and political expediency.[31] Concern about the potential effect of the new wave of small farmer disaffection embodied in the Charlestown Committee on Fianna Fáil's electoral support was also expressed by one of the party's rising western stars. Seán Flanagan wrote to Lemass in June 1964 that he was 'deeply concerned about the present situation':

> Since some of the more important men in the Charlestown Committee have been our best supporters in the past, they can do a great deal of damage merely by being lukewarm now. As for the others – and this has been Fr McDyer's approach right through – they will spread discontent with all politics and politicians.[32]

Unwilling to countenance electoral intervention, Father McDyer would later regret not having agreed to organise a march on Dublin from the West of Ireland –'at least it would have drawn attention to the pressure building up behind the proposal to form a Western political party'. He then derived consolation from the reflection that 'it is almost certain that the intensity of this campaign in the west did highlight the neglected condition of the more remote counties and certainly galvanised the government into making a greater effort on their behalf'.[33] Action and inaction during this period in the social welfare field appear to lend support to his contention. Fianna Fáil feared electoral damage from the western movement but was in the wider national context insulated from opposition party critiques of its social welfare neglect by those parties' unwillingness to coalesce and form an alternative government.[34]

Alongside the advent of new measures came the emergence of a new man. In October 1964 the Minister for Agriculture, Patrick Smith, resigned his post. Charles Haughey, who took Smith's place, brought new energy and a greater personal willingness to engage in governmental dealings with western disaffection.[35] Welfare concessions supplemented by a ministerial charm offensive, multiple consultation exercises and a new western regional focus within the Department of Agriculture mollified the more reconcilable elements of the Charlestown Committee support base.[36] 'Physically unable to bear the pressure' that his central inspirational role in Save the West campaigning had heaped upon him 'but also because there was a danger that the momentum would be lost in Glencolumbkille', Father

McDyer stepped away from his involvement in 1968, a loss that triggered the movement's disintegration.[37]

RURAL ENTHUSIASM FOR PLANNING: THE CASE OF MUINTIR NA TÍRE

The Charlestown Committee Broadsheet view that 'policy-making Civil Service cadres' were pursuing large-scale land clearance to serve the interests of industry, banking, and big business was not universally subscribed to by those pursuing rural Ireland's preservation. An important rural organisation that offered strong support to the economic planning enterprise was Muintir na Tíre (Muintir). Yet this support was not reciprocated from the government side and the movement ended the planning period in a state of deep crisis.

Founded in 1937 by a Tipperary priest, Father John Hayes, Muintir proclaimed itself to be 'a Movement for the promotion of the true welfare, spiritual, cultural and material of Ireland and, in particular, of its rural people, through the application of Christian social principles'.[38] Muintir's parish guilds quickly came to the fore in the local organisation of the (Second World War) Emergency period's drives to try to make up shortfalls in food and fuel supplies. The Department of Agriculture then recommended that Muintir should receive an annual grant through its Vote, but de Valera's reaction to this suggestion was that this 'would constitute nothing short of a disservice to the Association, because it would deprive it of the spirit of self-reliance and self-help so sorely needed in this country as a whole and among the farmers in particular'.[39] With the advent of the Marshall Plan, US aid providers were also favourably impressed by Muintir, earmarking it along with the Irish Countrywomen's Association (ICA) and Macra na Feirme (Macra) for Grant Counterpart Fund allocations to strengthen their organisational capacities.

However, divergences between Muintir's project of an all-embracing community movement and what it perceived as the sectional interest projects of its fellow funding beneficiaries were arguably as significant as the aims these movements shared in common.[40] During the 1950s these divergences were to be brought into the open by conflict over the Parish Plan for the organisation of agricultural advisory services. Originally devised by members of Muintir's National Executive, the Parish Plan was partially implemented in an adapted form by James Dillon during his stints as Minister for Agriculture in the first (1948–51) and second (1954–7) Inter-Party Governments.[41] Muintir was ultimately to distance itself from Dillon's initiatives in order to avoid damaging defections from its own ranks, but not before it came under sustained attack from Macra and its offshoot, the National Farmers' Association (NFA).[42]

Canon Hayes's death in January 1957 preceded by a few months a return to office of Fianna Fáil. That party had never regarded the Parish Plan with much enthusiasm while Whitaker and his Civil Service associates were-like minded. Such implementation as had been put in place of the Parish Plan was gradually wound down with sole responsibility for the delivery of advisory services being vested in the County Committees of Agriculture.

Deprived of its charismatic founder and bruised by the recrimination which it had experienced in the course of Parish Plan controversies, Muintir's leading figures now embraced as its twin focal points Community Development and Rural Sociology. Both were clearly in evidence when Reverend Professor Jeremiah Newman delivered the first Canon Hayes Memorial Lecture in February 1958. Here Newman engaged in a critique of the

1954 Report of the Commission on Emigration, arguing that the Commission had failed to properly analyse Irish emigration's social context and had treated rural depopulation as a problem peculiar to Ireland. Drawing on British and Dutch sociological research, he argued that it was possible to tackle rural decline by a positive planning approach to economic and social change.[43] Muintir now sought to establish expert community development credentials by forging international links with a variety of agencies and academics.[44] In an early 1960s submission to the government it criticised the lop-sidedness of the knowledge base of the newly established Agricultural Institute (An Foras Talúntais) and of the Economic Research Institute, calling for this to be redressed by the establishment under Muintir's own direction of a Rural Sociology Centre.[45] Whereas supporters of the Charlestown Committee could be accused of indulging in impractical nostalgia, leading Muintir figures displayed a supportive familiarity with the lexicon of planning and claimed to have seen in the international literature of community development and rural sociology a future that would work for rural Ireland. This process culminated when Muintir na Tíre sent the Taoiseach 'A Plan for Community Development in Ireland Submitted to the Government as an aid to the implementation of the Second Programme for Economic Expansion' in October 1964:

> Muintir na Tíre welcomes the new spirit abroad in Ireland – what An Taoiseach calls 'the new and positive attitude to progress' – since the advent of the First Programme for Economic Expansion. It acknowledges the stimulation and impetus given to our people by a realistic approach to our economic problems on the part of the Government. It is glad to find even more detailed programming and target-setting, especially in the field of agriculture, in the Second Programme for Economic Expansion.

Muintir's 'Plan for Community Development in Ireland' went on to say that:

> This present contribution from the National Executive of Muintir na Tíre is respectfully presented as a complement to the Second Programme, a sincere endeavour from one of the oldest of Ireland's voluntary rural organisations to gear itself to a rapidly-changing rural scene and to ensure that national programming will not fail for lack of local, virile communities. To this task Muintir na Tíre willingly re-dedicates the strength of its 398 guilds throughout the country. Never before was the application of a genuine Community Development approach to rural problems a matter of such urgency.[46]

Joint action was to be based on the creation within Muintir – an organisation that then had only a rudimentary national headquarters based in Tipperary town – of a cadre of full-time and part-time educators, administrators and community development field workers that would enable it to function as a comprehensive interface organisation linking the statutory and the voluntary sectors across the state. The Taoiseach was positively disposed to Muintir's initiative, stating that:

> it is desirable that there should be a positive approach in all Departments to the proposals on the understanding that the Government will wish to go along with them, unless they can be shown to be impracticable or undesirable or better means of achieving the same purposes can be suggested.[47]

However the departmental responses were overwhelmingly negative with a consistent tendency to characterise the proposals as impracticable, undesirable or sub-optimal. The proposer also found itself in the firing line in the Department of Agriculture's comment:

> Muintir na Tíre is disappointing as an organisation in the promotion of agriculture. Theoretically it covers a very wide field of activities but in practice there is very little effective work done by the organisation and in many types of activity in the field of agriculture it tends to be outshone by other rural organisations e.g. Macra na Feirme, Macra na Tuaithe, I.C.A., N.F.A.[48]

Lemass came to the movement's defence, writing that Muintir was not:

> just another rural organisation trying to cut in on work now being done by other similar organisations in the agricultural field… [it is] concerned with social activities of various kinds, and not merely agricultural problems… [it] has, notwithstanding its weakness in organisation, already done something significant in creating community consciousness and self confidence, as well as in promoting understanding of, and respect for, the social teachings of the church.[49]

However this intervention was no more successful than his earlier Minute had been in eliciting departmental expressions of support for the Muintir Plan's proposals.

What eventuated from governmental consideration of the Muintir Plan was a small annual grant from the Department of Education Vote to help Muintir improve its organisation. This primarily resulted in the creation of a full-time National Director post. When the remit of the Economic Research Institute was extended to take in a broader range of social sciences, the movement that had criticised the original omission and had sought to partially fill the gap was left without any linkage into the new agency. When, turning abroad, Muintir sought to salvage one element of the bigger 1964 plan – the Canon Hayes Institute of Community Development and Rural Sociology – its efforts to secure UN technical assistance or US foundation funding were effectively blocked by government departments' withholding of support and its applications ended in failure.[50] Enthusiastic about government planning, Muintir was nobody's child when it came to departmental sponsorship. Agriculture, to which it was linked from the time of the Marshall Plan, dealt with farmers. Education, into whose ambit it moved in the mid-1960s, dealt with schools and colleges. Finance, which exhibited active interest in both community development and social research, sought to use the civil service network that had launched Irish planning to shape the Economic and Social Research Institute into the supplier of the social science inputs that more technically sophisticated plans were recognised to require.

By the end of the 1960s, Muintir's second National Director, Tomás Roseingrave, was desperately seeking to shore up its finances through a mixture of internal income generation and appeals to government for an increased grant-in-aid. When a British academic admirer published an account of the movement in 1967 the figure for Parish Guilds he provided was half the almost 400 that had been given in the 1964 Plan presented to the government. The following year another very sympathetic observer could write that 'there is no one connected with Muintir na Tíre that does not feel that it has reached a crisis in its life. It is in serious danger of becoming irrelevant'.[51] Ill-fated initiatives such as the launching of a short-lived Canon Hayes Institute at Foynes and a Community Organisation Officer scheme, for which the hoped-for local business funding failed to materialise, served only to further drain Muintir's depleted coffers.[52] Searching for both financial viability and renewed relevance, the movement turned to 'a committee of distinguished people' drawn from outside its ranks to formulate the basis of a five year plan for its development. The upshot was a substantial narrowing of the scope of Muintir's community development role that did not succeed in opening up a way to secure any substantial state funding. The Irish planning period thus drew to a close with Muintir – its most enthusiastic, 'realism' embracing constituency of rural support – in scarcely a more healthy state than planning's western small farm champion critics who had partially regrouped in the face of a perceived new threat to the smallholder, the Mansholt Plan of the EEC.[53]

CONCLUSIONS

Technocratic planners could be emotionally detached from the changes they presided over, as exemplified by Whitaker's remarks to an audience of trade unionists in 1967:

> In recent years the numbers who left agriculture have been almost balanced by those who found new jobs in industry and services. The former had not been employed, except in an artificial, statistical sense, in agriculture; they left the land, in fact, because they had no acceptable income from it and production has not suffered in consequence. The stability of the aggregate figure for 'employment' in recent years conceals a marked change for the better in the character of this employment – a change from low-income under-employment to worthwhile self-sustaining employment.[54]

A prophet from whom official honour was about to be steadily withdrawn, Muintir counselled the government in December 1962 that 'economics alone does not envisage all aspects of the [land reform] question…for any administrator to lay a native Irish government open to being labelled 'confiscator' or 'exterminator' would be to pay a price which, by its undermining of confidence in the government would make the game far from being worth the candle'.[55] When the Charlestown Committee resorted to labelling of the kind Muintir had anticipated, the government proved itself politically adept at deflecting the charges. Political imperatives continued to require that prescriptions derived from economics be tempered by obeisance to what has been called Irish rural fundamentalism.[56]

Hannan and Commins note that the independent Irish state inherited 'powerful strains of rural fundamentalist ideology' which they define as:

> 'a set of values and beliefs which stressed (i) the advantages of family-owned, family-operated farms and of a numerous class of landholders (ii) the healthy nature of farming as an occupation and open country farming communities as ideal settlement models and (iii) agriculture as a basis of national prosperity'.[57]

Within a context of state policies shaped by the collision of economics-based planning and rural fundamentalism, Hannan and Commins identify three small farm sub-groups emerging between the 1960s and the 1990s – a minority generating a viable household income from farming; 'pluriactive' households with different sources of earnings spread across different household members and impoverished households dependent on social welfare payments though with some farm income. Planning consistently emphasised the economic viability of farms while enhancing social welfare support to defuse the threat of opposition from those falling below its threshold. But pluriactivity perhaps owed most to the planners and their broader approach to rural development. The hopes of this type of household, historically pinned on land redistribution policy,[58] were refocused as they went on to use the key planning legacy of an expanded education system very effectively to gain access for their children to a high proportion of the available off-farm employment opportunities.

CLERICAL POWER AND
RURAL CIVIL SOCIETY

Community Development Visionary or Social Conservative? Canon John Hayes Reassessed

Eoin Devereux

The contribution of Father (later Canon) John Hayes, the founder and leader of Muintir na Tíre (People of the Land), a Catholic and populist rural social movement that first appeared as a co-operative society in 1931,[1] is reassessed in this chapter. My discussion is guided by a critical theoretical perspective that highlights the existence in rural society of unequal power relationships and their potential to impact negatively on community development efforts.[2] Unlike earlier largely uncritical accounts,[3] a more searching gaze is cast on Father Hayes's efforts at rural renewal through the application of Catholic social principles. A number of particular questions are posed to guide our discussion. To what extent could 'a sense of community' be said to truly exist in a rural society so ravaged – as was Ireland's during the interwar and post-war decades – by economic depression, class inequalities, out-migration and where familism – as opposed to communitarianism – reigned supreme? Was, given such major constraints, Father Hayes's belief concerning the capacity of rural parishes to engage effectively in self-help – driven as it was by nostalgia for the Land League and by an exaggerated estimation of the ideal of self-sufficiency as expounded by Arthur Griffith and others – misguided? And, finally, how realistic were his expectations as to what might be achieved practically by a movement so heavily dependent on voluntary effort?

By way of answering these questions, the formative influences that shaped John Hayes's outlook, and the circumstances in which he came to launch Muintir na Tíre in the 1930s, are first examined. To assess his strengths and weaknesses as a community development leader, an outline of the history of Muintir na Tíre's two key organisational forms – as a co-operative society in 1931 and as a vocationalist community movement from 1937 on – is then presented. There then follows two sections where I scrutinise Father Hayes's efforts to come to terms with the challenges Muintir na Tíre's two different approaches to organising rural communities faced from class divisions in rural society and from his movement's relations with the Irish state.

FORMATIVE INFLUENCES 1887–1931

Three formative influences stand out as especially important in shaping John Hayes's worldview and his activist career: his childhood experiences in County Limerick; his training as a clerical student in France; and his tentative forays into community and youth work as a young curate in Ireland and England. Originally farming in the northeast Limerick townland of Ballyvoreen, Murroe, Daniel Hayes – John Hayes's paternal great grandfather – moved to nearby Moher in 1780.[4] When Daniel's grandson Michael Hayes married Hanora McCormack from Madaboy in 1872, the family was farming a 49-acre farm – about half of which was unreclaimed land – on the estate of Lord Cloncurry (Valentine Frederick Lawless). In response to the fall in agricultural prices, Cloncurry's tenants requested a 20 per cent rent reduction in 1881, but the landlord refused their request and the Hayes family (with their six children) were among 32 tenants evicted in April 1882. The local Land League moved quickly to erect huts for the evicted families.[5]

The Hayes family, now living in their Land League hut on Terence McCormack's land in nearby Ballyvoreen, were reliant for subsistence on damp and poor land. Four more children were born to Michael and Hanora Hayes (including John Martin in 1887) during their Ballyvoreen years. Reflecting the family's poverty, a total of three of the children died in infancy, most probably from diphtheria.[6] All the younger children suffered from childhood rickets, a disease that left John Hayes with a slightly stunted physique in later life. For nearly 13 years the family was obliged to live in poor circumstances in Ballyvoreen before returning to their ruined Moher homestead in 1894.[7]

John Hayes's childhood left an indelible mark in shaping his sense of social justice and his desire to look out for the underdog. The Land League's actions in Murroe convinced him of the positive impacts of popular collective action in rural Ireland; and his family's experience as reinstated evicted tenants possibly explains his later reservations about any land redistribution policy being pursued too vigorously by the native state.[8] Childhood experiences were also significant in fostering a strong sense of patriotism in both John Hayes and his brother Mick. As young students at the Jesuit Crescent College in Limerick city, the Hayes brothers came under the spell of the Gaelic Revival and of Arthur Griffith's Sinn Féin. During lunch breaks or before travelling home to Moher, they regularly read *The Irish People* (edited by Griffith) in the Limerick Free Library. Mick Hayes would go on to be a republican activist and organiser in the Murroe district,[9] while his priest brother would in time put his nationalism into practice through rural community development initiatives. Later in life John Hayes regularly invoked the idea of patriotism having its roots at parish level in terms such as these:

> The cry is that a parish will not solve a nation's problems, but when it helps to solve its own problems, it will truly have helped to solve the national ones. Let us begin below and build upwards and have patience and trust in God.[10]

From 1937 the notion that parish councils were in effect a 'parish parliament' frequently surfaced in Hayes's movement-building promotional drives.[11]

EARLY CAREER

Before proceeding to the Irish College in Paris, John Hayes received his initial training for the priesthood in St Patrick's College, Thurles, where he had enrolled as a clerical student in 1905. His years in France would expose him to the teachings of the papal encyclical

Rerum Novarum (1891) as well as to the practical work of Catholic rural groups such as the Belgian Boerenbond (1890) and the French Catholic Forum that commenced organising *Semaines Rurales* (Rural Weeks) in 1904.[12] As was true of Muintir na Tíre later on, Catholic priests were prominently active in these continental groups. Once ordained in 1913 John Hayes began his ministry in Kilbeg, County Meath, and while there he came to public notice locally for challenging the practice of wealthier families having reserved seating in the church. He was, as one of Stephen Rynne's informants later recalled, 'greatly for the poor' and 'greatly down on the ranchers'.[13] While in Kilbeg the young curate further busied himself in forming a branch of Redmond's Volunteers, organising bazaars, dances, a sports day along with a scheme to provide local children with warm milk after Sunday mass.[14]

Sent to Liverpool in 1915 to minister in the Parish of Our Lady of Mount Carmel, Father Hayes quickly set about organising activities to assist his parishioners.[15] On Merseyside, where he engaged with members of the Protestant faith,[16] he organised a boys' club in Peel Street, a Papal Cadets Corps, a Catholic scout troop, a men's sodality, and a brass band.[17] Time was also devoted to establishing a Council of the Knights of Saint Columbanus, a St Vincent De Paul Society and a Social Study Group.[18] His English experience helped convince him of the need to reduce Irish emigration by halting rural decline. First-hand knowledge of the poor living conditions of many Irish immigrants in urban industrial Britain possibly also helps account for a strain of anti-urbanism later evident in Muintir na Tíre's ideology.[19]

On being recalled from Liverpool in 1924 the 36-year-old curate ministered in Templemore, in Ballybricken in County Limerick (1925–7) before being sent to Castleiny in County Tipperary (1927–34). Finding himself in a severely economically depressed rural Ireland – and one deeply divided by a recent civil war – he again took up community organising. In Castleiny he encouraged tobacco growing and Angora rabbit-rearing. His activism also stretched beyond the locality; from 1927 he was active in the Athy-based Irish Grain Growers' Association (IGGA) and served as its national chairman in 1930 and 1931. Eventually in 1933 the IGGA's financial difficulties caused it to become subsumed as a sub-committee into Muintir na Tíre, Ltd before ceasing to exist in 1935.[20]

Muintir na Tíre, Ltd

Muintir na Tíre, Ltd appeared on 8 May 1931 as an umbrella body of organised rural commodity producers. Besides claiming to be apolitical, a central aim of the new group was 'saving' rural Ireland by such means as improving agriculture and rural life as well as by building a sense of unity between farmers and farm labourers. Influenced by the Belgian Boerenbond and the French *La Jeunesse agricole catholique* (rather than Horace Plunkett's co-operative movement), the new body was formally registered as a co-operative society that issued ten-shilling shares.[21] Contrary to Hayes's later assertion that the co-operative had '…two years of gratifying success',[22] it failed in fact to make any serious impact on rural Ireland. Clearly the new co-operative was not helped by the depressed economic conditions of the 1930s. At the outset there were 81 shareholders with a shareholding of £68 10s, and by 1936 total share capital amounted to just £151, contributed by 211 paid-up members.[23] And with its affiliated commodity organisations confined to Tipperary, Kilkenny, Laois and Kildare, the movement had yet to establish a national presence for itself. Partisan conflict also impinged negatively on Muintir Na Tíre Ltd. At the 1934 AGM a row broke out between the supporters of the two main political parties, something that led John Hayes to controversially select the Committee of Management himself.[24]

A major unanticipated development in Catholic social thinking would also pose challenges for Muintir na Tíre, Ltd. Just eight days after the new body's launch, *Quadragesimo Anno* was published. This influential papal encyclical letter restated the Catholic Church's position on the principle of subsidiarity where state-civil society relations were concerned,[25] and proposed the formation of corporations or guilds of employers and workers so as to overcome class divisions and combat class conflict. Under *Quadragesimo Anno's* growing influence the challenge for Father Hayes became how corporatism might be adapted for use in organising rural Ireland. Of course, Christian beliefs had been influencing Muintir na Tíre Ltd from early on; an emblem featuring a cross superimposed on a plough was chosen to convey its Christian character. And the perceived early challenge was to use the new organisation to pursue rural change that was consciously based on Catholic social principles. Referring to the papal encyclical *Rerum Novarum*, Father Hayes stated in 1931 that: 'On the principles laid down by the Pope, we wish today to unite the rural workers of this country and save them from the destructive elements now raging in the vast expansion of industrial pursuits'.[26]

The influence of the French Catholic *Semaine Rurales* on Father Hayes's activism is also evident in the 'rural weekends' he organised in the 1930s. Conceived as residential study groups, these gatherings were held in different locations to propagate the new co-operative venture, to discuss the impediments to desirable rural change, and to tease out the implications of papal social teaching for how Irish rural interests might be organised.[27] The first Rural Weekend took place in 1933 in Mount St Joseph's in Roscrea, with 'Catholic Action in Practice' as its main theme.[28] To make the discussion attractive to progressive farmers, time was devoted in Roscrea to offering practical agricultural advice relating to more efficient production techniques. By helping to build the public profile of Father Hayes and his movement these Rural Weekends prepared the way for the more broadly based vocationalist community movement that would materialise in 1937.

From the early days concerns were being raised – as was true of contemporary Irish Catholicism more generally – concerning certain 'evils' believed to be impacting negatively on Irish life. For Hayes in 1933 such 'evils' included the cinema, novels, newspapers and 'inappropriate' advertising images.[29] Interestingly, he differentiated between the impact of these 'evil influences' on rural and urban Ireland. Perhaps, as he put it, '…these things do not affect city life – as an old friend used to say – "they are manured to them" but our rural morals are not civilised enough for such stuff and the results are disastrous'.[30] The perceived threats of communism and state encroachment also loomed large in discussions at the Rural Weekends.[31]

VOCATIONALISM AND THE LOCAL COMMUNITY

Muintir na Tíre Ltd may have formally existed until 1938, but the 'Ltd' tag had been dropped by then and closing down proceedings set in train with the Registrar of Friendly Societies. The new Muintir na Tíre's first constitution presented the movement to the world in 1938 as an 'Association for the promotion of the true welfare, spiritual, cultural and material of Ireland and in particular its rural people, through the application of Christian Social Principles.'[32] The central aim of revitalising rural Ireland was to be pursued by 'Improving conditions of life in rural areas and in securing a just recompense for the vital services rendered by the rural population to the whole community.'[33]

Ideologically, the new Muintir na Tíre remained as opposed as ever to conflict of a class or partisan nature. The movement's conversion to vocationalism saw its aims being broadened around the ideal of organising the different occupational groups of the Catholic parishes into a single 'guild'. A typical guild was made up of 'sections' comprising farmers, farm labourers, merchants, professionals, women and youths. From the representatives of these sections a parish council was assembled to oversee local improvement activities – in a process that later became known as 'community development'. In spite of a strain of anti-urbanism in Muintir na Tíre's thinking, provision was also made for cities and towns to become 'associate guilds'.

How was a movement of parish guilds and councils to be built? Word of the new movement was spread by means of regular public meetings and by annual 'rural weeks' that were an extension on the earlier Rural Weekends. As a locus for the exchange of ideas among a gathering of Catholic Intellectuals, local activists, idealists and eccentrics, much attention was paid in the Rural Weeks to propagating the idea of how well suited the Catholic parishes were to rural organising and planning. At the 1942 Rural Week held in Mungret College in Limerick, for instance, papers were read by Father Edward Coyne on 'The Parish as a Unit of Rural Organisation' and by Michael Murphy, MA, on 'The Parish on the Unit of Economic Planning'.[34]

Media coverage of the Rural Weeks played a vital part in helping build Muintir na Tíre's national profile (and that of its founder), as did the movement's efforts at providing relief work during the 1939–45 wartime Emergency, promoting the rural electrification scheme from 1945 on, initiating the Parish Plan for Agriculture in 1947, and running a mobile film society. The founder was also a regular contributor to Radió Éireann, delivering talks on Muintir na Tíre's activities and the challenges facing rural Ireland more generally.[35] Local and national level activities and achievements were chronicled in *The Handbook*, in *Rural Ireland*, and in *The Landmark*, the movement's publications to which Father Hayes – in the guise of his alter-ego 'Phil Lahy' – was a regular contributor. Anti-urbanism was a recurring theme for some contributors to these publications.[36]

The more active local guilds took on a range of social and economic improvements. We find the *Landmark* and *Rural Ireland* documenting their work in providing water schemes, organising sports days, and in arranging adult education classes. Many of the stronger guilds built and ran parish halls. Some guilds were active as well in local job creation, with Father Hayes himself centrally involved in launching a floorcovering factory in Tipperary Town and a jam factory in nearby Bansha close to Tipperary Town (his last parish).[37]

CLASS DIVISIONS AND COMMUNITY ORGANISING

Two distinct positions on the question of social class can be identified in Father Hayes's thinking and in that of leading figures of his movement. One position tended to ignore the presence of classes and the likelihood of class conflict in rural (as against urban and industrial) Ireland. A second position acknowledged the existence of a rural class structure and the potential for class conflict but contended that the threat such conflict posed could be successfully overcome through 'brotherhood' and vocationalism. John Hayes's own stance veered between these two positions. On one occasion he claimed that 'We have a glorious tradition in rural Ireland of the Christian Brotherhood between farmers and their labourers and that tradition we hope to perpetuate'.[38] Writing in the *Landmark* in 1947 he suggested that Muintir na Tíre had always desired to see people '…helping one another in pulling together and driving out class distinction,'[39] adding that

> The farmer and the labourer were bound in a common spirit of brotherhood, working side by side. That spirit had gone from the cities, and it was up to the people of the land to revive it. The people of the land, however, must not allow anybody to come into their parishes to preach the gospel of class work (sic) for the purpose of creating trouble amongst each other.[40]

As his public profile grew, John Hayes's commitment to using vocationalism to actively suppress class conflicts wasn't confined to the civil society sphere. We find him mediating in a strike between butchers and their employers in Limerick in 1949.[41] And in 1947 he successfully negotiated with striking workers in the four state-owned sugar factories. On that occasion he had asked the workers to 'Make a sacrifice for their fellow workers, farmers, agricultural labourers and men and women in the factories…We know the high ideals of Irish workers…and we appeal to you to bury your own interests'.[42] His intervention in the sugar factories' dispute didn't meet with universal approval. Connolly Association activists questioned why workers (rather than employers) should always be the ones being asked to make the sacrifice.[43]

Even before the appearance of the vocationalist guilds and parish councils, difficulties posed by economic differences and conflicts had been encountered in Muintir's efforts to build new forms of rural organisation. Tensions between different types of farmers – pig farmers, for instance, competed with grain growers over cereal prices – made for difficulties within the co-operatively organised producers' federation. And it transpired that the co-operative's biggest shareholders and board members were not farmers at all but mostly urban- or town-based professionals (solicitors, doctors, politicians, and clergymen in particular) as well as merchants (such as William Dwan of Thurles). Some members of the Anglo-Irish gentry – most notably Lord ffrench – also purchased shares in the co-operative.[44]

Along with its low levels of share membership and its limited appeal to farmers, Muintir na Tíre Ltd encountered poor participation rates among farm labourers. Despite the initial inducement of free membership – and a later offer of reduced rate membership – farm labourers declined to participate in any numbers. And, as it turned out, inequality and class tensions between farmers and farm labourers became a key reason why the co-operative failed to make progress. All these setbacks proved salutary in convincing Father Hayes and his followers of the need to re-organise their movement along alternative vocationalist lines.

The shift to vocationalism and the new effort to maximise community participation – through the use of the guild/parish council structure – saw a renewed attempt to smooth out class differences in rural society. It may have been common for guilds to provide farm labourers with their own dedicated 'section', but how actively did farm labourers participate in Muintir na Tíre local activities? An internal survey of 99 guilds, undertaken by the movement's head office in 1950–2, provides an insight into who occupied leadership positions on the parish councils. The survey contains 67 responses relating to who occupied the role of 'parish council chairman'. The most prominent chairmen were farmers (26 in all), followed by curates and parish priests (17 and 7 respectively) along with farm labourers, doctors and shopkeepers who were chairing two guilds each.[45]

RELATIONS WITH THE STATE

The strong admiration John Hayes developed for Benito Mussolini while still a young man was most likely the product of the economic and political turmoil of the interwar years, along with the wider public support for Catholic fascist leaders such as Franco and Salazar in Ireland. The indications are that this admiration ran deep. When invited to preach during Advent in 1930 at San Silvestro – the Pallottine House of Studies in Rome – the young curate managed to meet not only the Pope but Il Duce himself. In later years John Hayes often fondly recalled his meeting with the fascist leader, noting how he had told him: 'We in Ireland love and admire what you have done in Italy, and I pray for you'.[46] An autographed photo of Mussolini – inscribed 'Al Reverendo J. M. Hayes...Cordialiter' – was a treasured possession given prominent display in parochial houses in Castleiny, Tipperary Town, and Bansha.[47] In a later account, Hayes recalled the fascist leader as '...a kind man, a human man, a man with the grace of God shining through his eyes; and I carried with me a mental picture which I feel will serve me for many a day. I feel a better man through meeting that noble, human Mussolini'.[48] That his admiration of Il Duce was to continue despite Italy's alliance with Hitler's Germany, and the excesses of fascism becoming more widely known, is demonstrated by a letter sent to the Italian ambassador in Dublin on the bombing of Rome in July 1943. The ambassador wrote in reply: 'It is indeed gratifying to find your admiration of Duce is so sincere and so complete'.[49]

But did Father Hayes's admiration for Mussolini signify an attachment to the autocratic state more generally? Early on he had realised that his rural movement could only survive in such a politically divided society as 1930s Ireland by remaining strictly non-political. Already in 1931 he made it clear that Muintir na Tíre Ltd would have 'no politics in the ordinary sense of the word, but would in time consider its position in the administration of the nation'.[50] Of course, remaining free of party politics – as the 1934 AGM illustrates – was not always possible. And in spite of Hayes's belief that partisan differences in post-civil war Ireland could be overcome through use of the guild structure, David P. Lynch's unpublished survey of the Muintir guilds between 1950 and 1962 cites some examples of guilds failing because of internal party political conflict.[51]

When Muintir na Tíre activists and sympathisers spoke and wrote on the state's 'proper' role in society, their positions tended to oscillate between two polar opposites. Giving a platform to those fearful of the interventionist state, the *Landmark* published a number of articles and editorials contending that the welfare state, socialism (and the 'descent into socialism'), communism and a one-party state were all to be regarded as serious threats in Ireland. The Irish state itself, in response to the growing number of voters residing in cities and towns, was even accused of being urban-centric.[52] At the other end of the spectrum of opinion, Father Hayes adopted a more measured and pragmatic position. We find him, for instance, suggesting in 1944 that:

... a real vocational order springs from below [...] from the people. It may need a helping hand by the state, but to be a genuine vocationalism it must be accepted by the people if its growth and survival are to be assured. It can thrive with a political and democratic form of government, but should itself be free from party politics, which have their own place in the state.[53]

Despite the importance Catholic social teaching regarding the state gave to the principle of subsidiarity, Father Hayes was ready to engage positively in practice with the state and to rely heavily on it for recognition and financial assistance. State support was sought for Muintir na Tíre in both its co-operative and vocationalist forms. It is clear that Father Hayes had a particular affinity for Fianna Fáil under de Valera's leadership and he was ready to lobby him personally for financial support.[54] In the very early days he made an unsuccessful attempt to secure official state recognition and financial support. An undated submission (probably written in 1932) requested: '...the Government to give official recognition to Muintir na Tíre Ltd, and to provide in the estimates for a subsidy of £1,000 per annum to enable the society with its programme of agricultural organisation'.[55]

Initially Hayes responded favourably to an offer of state support of £3,000 in 1941,[56] the funding being provided to support parish councils set up during the Emergency. However, after some wavering, it was decided not to accept this state support as it would compromise Muintir's stance on the principle of subsidiarity.[57] That is not to say that the organisation refused financial support from the state. During the Emergency they were successful in attracting funding from the Department of Local Government to operate fuel and allotment schemes.[58] Indeed, seeking state support would later become a priority for Muintir as is evidenced in the Parish Plan for Agriculture and its participation in promoting the state's rural electrification scheme.

Nor did fears expressed within Muintir na Tíre, and the Catholic Action movement more generally, concerning the dangers of state encroachment stop the local guilds/parish councils from regularly interacting with local and national branches of the Irish state. State bodies were routinely approached to provide local infrastructure (such as road works) and services (such as soil testing, post-office facilities and electrification). Such pursuits permitted close working relations to be built up with officials of the local authorities, the Vocational Education Committees and the Department of Agriculture in particular.

CONCLUSIONS

Was then John Hayes a visionary or a social conservative? He was in reality a mixture of both these things. While he may have been weak in terms of having an overall plan or strategy for Muintir Na Tíre, the multitude of projects he pioneered both in Ireland and in Liverpool provides much evidence of a man of imagination, idealism, and enterprise. That said, his ideological touchstones and his many statements concerning social change, modernity, the role of the state, urban living, and class structure carry the hallmarks of a deep-rooted conservatism reflecting the Catholic social thinking of his time.

Muintir na Tíre experienced mixed fortunes under its founder's leadership. While acknowledging that his personal charisma opened many doors, the movement's national promotion still rested very heavily on the founder's shoulders and those of a relatively small group of voluntary activists based mainly in Munster. At the time of his death in 1957 – and some 20 years after the shift in direction introduced by the guild/parish councils – Muintir na Tíre's local presence was still heavily concentrated in the Munster counties of Cork, Limerick and Tipperary. This in large part was testimony to both John Hayes's popularity in these southern counties, his acceptance by local members of the hierarchy who had the final say as to whether guilds could be formed in their dioceses or archdioceses,[59] and the heaviest concentration of voluntary effort in these three counties.

A case can be made that Muintir na Tíre was held back by Father Hayes's lack of a well-developed strategic plan to spread the movement. But were there more fundamental difficulties at work as well? Even in the best of circumstances, the movement's approach to community development drew upon a consensus approach that proved very difficult to implement in practice. The founder's populist desire to speak for all of the people in rural Ireland needs to be weighed up against the existence in rural communities of a class structure capable of impacting negatively on 'the people's' capacity and willingness to participate in the sorts of rural development efforts he was proposing. Farm labourers were noticeably absent from the ranks of Muintir na Tíre Ltd, and very few of them took up leadership roles in the vocationalist parish councils later on. What was also true of course was that farm modernisation and heavy out-migration – each of which was greatly accelerating in the 1950s – were all the while further reducing the size of the farm labourer population. This exodus, which Father Hayes and his movement's other leaders lamented but were unable to halt, emerged as a major reason for rural Ireland's steady social decline in the 1940s and 1950s.

Besides Muintir na Tíre's activities often being impacted negatively by class divisions and resentments, the movement's failure to address differences between propertied and non-propertied classes in particular may be seen as indicative of its underlying social conservatism. Such conservatism signified that the kind of rural Ireland the movement was intent on 'saving' (if it ever actually existed) was not to be made available for everyone.

What is also the case is that Father Hayes's hope of bringing all members of rural communities together under a single organisational umbrella encountered opposition from other organised interests in rural society. During the rural electrification campaign in Tipperary, and again when it came to the Parish Plan for Agriculture, the movement found itself competing in particular with Macra na Feirme over who had the best right to represent farmers.[60] Equally, as McNabb documented in east Limerick in the late 1950s,[61] the existence of other rural organisations claiming to speak for specific groups in rural Ireland – such as the Irish Creamery Milk Suppliers' Association (ICMSA) and the Irish Countrywomen's Association (ICA) – posed a continuing challenge to Muintir na Tíre's desire to represent rural communities as a whole.

After its founder's death in 1957 Muintir na Tíre's character changed significantly. The movement professionalised by embracing social science, by undertaking an ambitious set of community studies in east Limerick),[62] and eventually by employing full-time community development officers in the 1970s. A major development saw the movement's organisational structure change from the guild/parish council to the elected community council. A modest presence was even established in urban Ireland – most notably in the Clondalkin area of Dublin. Lively debates on local government reform, regionalism and community development, and Ireland's membership of the Common Market helped reinvigorate the movement as a whole in the 1960s and 70s. However, many of the core challenges Muintir na Tíre faced during its founder's lifetime were to persist, often with negative effects for its community development work. Prominent among such obstacles were class divisions at local level, competition with other rural interest groups, community apathy, lack of strategic planning, a dearth of funding, and the difficulties generated by the accelerating pace of modernisation and urbanisation in the 1960s and 1970s.

Cultivating Vocational Solidarity: The Class and Gender Politics of Organising Irish Agriculture

Tony Varley

Attempts at organising those who work in agriculture never occur in an historical vacuum and efforts at organising them in interwar southern Ireland were to be no exception in this regard. Dominating the political background were the recent civil war, a still contentious statehood, along with Fianna Fáil's rapid rise and emergence as a ruling party in 1932. The post-war slump, the Great Depression, and the economic war (1932–8) stand out as successive and overlapping phases of the mostly adverse economic context in which the three popular mobilisations featured in our discussion appeared. Looming large on the social front was a renewed social Catholicism much concerned with staving off the threat of class war (and communism) by cultivating solidarity (or a sense of togetherness) within and between social classes.

The desire to cultivate 'vocational' solidarity in local communities so as to bolster the social and political order became an abiding concern of Father John Hayes the founder of Muintir na Tíre (People of the Land), a movement that emerged as the prime expression of Catholic social action in the interwar Irish countryside. Loosely modelled on the Flemish Catholic Farmers' League (the Boerenbond), Muintir na Tíre (or Muintir) first appeared in 1931 as a would-be co-operatively organised national federation of agricultural producer groups. After its reinvention as a vocationalist local community movement in 1937, organising rural women alongside farmers and rural workers became a guiding concern of the movement's founder.

Something the main leaders of two new farmers' movements appearing in the 1930s – Frank MacDermot of the National Farmers' and Ratepayers' League (NFRL)/National Centre Party (NCP) (1932–3) and Michael Donnellan of Clann na Talmhan (Family of the Land) (1938/9–65) – assumed along with John Hayes was that organising Irish farmers anew would bring them together not just for their own good but for the greater good of rural Ireland (including the waged farm workers) and indeed of the Irish nation. A common challenge was to harness what farmer solidarity already existed in organising them to counter the various forces and pressures (whether external or internal to rural Ireland) perceived to be threatening agricultural and rural interests. At the outset cultivating solidarity via organisation was viewed in all three cases as generating a progressively more powerful capacity for collective agency.

Where our three leaders parted company was in who among those who worked in agriculture they wished to organise. While MacDermot and Donnellan saw paid farmworkers and farm women benefitting from their efforts at organising farmers, they didn't (unlike Father Hayes) set out specifically to organise them. Our three leaders further differed in their analyses of the difficulties Irish farmers were experiencing, their assessments of how much their troubles were attributable to Fianna Fáil rule or misrule, and in their characterisations of farmers either in 'vocational' or 'class' terms. They also diverged in their views of the forms the organisation of Irish farmers should take and of how organised farmers should interact with the ruling party. Such differences inevitably made for somewhat different conceptions of farmer solidarity. Besides comparing how our three leaders analysed the crisis conditions of the 1930s, gauged the contribution of ruling politicians to their genesis, and set about countering them by seeking to organise those who worked in agriculture and so cultivate solidarity among them, our discussion will examine how they and their movements were received within Fianna Fáil, and how much this reception (along with other relevant circumstances) impacted on their effectiveness and ultimate survival prospects.

ANALYSING THE RURAL CRISIS

Speaking in Cork in April 1932 (during the Great Depression) Father Hayes observed how 'We have been accustomed to look upon ourselves as the most distressful country that we can scarcely realise today that we are in a much better position than those nations which built their economic and social fabric on a mechanical industrialism'.[1] John Hayes may have been an 'unsinkable optimist' but for all that he must still in the early 1930s be counted among those disappointed at the way native rule was turning out.[2] The post-war slump and the Great Depression had left the new farmer-owners hard-pressed to reap the economic benefits of land ownership while the now unorganised paid farmworkers found themselves sinking deeper into poverty.[3] As a curate in Castleiny from 1927, he had witnessed at first-hand the devastating effects of cheap imported maize on his barley-growing north Tipperary parishioners.[4] In his Cork address of April 1932, he was moved to declare that: 'The land must not produce a nation of slaves, but of free men. Those who work the land must have a decent living on the land, otherwise they will not remain...'.[5]

From the earliest days the intention was to include paid farmworkers in the new organisation. 'The spirit of fraternal charity enunciated by the Pope', John Hayes pointed out in his 1932 Cork address, 'is the broad basis of our organisation for we wish no longer to have employer and employee divided but united in their common vocation'.[6] Another early conviction was that the difficulties afflicting Irish rural life were not just economic in nature. Any adequate response would therefore have 'to recognise and actualise the interdependency of the social, cultural and economic aspects of rural life'.[7] Accepting that 'the maintenance of a numerous, virile and contented rural population is essential to the health and stability of the nation as a whole', the movement's memorandum submitted to the Commission on Vocational Organisation (CVO) in 1940 observed how 'within the last 25 or 30 years' the sad reality was that 'purely social and cultural life in rural Ireland [has been] at a low ebb' and 'has been inclined to run in channels which lead to serious physical and moral defects'.[8]

But what of the economic impacts of the prevailing political conditions? Did John Hayes blame the governing parties for the interwar agricultural crisis? Impatient he may have been 'with political divisions' and ready to ride 'roughshod over the hypersensitive feelings of party men' while a young curate in Castleiny between 1927 and 1934,[9] but after Muintir na Tíre Ltd's launch in 1931 the founder's practice was to shy away from singling out politicians and the state for public censure. At the same time the traumatic market conditions experienced by his Castleiny barley-growing parishioners had to reflect poorly on Cumann na nGaedheal's trade policy. His private view of Fianna Fáil's advance to power – in stark contrast to those of MacDermot and Donnellan – was broadly benign. What impressed him greatly was Fianna Fáil's commitment to national self-sufficiency and to a managed and protected home market that would give preference to Irish producers.[10] There were other reasons as well why Father Hayes should look with favour on the rise of Fianna Fáil. His family background as evicted tenants, his sympathy with the rural 'small man' and labourer, and family support for the anti-Treaty party all made for a strong affinity with Fianna Fáil's early 'small man' populism.[11] Apparently he was on friendly terms with Éamon de Valera before his party had assumed office in March 1932; and subsequently James Ryan, Fianna Fáil's first Minister for Agriculture, was on his 'presbytery list of visitors'.[12] Shortly after the 1932 general election he nonetheless expressed himself adamant that '…we must look to no party within or without the country, to enable us to [secure a decent living on the land], we must look to ourselves'.[13]

How did MacDermot and Donnellan regard agricultural conditions in interwar Ireland and the Free State's governing politicians? MacDermot's early assessment of the interwar rural crisis owed much to the analysis of Monsignor Thomas H. Cummins, an influential advisor of the Roscommon Farmers' and Ratepayers' Association (RFRA). So bad did Cummins consider agricultural conditions while Cumann na nGaedheal was still in office that he was ready in January 1932 to describe the farmers as the 'slaves' of Ireland,[14] an image Hayes was to make use of a few months later and that Donnellan in turn invoked in 1939.[15] Blame for the farmers' difficulties was laid squarely at the door of the main nationalist parties. Standing as an independent candidate at the RFRA's invitation in the 1932 election, MacDermot's election address declared that 'the country is sick of both political parties and of the controversies that absorb their attention, and that it is time we got out of the party rut'.[16] The economic war greatly sharpened the edge of MacDermot's and Donnellan's attacks on the Fianna Fáil government. Once elected the independently wealthy MacDermot swiftly became a thorn in the government's side, going so far in a Dáil speech of July 1933 to rank de Valera second only to Oliver Cromwell in his record of inflicting 'harm on this country'.[17] Ten years later Michael Donnellan's view was that Clann most likely would never have been heard of were it not for Minister Ryan's 'unsatisfactory attitude…towards the rural population' and the policies introduced over the previous decade.[18]

Something else setting the Farmers' Party leaders apart from John Hayes was their readiness to attack ruling politicians for prioritising town and city needs over rural ones. For MacDermot in 1932 a deplorable consequence of the 'Dublin mentality' pervading the main nationalist parties was that the countryside was 'being drained to provide unnecessary jobs and salaries, while the Party leaders grow daily more self-satisfied and autocratic'.[19] Late in 1942 at an open-air farmers' rally in the Mayo village of Kilkelly, Patrick Cogan

TD (soon to become Clann's deputy leader) blamed politicians for favouring city and town interests over rural ones. 'The men elected', in Cogan's view, 'were only the mouthpieces of the cities and towns. They went around the country in their high power motor cars and then back again to the cities without the most hazy idea of how the rural population lived. They carried out a policy in accordance with the ideas of the Irish city dwellers'.[20]

A year later we find Father Hayes sounding a very different note in declining to pit rural against urban interests. 'Whilst we wish', he wrote,

> to raise and improve the position of the people of the land, we have no intention of creating conflict between people of the land and people of the towns. In many of our towns we have associate bodies…All this is only an unfolding of the spirit of organisation, bringing unity and co-operation, not merely into every parish but spreading it from parish to parish, linking up together parish and parish in a national organisation and bringing in at the same time the people of the cities and the towns in associate bodies.[21]

BUILDING ORGANISATION

Already a seasoned and resourceful community activist before arriving in north Tipperary in 1927, dismay at the poor (and worsening) home market available to Irish grain and fruit growers led John Hayes to work to improve market conditions with like-minded allies such as J. J. Bergin of the Irish Grain Growers' Association (IGGA). A branch of the IGGA was formed in Castleiny, as was a branch of the Fruit Growers' Association,[22] and seemingly out of these beginnings came the idea for a would-be national federation of producers launched as Muintir na Tíre Ltd in 1931.[23] In the face of this body's inability to make much headway, it gradually dawned on John Hayes that any approach based solely on 'promoting sectional interests' was unlikely to succeed.[24] 'The road of farmers' organisations', as he ruefully put it in 1937, 'was white with skeletons'.[25] For all its difficulties his failing producers' federation allowed him to enlist a cadre of loyal and dedicated activists,[26] and as its star waned a series of at least seven 'Rural Weekends' provided a forum to search for an alternative approach to organising rural interests.[27]

In this search Father Hayes was advised by the Knights of Saint Columbanus who were keen on promoting 'parish guilds and councils';[28] and he himself was part of the push to embrace the corporatism (or vocationalism) reintroduced in the 1931 papal encyclical *Quadragesimo Anno*. Apparently it was at the Fermoy Rural Weekend of August 1935 that 'the parish guild was adopted as the basis of all endeavour'.[29] Hayes's hope for these parish guilds (and councils) was that they would enable local people to bring 'about a healthy civic spirit' by 'putting into practice the Christian principles enunciated by the Papal Encyclicals'.[30] By way of desirable social change what the guilds could do 'above all', he suggested in 1940, was 'promote harmony and peace. They can keep out class war. By bringing together all classes, they will educate people to understand sympathetically other peoples' views'.[31] As much as local improvements would be the day-to-day business of the new parish guilds/councils, John Hayes was thinking more ambitiously of his parish-based and corporatist-organised civic activity as a central pillar of an ongoing educational process in which citizens of the new state could work together to build 'a truly Christian and Irish nation'.[32] Realising this ambition would require not just the effective mobilisation of local parish-based communities across the land but the creation of stable and mutually advantageous working relations with the state in all its institutional guises.

Just as John Hayes depended on allies to get his producers' federation off the ground, having powerful allies and backers became a key asset in building his new vocationalist community movement. While personally keen that it avoid becoming excessively clericalist in its leadership,[33] Muintir nonetheless relied heavily on the local parish clergy (curates especially) to lead the way.[34] While some bishops – Michael Browne of Galway in particular – were strongly supportive, a determined critic was Bishop Michael Fogarty of Killaloe who refused Muintir permission to organise in his dioceses. Writing to Father Hayes in 1940 Fogarty was unable to see how Muintir could be of 'much effective benefit to the farming community; it is too academic'; and he complained that it was 'vain to talk of local improvements as long as the people are being drained out by excessive taxation and economic meddling', issues he felt Muintir was deafeningly silent on.[35] Archbishop John Charles McQuaid of Dublin's objection to Muintir was that its professed 'Christian' identity left it insufficiently Catholic for his liking.[36]

In many ways the recent historical context, along with the class and political turmoil of the early 1930s, were anything but favourable to Father Hayes's evolving vocationalist community movement. The revolutionary period had seen a major upsurge in farmer-labourer class conflict with about 50,000 farm labourers organised along class-against-class lines by early 1920. In the 'strikes for wage increases and improved working conditions' of 1919 and 1920, 'the emblems, anthems and rhetoric of revolutionary socialism were fully employed'.[37] And not alone had the farmers been left divided politically by the Treaty split and the civil war but their political and class divisions had tended to align as the tendencies for bigger farmers to back the Treaty and smallholders (particularly so in the west) to gravitate to the anti-Treaty side became more deeply ingrained.[38] In response to the 1932 election result, elements in Cumann na nGaedheal feared that a Bolshevist-leaning Fianna Fáil government was dead set on destroying the strong farmer class.[39] And as the effects of the economic war bit deeper the Blueshirt movement came to rely heavily on anxious and angry farmers (strong farmers especially) for much of its popular following.[40]

Within such a deeply class-divided and politically polarised rural Ireland John Hayes found himself walking a tightrope. At the height of the economic war he insisted on depicting his still unformed movement as a strictly 'non-political' venture in which members would be required to bracket their political and social differences so as to work together for the good of the country.[41] For all that Muintir na Tíre Ltd's management committee wasn't spared being riven by factional infighting. When called upon to restore order by selecting a new 20-man committee in June 1934, Hayes's response was to use the opportunity to effect 'a famous purge of political-minded undesirables'.[42] This sweep-out may have improved the prospects for his still embryonic vocationalist community movement, but what helped even more were the Coal-Cattle Pacts of 1935–7. These pacts revived the cattle economy, took much of the heat out of the economic war, and contributed to a rapid fizzling out of the Blueshirt movement.[43]

Farmers and rural workers (though not rural women) were given centre stage in the vocationalist model of representation John Hayes adopted for his new community movement of 1937. Initially it was 'thought that for most rural parishes three sections would suit – farmers, rural labourers, and those who were neither', though guilds were left free in practice to decide their own number of sections.[44] 'Muintir na Tíre', John Hayes observed in 1941, 'has a place for the women of the parish also. It has never forgotten their importance. In some Guilds and Councils they have their own sections and in others they take their place representing the sections of their calling'.[45] Two years later he reminded his readers how 'we are endeavouring to obtain the amenities of life for the hard-worked woman in the country homestead'.[46]

To secure formal equality of representation, the members of the guilds' different sections were advised to select an equal number of representatives to sit on a parish council.[47] Reflecting his optimistic assumptions that such formal representational equality – along with a paternalistic 'spirit of fraternal charity' and a widely shared (if often dormant) sense of local civic pride – would make for a meeting of minds when it came to identifying the common good, his early view was that consensual decision-making was both the normative ideal and the everyday reality in the parish councils. In 1941 we thus find him writing confidently how '...never once was a vote necessary at our Council meetings [in Tipperary Town], and I believe this to be true of every Muintir na Tíre Council in Ireland'.[48]

Did the unity-loving and consensualist Father Hayes of 1941 differ from his more oppositional earlier self? 'Curates', Stephen Rynne remarks of him while a curate in Castleiny from 1927, '...were supposed to be big farmers' men, and this priest was a small man's man'.[49] One of Rynne's Castleiny interviewees observed how he 'could give offence. He was no respecter of big farmers and was unwilling to keep labourers in their so-called place'.[50] Yet Muintir's memorandum submitted to the CVO in 1940 depicted Irish farmers as a single undifferentiated 'element' or 'sectional interest' alongside the expressly differentiated artisans, professionals, and small businesspeople of rural society.[51] The same document declared that 'although the interests of these different elements of the rural population sometimes appear to be in opposition, actually they are in the main, identical, and from the broad national view-point...must be looked on as being identical'.[52] Taking farmers as a single vocational element with mainly identical interests facilitated placing small and large farmers on a formally equal footing for purposes of representation on the parish councils. And to take the span of vocational elements as having mainly identical interests was to help suppress any talk of dominant and subordinate sectional elements more broadly.[53] Shunned in Muintir's CVO memorandum of 1940 indeed was any use of 'class' to describe the different vocational elements or interests and the relations within and between them.[54]

As set forth in 1940 Father Hayes's favoured normative vision of rural society was therefore not as a structure of competing classes or even as a status hierarchy but as a set of vocational elements, sections or interests whose formal numerical equality on the parish councils derived fundamentally from the way the interests of the different elements were assumed to be mainly identical. Of course, numerical equality among groups of representatives on the parish councils didn't imply any immediate erasure of social and economic differences and inequalities within and between sectional interests and their representatives. These taken-for-granted differences and inequalities would continue (and indeed be reproduced), even if the founder's optimistic expectation was that mixing together and staying together in the local guilds and councils would over time take many of the sharp edges off social differences and inequalities. And, in its turn, rising agricultural prosperity would ideally do the same for economic differences and inequalities. Given such optimistic assumptions, an agreed and shared conception of the community interest and the common good – to be arrived at discursively in a deliberative decision-making process between numerically equal representatives on the parish councils – was therefore eminently achievable. It might on occasion require the subordination of the interests of individual sections to the community interest and the common good,[55] but as time passed and local organisation strengthened shared feelings of community-centred (as against oppositional class-centred) collective solidarity could be expected to put down deeper roots. A better life within a reconstructed civil society was therefore both imaginable and practicable, one in which Christian patriots could learn to truly live for their native land.[56] Becoming well organised at local level along Muintir lines was only the beginning for Father Hayes: higher layers of organisation would need to be built upon lower ones with the whole edifice having the effect of greatly boosting the bargaining power of vocationally organised agricultural interests. Substantially prefiguring some of the CVO's proposals of 1944, this was how he saw the future unfolding in April 1937:

> The parochial guilds will form a diocesan organisation which in turn will be unified by a Provincial Council. The Provincial Councils will form a National Body, It will be the duty of the Provincial and National Councils to set up Provincial and National Chambers of Agriculture. These chambers will act as practical advisory bodies whose advice no government dare reject. They will truly represent every class in rural Ireland and will be more capable of advising than those whose knowledge of the country comes from false information and agricultural statistics.[57]

Depressed agricultural conditions were what fundamentally led our two Farmers' Party leaders to see the necessity of building new farmers' movements. In view of the recent collapse of the Farmers' Party and the Irish Farmers' Union (IFU), Frank MacDermot and Michael Donnellan were understandably hesitant at first to form new farmers' parties. With Fianna Fáil settled into office, and the economic war under way, an initially non-political NFRL (with MacDermot as President) appeared in October 1932. Its declared aims were to 'restore access to the British market, to reduce government expenditure, and to maintain property rights'.[58] MacDermot further pledged the NFRL – in a Dungarvan speech of November 1932 – 'to exalt agriculture, to get away from the memories and hatreds of the civil war, and to promote Irish unity'.[59] Shortly afterwards the NFRL's standing committee decided on forming a new political party and 'declared membership of the League to be incompatible with membership of Cumann na nGaedheal, Fianna Fáil or the Labour Party'.[60] With a view to broadening the NFRL's appeal and to carving out a centrist space in Irish politics, a National Centre Party – under the joint leadership of MacDermot and James Dillon (neither of whom were farmers) – emerged alongside the NFRL early in 1933.[61]

Donnellan's first idea as Clann took shape in Galway in 1938–9 was to steer clear of electoral politics by organising along 'trade union' lines in the manner of the 'non-political' Irish Farmers' Federation formed in 1937.[62] Soon, however, the prospect of a by-election in Galway West in 1939–40 prompted a change of course. In the summer of 1942 Patrick Cogan, the Wicklow independent TD and IFF activist, had formed the National Agricultural Party and, with a general election looming, this new party joined forces with the westerners to form 'Clann na Talmhan – the National Agricultural Party' early in 1943.[63]

Despite having crossed the threshold into party politics, Donnellan was still viewing Clann in 1940 as a 'non-political' vocational party that stood for 'the prohibition of all political organisations not recruited on a vocational basis, as it regards the dissensions created by former and present political parties as disastrous to the Nation, both spiritually and materially'.[64] None of this prevented the CVO from criticising Irish farmers' parties for pursuing 'political objectives which easily aroused enthusiasm' but which 'lessened interest in organisation for purely social and economic purposes'.[65] In the CVO Report's discussion of other obstacles militating against the 'vocational organisation of farmers in Ireland',[66] no mention was made of the obstacles presented by the institution of private property in land that provided the farmers' possessive individualism and familism (or family-centredness) with their material bedrock,[67] the unequal distribution of land and the cattle economy's division of labour that at once reflected and reinforced class differentiation among big and small farmers, the division of the farmers along party lines (together with the tendency for class and party differences to align) in the aftermath of the Treaty split and civil war, and the regular politicisation of class differences among farmers by anti-Treaty politicians in particular. Something else the CVO Report was tellingly silent on was the legacy of mutual suspicion left by the upsurge of class conflict between farm labourers and farmers during the revolutionary and civil war years.

For MacDermot and Donnellan the very real existence of different farmer classes meant that for them the equally highly desirable normative ideal of Irish farmers forming a single unified class or 'sectional interest' was still a long way off realisation in the real world. A shared challenge therefore was to build alliances between different classes of farmers – between big and small farmers in particular – by accentuating what they could agree on and by downplaying, bracketing or suppressing contentious or potentially contentious issues. And while the NFRL and NCP (like the earlier Farmers' Party) have frequently been linked with large farmers,[68] MacDermot was anxious to throw the net wider in seeking small farmer and even farm labourer support. At an NFRL standing committee meeting of 3 June 1933 it was stated that the NFRL '…includes all classes of farmers, farm labourers etc. and…the agricultural community as a whole'.[69] A week later the movement's desire to represent 'the agricultural community as a whole' was developed further when MacDermot reminded his colleagues '…that when the organisation was founded a pledge was given that when the interests of large farmers, small farmers and agricultural labourers might conflict, the League would endeavour to hold the balance between them and not favour one rather than another'.[70]

In its turn Clann has been viewed with good reason as the party of the western smallholders,[71] but the early movement was led by large farmers in the main and was seen by Michael Donnellan and others as appealing to 'working farmers' (as against ranchers and gentlemen farmers) across the country. 'While we come mainly from Connacht', he declared in 1941, 'we represent, in a way, the working farmers elsewhere – that is to say the farmers of from £20 to £40 valuation'.[72] In a speech the previous March, Donnellan had been at pains to distinguish the 'large farmer' and 'small farmer' from the 'rancher', declaring that his party stood 'for fair treatment to all, whether large farmer, small farmer, or farm labourer' while standing at the same time 'four square for the division of the ranches'.[73]

If organising farm women was at least a question for Father Hayes, the same can hardly be said of either MacDermot or Donnellan, each of whom (with John Hayes) took it for granted that Irish farmers were men first and foremost and that the business of representing farmers was primarily men's business.[74] Just how much this assumption concealed the vital contribution of unpaid female and family labour to Irish farming comes across in Stephen Rynne's observation of 1950 that: 'To-day, as yesterday, there are two sorts of successful farmers: the man with ample capital, and the man who works the land with free family labour'.[75]

RULING PARTY RESPONSES

Whether perceived as friends or foes went far in deciding how Fianna Fáil leaders and activists regarded organised interests in interwar and wartime Ireland. As a well-known activist Catholic priest and authority figure, sympathetic to the underlying tenor of Fianna Fáil's economic and social policies at a time when some bishops were publicly critical of the ruling party's leader,[76] there were good reasons for de Valera to look favourably on Father Hayes and Muintir. Clearly the patriotic and civic collective consciousness and solidarity Father Hayes was keen on cultivating – even before his vocationalist community movement was formally launched in 1937 – resonated with de Valera's own preferences as to the sort of society in which the Irish nation could best develop and realise itself.[77] From time to time de Valera as government leader either appeared or spoke at Muintir gatherings.[78]

Wartime conditions presented Muintir with a slew of new difficulties, not least of which was the competition its parish guilds/councils faced from the new state-assisted parish councils. For fear of co-optation Muintir's national leadership had declined to join the state's wartime parish council scheme,[79] though this decision didn't mark any transition from a collaborative to an oppositional stance and identity. Nor did it create a rift with de Valera. Addressing a Muintir Rural Weekend in 1941, the Taoiseach deftly invoked the principle of subsidiarity in counselling Muintir against becoming overly dependent on state funding.[80]

The questions of the movement's future direction, its relations with the Fianna Fáil-controlled state, and the centrality of farmers and farm workers to its concerns all came up forcefully in the CVO's deliberations. Very much influenced by Muintir's approach, the CVO proposed a new community-centred or communitarian vocationalist model of partly overlapping rural and agricultural interests organised on a voluntary basis within the Catholic parishes.[81] The case for the Catholic parishes to be regarded as the 'basic territorial unit of rural organisation' rested on a taken-for-granted acceptance that the parish was 'a self-conscious community with common interests and common purposes'.[82] Equated with the parish community was the 'parish guild', each one with 'two or more' sections made up of 'farmers', 'agricultural labourers', 'rural craftsmen', professionals (such as 'clergy, doctors, teachers') and household-based 'women of the parish'.[83] The CVO's upbeat view was that the parish guild '…would correspond in some way to a miniature local parliament, a perfect democracy where every adult citizen could make his or her voice heard'.[84] Muintir's national organisation was considered well positioned to co-ordinate parish guild activity and to supply the guilds with useful information.[85] Another key proposal of the CVO was that the state grant '…sufficient powers…to enable the Parish Guild to discharge efficiently certain important functions, cultural, administrative and economic'.[86] Conferring such powers on the guilds/parish councils was believed to be possible without compromising their ability to function independently as voluntary bodies.[87]

Accepting that agricultural interests would continue to be organised along commodity lines, the CVO still proposed that the 'Catholic parish should be taken as the primary territorial unit of organisation for agriculturalists'.[88] The voluntary 'parish agricultural groups' it proposed would have sections composed '…of farmers, owner or tenant, but also of adult sons and daughters actually working on their parents' farms, and of agricultural labourers, male and female'.[89] The CVO saw 'no reason why each of these sections could not be integrated into the rural organisation and form a constituent section of…the Parish Guild'.[90] From these 'parish vocational units' the CVO saw county- and national-level corporatist organisation being 'built up' layer upon layer.[91]

The CVO Report's high hopes for rebuilding rural civil society around the Catholic parishes were tempered by a recognition of 'several difficulties or dangers' potentially besetting its 'scheme of parish organisation'. Among the identified difficulties were a possible shortage of public-spirited volunteers, 'private interests, family considerations and the like playing an undue part', the disinterest or 'even suspicion' or 'hostility' of the 'central administration',[92] and 'the ever-present danger of irrelevant party political considerations intruding into purely local problems' (for this reason the CVO thought it proper that politicians should exclude themselves from the parish guilds, councils and agricultural groups).[93] Conscious that its proposals for re-organising local rural and agricultural interests around the Catholic parishes would very likely not sit well with the long-established Irish 'tradition' of clientelist politics, the Commission issued a word of warning:

> If Parish Guilds and Agricultural Groups are treated in government departments as interlopers and their requests consistently ignored, while political clubs and TDs are received as the authentic exponents of local requirements, there will not be any sustained local enthusiasm for non-political parish organisation and the ideal of union and co-operation will be sacrificed.[94]

The overall message was therefore clear: any effective vocational re-organisation of rural civil society would require that the relevant 'difficulties or dangers' be watched out for, managed, or avoided if at all possible.

As much as the CVO desired 'that politics should be kept out of vocationalism and vocationalism out of politics',[95] this promptly proved to be a forlorn hope. The CVO Report's trenchant criticism of bureaucratic domination and democratic contraction and decay in Ireland, along with its root-and-branch restructuring proposals, didn't impress some leading figures of the ruling party and its proposals were shelved in a storm of controversy.[96] Late in October 1944 Minister Ryan drew attention to the transience of many voluntary parish guilds and councils – particularly those organised outside Muintir and 'at the beginning of the emergency' – and he questioned the degree of voluntary commitment there was to building local vocational guilds and councils.[97]

How did Fianna Fáil respond to MacDermot's and Donnellan's efforts at organising new farmers' parties? A crucial legacy of the alliance forged between nationalists and tenant-farmers during the 1879–82 Land War was that the political representation of farming interests stayed firmly in the hands of nationalist politicians. In the heavily agricultural post-partition south many nationalist parliamentarians were farmers by occupation and – besides having their own agricultural policies and owing their position largely to 'agricultural support' – these nationalists could readily present their parties as 'farmers' parties' worthy of the name.[98]

Our two farmers' parties derived much of their oppositional identity from their hostility to nationalist politicians, from stressing the damage government policies had inflicted on farmers, and from regularly insisting that Fianna Fáil in particular had shown itself to be entirely untrustworthy as a party purporting to represent farming interests. All this had predictable implications for how they were received by members of the ruling party. Competition for votes and seats, together with regular attacks on its leaders and policies, placed the farmers' parties and Fianna Fáil leaders and activists on a collision course. Donnellan, as a former Fianna Fáil county councillor, was viewed as a renegade by many in his former party and this was to give the response to him within Fianna Fáil an extra sharpness.

To see off the threat posed by its farmer challengers, the ruling party's leadership relied heavily (and effectively) on the calling of snap elections in 1933 and in 1944. During election campaigns Fianna Fáil attacks on their farmer challengers intensified and made a particular point of discrediting their 'class unity' aspirations for Irish farmers. In stark contrast to Father Hayes's desire that farmers should comprise a single vocational element for Muintir purposes, small and big farmers (especially 'ranchers') were routinely pitted against each other in Fianna Fáil's political rhetoric and in its activists' reactions to the farmers' parties. These parties were frequently portrayed as representing mainly the relatively small segment of well-heeled big farmers and ranchers.[99] Convinced in particular that big and small farmer classes had conflicting class interests when it came to redistributive land reform, many Fianna Fáil activists sided with land-hungry smallholders and landless men and looked forward to land division being greatly accelerated once the party was in power.

Besides seeking to amplify class differences, the class backgrounds of some leading farmer activists aroused particular suspicion in Fianna Fáil circles. Associating the farmers' leadership with the remnants of a long-dominant and negatively defined landed gentry that had functioned historically as an anti-Irish garrison class, Minister Ryan in a speech delivered in Wicklow in 1938 said of farmer activists how '…they were always against us. Farmers' Union, Farmers' Federation, Centre Party, they are a motley group; the men at their heads are descendants of those who came here in one or other of the confiscations'.[100] MacDermot may have been descended from a ruling Gaelic sept that had remained staunchly Catholic, but in the bitterly contested 1933 election in Roscommon this didn't stop his Fianna Fáil opponents accusing his family of being bad landlords who had evicted tenants in famine times and created a ranch out of their holdings. MacDermot was further vilified for his Home Rule and 'Cawstle Catholic' family background, for being pro-Commonwealth in his politics, for being 'the idol of the English Government and the English Press', and for being a British spy.[101] Stoutly rejecting as 'pure invention' the claims that his family had been bad landlords who had cleared tenants to create a 'ranch' during the Famine, MacDermot further countered by describing 'the great majority' of NFRL members not as 'big farmers and ranchers' but as 'small farmers. In County Roscommon they are mostly very small farmers indeed'.[102]

The gentry card may have been harder to play against Clann's top leadership, though in south Galway where Seán D. O'Kelly (Donnellan's running mate in the 1943 general election) and other members of the local gentry were active in the new farmers' movement, it quickly came to be dubbed the party of the 'landlords' as well as the 'Blueshirts' by local Fianna Fáil activists.[103] And as much as Donnellan insisted that Clann stood 'four square for the division of the ranches',[104] his political enemies were still eager to present his party as a ranchers' movement at heart. Late in the 1940s Donnellan recalled how during the 1943 election campaign the approach roads to Menlough in north Galway had been painted with anti-Clann na Talmhan slogans that read: 'Don't Support the Graziers', 'Don't Support the Ranchers', and 'Don't Support the Grabbers'.[105]

CHALLENGING HEADWINDS

How well then did our three leaders get on in building organisation and in using it to cultivate vocational or class solidarity? And what circumstances helped or hindered their efforts in this regard? 'Hayes', in Don O'Leary's view, 'did more than any other vocationalist in Ireland to give practical effect to *Quadragesimo Anno*'.[106] As Muintir made its way, his friendly relations with members of the ruling party elite helped gain recognition for his new movement and confer a certain legitimacy on it. At the same time what was undoubtedly Muintir's most hurting early setback can be related directly to the state. As a dedicated vocationalist, Father Hayes evidently came to see Muintir's longer term prospects as heavily dependent on the ruling party accepting the CVO's proposals for the reorganisation of local rural and agricultural interests along Muintir's vocationalist lines. While determined to preserve Muintir's autonomy to function independently, state recognition and the devolving of certain local administrative and developmental powers to rural guilds/councils were still viewed as empowering by virtue of bestowing standing, legitimacy, and resources on them. Another consideration in reaching out to the state was the slow progress recorded in spreading the new movement across the country. Only 20 guilds/councils had been formed between 1937 and the autumn of 1939. And as many as 50 of the 70 guilds/councils Muintir was declaring in 1940 had appeared in the previous 12 months;[107] with 'roughly about 80 per cent' of their total number located in Munster.[108] The rejection of the CVO's proposals didn't end Father Hayes's interest in the well-being of Irish agriculture. In the early post-war years his desire to see it modernise remained strong as he actively championed rural electrification, involved Muintir in holding a summer school for farmers and farm labourers at Pallaskenry, and eventually secured state acceptance for a Parish Plan for Agriculture that showed some early promise before succumbing to a series of reverses in the 1950s.[109] In the event, however, farm modernisation would soon be undermining one key strand of John Hayes's conception of rural social structure – the farm labourers. A predictable (if still highly consequential) effect of the post-war rural electrification and tractor-based farm motorisation was to greatly speed up the labour-shedding process in Ireland's labour-employing agricultural regions.[110]

Clearly not all of Muintir's difficulties in the agricultural sphere during the founder's lifetime related directly to state actions or inactions. Even with the policy climate becoming more favourable to some home producers in 1932 and Father Hayes being on friendly terms with members of the new government, his producers' federation of 1931 (Muintir na Tíre Ltd) sank under the cumulative weight of a number of crippling difficulties. One crucial thing going against it was its inability to get the powerful Beet Growers' Association to affiliate with it.[111] Undercapitalisation has also been seen as weakening it,[112] as have conflicts of interest between different sets of farmer producers,[113] the general disinterest of farm labourers,[114] and the failure 'to give a thorough grounding in co-operative theory and practice to all its members'.[115] Another difficulty was factional infighting in the federation's management committee which spurred the founder to get rid of 'political-minded undesirables' in 1934.[116]

How well did Muintir's local community organising and solidarity-cultivating efforts live up in practice to the founder's normative ideal of deliberative democratic decision-making among numerically equal parish council representatives? Most revealing here is Patrick McNabb's study of rural east Limerick in the late 1950s that explores how the local 'social structure' – with its rigid (if changing) class and gender divisions built heavily around male ownership of family land – was impacting on Muintir's local organising efforts. Much revealing light on participation and decision-making processes in local community life is shed by the way public meetings tended to be conducted in east Limerick. With meeting-goers seating themselves 'according to rank, age and sex' in the local parish halls, the first two rows of seating were typically occupied by

> middle-aged people of the professional or business class and farmers of high standing. These people were the spokesmen and answered for the whole community. While they were present, it was difficult to get other members of the audience to participate in discussion.[117]

McNabb further relates how despite rural workers having

> …equal representation on the parish council with other groups…the local policy of Muintir is influenced by those members of the Council whose opinions carry the most weight. They are usually people of social standing, or people who are good at expressing themselves. Neither would include the farm worker.[118]

From their positioning in the hall and their silence at parish meetings McNabb concludes that 'although the farm worker is in revolt against the traditional class attitudes, he does not feel strong enough to challenge them in public'.[119]

Evidently the relatively powerful east Limerick farmers McNabb describes didn't regard themselves as social and economic equals with landless workers; and the notion of engaging in full and frank discussion with class subordinates with a view to coming to an agreed conception of the common good was evidently way beyond their ken.[120] Rural east Limerick's traditional social structure may have been inimical to Father Hayes's normative ideals of equal representation and deliberative democratic decision-making among section equals, yet McNabb still deems Muintir – which he groups along with other modernising nationally-organised rural and farmer associations – as 'gradually succeeding' in advancing its aim of 'restoring a spirit of cooperation and self-help'.[121] In contrast to McNabb's rigidly class-stratified east Limerick, John Scully's very much less detailed early 1960s account of Father Hayes's final parish of Bansha in South Tipperary suggests that under his leadership local Muintir had actually made major strides in eroding local 'class distinction'. Writing as someone who had spent more than four years working as an agricultural advisor locally, Scully maintained that the local community:

> ...is no longer stratified into distinctive social classes, thanks to the efforts of Muintir na Tíre. Certainly, there are many members of the community who still believe in a society composed of separate social classes, but nowadays these are the exception rather than the rule in Bansha.[122]

How well did Father Hayes and Muintir fare in attracting women to the new vocationalist community movement of 1937? At the first 'Rural Week' in Ardmore in 1937 it was apparently 'only the women [who] made newspaper headlines. "Woman the Important Factor in Rural Ireland. Overwork and Drudgery Driving Her from the Land."' Raising awareness around these issues led Rynne to suggest that 'a feminist war was launched at Ardmore that was eventually to win two major rural victories: the electrification scheme and the State-aided scheme for bringing piped water to farm-house kitchens'.[123] These 'rural victories' were nonetheless slow in coming. Four years later Josephine McNeill (a Dublin Town Association Irish Countrywomen's Association (ICA) activist) was asking the 'men of Muintir na Tíre' to consider whether 'the townswomen are getting ahead of your womenfolk, streets ahead'. While town women had 'running water' and 'electric light', rural women still had to draw water from the well and to light their oil-lamps as darkness fell.[124] As long as such backward conditions obtained, young women were sure to avail of education to abandon the land for the city. A progressive step for McNeill would therefore be for Muintir 'to help us in extending the work of the Irish Countrywomen's Association'.[125]

John Hayes may have been keen in principle to see women involved in Muintir, but there were no women on Muintir's two diocesan federations (Cork and Cashel) in 1940 and but one woman on its Central Council.[126] And seemingly it took 'several years' for Tipperary Town's guild to have a women's section.[127] It was publicly acknowledged in 1940 that 'some places' had proved difficult to attract women's participation.[128] Nor, evidently, was Muintir's national organising secretary making any special effort to encourage women to participate actively in the local organisation. In his 1940 account of what 'usually happens' in organising new parish guilds/councils, J. O. Barry Walsh described how his practice was to ask those present at a public meeting '...to form themselves into three different sections in the hall, farmers, labourers, and others. I go to each separately and tell them that the purpose is to select the five best men amongst them to represent them on the council, and not to have any voting in the matter'.[129]

We are further told in 1940 how 'usually when there is a separate section for women they do not bother to go into the others'.[130] Why this was so, and why Muintir was apparently so heavily male-centred and male-dominated, were explored when some ICA women appeared before the CVO on 21 November 1940. In response to the suggestion that Muintir 'at present seems to be severely masculine', Josephine Mangan replied that 'I do not think that they want to be but men generally seem to do the talking. It is a fact that where there are men and women in a society, it is really the men who get the representation'.[131] It followed therefore that 'individual women on parish councils...would be very little help' to Muintir compared to women who were already ICA members.[132] Muriel Gahan agreed that non-ICA women joining Muintir as 'ordinary' members wouldn't 'get any representation. They would like to be considered as farmers, as business people and, in addition to be represented as country women with their special needs'.[133] Accepting that both the ICA and Muintir were 'doing important work for the organisation of women in rural areas', the CVO's final report nonetheless offered substantial support for the Muintir approach by concluding that 'the formation of women's sections in parish or local councils has been found a suitable method of organisation in many places'.[134]

John Hayes may have abandoned his attempts to organise Irish agriculturalists separately by 1937, but others were taking a very different view. The IFF had begun to organise farmers (as well as farm labourers) as a federation of organised agricultural interests in 1937.[135] Its presence, but more particularly the momentum generated by the advances of the young farmers' movement Macra na Feirme (Macra), the Irish Creamery Milk Suppliers' Association (ICMSA) and the National Farmers' Association (NFA) in the 40s and 50s, resulted in the purely farmer-centred approach clashing head-on with Muintir's community-centred approach and ultimately marginalising and displacing it as an effective means of organising farmers and representing their economic interests.[136] Not alone did the new farmer activists, along with those of the IFF earlier, believe that farmers were best organised separately but they tended to hold that farmers (rather than priests or other professionals) were the best qualified to speak for farmers and to lead attempts at organising them.[137] Muintir's community-centred approach was considered too general and diffuse to be an adequate means of organising and representing Irish farmers and of influencing state policy.[138]

Our two farmers' parties may also have opted for a separatist approach in organising Irish farmers, but by engaging directly in electoral competition they differed radically from the likes of the IFF, Macra, the ICMSA and the NFA. Ultimately their prospects came therefore to depend critically on how well they fared when their popular support was put to the test in general elections. And here not only did MacDermot and Donnellan come up against a superbly organised ruling party, but they had to contend with one whose leaders viewed it as more entitled and better able to represent farmers than any of its political rivals (including so-called farmers' parties). Nor was Fianna Fáil slow in using its control of state power from 1932 to commence building a new agricultural economy and to take steps to improve the position of farm labourers.[139] To go by the seats won, their share of the first preference vote, and the spatial distribution of their seats, the NFRL/CP and Clann nonetheless showed some promise on their first electoral outings but subsequently they couldn't develop into major parties. Five of the eleven seats the NFRL/CP won in the 1933 election resulted from Cumann na nGaedheal losses and no seat was gained at Fianna Fáil's expense.[140] Five of Clann's ten seats in the 1943 election were held by sitting Fine Gael TDs, though on this occasion the farmers took seats off Fianna Fáil in their western heartlands (one in Mayo South and one in Roscommon).[141] The ten seats Clann won in the 1943 election left it holding the balance of power in the new Dáil, though ultimately the farmers – swayed by the need to preserve wartime political stability – didn't block Fianna Fáil's efforts to form a single-party minority government. Joseph Blowick replaced Donnellan as party leader in 1944; and the loss of one of its two Roscommon seats (to

Fianna Fáil) in the 1944 snap election began a pattern of the party losing seats at successive elections. Eventually Clann transitioned from being a party of protest to being a party of power, but participation in the 1948–51 and 1954–7 inter-party governments brought the party dangerously closer to Fine Gael and greatly hastened its electoral decline.

Were there reasons other than a hostile ruling party why our two farmers' parties struggled to use organisation to cultivate farmer collective solidarity? The class differentiation that gave rise to tensions between big and small farmers in particular cannot be regarded as a mere figment of Fianna Fáil's political rhetoric. By early 1935 MacDermot was publicly accepting that Irish farmers were too internally divided to form a coherent economic and political class. In 'many parts of the country', he observed, 'the small farmers are hostile to the larger farmers, and refuse to recognise any solidarity of interest with them'.[142] Class divisions and tensions between big and small farmers proved to be a difficulty for Clann as well. During the 1943 election campaign serious strains in Clann's alliance of big and small farmers became apparent in policy differences over land redistribution. The big farmer element tended to view land redistribution as a serious threat to the principle of security of tenure and – for the sake of some semblance of unity – the westerners agreed to accept this principle in the party's 1943 election manifesto alongside a commitment to land division. With Patrick Cogan's departure from Clann in 1946–7 – following two of Clann's leading figures in Mayo (both sitting TDs) serving a month in jail for their part in a local land agitation – Clann's link with the IFF and its followers that took security of tenure as a core value was broken.

Conclusions

What set John Hayes apart from our Farmers' Party leaders was his clerical leadership, his analysis of Ireland's interwar rural crisis conditions, his commitment to bringing farmers, rural labourers, other occupational groups, and rural women together in the same organisation in the new Muintir of 1937, his inclination to see farmers as a single unified vocational interest for Muintir purposes by the late 1930s, and his desire to see the local community's different vocational sections working together to build a unified parish guild/council. Separating our two farmers' leaders from Father Hayes was an exclusive focus on organising farmers, an analysis that regarded them as divided into different classes and that took the building of alliances – especially between big and small farmer classes – as crucial in using organisation to forge unity, manage disagreements, and to cultivate class and vocational solidarity among them. The decision to compete with the ruling party (and other rival parties) by contesting elections profoundly influenced MacDermot's and Donnellan's analyses of rural crisis conditions, their organisational and tactical preferences, the sorts of relationships they came to have with Fianna Fáil leaders and activists, and the sort of farmer solidarity they sought to cultivate via organisation.

Based on what we have seen so far how are we to characterise the styles of cultivating solidarity of John Hayes and our two Farmers' Party leaders? John Hayes's strong desire to collaborate with the ruling party – and the broadly positive reception he and his movement got from leading governing politicians at first – suggests that the solidarity he wished to cultivate can best be described as collaborative. Along with the wish to collaborate with the state and its ruling party, the desire to see local sectional interests subordinating themselves to the community interest and the common good was what gave shape to the sort of vocational solidarity Father Hayes wished to cultivate via organisation in the new Muintir of 1937. This solidarity was conceived as wholly integrationist in that farmers, rural workers (the paid farmworkers especially), rural women (especially married farm women) along with other recognised vocational sections were to be formally integrated internally as vocational interests within the Muintir guilds. And the representatives of the different vocational sections were to function as numerical equals within the parish councils.

Father Hayes's desire was to see Muintir's local organisation integrated not just internally but externally into the wider society and polity as well. External integration was to be achieved on the strength of Muintir activists across the country acquiring a new sense of patriotic duty via local activism geared towards civic improvements and revolving around organised neighbourliness. A related necessary condition for the attainment of external integration was that the state reciprocate by recognising Muintir's practical usefulness along with its national- and local-level autonomy. Compared to Hayes's preferred integrationist-collaborative solidarity, the farmer solidarity MacDermot and Donnellan desired and sought to cultivate can best be described as integrationist-oppositional in character. It was integrationist insofar as it depended on organising inclusive cross-class farmer alliances while – reflecting the realities of electoral competition and a common opposition to the ruling Fianna Fáil Party – it was simultaneously heavily oppositional.

But how did our three attempts at empowering farmers – by means of building organisation and cultivating vocational or class solidarity – ultimately fare? All three mobilisations were unable to spread themselves evenly across the country and so become genuinely nationwide movements in that sense. They further shared the experience of being critically impeded by the actions of the ruling party's leaders. The rejection of the CVO's proposals for the reorganising of rural and agricultural interests at the local level delivered a lethal blow to the CVO's (and Muintir's) vocationalist project of reconstructing rural civil society around the primacy of the Catholic parishes. For their part, our two farmers' parties struggled in vain to get the better of a formidably powerful ruling party. Certain forces internal to the countryside also hampered the efforts of our three leaders. The appearance of Macra, the ICMSA and the NFA put Muintir's vocationalism, and the approach of our two farmers' parties, under severe challenge in the 1940s and 50s. Much the same can be said of the competition Muintir faced from the ICA in its attempts to organise women along vocationalist community lines. Something else that had a big bearing on outcomes were the difficulties experienced in transcending class divisions and in managing tensions and conflicts among farmers in the case of our two farmers' parties, and between farmers and farm labourers in Muintir's case. McNabb's research in particular questions the realism of Father Hayes's optimistic assumption that economic and social differences outside the parish councils could be bracketed inside them on the strength of formally equal section representatives building – in a spirit of Christian harmony and unity – an agreed and universally shared conception of the community interest and the common good.[143]

In the end the NFRL/CP lasted for less than a year before disappearing in the merger that saw the creation of the United Ireland Party/Fine Gael in September 1933.[144] Clann lingered on into the 1960s by which time its heyday wartime years were long over. Muintir would survive as a movement to the present day by adapting to changing conditions and especially by embracing 'community development' from the late 1950s.[145] In the longer run Father Hayes's communitarian vocationalist project of reorganising Irish agricultural interests around the Catholic parishes with a view to cultivating vocational solidarity wasn't to prosper. Indeed, the progressive abandonment of his version of communitarian vocationalism became a vital part of Muintir's adjustment to rapidly changing internal and external conditions following the Tipperary priest's death in 1957. From that point on the focus on agriculture diminished within the movement he had founded and faded further as its vocationalist guilds/parish councils began to be replaced by 'representative community councils' in the early 1970s.

Power and the Politics of Persuasion: Comparing Muintir na Tíre's and Tuairim's Relationships with Church and State in Post-War Ireland

Tomás Finn

At first glance Muintir na Tíre (1937–) and Tuairim (1954–75) would appear to be very different social movements with very little in common, even if their founders chose Irish names for each of them.[1] Established in 1937, Muintir na Tíre's early activities centred on the creation of voluntary 'guilds' and parish councils, the provision of parish halls, seeking improvements in community services and amenities, the holding of 'Rural Weeks', and undertaking the publication of a range of rural-themed periodicals (such as *Rural Ireland* and *The Landmark*). All these efforts were focused on making rural Ireland a more attractive place in which to live. By the early 1960s Muintir na Tíre (hereafter, Muintir) had begun to focus its efforts increasingly on the promotion of 'community development'. Tuairim, on the other hand was secular, independent of the Catholic Church and political parties, and its members, concentrated in urban areas, sought to influence the political establishment in a broadly liberal direction by such means as public meetings, study weekends and the publication of pamphlets. In broad terms, Tuairim set itself the ambitious task of generating an intellectual climate that would allow the Irish people (and its ruling elites) to get to grips with the many social, cultural, economic and political problems facing a rapidly urbanising and industrialising society.

Both movements generated considerable publicity for their activities, although by their very natures they differed in the projects they pursued, the types of activists they attracted, and in the constituencies they appealed to. As a movement founded by a Catholic priest and active at the parochial level in an overwhelmingly Catholic country, Muintir's *raison d'être* was from the outset the protection and preservation of rural Ireland. Particularly in its early decades Catholic bishops and priests were much to the fore in the movement as leaders and activists; and the movement succeeded in securing considerable support among rural Ireland's middle class.

By contrast, the issues Tuairim's activists and members debated were those emerging as southern Ireland underwent rapid urbanisation and industrialisation from the late 1950s. As primarily an urban-based movement, Tuairim's activists were overwhelmingly drawn from the urban professional middle class. Reflecting a determination to move beyond civil war politics, Tuairim appealed especially to younger adults and went so far as to set 40 as an upper age limit for its executive members and officers.

So as to be able to influence the course of social change, both movements had of necessity to build relations with two major power blocs in Irish society – the Catholic Church and the Irish state. It is these relations that this chapter explores particularly by comparing Muintir's and Tuairim's relations with members of the Catholic hierarchy and with ruling politicians. As Muintir was already almost 20 years in existence by the time Tuairim appeared on the scene, and as certain patterns and path dependencies had already emerged in its relations with members of the Catholic hierarchy and with ruling politicians, it makes sense to consider these earlier patterns to some degree.

RELATIONS WITH THE CATHOLIC CHURCH

While Tuairim was not constrained in where it could establish its branches, in the early decades Muintir's guilds required clerical approval. Among the movement's foremost post-war advocates were Father (later Canon) John Hayes (Muintir's founder), Archbishop Thomas Morris of Cashel and Emly, Bishop Michael Browne of Galway, Bishop Cornelius Lucey of Cork and Ross and (from the late 1950s) Jeremiah Newman, the professor of sociology at Maynooth and future Bishop of Limerick. An energetic supporter from the outset, Bishop Browne opened a Rural Week in Galway in 1939 with a mass in the Pro-Cathedral. In his homily Browne expressed the view that there was 'plenty of work for Muintir na Tíre to do for farmers…to develop among their children…love of Ireland that they would be prepared to work for Ireland, and, at least, live in Ireland'.[2] While occupying the chair of philosophy and political theory at Maynooth University, Cornelius Lucey frequently expressed his alarm at the condition of the small farmers and the consequent 'flight from the land', a theme he developed most notably in his minority report for the 1954 Commission on Emigration and other Population Problems. Just as Lucey's appointment as Bishop of Cork and Ross contributed to Muintir's continuing strength within the southern county, Browne's support enabled the organisation to gain a gradual foothold in Galway. By 1968 it had at least 11 guilds – mostly established after 1955 – and with the one in Maree, Oranmore, being particularly active from 1948.[3]

Archbishop John Charles McQuaid of Dublin, on the other hand, summarised his enduring disapproval of Muintir in 1959 when he observed once again how it was an 'interdenominational' body.[4] Once appointed archbishop, McQuaid saw his priority as ensuring Protestantism did not undermine the Catholic way of life. And as archbishop his view was that since Muintir was not wholly Catholic in its composition it could not be trusted to represent Catholic farmers or the Catholic people of rural Ireland more generally. Furthermore, McQuaid's view of Muintir was different to Lucey's and Browne's in that he did not perceive the movement as important in countering emigration from rural areas. Neither, for that matter, did he perceive emigration as the greatest national crisis, nor saving rural Ireland as critical to the country's future in the same way that Browne or Lucey did. Archbishop McQuaid was at least consistent in his view of Muintir. In 1941 he had refused to give any message of support to a 'Rural Weekend' in Lucan, a gathering for which the Muintir leadership had not sought his prior approval.

Most significantly for Muintir was McQuaid's refusal to sanction the establishment of guilds in the Archdiocese of Dublin. This sanction was withheld despite Hayes's pleas to him and despite his earlier praise for Muintir while President of Blackrock College. In the course of a sermon in his native Cavan in 1932 on the theme 'Our divine Lord Jesus Christ or Satan: The Real Struggle in the Modern World', McQuaid had identified Muintir as 'worthy of special mention'. This was particularly so insofar as it resembled Belgium's Boerenbond (1890), an 'astonishing organisation of the young, both boys and girls, rich and poor'.[5] In keeping with his strong support for the Catholic Action movement emerging in Ireland and continental Europe, McQuaid seemed especially pleased that Muintir was taking rural Ireland as its focus. The perceived importance of lay Catholics and study groups in the struggle against Satan was such that he believed their 'presence makes Communism virtually impossible'.[6] Once he became archbishop, however, McQuaid expressed himself in 1941 as 'not convinced that the association has yet proved it deserves a place in this diocese, the county or the city'.[7] How is this change of stance to be explained? In contrast to his previous position where 'as a schoolmaster [he was], of necessity, removed from a very active share in the daily life of the world',[8] as Archbishop McQuaid insisted on assuming full responsibility for ensuring his people led good Catholic lives. And whereas Muintir had only recently appeared in 1931, by the early 1940s it had evolved and come to welcome Protestants as well as Catholics to its movement. Apart from being unacceptable to him for this reason, Muintir apparently also represented a 'rival to [McQuaid's] Catholic Social Service Conference, which was firmly under his control'.[9]

Sandymount in 1942 provides a revealing example of how hostile a terrain Dublin was for Muintir in the early 1940s. In that year the local parish priest Father T. F. Ryan made it clear that a local parish council – recently established under the provisions of the 1941 Local Government Act – was a non-Catholic body and thus did 'not have the approval of the Church'. According to a letter to McQuaid from P. McDonald, the new council's secretary, Father Ryan, during a sermon had 'made a number of remarks about Masons, Lepers and bigotry in Northern Ireland', thus making it clear that the 'Council was being run on non-Catholic lines and for anti-Catholic purposes'.[10] In the event McQuaid was not swayed by the expressed hope of the new Sandymount council to become affiliated to Muintir, or the attention it drew to the 'benevolent interest taken in the Muintir na Tíre organisation by eminent Church dignitaries'. Most decisive of all for McQuaid was that the Sandymount council included six non-Catholic members. Predictably, McQuaid made it clear that he would not authorise any meeting or approve the establishment of a Muintir branch in his archdiocese.[11]

McQuaid's view of Tuairim evolved from early toleration to later rejection. Early on he was ready to offer Donal Barrington, a founding member of Tuairim, £6000 to establish a Catholic newspaper, a proposal inconsistent with Tuairim's preference to see a liberal review published in Ireland.[12] Soon the archbishop's initial hopes for Tuairim had given way to concern that the body was interdenominational, something that led him to seek further information about it from Father Bertram Crowe, a lecturer in moral philosophy at UCD. What had sparked his alarm about Tuairim was its raising of the questions of denominational education and the management of schools.[13] Nor did McQuaid find endearing Tuairim's support for ecumenical developments and that its membership which included Protestants and Jews along with high profile liberal Catholic clerics such as Father Enda McDonagh and Sister Margaret MacCurtain.

Browne and Lucey shared McQuaid's negative view of Tuairim with neither of them being happy with Tuairim's preferences as to the future shape of modern Ireland. Browne, for example, was outspoken in his support for the Fethard-on-Sea boycott and in that context was strongly critical of Barrington, then a young barrister, while Lucey argued for a more robust Irish censorship regime. That not all the junior clergy agreed with the likes of Browne and Lucey on social issues highlights the need for us not to treat the Irish Catholic Church as a monolith in the late 1950s. Father Peter Connolly, for instance, agreed with Tuairim as to the need to liberalise the censorship regime. Along with Tuairim, Connolly favoured an intellectual Catholicism, one that could respond and adapt to new ideas rather than seek to prevent them from ever entering the country.[14]

McQuaid's hostility towards Tuairim was not to change, as can be seen from his decision in 1971 to turn down an invitation to speak at an interdenominational event. Renewed attempts by Muintir leaders – specifically Hayes and Stephen Rynne (a long-term activist as well as the future biographer of Father Hayes) – to convince the archbishop of the value of the movement's work failed to persuade him to change his stance. In response to Rynne's request in 1955 for permission to establish guilds in the Dublin archdiocese, McQuaid again expressed his opposition to the possibility that any organisation – including ones that were 'far less desirable' – could be set up without the Catholic clergy's permission.[15] As with his approach in dealing with Tuairim, McQuaid in his replies to Rynne requested further information concerning Muintir while making clear that no requests to establish branches had been forwarded to him through 'the Parish Priest, the acknowledged spiritual head of each Parish'.[16] McQuaid's comment that if 'Muintir na Tíre is an organisation of Parish Guilds it is purely singular' is certainly ironic given that his determination to prevent Muintir establishing an organisational presence in Dublin left him at odds, not only with Hayes, Browne, Lucey and other senior members of the Catholic hierarchy, but with Pope Pius XII himself.

In 1954 the Pope had praised Hayes for 'rightly' choosing the 'Parish as the basic unit of a Christian social order' and had conferred a 'special Apostolic Benediction' on Hayes and the members of Muintir na Tíre for seeking to 'put Christian social practice into practice'.[17] The papal reference here to 'Christian' rather than 'Catholic' is notable, but it should not blind us to the strongly Catholic ethos that continued to be present in Muintir. The zeal for promoting a Catholic ethos could lead such Muintir supporters and activists as Father Edward Coyne to claim to be articulating the needs of 95 per cent of the people, to Alfred O'Rahilly (the UCC President) praising the spirit in Mussolini's Italy, and to Hayes quoting Portugal's Salazar as to the need for 'men of spirit'.[18] For many in Muintir the centre of Catholic Ireland was to be found in rural Ireland, even if Hayes stressed the 'symbiotic' relationship between urban and rural Ireland.[19]

Muintir may have had to wait until 1954 to be praised publicly by Pope Pius XII but at different times public endorsements of the movement had been voiced in Ireland by Archbishop Harty of Cashel, by Bishop Keogh of Kildare who commended it for giving the country 'new life', and by Archbishop Walsh of Tuam who described it as 'one of the most valuable movements started in Ireland for many years'.[20] These papal and episcopal commendations must have been re-assuring to John Hayes after his years spent seeking to build a movement that could embrace all classes and Christian creeds while putting into practice a vocationalism derived from the papal encyclicals. A member of the Commission on Vocationalist Organisation, Hayes remained throughout his life a strong advocate of vocationalism. As an alternative to Marxism and Communism and as a means to prevent class war, vocationalism, for Hayes, offered a Christian model to organise different sectors of society and the economy and to govern the country. Yet, for all the talk about it as an ideal, the possible implications of vocationalism for Irish democracy received little detailed scrutiny at Muintir gatherings. When it was considered, the main view put forward was that Muintir's parish guilds and councils constituted a particularly effective way to 'promote Christian communal cooperation', and thus offered something of an alternative to the adversarial system in which political parties operated.[21] For his part McQuaid had misgivings about the potential implications of vocationalism for the pre-existing conservative consensus of church and state in Ireland and for the Catholic church's capacity to influence public policy.[22]

As Irish society began to change rapidly from the late 1950s McQuaid's antipathy towards Protestants and Catholics sharing membership of the same associations came under greater challenge. With Vatican II change was also coming to the Catholic Church as a greater openness to individuals from different religions working together in the civic sphere developed. However, McQuaid's opposition to Muintir remained unchanged. Still opposed to the movement as an interdenominational body, he deemed Muintir unsuitable to work with the Young Farmers and the National Farmers' Association [NFA], and to act as a 'liaison body' in a 'Catholic body to represent Irish farmers and rural people in a proposed Catholic International Rural body'.[23] His one concession to Muintir came in 1959 when he agreed to Archbishop Thomas Morris's proposal for Father James Holoway to undertake an MA in sociology at UCD.[24]

After Canon Hayes's death in 1957 state planning and improved relations with the state came to be seen within Muintir as central to its effectiveness as a rural movement. Vocationalism's doctrine of subsidiarity (the need for decisions to be taken at the most local level possible) rapidly faded in importance within the movement. When Tomás Roseingrave, Muintir's National Director, participated in a wide-ranging Tuairm conference on the role of Government and civil society in 1969,[25] he explicitly emphasised the need for institutional reform and better communication and working relations between the state and voluntary associations. Of course, the local community was still central for Roseingrave who insisted on taking the health of different voluntary groups in the community as the 'essence of democracy'.[26]

It was perhaps surprising that Tuairim, a body whose mission was the renewal of Irish democracy and intellectual life, had very little to say about Irish Catholicism's advocacy of vocationalism. Its silence reflected how Catholic vocationalism had lost much of its appeal by the late 1950s, though questions of church-state relations still remained prominent. Barrington, a future Supreme Court judge, suggested that church-state relations in Ireland could be interpreted with reference to the constitution as having potentially revolutionary implications.[27] When arguing for a greatly expanded role for the state in the economy and society in the 1950s, Barrington implied that the Catholic Church's 'special position' in the Constitution could allow Canon Law to take precedence over Civil Law in certain circumstances. This was a position which Maynooth's Jeremiah Newman might concur with but Barrington – perhaps influenced by Enda McDonagh also of Maynooth – later countered by arguing that the Catholic Church's position 'flow[ed] from the factual...not the juridical position'.[28]

RELATIONS WITH THE IRISH STATE

At the Lucan Rural Weekend in 1941, which McQuaid had declined to support, both the Taoiseach Éamon de Valera and the leader of the opposition William T. Cosgrave attended and spoke.[29] This event somewhat eased reservations over the 1941 Local Government Act that provided for the official recognition of parish-based local councils. The possible implications the 1941 legislation had for Muintir's independence had been the cause of some controversy. By 1940, however, Hayes believed that the government had accepted the 'voluntary system' and had paid the 'best possible tribute to the idea of Muintir na Tíre by using the parish as the basis to form emergency committees'.[30] He further claimed that the government agreed with him that Muintir should not be incorporated into any state system. Certainly de Valera took the view in 1941 that Muintir's 'Guilds would be better without state interference...that the whole movement would be destroyed if the State endeavoured to make the parish groups a part of the general State organisation'.[31] Consistent with such a stance, the Taoiseach had refused to give Muintir a grant in 1939 as his view was that to be 'successful the work must be altogether voluntary'.[32] De Valera spoke very highly in public of Muintir in 1940 when describing it as 'the ideal type of organisation, not waiting for directions from the top, but taking the initiatives in its own area'. In 1941 he wished the movement every 'success' and again in 1958 when he noted how he had been going to the Rural Weeks for 21 years.[33]

Hayes himself remained steadfast in his view that Muintir had to remain voluntary and that state control would destroy the independence his movement needed to do its work. Despite such comments, P. J. Ruttledge, the Minister for Local Government and Public Health, claimed that much of the work of the state-approved '600 parish councils' which had been established by 1941 was done 'under the auspices of Muintir na Tíre'.[34] Early examples of such councils included Tuam, Terenure and Trim. At a meeting in Tuam, Hayes explained that Muintir would help the country during the war, before proceeding to urge 'people not to lose their heads in the crisis'.[35] Not only did the wartime emergency facilitate Muintir's growth but it showed its ability to adapt to changing circumstances. With the war ending in 1945 whatever threat the conflict posed to the organisation and to its independence passed without resulting in any lasting damage.

Following the war, as the crisis facing rural Ireland became more pressing, Muintir proceeded to reinvent itself by taking on new activities. Its proposals for a 'Parish Plan' to increase production in agriculture gained the support of Taoiseach John A. Costello and James Dillon, the Minister for Agriculture in the two inter-party governments of 1948–51 and 1954–7. Essential to Muintir's Parish Plan scheme was the provision by the state of special agricultural instruction at the parish level.[36] From an early stage difficulties arose over the size of the Parish Plan areas and the advisory personnel to be used in the effort. There were also divisions between the main political parties regarding the value of the scheme. Significantly, Macra na Feirme was opposed to the Parish Plan; and in a note to McQuaid his secretary highlighted the opposition of Macra as a reason not to support

Muintir.[37] Interestingly, Bishop Lucey of Cork echoed the fears of Macra and some Muintir members concerning the scheme's potential for state control.[38]

Fianna Fáil pointed to the practical difficulties of finding a sufficient number of agricultural instructors to operate the Parish Plan.[39] And despite the inter party government's efforts and some evidence of cooperation between County Committees and voluntary organisations such as Muintir, many County Committees of Agriculture felt threatened by the Parish Plan's potential to intrude on their own area of responsibility.[40] By contrast, rural electrification was relatively free of controversy and proved to be of immense value to Muintir's post-war efforts to expand its guild organisation. There was a great deal of co-operation between the Muintir guilds and the relevant state bodies in advancing rural electrification and – inevitably given the scale of the project – some overlap of membership occurred between the various bodies that added to the campaign's momentum.

As 'community development' emerged internationally in the 1950s, Muintir could claim to have had long practical experience with this sort of activity. Interest began to be shown in Muintir in the USA, in parts of Europe as well as further afield. There was even an unsuccessful request in 1956 to the then Taoiseach, John A. Costello, for a letter of support to help to establish Muintir in South Vietnam as an 'antidote to Communism'.[41] As a reflection of the strides it was making in building a profile for itself in promoting Irish community development, Muintir was able to host an international seminar on the topic of 'Organising Resources for Community Development' at Gormanston College in 1962.[42] The state grant of £3000 provided to Muintir for its Gormanston seminar, and Lemass's willingness to launch the *Limerick Rural Survey* in 1964, offers evidence of greater receptiveness to Muintir in ruling circles. As regards the *Limerick Rural Survey*, civil servants praised Newman's contribution but criticised the main part of the report for its perceived impracticality.[43] Muintir's arguments that local voluntary bodies be included in the membership of the state's new County Development Teams (CDTs) were rejected in 1964, but provision was made for holding regular meetings between the CDTs and local voluntary groups.[44]

Archbishop Morris, a strong supporter of ecumenism, and Newman, 'at best, ambivalent' to it,[45] may have differed in their attitudes towards Vatican II, but they were at one in seeing Muintir as having a valuable educational role to play, especially in promoting community development and rural-related sociological research. The government accepted the need for more research but, as a memorandum put it in 1961, the challenge was to decide the proper balance between voluntary organisations and state activity in carrying it out. Apparently as a 'result of representations [made] by…Muintir na Tíre [and the West Cork Development Association], An Foras Talúntais decided to carry out a survey of the problems of West Cork'.[46] Criticism of Muintir's surveys related to the movement's limited engagement with the local population and highlighted more broadly the state's and wider society's different priorities.[47]

Lemass praised Muintir for its work in seeking to provide a more holistic way forward in response to the problems of rural Ireland. Such praise for Muintir's plan for community development (including its proposal for an Institute for Rural Sociology) prompted the Department of Agriculture to observe in 1964 that Muintir was 'not a very effective organisation at local level'.[48] In response the Taoiseach claimed that the department had not been 'quite fair' in treating Muintir as if it was the same as other rural organisations, pointing out that Muintir's approach was more comprehensive by focusing on the social as well as the agricultural problems facing rural Ireland.[49] Lemass went on to urge his ministers to consider Muintir's proposals more positively.

The ensuing departmental responses, however, pointed to problems of duplication in the educational sector, to the cost implications of Muintir's proposals, and to Muintir's inability to run its proposed research centre. These criticisms and reservations did not stop Lemass's government sanctioning an annual grant of £5000 to Muintir in 1964, the funding to be administered by the Department of Education rather than the Department of Agriculture.[50] As its educational role differentiated Muintir from other rural bodies, it made sense that Education (rather than Agriculture) be given responsibility for administering its new funding. More than anything, the decision to fund Muintir's work – one made against the advice of the Department of Agriculture – reflected in particular Lemass's acceptance that Muintir had a valuable contribution to make to 'education in the broadest sense'.[51]

Where state support for Muintir was concerned Lemass's pragmatism contrasted with de Valera's frugality. The Parish Plan can be said to have been crucial in moving state-Muintir relations closer to the full partnership some in Muintir now desired. What also contributed to the new relationship was the steep decline in enthusiasm for vocationalism, the related gradual breakdown of the suspicion many within rural Ireland had of the state, and the state itself adopting an increasingly interventionist role in the economy and society.

What can be said of Tuairim's relations with modernisation-minded Irish state elites from the late 1950s on? Through its pamphlets and meetings, Tuairim put forward a range of arguments that sought to give modern Ireland a more liberal shape and that impacted upon the political establishment. In different ways, Seán Lemass, as Taoiseach from 1959, praised Tuairim's role in seeking solutions to the issues facing the country and recognised it as part of a 'new spirit'.[52] This is not to say that there was no resistance to the sort of questioning culture Tuairim favoured, particularly when its commentary touched on the performance of Ireland's political parties. Fianna Fáil's Seán MacEntee, who generally held Tuairim in high regard, criticised the movement for its independence of political parties and for attacking his own party. Yet, once the context in which the governing Fianna Fáil Party had been criticised was made clear to him, MacEntee apologised for questioning the movement's impartiality. Fine Gael's John A. Costello referred to Tuairim's 'aloof neutrality' and for discouraging young people from joining political parties.[53] Yet Costello himself, who for much of his career did little to change his party, came to recognise the need to improve Fine Gael's image and make it more appealing to younger people. Following a meeting (probably in late 1959) with young students at University College Dublin, Costello supported the creation of a Fine Gael branch in UCD.[54] And after it came into being in 1962 the UCD branch became the most active of any Fine Gael Party branch during the 1960s.

The fate of rural Ireland was never one of Tuairim's prominent issues, though the case for a farm apprenticeship scheme being proposed by the NFA and Macra na Feirme was considered at one of its conferences.[55] In the event the farm apprenticeship scheme that materialised failed to result in any significant change in patterns of farm ownership and management.[56] Plans were discussed at other Tuairim conferences for greater cooperation between local development bodies, a discussion encouraged by Lemass's support for them to affiliate with the National Agricultural and Industrial Development Association.

Professor Patrick Lynch's *Planning for Economic Development* – a pamphlet Tuairim published in 1959 – criticised certain traditional rural attitudes and practices such as those that saw farmers leaving their farms to their less intellectually capable sons. In a response Jeremiah Newman, who from the late 1950s was increasingly prominent in Muintir, questioned whether Lynch believed that the Church's scope of influence should be limited to faith and morals. Lynch's response to Newman suggested that those in positions of authority, whether lay or ecclesiastical, should respond in a constructive fashion to the pressing challenges of the day.[57] More controversial was the case made for larger schools in Tuairim's London branch in 1962. In his response to this case Newman took the view that the 'village [had] to be preserved as the proper framework for elementary education, church life and…daily needs'.[58]

CONCLUSIONS

Unlike Tuairim, Muintir's early success depended heavily on the attitude of the Catholic clergy, both bishops and priests, something that had a major bearing on its ability to become a genuinely nationwide movement. The range of reaction to Muintir among members of the hierarchy extended from support, activism and leadership on the one hand to indifference, opposition and even hostility on the other. Foremost among those at the hostile end of the spectrum was Archbishop McQuaid. Even if there was less diversity of attitudes towards Muintir among governing politicians, the contrast between Éamon de Valera's and Seán Lemass's responses to the movement is nonetheless instructive. Reflecting the strength of the ideal of a self-sufficient Ireland and Muintir's early commitment to the ideal of subsidiarity, de Valera saw Muintir's strength as rooted in its self-help and self-reliance capacities. Excessive dependence on state support might erode such capacities. By the time of Lemass's premiership Muintir's early suspiciousness of the interventionist state had substantially been replaced by a desire for partnership with state bodies. Lemass, who arranged for Muintir to receive annual state funding in 1964, viewed the movement's value in its ability to promote community development and so advance the state's modernising project (especially in its social and educational dimensions) in the Irish countryside.

Even if Muintir had good relationships with many powerful individuals in church and state, its potential to influence public policy was always substantially less than might be expected. One difficulty the movement always faced was how its activities at local level were to be understood and categorised. In the early 1960s Archbishop Morris could observe how Muintir was a '"maverick" organisation' in that it was 'not simply a farmers' organisation [nor] a youth organisation, nor was it devoted simply to sporting or cultural pursuits'.[59] Initially inspired by Catholic social teaching, its vocationalist local activism lasted for more than two decades before community development became its chief pursuit from the late 1950s. The ambitious project of representing and organising the local community made for numerous challenges and gave Muintir a complex identity. Such complexity can be seen in the way the movement regularly found itself competing with other community-based interests, such as Macra na Feirme in the 1940s and 50s. The movement's inability to become a genuinely nationwide organisation was another source of weakness. Considerations of timing were also significant. By the time Muintir identified with community development, the direction of state policy was already set with a rapidly modernising state unequivocally driving the policy agenda.

Tuairim's fundamental significance lies in the contribution it made to an accelerated process in which not only the state but also the Catholic church and the wider society began rapidly to open up to new ideas. By providing a distinctive forum for debating the many social and economic policy issues raised by the process of accelerating change, Tuairm became a modernising force in its own right. As such it helped build a consensus around the necessity of Irish policy-makers (and the Irish public more widely) embracing the modernising challenges posed by rapid industrialisation and urbanisation, Irish membership of the EEC, free trade, and a massive expansion in the educational system. As with Muintir, Tuairim found in Lemass a political leader quite amenable to its ideas. This is not to say that Tuairim didn't find it increasingly difficult to influence the changing policy-making environment as the 1960s progressed, a difficulty that ultimately contributed much to the movement's demise in 1975. In 'an increasingly crowded market place for ideas',[60] Tuairim found itself competing with such state bodies as the Economic and Social Research Institute, An Foras Forbartha, An Foras Talúntais, the Institute of Public Administration and the National Industrial and Economic Council.

Regardless of the many differences between them, both Muintir and Tuairim were intent on becoming instruments of change at a time in post-war Ireland when the nature of change itself had begun to shift radically (compared to what had gone before) and its pace picked up dramatically. As far as organisational matters went, both movements experienced comparable difficulties in attempting to stay alive and in remaining vibrant and relevant over the longer run. These difficulties reflected the ambitious aims the leaders of the two movements set for themselves and their members, the challenges of attracting new members as well as ensuring that local branches remained active enough to keep going in the longer run. What ultimately separates the two organisations is that Muintir, unlike Tuairim, managed to overcome many obstacles and to stay alive as a movement to the present day.

Delegates at Rural Week, held at St. Patrick's College, Thurles, August 1962 [Muintir na Tíre Collection, P134/14/273].

Delegates enjoying an outdoor seminar at Rural Week, held at St. Maccartan's seminary, Monaghan, August 1947 [Muintir na Tíre Collection, P134/15/261].

Fr Hayes addressing delegates at Rural Week, held in Mungret College, Limerick. Pictured (l to r) Fr McMahon, Rector of Mungret College; P. J. Meghen; Fr Hayes; Most Rev. Patrick O'Neill, Bishop of Limerick; Minister Keyes T.D.; Dr. McKevitt Maynooth. August 1949 [Muintir na Tíre Collection, P134/15/124].

Some of the walkers on Wexford's first sponsored charity walk for Muintir, August 1973 [Muintir na Tíre Collection, P134/15/92].

Fr Hayes pictured with Archbishop Cushing and friends at the Archbishop's house in Boston (l to r) Mr. J. Bergin, Boston; Rev. J. Bergin, C.C., Thurles; Very Rev. M. J. Houlihan, St. Patrick's Seminary; Mrs. J. Bergin, Boston; Mr. Joseph Shields, Irish Consul; Fr Hayes; Archbishop Cushing; Paul Tierney, President, Boston A.O.H.; Dr. James Russell and Mrs. Russell, December 1949 [Muintir na Tíre Collection, P134/15/247].

Meeting of Muintir supporters and staff. Included in the photograph are William Looby, Muintir HQ staff; Fr Joe Bergin; W. F. Roe, Chairman ESB; Fr Hayes; Seamus O'Farrell, Editor of *The Landmark*; Paddy Carey, Dublin Muintir Guild and Tom Fitzgerald, Muintir HQ Staff. *c.*1950 [Muintir na Tíre Collection, P134/15/289].

Fr Hayes in the Dorothy Quincy Suite, John Handcock Hall, Boston, Massachusetts, at a reception held in his honour by Archbishop Richard J. Cushing. Also in the picture are Dr. & Mrs. Russell, Bansha, Co. Tipperary, Dr. and Mrs. Russell, Slaterstown, Massachusetts, Mr. & Mrs. Paul Tierney (John Handcock Auditor), Mr. & Mrs. Bergin, Rev. Joseph Bergin, M. Frances Fox (an admirer of Mr. de Valera, and also a John Hancock associate) 1949 [Muintir na Tíre Collection, P134/15/85].

The photograph depicts one of the UNESCO instructors at ENIR, Yaoundé. The aim is to develop a new type of rural teacher, who would help in the community and on the land, as well as in the classroom. February 1971 [Muintir na Tíre Collection, P134/15/81].

The photograph depicts growing and harvesting crops as part of the teacher's training. The methods learned were to be passed on in the communities where they worked, February 1971 [Muintir na Tíre Collection, P134/15/82].

Fr Raymond Browne, Muintir's National Chairman and Andy Roche, National PRO, meeting Senator Ted Kennedy in Washington. June 1965 [Muintir na Tíre Collection, P134/15/56].

Photograph of promotion stand of Muintir's Cork County federation featuring two women members of the federation, 1971 [Muintir na Tíre Collection, P134/15/30].

Group at Rural Week, Virginia, Co. Cavan, August 11-18th, 1940. Included are Most Reverend ...ons, Bishop of Kilmore, Father Hayes, Founder of Muintir na Tire, Lord ffrench, Vice-...t, Prof. A. O'Rahilly, U.C.C.; Rev. Dr. C. Lucey, M.A., Ph.D., Maynooth; Rev. Dr. Comey, P.P., Virginia.

Rural Week, Virginia, Co Cavan. The photo includes the Most Rev. Dr. P. Lyons, Bishop of Kilmore, Fr Hayes, Lord ffrench, Vice-President of Muintir, Prof A. O'Rahilly, UCC, Rev. Dr. C. Lucey, Maynooth and Rev. Dr. Comey, August 1940 [Muintir na Tíre Collection, P134/15/10].

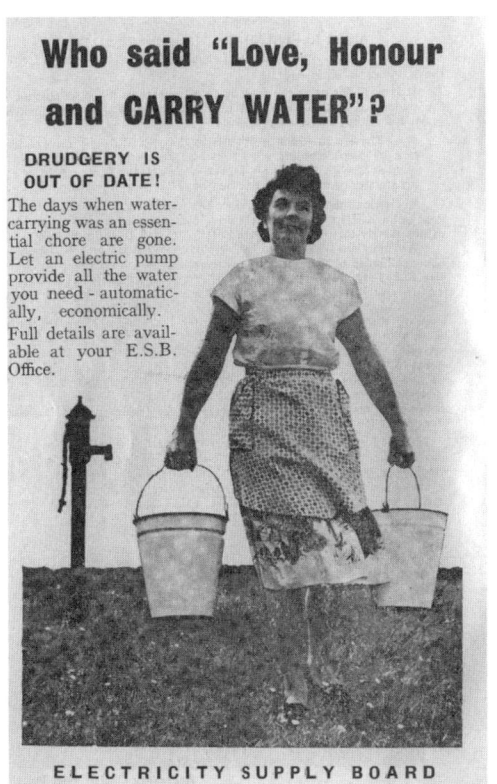

Advert from "Rural Ireland", *c.*1950 [Muintir na Tíre Collection, P134/15/618].

Delegates at a social event during Rural Week, held at Wesport, 1972 [Muintir na Tíre Collection, P134/15/616].

Liam Maher, Fr Hayes, Frank Lyddy and Fr Morris, *c.*1953 [Muintir na Tíre Collection, P134/15/615].

Muintir na Tíre Hall, Murroe, Co. Limerick, *c.*1950 [Muintir na Tíre Collection, P134/15/614].

Fr Hayes meeting Pope Pius XI in the Vatican, 1953 [Muintir na Tíre Collection, P134/15/607].

Fr Hayes with Éamon de Valera and others attending at a Rural Week, Knockbeg College, Co. Carlow, August 1948 [Muintir na Tíre Collection, P134/15/603].

Fr Hayes, National Chairman of Muintir na Tíre with Éamon de Valera and a group of priests, with Mr. Martin Madden of Cappawhite, Co. Tipperary, *c.*1950 [Muintir na Tíre Collection, P134/15/290].

Fr Hayes, Fr Bergin, Archdeacon Nolan and Fr Kelly with a group of Muintir supporters in Tipperary town, 1930s [Muintir na Tíre Collection, P134/15/220].

INTELLECTUALS, RURAL IDYLLS
AND GRITTY REALITIES

Contemporary Rural Life in
Irish Fiction of the 1940s

Caitriona Clear

The newly-independent Irish were great readers.[1] Elizabeth Russell argues that even though there was a shortage of bookshops and libraries in the small towns of the new state, newsagents and other outlets sold books as well as newspapers and periodicals, to an avid public. Irish people relished the escapism of romance and cowboy fiction, but they also liked to see the atmosphere of their everyday lives reflected in what they read.[2] In the mid-twentieth century over 60 per cent of Ireland's population lived either in the country or in towns of less than 1,500 people, so it was natural that the small town and its rural hinterland would be a locale for fiction.

Not all Irish writers wrote about rural life, or wrote about it all the time. Popular authors John D. Sheridan, Elizabeth Brennan, M. L. Stewart and William Hand set their fiction mainly in Dublin. Mary Lavin, Maura Laverty and Olivia Robertson shifted their settings from rural to urban and back again. The bestselling novels of Annie M. P. Smithson are set either in Dublin or in a rural hinterland occupied by professionals and upper-middle-class people, and the same is true of Kate O'Brien's works.[3] Norah Hoult, Molly Keane ('M. J. Farrell') and Elizabeth Bowen, three other prolific Irish writers of this period, set their Irish fiction either in 'big houses' or in an urban middle-class milieu – although Norah Hoult made the occasional successful foray into Irish small-town/rural life.[4]

This chapter looks at how rural Ireland and rural people of the 1940s were depicted in the fiction of a selection of popular contemporary authors.[5] The selection of books was made by looking at all the book review pages of the two bestselling daily newspapers, the *Irish Press* and the *Irish Independent* for the decade, and by scrutiny of *Easons Bulletin*, a trade magazine which contained information on new books and interviews with authors. Easons, the main book distributors for the country as a whole, were in tune with – no doubt helped to form – popular taste. Second-hand bookshops and charity shops throughout the country were also visited regularly.[6] The focus is on fiction in which rural and small-town people are the main characters, rather than stroll-on local colour or dialect-speaking servants.[7] Protestants as well as Catholics are included, but Northern Ireland is left out, because it was a different jurisdiction with a different censorship regime. Preference is given to unbanned books which were accessible to a large audience, although Patrick Kavanagh's *Tarry Flynn* (1948: hereafter *Flynn*), banned for a brief period, is included, because it has achieved status as a classic of rural life. Maura Laverty's *Alone We Embark* (1943: hereafter

Alone), also banned, is also included because she was a well-known broadcaster and journalist at that time.[8]

Was the Bog of Allen ever described as lovingly as it is in Laverty's *Alone,* as a sea that 'comes in smoothly and sweetly, to break in gold-crested waves at Tullynawlin's feet'? In another midlands location, John Lee in Francis MacManus's *Flow On Lovely River* (1940: hereafter *River*), sees:

> The light had dribbled then to a corner of the sky, and the loveliest of rivers was like glass flushed faintly, in which the reeds, the sky and the willows and even a sloping field of wheat stooks swayed gently, a rosy, lost world...[9]

This 'loveliest of rivers' is the Nore (not the Suir of the song, 'The Rose of Mooncoin' from which the novel's title is taken). For Eily Gorman in Patrick Purcell's *A Keeper of Swans* (1942: hereafter *Swans*) the beauties of the south Kilkenny landscape are a mockery:

> [She] paid no heed to the scents of high summer, although she passed the squat rose-trees, beauty-bloomed...She spared neither look nor thought for the mirrored river, red beneath her in the slanting sun-rays.

This river is the Suir.[10] Kavanagh's *Flynn* has many sensual descriptions of rural Cavan, as for example:

> And as he sat there the scents of a thousand flowers and the still stronger scents of the clay at the roots of turnips buried him in a fog of enchantment.[11]

Sheila Pim in *The Flowering Shamrock* (1947: hereafter *Shamrock*), writing about the midlands, is more prosaic:

> ...real lakes in the deep depressions, artificial lakes where old quarries had filled up with water, and seasonal lakes on flat, rushy stretches that appeared in wet weather.[12]

Mary Purcell's *The Pilgrim Came Late* (1947: hereafter *Pilgrim)*, set in Leinster, has no lush descriptions of either the town or its rural hinterland, and the farmers' wives, teachers and village shopkeepers who populate the novel are as likely to be mean and gossipy as good and kind. In this, as in all the other novels discussed here, rural and small-town people are a mixed bunch, neither caricatured nor idealised.[13] According to Keith Snell, popular British detective fiction of the interwar period by Agatha Christie, Dorothy L. Sayers and others, portrayed villages and rural people as pathologically 'backward and inward-looking'.[14] Characters in the Irish novels looked at here are acutely anxious not to be like this. Packey Regan, the choric road worker in Purcell's *Swans*, complains about some farmers that he can see the 'ignorance' shining out through their faces 'like cow dung through the polish on their boots'.[15] When a character in another of Purcell's novels, *Hanrahan's Daughter* (1940: hereafter *Hanrahan's*) comments that the 'schools and the newspapers have this country ruined between them' for raising people's expectations, we are meant to think of him as hidebound and narrow-minded.[16] While tradition is respected, modern facilities and services are greeted enthusiastically, and lack of interest in the world beyond the town, townland and parish is always mocked and derided.

MODERNISATION OF RURAL LIFE

Rural does not mean remote; country people in these novels are well up in international affairs. The Second World War is referred to in McManus's *Watergate* (1942) and *River*, in Laverty's *Alone*, Patrick Purcell's *Swans*, Temple Lane's *Friday's Well* (1943: hereafter *Well*), Mary Purcell's *Pilgrim* and Pim's *Shamrock*. When a character in Philip Rooney's *Singing River* (1944: hereafter *Singing*) instances an American accent, he refers to Raymond Gram Swing, an American war correspondent for the BBC.[17]

Cities and towns are visited often, for shopping, medical appointments, entertainment, even a little luxury. A 'real restaurant with uniformed waitresses and glass-topped tables' in Waterford city is a treat for farmer's daughter Eily Gorman, cycling in from her south Kilkenny farm. The anti-urban bias of some British writers of the interwar period is markedly absent from most of these books; Dublin is described in *Watergate* as 'a golden city glowing in the sun'.[18]

Urban centres are reached by train or bicycle (by far the most common means of transport), or more rarely, by motor car. The car has not fully replaced the trap and pony in getting around; in *Singing*, several characters drive cars, but a visitor to the town, pragmatically rather than nostalgically, uses a trap and pony. The motor car that brings them to Mass is the only luxury the tight-fisted Gormans allow themselves in *Swans*, but the equally big-farming Prendergasts in *Well* still use a trap and pony – though other characters in the novel have cars. The use of a car accident as a plot device in four of the novels looked at, suggests the novelty of this means of transport.[19]

Some of the houses, even if not electrified and aquafied, are well furnished – thus, the Lennon farmhouse in *River*:

> ....the mellow-lit kitchen shining with crockery and hanging milk-cans and scrubbed timber... the brown, green-bordered staircase...Why don't Irishmen [i.e. artists] forsake the eternal bog and bleak mountain roads for a while...for something like this...

A prosperous farmhouse visited in *Hanrahan's* boasts a gravel drive, a row of neat, whitewashed outhouses and a small, snug parlour with:

> ...two big armchairs...a painting on the wall of a not-so-recent pope...There was the usual stuffed pheasant on the sideboard, complete with the inevitable brass tag giving place, date and executioner.

There are also family photographs, 'occasional tables' and all the paraphernalia of the traditional parlour, lit by candles and oil lamps. People furnished their houses as they could, for comfort and convenience. Hermione, the English visitor in *Shamrock*, amuses her Irish hosts with her disappointment at the 'hideous' cheap modern furniture she finds in a rural labourer's house. In *Field of the Stranger* (1946: hereafter *Stranger*) Olivia Robertson ridicules a bohemian English visitor for deploring the 'prefabricated bungalows and all-electric kitchens' which are the heart's desire of every young Irish (and indeed, British) couple, at this time.[20]

In some of these novels, rural wealth is no guarantee of elegance, or even of ease. Tarry's family in *Flynn* are among the biggest farmers in their townland, but poultry are underfoot in the kitchen, and a 'vessel' used overnight in the bedroom is used later in the day for feeding the calves. The Gormans in *Swans* are the 'snuggest [i.e. biggest] farmers round Carriglea', but this does not make their everyday lives more pleasant, as Eily reflects bitterly.[21]

Modernisation is uneven. Neither of the comfortable Kilkenny farmhouses described above has piped water or electricity. In *Well*, the Prendergasts' Munster farmhouse has electricity but is not fully aquafied – rainwater is used for washing, and spring water is drawn from a well for drinking and cooking. The electricity is referred to as 'the switches of the Shannon Scheme'.[22] Almost exactly the same phrase is used by Olivia Robertson in *Stranger*; in Wicklow/Carlow, where this novel is set, the power would have come at this stage from Poulaphouca, but the flagship project of the fledgling state is nonetheless referred to with the same pride.[23]

As with houses, so with clothes – the more up-to-date, the better. Tarry Flynn, who has hopes of cutting a dash in the day-to-day life of the parish, is mortified by the patched trousers his mother leaves out for him. Going into town means dressing up; a trip to Kilkenny in MacManus's *Watergate* has the two farm women with curlers in their hair all morning: '....the fuss started with grabs for boot brushes and polish and hot water and there was a thumping din of feet across the bedroom floor'. A young woman in *Hanrahan's* is dressed for town in 'a frock of some black silk stuff, kilted with a red belt at the waist, and a red flower at her throat in a collar of lace'. Village shopkeeper's daughter Linda Tyrrell in *Stranger* dresses up in a 'smart black coat and skirt, a white-veined satin blouse, with a gold 'Tara' brooch at the neck, and new brown laced shoes'. Brooches give the finish to a 'rigout'; Máire, in *Shamrock*, wears a 'soft dark-green [frock] [with an] ancient Irish brooch'. Miss Rawley, chatelaine of the local 'big house' in *Well*, dresses for dinner in 'a black wool dinner dress nearly down to the carpet with a pink velvet rose in the opening of the neck, held in with a diamond bar'. Anna, the farmer's 'assisting relative' invited to the big house, is amused when asked to 'pack evening clothes': '"I'll pack the old dress I wore at the threshing...That has no sleeves".' In the end, she musters up a suitable dark dress, with clasps of rhinestone rather than diamond. Brighter colours are for the young.

John Lee finds Statia Lennon in *River* quite attractive in her 'tight scarlet jumper', even when she is hot and bothered after cooking and serving a threshing supper. The nineteen-year-old Mary Reilly, for whom Tarry Flynn yearns, wears a 'light-blue cotton dress'. At the barn dance in *Hanrahan's*, the heroine sweeps by in another man's arms in a 'soft frock of St Patrick's blue', and all the young women are in their Summer frocks; returned emigrants are sleeveless, with permed hair, and the young men are in serge suits of brown and blue. Only the men from the 'remotest villages' wear long coat-tails and 'are bereft of collar and tie' – there is an insight here into pockets of rural life as yet untouched by modernisation.[24]

Entertainment

The dancehall was important. Eily in *Swans* regularly cycles to dances in Waterford city, and a character in the same novel, when extolling the delights of Limerick, mentions the legendary Stella Ballroom in the same breath as 'sweet Adare'. In the south Kilkenny dancehall in *Hanrahan's* there is a 'haze of dust and tobacco smoke'. Informal house-dances, of the 'round-the-kitchen-and-mind-the-dresser' kind, feature often, and the music for these occasions is as likely to come from the radio or gramophone as from a live musician. Neither required mains electricity – the wireless could be run on a wet or dry battery, and the gramophone could be wound up. The Dooleys in *Stranger* apologise for having to use a melodeon for an impromptu house dance; their wireless battery is flat. The same use is made of the wireless not only in the Kilkenny homes described by MacManus, but in an idealised rural community depicted by Kathleen Joyce-Prendergast.[25]

As in all novels of the period, British and Irish, a local concert is a good plot device to throw characters together. The variety concert/dance in *Flynn*, for example, complicates the hero's romantic hopes, as does the dance in *Hanrahan's*. But a glance through any provincial newspaper from these decades will confirm that charity dances, concerts and other public entertainments were a regular feature of Irish rural and small-town life in the 1940s. Amateur drama was becoming so popular that an annual festival-competition featuring acts from all over the country would be inaugurated in Athlone in 1953, and the *Irish Independent* would feature, once a month on its book-review pages, an amateur drama report. The Christmas concert in *Swans* features Adeste Fideles, Silent Night, songs and ballads of all sorts, a few tunes on the melodeon, a sketch in the Irish language which is received respectfully, and a short comic sketch by the dramatic society, 'It Never Rains But It Pours'. Fr Rice in *River* is resented by the narrator for insisting that the concert organised by the National teachers consist of all Irish songs – The Minstrel Boy, Let Erin Remember, The Harp That Once, concluding with the national anthem. The priest grudgingly accepts the accompaniment of the piano-accordion, which he considers 'a vulgar instrument... from the music-halls'. In a concert in Laverty's *Alone*, a mature woman sings 'When You Come Home, Dear', a parlour ballad of the period; a young fiddler plays some classical music, a stout, light-footed young woman step-dances, someone recites 'The Convict of Clonmel', and 'a frightened-looking girl from the bog sang 'Danny Boy'...and ended up somewhere above the chapel spire'.[26]

The cinema is also central; the small towns of Ireland, a character comments in *Pilgrim*, are keeping Hollywood in business. In *Stranger*, set in rural Wicklow, the country girls are able to 'fly up' hills on bicycles without effort, because of the practice they get cycling to the 'picture-house' in Carnew. An evening at the pictures in town was 'like a bit of heaven', a character in *Watergate* explains, for a hard-working woman of the house. Helen Byrne's oral history research on Waterford in the 1940s and 50s shows how important the 'pictures' were, as relaxation and escapism, for women in particular.[27]

Novels also offered pleasant entertainment; farmer's wife Mrs Lennon in *River* loses herself in a novel called *The Profitable Kiss*. Although its author is not given, it was probably not published by An Gúm. Cultural influences on the characters are as likely to be English and American, as Irish, and clues about authors' favourite writers are provided in descriptions of characters' bookshelves. Janie Spillane in Mary Purcell's *Pilgrim* likes

English novelists Storm Jameson and Margaret Pedler. National teacher Seamus Conroy in Patrick Purcell's *Swans* like Dickens, Dostoevsky, Canon Sheehan, Walter Scott and Francis Brett Young. Is Francis McManus swanking it a little, having John Lee in *River* reading Ó Dálaigh Fionn, Keats, and Dante in the original? The authors discussed here are likely to have been as influenced by British and American authors, as by Irish ones. Irish readers also, as Russell has shown, read Anglophone authors from other countries, or at least, as many as the censorship permitted them to do.[28]

The people in these books appreciate music of all kinds. In *Alone*, one of the strolling players sings Schumann's *'Träumerei'*. Laverty is confident that her readers, like the Tullynawlin audience, will not only be familiar with it, but will appreciate the critical comment made by one of the supercilious Misses Devine: '"Treacle – and poorly administered".'[29]

None of the authors have anything positive to say about jazz, Pim and Laverty in particular, deploring it. Many priests and prelates would have agreed.[30]

PRIESTS AND RELIGION

In *River* the narrator is exasperated not only by Fr Rice's narrow cultural range (see above) but at his criticism of the women teachers smoking 'where the children can see them'. Laying down the law was something that young priests did too. In *Swans* the clerical student brother in Maynooth, Kieran, writes pompous letters home to his sister Eily counselling her on her marriage plans. '"The Land of Saints and Scholars! The Land of Slaves and Hypocrites, say I!"' a sympathetic character comments in disgust at this. Such comments and characters did not cause fiction to be banned, any more than good religious characters – and praise for religious-run institutions – prevented books from being banned.[31]

But priests can support women, too. In *Flynn* we are invited by Tarry to consider the parish priest something of a spoilsport for speaking out publicly against the young men who sexually assaulted a girl at a crossroads. Tarry's mother gives up her matchmaking plans for a daughter because a priest on the pilgrim station of Lough Derg advised her (the daughter) that it would be 'a sin' to marry an old man she did not love. To Tarry (whose sexual fantasies about girls in their early teens make unpleasant reading), all this was unacceptable clerical interference.[32]

A high level of Catholic practice is matter-of-factly described in the novels written by Catholics. In Laverty's *Alone*, two children break off their game to say the Angelus when it rings. '"Hurry up, we have the litany and all to say",' a young female teacher in Mary Purcell's *Pilgrim* reminds her office-worker friend when they are getting ready to say the Rosary before going out for the evening.[33]

Not all of these novels centre on Catholics; in Lane's *Well*, Robertson's *Stranger* and Pim's *Shamrock* the central characters are Protestant. In *Well*, Anna addresses her father as 'Dada', as did most middle- and working-class people at that time, urban and rural, Catholic and Protestant, and he talks, as does his old friend Mr. Quin, in a recognisable north-Munster idiom. Religious difference is not ignored; Olivia, in *Stranger*, moves with ease between Catholic and Protestant rural houses, but she makes fun of a Protestant Miss Pringle, who 'invariably referred to her fellow-countrymen as "the Irish" and to the government as "these present people".' Middle-class Protestant snobbery towards

Catholics of the same class is also mocked in Pim's *Shamrock*, when Mrs Gavin balks at asking her daughter's friend Kevin, a solicitor, to dinner: 'She said that Kev...would hardly fit in, and she rather thought his family did not dine but had high tea'.[34]

Catholic and Protestant family dynamics, however, are similar in these novels.

Families in General and Females in Particular

Although Tarry Flynn's sisters talk back to their mother, even on occasion telling her to 'shut up', many of the novels discussed here feature young (and middle-aged) people suffering under elder authority. This is also a very common theme of British novels in these decades, so we cannot infer from its prevalence as a theme in Irish fiction that there was either strong elder authority, or strong resistance to it, in Ireland at this time. In *Pilgrim*, Janie's decades-long servitude to her parents leads her, once they have died, to make a foolish life-changing decision. In *Stranger*, a couple walk out together for 20 years, each slow to break free of the parent dependent upon them. Both the Patrick Purcell novels discussed here involve, in different ways, young lovers defying elder opinion. However, although its plot resolution subverts established values, the narrative arc of Laverty's (banned) *Alone* is the cascade of problems resulting from Mary Sheehy's *rejection* of the strong-farmer suitor her mother approves of, and her impulsive marriage to a strolling musician who turns out to be just as bad as everybody warned her he would be.[35]

But Mary Sheehy is a free agent, because female self-determination is regarded as a good thing in all these novels. This reflects the changes of the times. Mid-twentieth-century Ireland saw more and more Irish women moving out of farm and house and into the workforce. Between 1926 and 1961 the number of females in Ireland 'assisting in agriculture' as farmers' daughters, sisters or in-laws fell by 65 per cent. Many of these country girls emigrated, but some got jobs in nearby towns in shops, offices and factories, and year on year, increasing numbers stayed on in secondary school so as to be eligible for the kind of jobs held by the narrator's housemates in Patrick Purcell's *Fiddler's Green* (1949):

> ....there are four females of the civil servant species on the premises. [This means] the bathroom locked for hours while they wash all kinds of unmentionables. The fire barricaded off with wet stockings every frosty night.[36]

In the fiction looked at, young women of rural origin are teachers, nurses, civil servants, typists, shop assistants and factory workers, sometimes living in the rural community, sometimes gone from it to the local town, to Dublin, or further afield. Several British historians have noted the appeal of 'nice and neat' clothes, houses and shops for mid-twentieth-century women, and many Irish women of rural origin shared this aspiration. Mary Lavin's short story *Lilacs* (1943) pokes fun at two boarding-school-educated women who are embarrassed at their father's lucrative dung business,[37] but Eily Gorman in *Swans* would have sympathised fervently. Although she is free to cycle into Waterford regularly – which implies that she has set time off – and has pocket money enough to go to dances and the pictures and to treat herself to lunch in town, she is aggrieved when she compares her life with that of her seminarian brother, 'with no puddles to plod through and no churns to scour and no contrary calves to feed'. Her sister, Cissie, a nurse in a Dublin hospital under equally rigorous authority, is also envied. Discipline is preferable to drudgery and dirt, and Eily falls in love with a teacher partly because marriage to him will rescue her forever from the farm. A female character in Olivia Robertson's *Stranger* makes a strong case for leaving the land:

> It's grand in Birmingham...No dirty countryside, all nice and modern with road-houses and cafes and smart saloon bars for ladies and dance halls and picture-houses and plenty of loudspeakers brightening up the place...music while you work![38]

Robertson deplores her attitude, but it is easy to see the attractions of urban, non-agricultural work when presented in this way. Not all Irish women felt like this – many married happily onto farms, relishing the skills and challenges involved in companionate agricultural partnerships. And even in the novels, there are contented farm women – Mrs Lennon in *River*, several female characters in *Hanrahan* and *Pilgrim*, and Anna in *Well*, who has left a teaching job in England without any regrets, to become an 'assisting relative' on her father's farm.

Anna is contented not only on the farm, but in her single status, when *Well* opens; female characters in these novels are not always pining after marriage and men. Statia Lennon is jilted by teacher John Lee in *River*, but in *Watergate*, a novel set later in time involving some of the same characters, Statia has gone to Waterford to teach domestic economy while Lee (rejected, in turn, by Kit Hennessy, who has entered a convent) remains bitterly single. For Miss Rawley in *Well*, romantic love is a lamentable deception, but for Janie Spillane, in *Pilgrim*, it is fatal. Janie is depicted by Mary Purcell (who remained single all her life) as pathetic because her self-worth depends upon the status of being married.[39]

Happily single women populate all these novels–the cheerful National teachers in both *Swans* and *River* known by their surnames ('O'Donnell' and 'Toomey'), several characters in *Pilgrim*, the narrator in *Stranger*, and Anna in *Well*. If novels set in urban as well as rural Ireland are taken into consideration, novels by the aforementioned authors Brennan, Sheridan, Stewart, Smithson and O'Brien all feature independent unmarried women.[40] The single woman making a good life for herself was also a staple of British fiction of the first half of the twentieth century. In both countries this reflected demographic realities.[41]

CONCLUSION

In interwar and wartime Britain, elegiac novels and memoirs of a lost rural world sold well, and urban life's inferior food, bad air, cramped accommodation and cheap, mass-produced entertainments, were much deplored.[42] Independent Ireland's cities and large towns, though they did not have industrial smog and slag heaps, had their own problems; Dublin had its tenements, Limerick, its lanes, and most country towns had at least one row of 'cottages' like Maiden Street in Newcastle West in the 1940s, described by Michael Hartnett: 'The walls were of mud and the roof it did leak/and our mice nearly died of starvation'. Rural life at any social level was healthier than urban life, as the National Nutrition Survey of the late 1940s found.[43]

How rural readers felt about the depiction of themselves in the books discussed above is beyond the scope of this article, although it is noteworthy that Laverty's *Never No More* caused widespread hurt in her native Rathangan, because she used easily-identifiable local characters (sometimes without changing the names) and true stories. Laverty made the mistake of thinking Irish rural and small-town people did not read books. Very popular in the English-speaking world – it went into several editions – Laverty's first novel was never widely-read in Ireland generally, perhaps because many of the living conditions in the 'lost' world it described (it was set in the years 1918–22) were still all too real for Irish people in the early 1940s. Eric Cross never imagined that the undiluted and raw rurality of Ned and Stasia Buckley's world which he described so sensitively and humorously in *The Tailor and Ansty* would offend local people and Irish people generally – but it did. Both books appeared in 1942. Kavanagh's *Tarry Flynn,* with its sometimes grotesque descriptions of rural life, was briefly banned, but it was never very popular either.[44]

The authors whose works are discussed in this article – Francis MacManus, Patrick and Mary Purcell (they were brother and sister), Temple Lane, Sheila Pim, Philip Rooney, Kathleen Joyce-Prendergast and Olivia Robertson set their novels partly or wholly in rural Ireland, but they did not make rurality a central theme. This is probably why their books, while they were no doubt liked or disliked in the normal way readers appreciate fiction, were never rejected by a rural readership.

Four decades later in a completely transformed Ireland, the half-doors, water-barrels, flour-bags, chamber-pots, pig-killings, and tea-dinners of mid-century rural life found a hugely popular chronicler in Alice Taylor.[45] But in the 1940s all these realities were too close for comfort for most Irish writers and readers.

Catholic Intellectuals and Rural Decline

Bryan Fanning

The focus of this chapter is on writings about rural decline in *Christus Rex,* a Catholic sociological journal primarily intended for a clerical audience engaged in rural pastoral work. The Christus Rex Society was founded in 1941 four years after Muintir na Tíre's appearance as a local community movement. *Christus Rex* was primarily a journal of applied Catholic thought. Many contributions were opinion pieces that reflected anxieties about social change rather than contributions to the sociological study of such change. Yet *Christus Rex* became preoccupied with 'real' sociological questions about the nature and consequences of social change, social cohesion, rural decline, urban alienation and poverty. It published a handful of pioneering empirical studies of Irish social problems that influenced both social policy and the development of the social sciences in Ireland.

The intellectual driving force of *Christus Rex* was the Revd Jeremiah Newman who garnered a reputation as an archconservative during the last phase of a career that included being President of St Patrick's College Maynooth and Bishop of Limerick. He was also perhaps the leading Irish sociologist during the lifetime of *Christus Rex* which ran until 1970. In *Christus Rex* the case for rural community development was often linked to a conservative Catholic critique of modernity, yet there was also a sense, expressed in the writings of Newman and some others, that Catholic influence and rural social cohesion could only be preserved through radical action to arrest social and economic rural decline.

Concerns and debates about rural decline were by no means the sole preoccupation of Catholic clerics. These also found expression in plays, short stories, novels, newspapers and in other intellectual outlets besides *Christus Rex.* For example, the anti-establishment literary journal *The Bell,* founded by Sean O'Faolain in 1940 published unvarnished examinations of rural society. These included extracts of *The Tailor and Ansty,* Eric Cross's earthy account of a rural marriage which was banned by the Censorship of Publications Board.[1] The aim of *The Bell,* O'Faolain wrote in a 1941 editorial was to 'project a picture of popular life'.[2] The audience of *The Bell,* O'Faolain was clear, was mostly Catholic:

> That the vast majority of the people here are Catholic is a matter of mathematics. That the country is in the main Nationalist is equally obvious, and that it has Isolationism in its blood must be evident to anybody who has even heard the words Sinn Féin…Nationalist, Democratic, and Catholic then: that appears to be the sum of what it is clear in the picture of Life here…[3]

In a 1943 editorial O'Faolain reflected that Ireland was a provincial place where, when Mussolini was deposed 'and the battle of Sicily was at its height', the first item on the Irish radio news concerned the pilgrimage of 10,000 people to Croagh Patrick. The second item gave an account of a Muintir na Tíre conference in Cork. Only when 'these things were given their pride of place' did attention turn to a pivotal moment in the Second World War.[4]

During much of the period covered by this chapter – the 1940s to the 1970s– Catholic thought on social questions was highly influential, although it came to be challenged by a liberal economic nation-building project from the late-1950s onwards. Yet Seán Lemass, the political leader of the new developmentalism, contributed to discussions in *Christus Rex* about emigration and the need for economic growth. An early 1990s account of the debates considered in this chapter emphasised the influence of 'powerful strains of rural fundamentalist ideology' that promoted family-operated farms and argued that national prosperity should be based upon an agricultural economy.[5] As an assessment this took little account of how debates about social change, including arguments in favour of economic development, played out amongst clerics and other Catholics who wrote about rural decline at the time.

MODERNISATION AND RURAL IRELAND

Histories of the twentieth century tend to foreground ideological conflicts between Catholic conservatism and liberalism more so than those between left and right. In sociological terms the tension is understood as one between rural communal and urban individualistic ideals of what constitutes the good society, with religion seen to flourish in the former and secularism in the latter. Ruralism also came to be idealised within nationalism for similar reasons as in other countries during the nineteenth century when romantic nationalists sought to imagine *their* nations as having deep primordial roots. In the writings of Patrick Pearse, and in the political rhetoric of Éamon de Valera, rural Ireland was the authentic embodiment of the Irish nation. The audience which attended the 1908 Dublin premier of *The Playboy of the Western World,* J. M. Synge's ribald comedy set amongst rural folk, rioted in protest against a perceived slur against the Irish character.

Even though the Church had set itself against modernity, it became integral to the modernisation of Irish society. What was commonly understood as traditional Irish society – the rural Ireland that for cultural nationalists was the real Ireland – was in many respects a modern post-Famine social order. In the *Last Conquest of Ireland (perhaps)* John Mitchel described how in the years following 1847 the numbers of rural smallholdings rapidly declined and indebted estates were sold off. However, Michel also noted that a decade later most of the lands that came up for sale were purchased by Catholic Irishmen. It could not be denied, Mitchel wrote, that some well-to-do elements in post-Famine Ireland had begun to live better.[6]

Another account of rural society, Arensberg and Kimball's *Family and Community in Ireland* noted that in 1841 County Clare had a population of about 250,000 persons in a society (coterminous with the later 26-county Free State) in which 43 per cent of men aged between 25 and 35 were single.[7] By 1926 County Clare had just 95,000 inhabitants with 88 per cent of its rural men aged 25–30 years (and 73 per cent of its rural men aged 30–35 years) still single.[8] The subdivision of smallholdings had practically ceased by1852 in order to protect family landholdings.[9] Social mores relating to marriage changed to reflect changes in inheritance.[10] The role of the Catholic Church in regulating sex and marriage, Arensberg and Kimball suggested, was an adjunct one. Catholic public morality concurred with rural social mores as distinct from defining them.[11] According to the sociologist Tom Inglis in *Moral Monopoly,* his account of how the Church came to dominate Irish public morality, communal proscriptions on marriage – except for those expected to inherit land – left many with the choice between celibacy, emigration or holy orders.[12]

A 1962 *Christus Rex* article titled 'The Family in Irish Tradition' written by a member of the Irish Folklore Commission explained that in 'traditional' rural society men and women remained under their parents' control until they were married. A young wife of 21 had attained her full status in the community whereas an unmarried woman of 35 had not. Matchmaking was restricted to those who would inherit land. A man likely to inherit a farm or a woman with a dowry could marry but not their siblings who remained in their family homes.[13]

Rural Ireland, as this was understood during the twentieth century, was a post-Famine construct that had been reshaped in many places by intense economic rationalisation and emigration. It came to be influenced during the second half of the nineteenth century by an assertive Church that had mobilised internationally to compete with Protestant evangelism, liberalism, socialism and secularism. In Ireland it stepped up to organise communal life in new ways.

Cardinal Cullen, the architect of the post-Famine Church which came to wield huge influence in Ireland for a century, was a protégé of Pius IX, the first Pope to be declared infallible and who presided during his 30-year papacy over the Church's intellectual response to modernity. Under Cullen's similarly long stewardship of the Church in Ireland there occurred an unprecedented level of standardisation of religious practice and priestly behaviour. New forms of religious practice – mostly of Roman origin – were emphasised during the post-1850 'devotional revolution'. These practices included the Rosary, novenas, benedictions, devotion to the Sacred Heart and the Immaculate Conception, processions and retreats. The Church built up a system of parish priest-controlled primary schools and parish priests were regarded as communal leaders.

During the late nineteenth century some clergy became champions of rural development and of the rural cooperative movement whilst preserving their antipathy to many aspects of liberalism and modernity. This aversion was described by Horace Plunkett, a (Protestant) champion of the same causes in his book *Ireland and the New Century* (1904):

> Roman Catholicism strikes an outsider as being in some of its tendencies non-economic, if not actually, anti-economic. These tendencies have, of course, much fuller play when they act on a people whose education has (through no fault of their own) been retarded or stunted...I am simply adverting to what has appeared to me, in the course of my experience in Ireland, to be a defect in the industrial character of Roman Catholics which, however caused, seems to me to have been intensified by their religion. The reliance of that religion on authority, its repression of individuality, and its complete shifting of what I may call the moral centre of gravity to a future existence – to mention no other characteristics – appear to me calculated, unless supplemented by other influences, to check the growth of the qualities of initiative and self-reliance, especially amongst a people whose lack of education unfits them for resisting the influence of what may present itself to such minds as a kind of fatalism with resignation as its paramount virtue.[14]

This analysis echoed contemporaneous writings by the German sociologist Max Weber regarding the role 'the Protestant ethic' played in conjuring into existence 'the spirit of capitalism'.[15] Unsurprisingly, Plunkett's tone sat poorly with Catholics. *Catholicy and Progress in Ireland* (1905), a rebuttal of Plunkett's book by Fr Michael O'Riordan criticised Plunkett for besmirching the character of a people whose condition was the result of generations of misgovernment, bigotry and discrimination.[16] Yet, Plunkett's assessment was a fair summary of the then intellectual climate.

SAVING RURAL IRELAND

Catholic understandings of the stakes involved in modernisation, as articulated in papal encyclicals from the late nineteenth century, exerted considerable influence on Irish Catholic thinking about rural society during the twentieth century. In *De la Division du travail social* (1893), published in English as *The Division of Labour in Society*, the French sociologist Emile Durkheim described the unravelling of pre-modern forms of social solidarity and their replacement by more complex modern social interdependencies that allowed for individual autonomy. Members of pre-modern communities had little individual autonomy and were expected not to deviate from communal norms and religious practices. For centuries generation after generation lived in the same villages and rural areas, and held the same things sacred.[17] Archetypically people lived and died in the village in which they were born, within visual range of the same church steeple, sharing the same beliefs. Durkheim's German contemporary Ferdinand Tönnies referred to this as *gemeinschaft*. This kind of social cohesion was thought to unravel when people moved to cities where they interacted with one another as individuals. In Durkeim's analysis urbanisation in modern society could be associated under certain conditions with a loss of social cohesion and traumatic dislocation.[18] From a Catholic perspective, according to Jeremiah Newman, urban life tended to lack '*gemeinschaft,* the community life of the family and the locality, of the village, the smaller town, the owner-occupied shop, the rural church'.[19] The Christian life, Newman and other Catholic intellectuals argued, was best incubated in such an environment.

What came to be called Catholic social thought (or 'Neo-Thomism') emerged during the late nineteenth century as an intellectual response to modernity aimed at competing with socialism and liberalism. It was rooted in understandings of natural law set down in the thirteenth-century writings of Thomas Aquinas which had in turn Christianised conceptions of natural law set out by Aristotle. From the late nineteenth century Neo-Thomism provided the basis for intellectual and political opposition to liberalism, socialism and secularism, but also served as a tool for engaging with social change.

Neo-Thomism found its first full expression in the 1891 papal encyclical *Rerum Novarum*'s principle of subsidiarity which held that a community of a higher order (meaning the state) should not interfere unnecessarily in the internal workings of a lower-order community (such as the family or the religious voluntary sector).[20] Simply put, the state should not interfere in families or communities except as a last resort. Such Catholic social thought influenced *Bunreacht na hÉireann,* the 1937 *Constitution of Ireland.* For example, Article 42 enshrined the subsidiarity rights of the family; it guaranteed the inalienable right and duty of parents to provide for the education of their children. Article 44.4 protected the subsidiarity of Catholic and other religious schools.

A subsequent papal encyclical *Quadragesimo Anno* of 1931 advocated political corporatism or vocationalism as an alternative to liberal democracy and state socialism but this had relatively little influence in the Irish case. The main political movement to advocate political corporatism in the Irish case, the Blueshirts (a movement emerging from the Army Comrades' Association and the later National Guard) imploded before contesting national elections. After the party's appearance in 1933 there were some in Fine Gael who continued the Blueshirts' advocacy of political corporatism. The sole political institution to be influenced by corporatism was the Seanad where different vocational 'panels', including 'the Agricultural Panel', were recognised and given representation. In Ireland the influence of Catholic social thought found expression less in the hardware of political institutions than as a form of intellectual software, a way of thinking about the world that could be disseminated through education.[21] For its part Muintir na Tíre developed a parish-based corporatist approach to local community organising from 1937.

Neo-Thomism became the intellectual basis of Catholic sociology taught in European Catholic universities such as Leuven where several Irish priests, including Jeremiah Newman and Peter McKevitt, were sent to obtain doctorates. McKevitt was appointed as the first Professor of Catholic Sociology at St Patrick's College Maynooth in 1937.[22] His *The Plan For Society*, sometimes described as Ireland's first sociological textbook, related general principles of Catholic social teaching to some specific Irish problems. These included emigration and rural decline. The latter in particular was seen as a threat to Catholicism.[23]

The first issue of *Christus Rex: An Irish Quarterly Journal of Sociology* appeared in 1947. McKevitt, the main founding editor, was succeeded as editor by Jeremiah Newman who became the journal's dominant intellectual figure. The imagined audience of the journal consisted of young priests interested in social work who had participated in study circles on social problems at Maynooth and had become members of the Christus Rex Society established by McKevitt in 1941. The objects of the society were (a) to promote amongst Irish diocesan clergy the study of the Church's social teaching, and (b) to encourage and assist priests in all forms of social work. Membership 'was to be open to all diocesan priests interested in social work'.[24] Its first Priests' Summer School of social study took place in Galway in August 1946. The theme was 'Justice for the Worker'. More than 70 priests attended, the society's constitution was finalised, and plans were drawn up for further events.[25]

Christus Rex was primarily a journal of applied Catholic thought. The first article in the first issue was titled 'Why Catholic Priests should Concern Themselves with Social and Economic Questions' by Michael J. Browne, Bishop of Galway. Browne argued that:

> the education of Irish public opinion in the social teaching of the Church is the right and duty of every priest. It depends on him whether the Catholic people – men and women of every class – will understand the issues and perform their duty at local and general elections and in their political clubs as Catholic citizens, or whether they will be ignorant and indifferent to everything but their own narrow, selfish interests.[26]

In another *Christus Rex* article in 1947 McKevitt argued that the role of study groups, run by priests, should be to identify the specific problems facing communities and to direct debate about these in keeping with Catholic principles. Priests faced with leading such groups would benefit from studying social science.[27]

Within *Christus Rex* practical advocacy of rural development jostled, to some extent, with the old yearnings for a distinctive Catholic social order. Many articles recycled formulaic expositions of social teaching alongside ad hominem attacks on the evils of statism. These were rarely married to any practical focus on social problems. In 1956, in 'Agriculture in a Vocational Order of Society', the pseudonymous 'Feirmeoir' (Farmer) argued that since the Army took control of Portugal in 1926 Salazar 'had given his people many salutary lessons in the art of living, not the least of which is the lesson of thrift'.[28] Corporatism, the nameless farmer declared, had 'brought about a condition of stability and tranquillity previously unknown in that turbulent country'.[29] Another article in the same issue by a devout economist Louis Smith who had worked to set up the National Farmers Association (NFA) in 1955 – and which subsequently would become the Irish Farmers Association – claimed that the ideal of a more Christian society was clearly in the minds of many NFA farmers and that there was no shortage of 'a genuinely supernatural motive as far as individuals are concerned'.[30]

Some articles maintained that austerity was an acceptable price to pay for national and spiritual survival – de Valera's position in his 1943 St Patrick's Day broadcast in other words. In a 1961 example the Revd Daniel Duffy depicted emigration as the economic consequence of a desire for higher living standards in Ireland.[31] Duffy argued that economic austerity and generally lower living standards than those enjoyed in richer countries had to be accepted if people were not to be displaced by emigration. As he put it:

> The pursuit of living standards, such as the affluent society demands, can only lead to an indefinite postponement of our economic salvation. It is no dishonour to be poor. It is foolish and contemptible to aim at the incomes and expenditures of those more prosperous than ourselves.[32]

Yet, many articles dissented from such frugalism. One published in 1959, 'Foundations of Social Justice in Ireland' identified three problems confronting Irish society, the chief of which was the economic one, followed by the Irish reluctance to marry – too few marriages and too late – and thirdly emigration: 'The number of boys and girls, born in Ireland, and now living in England', it was observed, 'has not been exactly determined, but no one can seriously quarrel with the figure, 800,000'.[33] Newman sided with those (such as Lemass) who promoted frank acknowledgement of social and economic problems. As Lemass put it:

> Our rural society is based on the family farm – a system which, unquestionably, is the best suited to the national character and which, incidentally, is fully in accord with the sociological concepts underlying the agricultural policy of the European Economic Community. We cannot, however, close our eyes to the mounting body of evidence that the rural generation today is no longer prepared to accept living standards based on land units on which their forefathers were compelled to eke out a subsistence livelihood.[34]

Newman argued that rural social cohesion depended on improving standards of living and he set about undertaking sociological research aimed at informing rural development plans. What came to be called 'The Limerick Rural Survey' was commissioned by Muintir na Tíre and its findings were published in and debated in *Christus Rex*. The first of several interim reports focused on emigration and was followed by reports on the physical geography of County Limerick and on the demographic and social structure of the county. The fourth interim report drew on the Dutch sociologist E. W. Hofstee's proposals for rural centres that had so very much impressed Newman. The fifth report – on Limerick's social history – was written by P. J. Meghen who had been Limerick's County Manager during the late 1950s and was a member of Muintir na Tíre's National Executive.[35] Earlier in his career Meghen held the post of Town Commissioner in Ennis County Clare during which time he became friendly with Conrad Arensberg who dedicated his 1937 book *The Irish Countryman* to him along with the anthropologist W. Lloyd Warner.[36] Although Catholic priests like Newman and Hayes led efforts to promote rural development, these debates also drew on international experience and expertise.

In 1958 Muintir na Tíre had affiliated to the European Society for Rural Sociology whose president Professor Hofstee advised on the preparation of the Limerick Rural Survey and arranged research training for its Irish research fieldworker. Hofstee gave a lecture to a Muintir conference in Roscrea in August 1958 that was published by *Christus Rex* in the following year. Drawing on his rural research in the Netherlands Hofstee argued that similar social research in Ireland could contribute to an understanding of the structural factors relating to how rural society might deal with inevitable social change. Hofstee's article described Dutch experiences of the use of agricultural vocational education and advisory services to raise farm incomes. Even when Dutch sociological research found that culturally traditional farmers had significantly lower incomes, it was not simply the case that less economically successful farmers were resisting modernisation. The more traditional farmers were found to live predominantly in isolated areas (measured by distance to good roads) which cut them off from modernising influences and supports.[37]

Hofstee further described research on Dutch rural extended families which found that young married couples were increasingly dissatisfied with having to live with parents in multi-generational households, and identified a solution of dividing the farmhouse into two separate living quarters.[38] In essence, Hofstee argued that a better understanding of the dynamics of rural families and communities could help with the design of supports which would make people happier to remain on the land. Hofstee contributed to the design of the Limerick Rural Survey and Patrick McNabb, the project's fieldwork researcher, received sociological training in Holland.

McNabb, in the third interim report on Limerick's rural demography, observed that since 1949 a significant percentage of farm labourers had left the land. As he put it 'the farm worker has opted out of the rural community'.[39] This suggested the need for rural communities to take positive action to make rural life more attractive to paid farm workers. As concluded by McNabb:

> In general, it may be said that the community is not prepared to meet the social and economic aspirations of the farm worker. It is equally clear that the farm worker has decided that the

community will not satisfy these aspirations in the future. Therefore, in planning his children's future, he does not take into account local opportunities.[40]

The fourth interim report written by Newman argued that the effects of rural depopulation had been 'absolutely staggering' in the smaller villages and in the more rural parishes. He warned that these would disappear unless some radical preventative action was taken. Newman's 'conclusion' was that the only way to conserve rural population was to develop a number of towns in each country equipped with adequate social and cultural facilities to serve their rural hinterlands. If the surrounding rural area was to remain viable, each town selected for development would need to be able to provide industrial employment for many people living within a radius of several miles as well as attractive social facilities. Much of the fourth interim report was given over to explaining how this plan for 'rural centrality' might work, The survey examined and ranked Limerick's towns and villages according to the presence in them of such facilities as churches, sports venues, libraries, social clubs, rail and bus services, banks, shops, and doctors' and solicitors' practices. Newman argued that development should focus on the towns that already ranked highly or had the potential to do so.[41] He maintained that without such central focal points the rural population would continue to diminish leaving large farms in thinly-populated 'rural deserts'. This, he declared, was not in the interest of the Church:

> The Church cannot benefit from this, for without people there is nothing she can do. It behoves us therefore, even at the expense of raising new pastoral problems, to encourage the transformation of the old-style into the new-style rural community, even to the extent of fostering the growth of a sufficient number of semi-rural towns. It is better to have people and problems than to have no problems because there are no people. If there are fewer vocations in urban areas than in rural, there will assuredly be fewer still in areas that have become depopulated.[42]

Newman and his associates in Muintir na Tíre who wrote in *Christus Rex* were no less champions of economic development than Seán Lemass, the political architect of Irish developmentalism and his chief civil servant T. K. Whitaker, the author of the seminal report *Economic Development* in 1958. A 1964 article by a civil servant in *Christus Rex* on 'Planning and National Development' explained that the Government's Second Programme for Economic Expansion was focused on national economic growth and reducing emigration. However, the article also acknowledged Newman's concern that growth would be concentrated into a few cities without arresting rural decline:

> The possibility is a real one, he says, that the future may see Ireland a prosperous nation, with a favourable balance of trade and little emigration, but with its people packed into a few huge cities and provincial centres and its countryside a prairie very sparsely peopled by wealthy farmers but haunted by the ghosts of dead towns and villages.[43]

Prosperity was not a problem in itself as long as rural Ireland also benefited. Newman did not attack the new economic development nation-building project politically led by Seán Lemass. In his 1961 *Christus Rex* article, the then Taoiseach blamed emigration on:

the insufficiency of our efforts to date to develop a completely attractive way of life for all the elements of the national community, and adequate opportunities of employing individual talents in Ireland to earn livelihoods equivalent to those which emigrants hope to find elsewhere.[44]

Unlike the Revd Duffy, whose aforementioned article appeared in the same issue, Lemass did not believe that emigration could be halted by urging people to willingly accept living standards less than could be obtained elsewhere.[45]

These debates were accompanied by some articles which parsed the papal encyclical *Mater et Magistra* (1961) on the topic of Christianity and social progress which, using the same natural law vantage point as *Rerum Novarum,* acknowledged social changes resulting from scientific advances, rising education levels, the emergence of the welfare state in many countries, the breakdown of Western colonialism and the diminishing role of agriculture in employment.[46] One such article by an Italian cleric and sociology professor (translated by two divinity students at Maynooth) noted that less than 20 per cent of Italian economic output now came from agriculture. According to the encyclical and the Pope, 'the farming community must take an active part in its own economic advancement, social progress and cultural betterment'.[47] Millions of workers around the world, including tillers of the fields, 'were condemned through the inadequacy of their wages to live with their families in utterly subhuman conditions'.[48] The remuneration of work was 'not something that can be left to the laws of the market' and 'those engaged in agriculture should receive a share of the national income...equal or almost equal to that enjoyed by other economic and professional categories of citizens'.[49]

Mater et Magistra specifically advocated instruction in farming methods to enable family farms to become economically viable as well as co-operation and solidarity within farming communities in keeping with the principle of subsidiarity.[50] In practical terms, the necessary minimum of state support which could be justified had risen considerably.

In the Irish case the bottom-up 'micro-corporatist' community development approach of Muintir na Tíre, was also in keeping with Catholic social thought which promoted the principle of subsidiarity.[51] Amongst Catholic intellectuals there was the general presumption that rural development would help to sustain spiritual welfare by supporting rural ways of life that were amenable to religiosity. Within the pages of *Christus Rex* the survival of Catholic rural Ireland came to be seen as requiring support from the state as well as communal mobilisation and self-reliance.

POSTSCRIPT

Legacies of the Catholic intellectual debates on saving rural Ireland include the work of priests such as Monsignor Horan who developed an international airport at Knock. A 1970-*Christus Rex* article by Fr Harry Bohan, proposed a synthesis of 'pastoral theology and empirical social sciences' in promoting community activism and community development.[52] Bohan is remembered as a rural housing innovator. A 1962 article in *Christus Rex* by a Welsh-based academic on the international recognition of the work of Muintir na Tíre discussed its approach to community development as a model for developing countries. The title of the article was 'Christian Witness in Community Development'. Citing a Muintir pamphlet, it declared that 'the small community acts as a buffer between the individual and the state' and worked to prevent too much reliance on the state and to control individualism.[53] Another article in the same issue by another Welsh-based academic, George Thomason, focused on leadership within Muintir na Tíre.[54] Thomason was the author of a pamphlet *Community Development in Ireland,* published by Muintir the previous year.[55] The approach to pursuing rural development advocated by Muintir na Tire and in *Christus Rex* was seen as a model for international missionary work.

However, by the time Newman stepped down as editor of *Christus Rex* in 1970 he seemed to have concluded that the battle to save Catholic Ireland could not be won in the countryside. The wider war would need to be fought on other fronts. Although the focus in this chapter has been on his work as a sociologist, Newman also wrote extensively as a political philosopher and theologian. Most of his writings addressed either the effects of social change on Catholicism or the secular ideas that challenged it. Newman's body of work included three major books on political philosophy–*Studies in Political Morality* (1962), *Conscience Versus Law* (1971) and *The Postmodern Church* (1990) – in each of which he developed and comprehensively articulated his arguments against secular modernity.[56] Newman also wrote a number of books aimed at the general Irish public and international Catholic audiences. These included *Race, Migration and Immigration* (1968), which examined racial segregation in the United States and the emergence of Apartheid in South Africa and the 'White Australia' policy. Newman was unambiguously opposed to Apartheid, racist immigration policies and restrictions on immigration that curbed family reunification.[57]

Keenly aware of the likely ongoing decline of Catholicism, Newman's writings from the late 1960s might be described as a fierce rearguard action aimed at showing this and the advance of secular influence to the greatest extent possible. Rural decline was just one of Newman's preoccupations in *Christus Rex.* In a 1967 article 'Vocations in Ireland' he undertook a comparative analysis of declining vocations in various European countries. At Maynooth ordinations had peaked in 1941 and Irish ordinations overall had peaked at 447 in 1961 and were now falling away. Newman was clear that further decline would follow. He attributed this decline to increased affluence and urbanisation (mirroring the conditions of other societies that experienced declining vocations) along with changes in the structure of the education system (resulting in the decreasing influence priests had upon young people).[58]

In his 1971 book *Conscience Versus Law* Newman outlined his sociological analysis of the crises facing the Church and society. This began by explaining the distinction made by Tönnies between 'community' (*Gemeinschaft*) and 'institution' (*Gesellschaft*) as organising principles of society.[59] With the decline of Irish *gemeinschaft,* and the communal mores that it enforced, Newman argued that a legally enforced public morality offered the only potential bulwark against the acceleration of secularisation. For example, he believed that the pressure for divorce legislation and for secularisation went hand in hand in Ireland. Catholic politicians who advocated divorce legislation needed to understand that they were also endorsing the secularisation of Irish society by undermining the extent to which Catholicism shaped public morality.[60] In *The State of Ireland* he argued that politicians who supported legalising divorce and contraception were undermining the institutionalisation of Catholic public morality in the constitution and under the law.[61]

The debate about saving rural Ireland that played out in the pages of *Christus Rex* did not dominate the journal. A content analysis of *Christus Rex* articles by general themes identifies just 15.5 per cent of journal pages devoted to rural Ireland; almost the same amount of attention (11.15 per cent of pages) as given to industrial relations.[62] In 1971 the journal changed its name from *Christus Rex* to *Social Studies,* and began to be edited by Fr Liam Ryan who (like Newman) went on to become president of Maynooth College. Ryan's most distinctive contribution to Irish sociology was based on urban rather than rural realities. Published in 1967, his hard-hitting major study of early school leavers in urban Limerick looked frankly at the lives of young people living in social housing in a poorer suburban estate of the city given the fictional name of 'Parkland'.[63] The 100 young people interviewed as part of the research were not the children of farmers but of families that had been unsuccessfully transplanted, through a process of slum clearance, from old overcrowded Georgian or Victorian buildings or from smaller houses 'in the back-lanes and alley-ways'.[64] Ryan described the difficulties encountered by interviewees in their own frank language. For example, he referred to the sex lives of frustrated young married couples who were forced to live with their relatives even when they had children of their own.[65]

Jeremiah Newman became Bishop of Limerick in 1974 and acquired a reputation as 'the most outspoken, controversial, and conservative member of the hierarchy'.[66] A *Magill* magazine profile described him as the 'Mullah of Limerick' in 1985. This moniker referred to a statement he made at the opening of an oratory (prayer room) in a Limerick shopping centre where he had tried to explain how religion should be integrated with life. It 'had to be admitted with shame', he observed, that Muslims had integrated religion better into their lives than had Irish Catholics.[67]

FARM WOMEN, THE STATE, AND NEGOTIATING POWERLESSNESS

Women and Patriarchal Power in Rural Ireland

Anne Byrne and Tanya Watson[1]

Patriarchy defined sociologically is a 'system of social structures, and practices in which men dominate, oppress and exploit women'.[2] Of course, patriarchal power can take a variety of forms in different social settings, can vary in its strength and persistence, and can become subject to a wide range of challenges over time. Since the 1970s patriarchal power in Irish society has been waning in certain respects as women and men have challenged it in many social, cultural, economic and political spheres. These challenges are evident in women's greater participation in the workforce, in their increased representation in leadership positions in public and civic life, along with the freedoms brought by legislative changes aimed at securing women's employment equality, rights to equal pay, divorce and access to contraception and control over their reproductive lives.[3] Rural (and in particular farm) women have also benefited from these advances, though they have simultaneously been held back by distinctive rural forms of patriarchal power.[4] Why this is the case has to be a critical line of gender-focused inquiry in Irish rural studies and it is the question that provides this chapter with its point of departure.

Our discussion will review leading contributions to the anthropological and sociological literatures from the 1930s to the 1990s to see what light these can shed on rural women's lives on and off the farm and on the challenges of achieving gender equality in the decades since political independence. As the primary site in which patriarchy is practiced, produced and reproduced, much attention has been paid by anthropologists and sociologists to family life on the land. Our review will therefore have much to say concerning what has been written about the gendered division of labour on Irish farms, the regulation of women's labour, subordinate and dominant gender relations in the family, on the farm and the historical exclusion of women from the occupational category of farmer. Against this backdrop we will review contemporary sociological farm family research that emphasises new opportunities available to women to become active agents in resisting different forms of patriarchal power on and off the family farm.

WOMEN IN 1930S RURAL CLARE

Arensberg and Kimball's classic ethnographic study of rural Clare between 1932–4 is clear about the father's dominance in family and farm being ultimately founded on land ownership.[5] The cultural valorisation of male farmer authority, along with sole male responsibility for the farm economy as property owner, is deeply embedded. In a general sense the husband-father's legitimacy in directing family labour and in structuring familial relations is recognised. It is the landowning man who:

> … comes to stand for the group which he heads; the farm is known by his name, and wife and children bear his name likewise. For the Irish family is patrilocal and patronymic…Farm, house, and most of the household goods descend from father to son with the patronym…[6]

Why country people only 'vaguely' recognise 'the right of a woman to hold property' reflects its incompatibility with the identification of family and land with the male landowner.[7]

The identities of 'father' and 'son' hold 'emotional symbols of very great power' in 1930s Clare.[8] A son gradually receives farming knowledge from his father, uncles, brothers 'at their hands' and eventually acquires on the farm 'the full training which makes him a member of his class and time'.[9] In important respects the transmission of farming skills is secondary to the acquisition of male authority and the reproduction of the practices that maintain the generational (and gendered) continuity of the family farm. An adult son at home never escapes his father's 'disciplinary force' first encountered as a child, and it is therefore difficult for any father-son 'intimacy to develop',[10] something that could lead to 'antagonisms' and serous conflict on occasion.[11] Women have some power in the care and socialisation of their sons and mother-son relationships are described as affectionate and as a bulwark against 'a too arbitrary exercise of his father's power'.[12] A daughter is subject to similar 'conditioning' as a son, equally subordinate, but spends her early life in close working contact with her mother and other women of the household and largely separated from her father. She learns to clean, bake, sew, care for and feed animals, look after other children and 'is at the older woman's command'.[13]

Conventional beliefs grounded in conceptions of what is natural underpin the division of labour between the sexes, adults and children. Where family, domestic and farm work are concerned women and men are seen as occupying strictly separate spheres, though spousal roles are described as 'complementary' with reciprocal obligations.[14] A husband's access to the public sphere – though limited by the daily demands of farm work – is considerably greater than that of a wife's. When the annual round of men's farm work is compared with women's daily round of domestic, farm and caring work, a distinguishing feature of farm women's lives is the repetitive and restricted character of their productive and reproductive labour, with little free time or space available for solitude or wider social pursuits.[15] Though tied to the agricultural season, men's work round is freer, more varied and is of 'greater valuation' in the community.[16] The anthropologists observe there is 'no formal taboo confining a woman to women's work' and 'in the case of a woman doing a man's work some of the praise bestowed upon surprising success meets her if she does it well'.[17] Despite this, attitudes of country people serve to bolster sex roles and the strict division of labour, and 'ridicule and laughter greet suggestions that either sex busy itself with the work of the other'.[18] While women's role is separate, women's farm labour is described as 'auxiliary' and 'women's work'.[19] Manual work that is based in the home, caring for others and animals, mending, making and provisioning is represented as less technical, less mechanical, less physically difficult than men's farm work, and is represented as a lesser form of support to the primary work of the farm household.

When it comes to marriage, considerations of social status and land ownership are uppermost. The anthropologists relate how:

> The nearly universal form of marriage in the Irish countryside unites transfer of economic control, land ownership, reformation of family ties, advance in family and community status, and entrance into adult procreative sex life.[20]

Yet Arensberg and Kimball's ethnography of traditional small farm family interpersonal relationships does alert readers to the forces of modernisation and change. While familism offered 'strong resistance to slow assault', the anthropologists predicted that change would come from within the family structure itself.[21] Enforced celibacy and delayed marriage were producing their own tensions that reflected a 'paradox' in Irish rural life stemming from the way 'a social system centring so strongly round the institution of the family condemns a large proportion of its members to celibacy and long-preserved virginity'.[22] Hierarchies of masculine privilege, status and power had the effect of marginalising unmarried family members, both men and women. For this reason, the structure and dynamics of the traditional farm family could not remain immune from wider societal influences in the longer run.

FARM WOMEN IN THE 1950s AND 1960s

Patrick McNabb's study of rural east Limerick in the late 1950s focuses on family life during a time of transition.[23] Again the 'chief institutions' that give McNabb's Limerick rural communities 'their specific form and function are so organised and related to each other as to guarantee the authority of the father and the conservation of property'.[24] A feature of east Limerick farming is the presence of hired labour and we hear how a table by the fire is reserved for the family, while 'a plain deal table near the door' is for 'the serving boy or girl or the hired workers'.[25]

The authority of the father – ultimately derived from his ownership and control of the family farm – allows him to act in the household as 'an autocrat, and his word, when he chooses, is law'.[26] The unsentimental relationship of 'mother and father' is noted, with the husband being neither 'companion nor lover' to his wife.[27] Where 'matters of finance and farm management' are concerned, the man of the house is 'loath to consult his wife or adult children'.[28] Paid in pocket money, adult sons at home are given no idea of their father's thinking regarding succession, a process described as 'blackmail' in which sons submit to the authority of the father with 'unquestioning obedience'.[29] The burden of work on farm women is especially heavy and the typical reality for unmarried daughters is that:

> ...if she remains on the farm, she must do a full day's work, and too often her life is one of unrelieved drudgery. There is an almost Oriental attitude to girls. They are favoured neither by father nor mother and accepted only on sufferance...they are loved but not thought of any great importance. They are educated consciously in a way which facilitates their exit from the home.[30]

It is women in east Limerick who oversee the education of children, and daughters are educated to leave as they are regarded as 'no longer essential to the farm economy'.[31] Young women's growing disenchantment with rural life is identified as a source of change given the way 'the modern country girl is turning away from the land'.[32] Even if the farmer father's authority remains strong, McNabb observes how emigration – particularly of farmers' daughters – presented a 'grave threat' to the farming community.[33] Better educational opportunities for women, poor marriage prospects, unending unpaid heavy work, and (in the event of marriage) dissatisfaction with the practice of the dowry being paid to in-laws rather than to the in-marrying woman, are all factors that loosen women's commitment to, and sense of fit within, a changing rural society.[34] Significantly 'the status of the farmer has gone down considerably in the eyes of the female population'.[35] When a woman agrees to marry a farmer she makes 'quite extraordinary demands' for 'modern conveniences, whatever the cost'; and her desire was to 'clear the house' of all relatives before marriage.[36] The well-being and 'standing' of families is tied to the influence and work of the married woman with children, hence 'a good mother is everything'.[37]

McNabb is optimistic about the modernising influence of the Irish Countrywomen's Association, recognising 'that for the first time women have the opportunity to assume an institutionalised role outside the home'.[38] The young farmers' organisation Macra na Feirme is presented as a form of 'organised opposition' by bachelors to the authority of the father and more traditional approaches to farming.[39]

Ethna Viney describes the grim lives of Irish farm women in the 1960s as a product of unrelenting physical domestic and farm labour with few material comforts, having large numbers of children, poor relations between spouses and between parents and children, and the lack of opportunities for rest, social contact or leisure. Mothers encourage their daughters' education to 'enable them to make their way in the world away from any other farm' and they seek to dissuade their daughters from marrying a farmer.[40]

Women's dissatisfaction with their lives is similarly a feature of John C. Messenger's 1960s ethnographic study of an Irish-speaking western island community.[41] Excluded from activities customarily prohibited to women, younger women emigrate to avoid living the restricted lives of older women, subject to the rule of husband or father.[42] The anthropologist Hugh Brody writes in the early 1970s of the 'rejection of rural life itself' in the Inishkillane community, and of 'country girls' who 'have refused to marry into local farms'.[43] For most young women indeed 'the prospect of marriage in the countryside is too absurd to consider…and do not take seriously any proposals which might entail a life in rural Ireland'.[44] Accordingly, the widening gap in material living standards between urban and rural communities, and perceived expanding occupational, social and marriage opportunities in the city, the demands imposed by farm life, weaken young women's commitment to life on the land.[45]

At a time of accelerating farming and social change, the survey research of Damian Hannan and Louise Katsiaouni in the 1970s explored changing relations within farm families since the 1930s.[46] Some of the features of family life Arensberg and Kimball had charted – in particular patriarchal authority and control, the gendered division of labour, and women's responsibility for socio-emotional and care labour in the household – hadn't disappeared by the 1970s. However, their legitimacy had begun to be contested by some family members as changes in rural beliefs and values encouraged people 'to take on the perspective of prestigeful urban reference groups'.[47] Inspired by a vision of urban middle-class marriage, some farm women were dissatisfied with the status quo and were intent on having more equal and affectionate relationships with their spouses. Power relations in such households were characterised by joint decision-making. Yet even if mothers' sole responsibility for childrearing was somewhat lessened, the economic provider role on farms remained predominantly male, limiting 'the degree of participation by the husband in household and child-rearing tasks'.[48] Hannan and Katsiaouni write that importantly 'the norms have changed. The husband is not ridiculed or sanctioned if he helps in the household and child-rearing tasks, rather it is expected that he will do so on a regular basis'.[49]

Acknowledging women's and children's contribution to farm work, and some women's preference for outdoor farm work, farm women remain overwhelmingly socially positioned in the domestic space of the house, ensuring that farm and domestic spheres remain separate. Hannan and Katsiaouni argue that the family farm model of 'traditional patriarchal dominance of decision making would be almost impossible to maintain' in a context of increasing modernisation in which the commercialisation of farming, and alternative career and lifestyle opportunities for young women and men, are forcing changes in family roles and relationships.[50] Opportunities for involvement in social and rural-based organisations disrupt attachment to traditional standards and values, particularly for women, even as changes in farm production and consumption patterns are 'instrumental in lessening or weakening the position of the wife in farm production'.[51]

Male farm ownership remains largely unquestioned, but Hannan and Katsiaouni's research is nonetheless significant for the evidence it presents of changing spousal power relations inside the farm family, of the expressed desire among some farm women for more equal gender roles, and of the creation of new spaces inside the farm family for the open expression of love, care and affection between family members. Despite the challenges of changing modes and technologies of farm production and new patterns of household consumption, closer spousal relations raise new possibilities for negotiating farm work and shared decision-making between wife and husband.

FEMINIST FARM FAMILY RESEARCH: GENDER, POWER AND PROPERTY

The anthropological and sociological studies of the 1960s and 1970s agree that male property ownership remains the main source of men's power, masculine identity and the farmer's social status. They further link women's increasing dissatisfaction with farm and rural life to unremunerated and endlessly repetitive domestic labour, to subordinate relations with fathers, husbands or brothers, to unfulfilling spousal relations and to a paucity of local social and economic opportunities. Gender features in these studies as an implicit category of analysis that signals the presence and operation of power among men, the deeply homosocial culture of agriculture, and the solid persistence of role differences between men and women. But, in the absence of an explicit feminist theoretical framework with gender as a primary analytical category, the institutionalised structures, practices and social relations that constrain women's lives are less than fully understood, women's power of agency is insufficiently visible and adaptive roles are misunderstood. The locus of patriarchal power in male land ownership, in unquestioned male authority to regulate and control family labour is identified, but its legitimacy is rarely questioned. The weakening of women's commitment to rural life and flight from the land are presented as threats or problems of rural depopulation for which women are held partly responsible rather than as a consequence of men's power over women, limited opportunities for marriage and women's marginal status in the family and rural economy. In the absence of gender as a primary category of analysis, women's skills in farming, in domestic, care and child-rearing work, and their presence as active participants in rural society, are neither fully recognised nor understood. There is a significant absence of a critique of men's traditional right to inherit land, of the dominance of the male breadwinner model in Irish family life, of the private and public power of men, or of the importance of the rural smallholder to Irish national identity. Women's access to land and in particular their right to inherit it or to be considered legitimate farm owners, are issues that are simply not addressed.

Informed by feminist concerns and a commitment to freedom and equality, gender in more recent Irish pioneering sociological research is central to understanding the division of labour and the consequences of sex roles that include institutionalised inequalities in the constitution and reproduction of male and female identities in farming. The links between patriarchal power and gender-based inequalities are traced. Patriarchy's negative effects on women are charted by Patricia O'Hara and Sally Shortall in particular. Patricia O'Hara presents her study as not just 'about' or 'on' women but is part of the feminist tradition of research 'for' women.[52] Her early 1990s research establishes that women are essential to Irish family farming, that the farm family is not a consensual unit, that men and women have different interests, and that there are distinguishable types of farm women. O'Hara argues that farm women – though subordinate to men in many ways – must still be seen as 'active agents involved in production, consumption and reproduction' on farms and in farm households.[53] Drawing on interviews with farm women and men, O'Hara's research explores the bases of patriarchal power in Irish farming, how it routinely works in everyday life, and how it has come to be accepted by some women and rejected by others. O'Hara asserts that 'by objective criteria and from a feminist perspective, family farming can be seen as oppressive to women'.[54] For O'Hara, power needs to be conceptualised 'as a negotiated process, often informal and unarticulated…there is always room to manoeuvre … the sources of women's power and influence are intertwined with their responses to subordination'.[55]

Women's tactical responses to their perceived subordination range from acceptance (and co-operation) to rejection (and resistance) as is evident from the ways they negotiate the gender-based division of labour in the house and on the farm. Four categories of farm women are distinguished with reference to the work (paid and unpaid) they do, how they perceive their own subordination, and how they connect this subordination with male power. These categories O'Hara identifies as the 'farm helper', the 'farm homemaker', 'farm women in paid work' and women 'working for the family farm'.[56]

The women 'farm helpers', who have significantly less access to farm income and less involvement in making decisions than the others, emerge as resentful of their taken-for-granted status, as unhappy about their lack of independence by virtue of having no income of their own, and as being weighed down by 'the sense of having no choice' in life.[57] Though these women may contribute 'up to half of the farm work they do so in the subordinate role of helper'.[58] The farm is referred to as the property of their husbands rather than a shared asset; and farming they view as their husbands' business rather than as a shared enterprise. These 'farm helpers' are characterised as having 'a strong consciousness of being constrained by patriarchal power relations and of having established a pattern of inferiority throughout their married lives which is almost impossible to change'.[59]

Childcare and domestic work are the principal concerns of 'the farm homemaker' whose farmer husband has off-farm work. Farm homemakers have no personal income, and typically have to ask for money and depend on an allowance from their husbands. Described as 'house-centred rather than farm-centred', homemakers are 'more likely' to join rural organisations such as the Irish Countrywomen's Association to relieve the 'boredom and monotony of housework'.[60]

'Farm women in paid work' are presented as having a distinctive occupational identity independent of the family farm. Earning their own income places these women 'in a much stronger position to challenge male domination in their relationships',[61] and to negotiate greater involvement of husbands/fathers in the care of children and housework.[62] Besides affirming their self-worth, having an independent income permits these women to improve their households' standard of living.

Why the women 'working for the family farm' are the most committed to farming life reflects the way farms are jointly run with women sharing control of material assets, having extensive involvement in making decisions and sharing responsibility for financial management. These arrangements allow women to experience an easing of traditional patriarchal constraints. Not feeling 'victimised' by childcare, domestic work and farming is something O'Hara explains as an outcome of their strong identification with the family farm.[63]

It is the women with off-farm paid work who emerge as the most inclined to contest and negotiate patriarchy. Particularly marked among women 'working for the family farm' and those with off-farm paid work is the tendency to reject the category of 'housewife' as a primary source of identity, based on unpaid domestic work. The dislike of housework gave rise to such negative comments as: 'there is nothing good about it', 'what I think of housework is unprintable...I hate housework', and 'a total waste of energy and time and I do as little as possible'.[64]

As regards the family farm's generational continuity and succession, O'Hara views women as mothers (rather than wives) as exercising 'the greatest influence on reproduction'.[65] Full-time housewives stand out as the most positively oriented to motherhood and provides 'their primary identity'.[66] A combination of the gendered division of labour in the field, the yard and in the kitchen, and the social construction of motherhood as women's sole responsibility for parenting, enables women to exercise influence over children in ways that prepare them for a future away from the family farm. Aware that farming (on smaller holdings in particular) is no longer a viable full-time occupation for heirs, mothers seek to ensure that their children are well educated so as to gain access to occupations outside farming. Control over socialisation, responsibility for caring for children and others, and the importance given to education become highly significant means 'of resisting patriarchal dominance and creating a separate sphere of influence'.[67] A major effect of encouraging their daughters to concentrate on occupational opportunities outside agriculture is that 'the cycle of dependent farm wife is fractured and that the women of the next generation have better choices', thereby threatening the traditional power of the male farmer to control labour and inheritance decisions.[68]

Focusing especially on linkages between power and land-based farm property ownership, Sally Shortall's 1990s pioneering research sets out to identify the factors 'which render women invisible in farming, and why women continue to subscribe to such a situation'.[69] The persistence of the gendered nature of farm ownership – based on land transfer between men – is identified as the key factor impacting on women's lives on and off the farm, in the family, in community and farming organisations.[70] Given that patrilineal inheritance is unquestioned, Shortall regards the term 'family farming' as 'contentious' insofar as 'it misrepresents the ownership structure that underlies the household'.[71] Since land ownership is individualised, family farming 'invariably refers to a family living on a farm owned by a man'.[72] The many disadvantages women face on Irish family farms – for instance, typically 'agricultural knowledge is male knowledge'[73] – originate in male land ownership. And as long as land continues to be transferred from father to son 'the struggle is likely to continue between the tenacious emotional attachment to the traditional structures of family farming and attempts to reform the essentially sexist assumptions on which family farming is based'.[74]

Nor is patriarchal power confined to the family farm. In considering the difficulties women face in being active in farming organisations, Shortall draws attention to how 'economic power that follows from property ownership...leads to enhanced political, ideological and organisational resources' for men in the public sphere.[75] What is further evident, as Shortall argues, is that patrilinealism inhibits the growth of a feminist rural movement advocating gender equality as a means of challenging gender-based inequalities and empowering women.

GENDER EQUALITY IN FARMING: THE LATER PHASE

Since the feminist-inspired research of O'Hara and Shortall in the 1990s there have been a number of significant policy initiatives to address gender inequality in agriculture and to support women's presence and participation in rural civil society groups. In 2000 the Report of the Advisory Committee on the Role of Women in Agriculture highlighted women's significant contribution to family farming, while contrasting this with the relatively few women earning independent incomes from farming, the dearth of landowning women and the relative absence of women holders of herd numbers.[76] The Committee recommended joint ownership of herd numbers to increase women's visibility as legitimate recipients of direct farm payments and as claimants for social welfare and pension entitlements.[77] Subsequently the Gender Equality Unit (GEU) established the Women in Agriculture Steering Committee to commission further statistical research to record and document women's position in Irish family farms and in rural development.[78] A 2004 GEU study found that men and women equally perceived women's work on farms to be largely undervalued and that 90 per cent of respondents approved of joint ownership of farm property. Yet traditional succession attitudes in naming a male heir remained strongly unchanged – only 17 per cent of women respondents identified themselves as joint owners with their husbands.[79] Over three decades women's sole legal ownership of farm property has increased by a mere 3.7 per cent, from just under ten per cent in 1991 to slightly over 13 per cent in 2020.[80] Of almost ten per cent of women farm holders in 1991, some 56 per cent became landowners on the death of a spouse, and just over a quarter (27 per cent) were daughters inheriting from their parents.[81]

In 2012 a Macra na Feirme-led survey of succession and inheritance practices found that where no successor was yet identified, nine per cent of farmer respondents explained they had only daughters as prospective heirs.[82] Since most farmers over 55 have not selected a successor, Macra na Feirme appointed a land mobility programme manager in 2013 to advise farmers on identifying a successor and to encourage participation in collaborative farming arrangements. This initiative did not explicitly promote the succession of daughters, but given the often problematic nature of Irish farm continuity, the issue of female succession is unlikely to fade away.

Anne Cassidy's interview-based research highlights the benefits to farming and agriculture of women successors.[83] In advance of decisions being made about succession, women with a connection to family farming emerge as regarding themselves worthy successors by reason of being frequently engaged in future planning for the farm, and being prepared to return to farming in a career change once the landowning farmer has retired. The case for women's succession is further strengthened in Cassidy's research in view of the abundance of new creative ideas that relate to how land might be farmed more sustainably (by addressing environmental concerns, exploring diversification and job creation opportunities) for the benefit of the land itself, farms, farm families and for the individual women.

The most recent sociological research suggests that while patriarchal practices have by no means disappeared on Irish farms, the gender order is nonetheless shifting in a process of 'feminisation' that is providing for more equitable working relationships between farming men and women.[84] Studies of the farm co-management agreements known as Joint Farming Ventures (JFVs) – launched first in 2002 in the form of the Milk Production Partnership aimed at improving the economic resilience of farms – have shown them to have been particularly important in facilitating the entry of women into farming, making visible and placing value on women's labour and knowledge, promoting joint decision-making and more equitable work relationships.[85] Initiated by sociologist Áine Macken-Walsh, research relying on narrative interviews with JFV participants reveal that traditional gender divisions around productive and reproductive work on the farm and in the household have lost much of their former rigidity.[86] The formal socio-legal space created by the JFVs have opened up new possibilities so that 'women and youth can exercise agency on the farm, resisting patriarchal control through an empowered sense of self'.[87] With the support of spouses and families, the JFVs have allowed women to identify themselves as farmers and to be recognised and represented as such. At the same time, farm partnerships are relatively recent developments and have yet to become a general feature of Irish agriculture. If they are to realise their full potential to prompt greater agency among farm women in a context where patriarchal norms and practices still exist in Irish agriculture, the JFVs will have to become more widespread and continuing ideological adjustment will be required from male spouses, family members and rural society more generally.[88] While JFVs, based on public socio-legal frameworks, have introduced real possibilities of change for farmer women, they may not be sufficient in and of themselves to transform the deeply-rooted sexist norms of patriarchal succession in Irish farming. Yet, when aligned with wider societal currents that challenge the inherent sexism of the familial, economic, social, cultural and political structures of patriarchy in Irish society – and with the state's commitment to pursue a gender equality agenda across all domains – the JFVs do offer an important platform for the rights of women farmers to be recognised, represented and advanced.

CONCLUSIONS

Since Arensberg and Kimball's ethnographic work in the 1930s much has been rightly made of the persisting strength of patrilineal inheritance as an economic and cultural norm in rural Ireland, of women's restricted access to land ownership, and of the economic and social power land ownership has conferred on men. In recognition of the power of male farmer agency, and the durability and legitimacy of patriarchy as a source of social, economic and cultural power, women emerge in the social science literature reviewed here as accepting, adapting to and resisting patriarchal power in various ways across the stages of the family cycle. Historically emigration has been a major means for younger farm women to fulfil a desire for independence within a family regime based on gender inequality and on social relations marked by economic, social and emotional dependence on men. What the 1970s survey research of Hannan and Katsiaouni, along with the feminist-informed studies of O'Hara and Shortall of the 1990s, show is that the earlier rigid forms of patriarchy were weakened by women's resistance to sexism inside the farm family and in society more broadly. Equality legislation, the rise of a feminist consciousness, the spread of liberal values, combined with economic threats to agriculture have all inspired demands for more equal gender relations on Irish farms.

Feminist sociological analyses of family farming are infused by a desire to secure the future sustainability of the Irish family farm and to 'de-legitimise patriarchal ideologies in a changing society'.[89] By challenging the principle of male farm ownership, Patricia O'Hara's and Sally Shortall's pioneering research of the 1990s has established the significance of gender as a critical analytical lens in the study of agriculture, rural society, agricultural policy formation and implementation. Áine Macken-Walsh's innovative sociological research provides evidence of women at farm level – particularly in the context of the new socio-legal JFV's – being able to negotiate power relations on the farm and in the family (based on property and gender) at different points in time across the family life cycle. Under the new conditions provided by the JFVs, patrilineal inheritance is challenged (and even disrupted), but much fundamental change is needed if the ideals of equality in gender relations inside and outside the farm family are to be fully realised. Women's experiences of interactions with support mechanisms for entering farming and planning a farming career, with a concentration on barriers and successes, are a promising focus for additional qualitative research directions.

Though in early stages of implementation within the agri-food and farming sectors, Equality, Diversity and Inclusivity (EDI) strategies can challenge and change the gendered status quo.[90] Formalisation and recognition of gender-specific strategies to create more favourable outcomes for women in farming, particularly in regards to equal succession rights, are crucial. The recent National Dialogue on Women in Agriculture Action Plan promotes gender awareness as a starting point in recognising the discrimination standing in the way of achieving gender equality for women.[91] The creation of EDI guidelines, based on a tested and achievable model that converts aspirations relating to gender equality into action, can be replicated by businesses and organisations within the sector, with some potential to influence gendered farm family dynamics, and promote programmes by and for women. Targeted supports are important in creating a more equitable setting for women who wish to own farmland, enter the sector and work as farmers, and so provide new opportunities for the partnership, leadership and innovation critical for the longer-term sustainability of Irish family farms. The research reviewed here points to the urgency of rethinking patrilineal succession not only for equality but crucially for the longer-term sustainability of Irish family farms. To conclude, patriarchy as a system of power is tenacious, ubiquitous and highly detrimental for the continuity and survival of the Irish family farm.

Challenging Patriarchal Power?
Women Advisors as Change Agents in
Twentieth-Century Irish Agriculture

Mícheál Ó Fathartaigh and Anne Cassidy

The relationship between female agricultural advisors and farming women – farmers' wives and daughters in particular – is the topic considered in this chapter. The history of this relationship, as a potentially key expression of female power (in the form of the collaborative agency between the women instructresses/advisors and Irish farming women), can be divided quite neatly into two parts during the twentieth century. In the very early decades of the last century collaborative female agency of the kind we consider was in the ascendant while thereafter it fell into decline. During the years of its ascendancy the collaborative relationship helped inspire a distinctive transformative phase of change in twentieth-century Irish agriculture. Why this transformative agency later faded away can be linked to restructuring processes in Irish agriculture, processes that allowed the relationship between male agricultural advisors and farming men to assert a new hegemony. An increasingly dominant male agency can indeed be viewed as absorbing much of the dynamism of the earlier female agency already present in the agricultural sphere. Another notable consequence of expanding male hegemony was the way it substantially erased earlier forms of collaborative female agency from popular memory.

The challenges Irish farming women and men were facing early in twentieth-century Ireland were formidable to say the least. Relative to many parts of Western Europe the country continued to be an agricultural backwater. The Great Famine of the 1840s had brutally laid bare serious shortcomings in the structures of Irish agriculture. As the subsistence crisis deepened, the existing system of land ownership, as well as the manner land was being farmed, proved themselves incapable of preventing mass distress and mortality among the impoverished rural classes dependent on a potato diet. Tenurial reform became a significant element of the post-Famine adjustment and by the early 1900s the transfer of land ownership from the Anglo-Irish gentry to Irish tenant farmers was well underway. Of course, land ownership remained nonetheless firmly in male hands. Given this fundamental patriarchal reality, and the backwardness of much of Irish agriculture, the chances of Irish farming women emerging as dynamic producers in their own right were hardly very bright in the early years of the last century.

For late nineteenth-century improvement-minded observers – most notably Horace Plunkett, the founder of Ireland's co-operative movement – land reform would change little in the absence of agricultural change. To combat the underdevelopment that made Ireland an agricultural backwater and to improve the position of farming women, Plunkett put his faith in a well-organised co-operative movement (with the dairying sector at its centre) working in dynamic partnership with the new Department of Agriculture and Technical Instruction (DATI) he had helped establish in 1899. From the 1890s Plunkett was regarding the provision of agricultural advice – via the deployment of a cadre of well-trained agricultural instructors (and instructresses as the women were titled officially till the 1960s) – as fundamental to any new state intervention aimed at modernising Irish agriculture. Only by deploying professional agricultural advisors might Irish farmers (women as well as men) learn to work the land more efficiently in accordance with modern scientific principles. Several previous attempts at agricultural instruction in rural Ireland had appeared since the eighteenth century, but Plunkett sought to radically change both the substance of agricultural advice and the manner of its delivery. His ultimate idea was to see DATI, in conjunction with the new county councils established in 1898, provide a countrywide county-based agricultural instruction or advisory service.[1] Once despatched to every corner of rural Ireland, Plunkett was confident that his agricultural instructors (women and men) would be effective in working closely with farmers to change their farming practices along up-to-date scientific lines. Broadly speaking Plunkett's optimistic conviction was substantially borne out in practice over the long run. DATI's advisory service became the fundamental institutional framework under whose influence Irish agriculture would undergo different phases of transformative change. The first such phase owed much to an evolving collaborative relationship between female instructresses and farming women.

At the outset in 1900 DATI's agricultural advisory service revolved around three distinctive strands of activity. One set of instructors specialised in the provision of general agricultural advice, another in horticultural and beekeeping advice, and a third set was tasked with the job of transferring poultry-keeping and butter-making knowledge and expertise. The first two sets of instructors were exclusively male while the third set was composed solely of women. Such a division of labour reflected the prevailing reality of Irish poultry-keeping and butter-making being regarded conventionally as female agricultural enterprises. It was consistent besides with general Victorian ideas regarding the proper working roles of farming women and men.[2]

As advisors had to be formally trained, and the educational infrastructure to train them was still under construction, it took several years for each county to recruit its full complement of agricultural instructors. Significantly, this delay impacted least on the recruitment of poultry-keeping and butter-making instructresses because their first training facility, the Munster Institute in Cork, had begun to produce women advisors in 1905.[3] And even before 1905 the Reading College Poultry School was graduating poultry-keeping instructors.[4] All this meant that the Irish counties could move quickly to recruit their quota of two poultry-keeping and butter-making instructors. The upshot was that the women advisors were actively at work approximately a decade before their male colleagues. Besides their relatively early arrival on the scene, the women instructresses' alacrity and assiduity in interacting with Irish farming women quickly became apparent.[5]

WOMEN AND POULTRY-KEEPING

As energetic as were the new women advisors, little headway could have been made had the farming women themselves not been so receptive to the advisors' message regarding poultry bloodlines and the quality of Irish eggs. In the take-up of agricultural advice gender differences quickly became apparent. For a long time Irish farming men tended to remain suspicious of the advisory service. They tended to see DATI's (and its successor's) unsolicited advice as an unwelcome encroachment on the private affairs of the family farm, ownership of which had but recently been transferred (or still awaited transferral) from the landlord class to the tenant-farmers.[6] In stark contrast, a rapport was quickly built up between the female instructors and Irish farming women.

A good illustration of this is found in east Galway where Nóra Keating was one of Galway's first three female poultry-keeping instructresses. Appointed in 1902, Keating was instrumental in 1903 in opening five egg-distribution centres in east Galway. These centres were quickly inundated with farming women who were eager to purchase the fertilised eggs of pure-bred poultry birds. Soon ten new centres had been added to the five original east Galway centres, thus making possible the distribution of the eggs of 18,000 pure-bred hens in 1903–4. All this development was the product of the courses Keating was running from 1902 throughout east Galway. Unencumbered by the scepticism of their menfolk, east Galway's farming women tended to respond with enthusiasm to Keating's simple message that better-quality birds would produce eggs of higher quality capable of fetching better market prices.[7]

It is difficult to be categorical as to why Keating's extension work attracted such an enthusiastic response, but clearly a small number of factors were at work. The egg market in the early decades of the twentieth century was generally buoyant.[8] Another significant reason why east Galway's farming women responded pragmatically to Keating's advice can be found in rural Ireland's social structure. The women who helped promote and operate the egg-distribution centres that Keating was setting up tended to come from the big or strong farmer class. One such centre in the Loughrea district, for instance, was run by Brigid Hogan of Kilrickle of east Galway.[9] The indications are that the partnerships between female advisors and locally influential farming women conferred a vital legitimacy on the new women instructresses and their pioneering early work. Considerations of social class were relevant in another fundamental sense as well. Not only was the 'egg money', as it was called, earned by women on even the smallest farms but early in the twentieth century it was often the only thing that stood between the poorest farming families and dire poverty. Here Nóra Keating observed perceptively how: 'The poorest people have hens, and acknowledge they live by them the greater part of the year'.[10]

Of much relevance as well is the way farming women were often the mainstay of rural families. In those 'congested districts' where seasonal migration was the norm, it was the women who regularly ran the small farms in the absence of the household's adult men who were away working seasonally on Britain's large commercial farms.[11] Typically these women managed the household budgets with a view to ensuring that the family as a whole benefited from whatever household income could be earned.[12] For farming women to be receiving the greatest proportion of the regular household income directly – in the form of 'egg money' – underpinned their economic worth and social power within the household.

In a somewhat paradoxical manner, this 'egg money' served to make women much more economically independent as individuals while simultaneously making them economically much more indispensable to their families.

That these farming women had a certain access to the public sphere in the form of the egg market could further boost their social power. Nóra Keating remarked in 1904 how: 'It is gratifying to notice the good-humoured smile of the women coming to market with their well filled baskets of eggs.'[13] This observation conveys an appreciation of just how emancipatory household-based commercial poultry-keeping was for the farming women of east Galway (and by extension in rural Ireland more generally) in the early twentieth century. For farming women keen to assert their autonomy in a strongly patriarchal society, the 'egg money' had become a crucial material and social resource that enhanced their standing both inside and outside the family farm.

So far we have considered the broadly positive reception of the farm women to the possibilities offered by the state's attempt to transform the Irish poultry economy. But what can we say about the contribution of the state's women instructresses themselves? The east Galway case reveals just how vital Nóra Keating's enthusiasm, energy and expertise were in stimulating the participation of farming women in what was an exclusively female-dominated branch of Irish agriculture. Looked at more broadly the value of the interactions between female advisors and poultry-farming women is also very evident. A national agricultural census reveals how in 1903, as Nóra Keating and her colleagues were commencing their extension activities, there were 18.2 million poultry birds on Irish farms. A decade later – just before the First World War and the boom in agricultural output the war inspired – there were 25.7 million poultry birds (an increase of over 40 per cent). By contrast in the previous ten years (1893–1903) poultry numbers had increased by a mere 13 per cent.[14] We can conclude from the combined evidence of advisors' local experience (such as in Nóra Keating's east Galway) and from the national statistics that collaborative female instructor-farming woman agency not just existed but had succeeded very early in the last century in initiating a transformative phase of Irish agricultural change.

The severe disruption resulting from the Irish Revolution and civil war (1917–23) along with the prolonged post-First World War agricultural slump, posed testing challenges for Irish farmers and for the new Free State in the 1920s. In response to those questioning the cost of maintaining the advisory service as a whole Louis Dalton (a Cumann na nGaedheal TD for Tipperary) singled out the work of the female poultry instructresses for special mention. 'A good many decried it at the time', he pointed out in 1924, 'and did not think it of any importance, but we know now its value in the number of eggs and poultry exported.'[15]

Not only was the advisory service retained but after Fianna Fáil came to power in 1932 the number of female poultry instructresses was increased from 45 in 1934 to 58 in 1939.[16] Geared especially to improving the viability of small- and medium-sized farms, the work of the poultry instructresses was indeed prioritised by successive Fianna Fáil governments both as a means of mitigating some of the negative effects of the Anglo-Irish 'economic war' (1932–8) and of helping to reconfigure Irish agriculture in favour of smaller farms. By the late 1930s Ireland had become self-sufficient in eggs and, in the absence of egg imports, the strong position of Irish poultry-farming women (mostly on smaller farms) in the domestic market compensated somewhat for the difficulties Irish farmers had experienced in accessing the British agricultural markets in the economic war years.[17] Such was the esteem in which the Department of Agriculture (and the government more widely) held the work of the female advisors that their number was increased further – from 58 to 61 – during the Second World War.[18]

Even if it was not recognised at the time, this latest expansion would be the high-water mark of Ireland's female-controlled small farm-centred egg economy in the twentieth century. From the late 1940s small-scale poultry-keeping was gradually being displaced by specialised poultry farms that over time were increasingly organised along industrial lines. In this transition women poultry farmers were the big losers as intensive large-scale poultry-keeping tended to become the preserve of male farmers. And as many farmers' daughters experienced economic displacement, the mid-century trend of rising female emigration from rural Ireland became firmly established.[19]

WOMEN AND BUTTER-MAKING

Although the poultry-keeping and butter-making advisory roles were largely combined from the early days of the advisory service this was not uniformly the case. In counties where dairying was practised widely or in counties that had pockets of dairying the butter-making role was initially a dedicated one, with many instructresses specialising when they left the Munster Institute. By the 1930s the distinction had virtually ceased, with only three of 45 female advisors exclusively butter-making instructresses in 1931.[20] Butter-making advice centred on hygiene and made a particular point of encouraging farming women to make butter in the sanitary environment of a standalone dairy. Following the foundation of the Irish state in 1922 the first Minister for Agriculture, Patrick Hogan, was zealously keen to see butter produced in only the optimal environment of the creamery, and from his time homemade butter was actively discouraged.[21] Consequently, butter-making female advisors quite quickly lost influence and suffered displacement as the move to creamery-made butter accelerated.

Annie Coyne was appointed alongside Nóra Keating as a butter-making instructress for Galway. She was soon reporting cheerfully that her classes held in the dairying districts of north and east Galway were immediately impactful:

> The people were very attentive to instruction, and anxious to learn. On the whole, the dairy industry shows marked signs of improvement. The new methods have been already adopted in many parts of the county.[22]

A decade later a departmental inspector, while praising her efforts, noted that attendance at her classes was poor. He noted, too, that the attendees were 'girls'.[23] Ever before Hogan's creamery crusade women from the strong farmer class do not appear to have involved themselves in promoting female butter-making, as was the case with poultry-keeping. And this has to be counted as another reason why butter-making instructresses were not as influential as the poultry-keeping instructresses in changing the patterns of Irish farming.

THE FARM HOME MANAGEMENT ADVISORS

With household-based poultry-keeping and butter-making no longer controlled by farming women, the farmhouse became the prime female dominion. Of course, housekeeping and child-minding had always been the sole responsibilities of farming women, but in the early post-1945 decades 'home economics' came to acquire a wider significance. Some commentators, reflecting on the changing order of things in 1960s rural Ireland, were viewing male farmers as bounding ahead while home-based farm women lagged behind, even to the point of impeding the progress of the farming men. One provincial newspaper, the *Nenagh Guardian*, felt compelled to observe in 1966 that:

> If the housewife on her side does not make equal progress she may slow up the development of the farm and thus make the life of the family less satisfying than it could be.[24]

Similarly in official circles in the second half of the twentieth century the idea gained momentum that the 'modernisation' of Irish farming had to happen inside as well as outside the farm household. One expression of such official thinking noted how:

> modernisation did not just need to happen on Irish farms themselves, it needed to happen in Irish farmhouses...If time, energy and money were all managed efficiently in Irish farmhouses, this would make a huge contribution to modernising Irish agriculture.[25]

The Department of Agriculture's recognition that 'the farm home' was at 'the heart of the farm' – and that it was 'from there the business is managed and worked' – implied that farm women would have to become more central to the efficient management of 'time, energy and money'.[26] No less than was the case with poultry-keeping and butter-making in earlier decades, the new official view was that farm women would need to be advised by dedicated advisors if they were to maximise their abilities to manage the farm household's 'time, energy and money' to best advantage. The interactions between the female agricultural advisors and Irish farming women would therefore require restructuring in line with the new official thinking. From 1962 we therefore find the role of the poultry-keeping and butter-making instructresses being reinvented as they began the transition to becoming Farm Home Management (FHM) advisors. With the change of title and direction, the interactive dynamic relationship between female advisors and farming women in rural Ireland entered a new phase.

FARM HOME MANAGEMENT

As with the poultry-keeping and butter-making instructresses from the earliest days, the FHM advisors were trained at the Munster Institute. Senior practitioners in home economics were brought in from Nebraska, Germany and Austria to help design the advisors' new course.[27] Almost at once the new course underwent significant expansion. While 13 female advisors were sent on a one-year course in 1962 some 57 of them commenced training in 1968, a year when three students also completed the first three-year course. In 1973 there were 112 women advisors still in the advisory service who had initially been trained as poultry-keeping and butter-making instructresses, and 82 of these women had been trained or retrained in FHM.[28] Several of them had also availed of additional training in Austria and Bavaria, the recognised centres of FHM excellence in Europe.[29] As of old these advisors continued to interact with farming women, but in both its substance and approach their work had changed fundamentally. No longer were they instructing farming women in local groups in such places as school halls. They were now visiting the homes of farm women and consulting with them individually on household-related matters that – very significantly – included the financial affairs of the farm enterprise.

There was also a recognition in Brussels in the 1970s that farming women were at the heart of the family farm. And under the EEC's scheme of vocational education – the so-called 161 courses that in 1975 subsumed all the educational programmes offered to Irish farmers (both male and female) from the early 1900s – the FHM advisors were assigned a leading role. Mary Duffy, an FHM advisor in Galway, recalled how the 161 courses '...were for farm women essentially'.[30] One significant feature of the new EEC-inspired educational regime was that female advisors were no longer confined to interacting solely just with farm women. Another key difference was that the responsibilities of the FHM advisors became much more diffuse. Joanne Banks describes how:

> Farm Home Management advisers were also involved in community development, encouraging local leadership and working with rural organisations and interest groups with education programmes. Farm Home Management advisers would work with whole families, advising them on education opportunities and community resources available to them.[31]

The impact of the FHM advisors on the development of rural Ireland can be traced in the visual transformation of many Irish farmhouses between 1962 and 1984. We find the FHM advisors for instance – anticipating the later priority given to home-based energy conservation – spearheading an innovative campaign to improve the insulation of Irish farmhouses in the early 1980s.[32]

Of course, the FHM advisors never operated in an economic and social vacuum. By no means was the 1962–84 period without its economic difficulties, but the wave of prosperity being experienced by some Irish farmers (particularly in the 1970s) allowed for the material improvement of many Irish farmhouses and for the building of many new farmhouses. This new prosperity – along with the longstanding relationship the female advisors had built with Irish farming women – allowed the FHM advisors to make a major contribution to the material improvement of Irish farmhouses that was especially marked during the later phases of the 1962–84 period.

WOMEN AS SOCIO-ECONOMIC ADVISORS

Despite the success of the FHM advisory role, a decision was taken in 1984 to shut down the service and to retrain the female advisors as socio-economic (or enterprise) advisors. Apparently this decision reflected, in important respects, the way the FHM advisory role had come to be perceived officially as the victim of its own success. ACOT (An Chomhairle Oiliúna Talmhaíochta), which became the management authority for the Irish state's agricultural advisory service in 1984, stated in a press release announcing the new socio-economic role how:

> It is in recognition of [the] inter-relationship between the farm business (the production unit) and the farm family (the consumption unit) that the Socio Economic Service has been established.[33]

And although female advisors would henceforth be titled socio-economic advisors (SEAs), in the eyes of the advisory service's managers they would now be seen as essentially enterprise advisors.

Just as today there is much official concern regarding the issue of succession on Irish family farms, so too in the 1980s there was much official anxiety about the way many farms were failing to manage intergenerational succession in a manner consistent with the demands of modern agriculture. The nub of the succession problem was that aging landowning men were insisting on running family farms into old age and refusing to hand over to a successor in a timely fashion. A related dimension of the problem was that delayed transfer of ownership and control was making the prospect of taking over the family farms unattractive to prospective successors. The new SEAs were given the formidable challenge of resolving the problem of farm succession.

Rather than relying on in-service training the new SEAs were obliged, as an essential part of the recalibration of their role, '… to attend a year-long course at the Department of Agricultural Extension in UCD. In many cases, female advisers with their own families had to attend month-long modules followed by intensive project work'.[34] Along with the logistical challenges this retraining entailed, the UCD course curriculum '…placed great emphasis on inheritance to limit the financial chaos and family disagreements which often resulted from farmers not making wills'.[35] As one of the first SEAs, Mary Duffy, recalled the female advisors' duties now shifted entirely from the broad home management purview to focus exclusively on 'succession, inheritance, farm transfers, wills, capital taxation, farm accounts and a certain element of social welfare, health board issues'.[36]

Once they began their work the experience of the new SEAs was that the succession issue on Irish farms was not merely widespread but also – regardless of what resources were devoted to dealing with it – highly intractable. In the face of the many obstacles to progress (a great many of which revolved around fears of financial insecurity), it soon became apparent that whatever prospects there were for better results being achievable would require a multiagency approach. Experience confirmed that it was simplistic to think that any major movement on the succession problem could be reached by sending in SEAs who – acting for all the world like shock troops – were expected to singlehandedly overcome the many difficulties. And as the SEAs struggled with the succession issue, the areas in which the women FHM advisors had excelled were neglected. Eighty years of fruitful collaborative agency between advisors and farming women, which had contributed very significantly to the development of rural Ireland, had been brought to a regrettable close.

The advent of the SEAs coincided with an important milestone in the history of the Irish agricultural advisory service. This milestone saw the service's gender-based division of labour coming to an end in the mid-1980s. The women advisors would in future be expected to perform the exact same roles within the advisory service as men. On the face of it this was long overdue progress by any yardstick. Yet – as things turned out – the gender imbalance in the advisory service remained firmly in place. While many of the women advisors made significant advances in their careers within the service, a persisting difficulty was that the proportion of women advisors did not change to achieve anything approaching gender equality.[37] Today, four decades on, the proportion of female advisors in Teagasc (within which the public advisory service has existed since 1988) continues to be approximately 20 per cent.[38] In the face of such a gender disparity the status of female advisors – even if many individual female advisors have enjoyed an increased prominence as individuals – has undoubtedly diminished both in terms of their identity and collective influence. Ever since the mid-1980s, the state's advisory service has been characterised by an effective bilateralism between a male-dominated advisory service and male farmers.

CONCLUSIONS

From early on Plunkett had been keen on involving women in the co-operative movement.[39] And, once it advanced and DATI was up and running, he looked to collaborative female agency to establish itself as a central pillar of a modernising Irish agriculture that could realistically aspire to be as progressive as any in Western Europe. But how well was Plunkett's vision regarding women's contribution to Irish agricultural modernisation realised in practice? And how much assistance did Irish farm women get from the women agricultural advisors in challenging patriarchy in Irish farming?

A strong case can be made that Irish farming women were quite centrally involved in production agriculture – both in butter-making and especially in the poultry economy – in the first half of the last century. In this early phase of development the poultry instructresses in particular made major strides in developing a collaborative agency between themselves and the women poultry-keepers that had the consequence of increasing the women producers' economic independence within patriarchal households while simultaneously establishing the egg economy as an important sector of Irish agriculture. Yet by mid-century women's involvement in poultry-keeping was rapidly disappearing as the women lost out to the new intensive large-scale poultry-keeping (mainly under male control) that came to replace dispersed small-scale poultry-keeping.[40] The consequent economic displacement experienced by many farmers' daughters came to be reflected in the high rates of female emigration from rural Ireland.

During the 1960s as the FHM service developed, the focus of the women advisors became one of adding to the agency of farm women in the household sphere. Insofar as account-keeping was viewed as women's work, women were by no means excluded entirely from the sphere of production agriculture under the FHM regime, though household-centred improvements did take centre stage.[41] A fundamental rationale of the FHM regime was that the household and family-based farming needed to come into a more dynamic and mutually supportive relationship if the family farm's potential for development was to be realised.

There were two stages in the decline of the female advisors' collective influence from the mid-1980s. First, there was their recasting as SEAs. This, given that it burdened them with the resolution of the intractable succession issue, all but guaranteed them a degree of ignominy. By helping farm women attain a degree of economic independence the early poultry instructresses were in their way building a challenge to patriarchy, but the SEAs found themselves grappling with the difficulties of a fundamentally male-centred farm succession system. Second, and with further irony, the absorption of female advisors into the wider agricultural advisory service led to a loss of identity and greater anonymity. Through the seeming introduction of full parity between men and women within the advisory service, female advisors could never collectively achieve full parity of esteem so long as they remained such a small minority of the advisory body. Owing to the success historically of the female poultry-keeping and butter-making advisors, Irish people tend to remember the state's agricultural advisory service for what it was – female-led in many of its activities and genuinely gender-mixed in its complexion. Today, however, owing to the manner the female advisors have been absorbed into the male-dominated advisory service, Irish people tend to regard the contemporary agricultural advisory service as essentially male-led and not conspicuously gender-mixed. Over the course of the twentieth century, the status of female agricultural advisors in Ireland seesawed appreciably, but ultimately it veered in a reverse direction to that taken by most women professionals in Irish public sector employment.

The trajectory of Ireland's rural development was driven appreciably upwards during the last century and at the core of this movement were interactions between female advisors and farming women. The lesson is obvious: relationships between women advisors and farming women were remarkably effective in the early decades of the last century. On this basis alone, a strong case can be made for women becoming more central to the interactions between the advisory service and farmers in rural Ireland. Such a course should not be justified for optical reasons but because it has been demonstrated historically as greatly improving the prospects of achieving a less patriarchal and more diverse Irish agriculture.

THE CONTEMPORARY COUNTRYSIDE

Emigration and Return: Limitations and Attractions of the Irish Countryside

Mary Cawley[1]

Outmigration from the countryside has been a recurrent theme in studies of Irish population change during the twentieth century and continues to attract attention.[2] For many young rural persons, especially during periods of national economic recession, emigration overseas was a pathway to employment or employment commensurate with their qualifications.[3] Emigration was also sometimes chosen to gain specialised employment, education and training or to pursue other forms of personal fulfilment.[4] Migration to towns and cities within the state was more an option for the better educated in the 1960s.[5] Stemming outmigration from the countryside by improving rural living conditions has received attention from Muintir na Tíre since its establishment as a community movement in 1937.[6]

The persisting challenge of retaining school-leavers and college graduates in areas outside commuting distance of larger centres of population and employment, was once again highlighted after the recession commencing in 2008.[7] Attracting outmigrants, including emigrants, to return to rural areas is recognised internationally as a strategy to offset demographic, economic and social decline.[8] Return migration from overseas to Ireland is documented in archival, interview and census sources; and the motivations of rural return emigrants have been explored in several case studies since the 1980s.[9] This chapter seeks to contribute to this literature by tracing – with reference to conceptions of 'structure' and 'agency' – the decision-making processes and experience of a sample of individual emigrants from emigration to return.

The research is based on the reported experience of 42 individuals who emigrated and later returned to different parts of rural Ireland between 1969 and 2012.[10] Such a timespan permits continuities and changes to be identified over time. The respondents' places of origin and return were usually the same and all had a population of less than 1500 people, and so qualified as 'aggregate rural areas' for Irish census purposes.[11] A biographical approach is followed that explores the experience of emigration from leaving Ireland to life following return. Detailed thematic analysis of replies to open-ended questions is conducted to reveal the structures within which emigrants acted as decision-making agents.[12] The decisions, as well as the experiences relating to emigration and return, emerged in a context of interrelated economic, sociocultural and environmental structures within which emigrants had varying levels of agency and influence.

The concepts of structure and agency draw on the work of sociologist Anthony Giddens and his ideas relating to 'discursive' and 'practical' consciousness underlying the motivations of individuals.[13] This approach allows us to explore 'the ways in which migrant geographies are both made by migrants, and at the same time embedded in wider social and economic structures...which in part define the conditions of their existence'.[14] A biographical approach has been suggested as a method of revealing the 'discursive' and 'practical' consciousness underpinning motivations for migration; and has been seen as requiring in-depth research to uncover the meanings of migration for individuals with reference to their wider life course.[15] The role of underlying structures in influencing decisions to migrate and return has been recognised in earlier Irish research, but the actions of emigrants and returnees within these structures have not been conceived explicitly as expressions of agency.[16] The research reported here seeks to locate the agency of the respondents within the structures influencing their reported decisions and experiences in Ireland and overseas. A brief background context to return migration to rural Ireland during my study period is provided initially. There then follows a discussion of my methodology, a profile of the sample, a presentation of my findings and a concluding section.

RETURN MIGRATION TO RURAL IRELAND IN CONTEXT

The census of population provides information (by the periods of return) relating to returned emigrants who were born in Ireland, spent one year or more residing outside the state and then returned to live here.[17] This information helps to contextualise my survey evidence. At the time of the census in 2022, returned emigrants numbered 436,541 persons (see Table 1). The numbers are likely to be an underestimate because of attrition through death in the earlier periods and repeat emigration among returnees in all periods. The more recent data are included for information purposes, although my sample relates to the years before 2016.

A broad relationship exists between the state of the Irish economy and the scale of emigration and return, with emigration increasing during years of recession and returning to Ireland being associated with periods of economic growth (see Table 1).[18] Return migration increased during the 1970s when the Irish economy was growing, increased markedly again between 1991 and 2006 as economic growth accelerated, declined between 2007 and 2011 (following recession in 2008), and increased again over the 2012–16 period (especially between 2014 and 2016) and between 2017 and 2022.[19] The United Kingdom (UK) was the principal source of returnees until 2000. Thereafter, the sources of returnees became more diverse, reflecting changing emigration destinations. During the recession beginning in 2008, emigration – reliant on short-term contracts in many cases – increased to Australia, Canada and New Zealand to meet labour deficits associated with economic growth.[20] The expiry of visas precipitated return, although some emigrants remained illegally.[21] Emigration on contracts to Middle Eastern and Asian countries also increased during these years of recession and contributes to the numbers returning from 'other countries'.[22] Return from the latter also includes church missionaries and development workers from African, Asian and South American states and the children of returning immigrants (born in Ireland).

Table 1. Census 2022: population aged one year and over, born in Ireland, usually resident and present, who lived outside the state for one year or more, by country of previous residence and years of taking up residence

	All countries	% UK	% Europe, excl. Ireland and the UK	% USA	% Australia	% Other countries	Total %
All years	436541	47.8	9.9	11.1	14.3	16.9	100.0
Pre 1951	481	76.9	2.1	5.8	0.4	14.8	100.0
1951–1960	3587	79.4	2.5	8.5	0.7	8.9	100.0
1961–1970	20005	77.1	3.2	9.6	0.8	9.3	100.0
1971–1980	37456	74.5	4.5	7.1	3.0	10.8	100.0
1981–1990	37510	58.6	8.5	12.9	7.0	13.1	100.0
1991–2000	96796	56.9	10.2	13.3	10.7	8.8	100.0
2001–2006	55401	42.8	11.3	15.0	20.4	10.4	100.0
2007–2011	36633	37.3	12.6	10.8	23.4	15.9	100.0
2012–2016	58938	32.2	11.3	9.3	25.3	21.9	100.0
2017–2019	40822	33.1	12.4	9.6	18.2	26.7	100.0
2020–2022	25400	33.0	14.5	9.8	14.9	27.7	100.0
2017–2022	66222	33.1	13.2	9.7	16.9	27.1	100.0
Not stated	23512	28.5	6.2	6.1	9.3	50.0	100.0
Total number	436541	208666	43208	48246	62511	73910	

Source: Central Statistics Office, Census 2022 summary results, FY018, last updated 30/05/2023 11:00:00. The CSO suggests that the relatively high proportion of 'not stated' from 'other countries' arises from a possible misinterpretation of the question.

European countries increased in importance from 1981 as sources of return, reflecting their roles as emigrant destinations for students, graduates and workers more generally, as new markets became available through Ireland's membership of the now European Union (EU).[23] Emigration to the USA declined during the 1950s, except in 1957–8,[24] but increased during the 1980s when many emigrants became undocumented.[25] Some undocumented emigrants had their position regularised in the late-1980s and the early-1990s through visas introduced via lotteries, known as Donnelly and Morrison visas respectively.[26] Returning increased during the 1990s, and in the first half of the 2000s, in response to economic growth. Since the attacks on the World Trade Towers and the Pentagon on 9 September 2001, emigration to the USA has been strictly regulated and monitored and severe penalties apply for breaches of the regulations.[27] Fixed-term visas have become more common which contributed to return.

The reasons for return migration to rural Ireland, as documented in several studies since the 1980s, point to family and societal factors outranking economic factors, although economic considerations enabled return to take place in most cases. Based on a large-scale study in eight western counties in the early 1980s, George Gmelch queried the economic model of return.[28] Similarly, Fiona McGrath's study of the impacts of returnees in Achill

Island in the late 1980s revealed a prioritisation of social reasons for return,[29] as did research by Richard Jones a decade later on the links between new industrialisation and return migration to County Mayo.[30] Using a life-course approach with a sample of 30- and 40-year-old returnees to southern and western counties during the 1990s and the early 2000s, Caitríona Ní Laoire found that return was framed within classical counter-urbanisation discourses, in which conceptions of a rural idyll, family and kinship relationships and a desire to bring up children in Ireland were interlinked.[31] Maura Farrell and her colleagues illustrated the complexities associated with more recent return, using County Roscommon as a context.[32] The present author and Stephen Galvin found evidence of both continuities and changes over an extended period in reasons for return migration to a wide range of rural areas.[33] The evidence reported below extends the discussion of motivations for emigration and return with reference to conceptions of 'structure' and 'agency'.

METHODOLOGY

In this study university geography students, studying migration as part of an academic module, interviewed 42 returned emigrants in 2013.[34] Statistical representativeness was not sought, but the study did seek to capture experiences of emigration and return over time across a range of age groups. The students interviewed a family member who had migrated from the Irish state as an adult, lived overseas for one year or more, and returned permanently or for a period of one year or more before migrating again (and possible returning again). The one-year provision follows the internationally agreed definition of migration.[35] All the interviewees had emigrated from and returned to settlements with fewer than 1500 persons.[36] In most cases these settlements were the place of origin and the experience of living there before emigration and after return could be compared. The interview schedule, which was provided for the students, profiled the social and employment attributes of interviewees at the time of emigration, while overseas, and upon return. Open questions queried, in the respondent's perceived order of priority, the motivations for emigration, the experience of living overseas, the reasons for return and the experience of residing in a rural area again. Transnational relationships with Irish people overseas and at home were further addressed, including return visits.[37] And details of repeat migration and repeat return were recorded.[38]

Most respondents gave several reasons as influencing their decision-making and some elaborated at considerable length. Their responses were analysed using an inductive thematic approach that involved in-depth reading and rereading of the text; and the linking of motivations and experiences – and the contexts in which they occurred – to attributes of individual respondents. This procedure allowed underlying 'structures' within which the respondents' actions and experiences took place, and the 'agency' they possessed within these structures, to be identified.[39] Three broad structures emerged as impacting over the various stages of an individual's emigration history – the economic, the sociocultural and the environmental. The environmental structure includes aspects of the natural and the built environments.[40] Responses indicated that the respondents exercised varying forms and degrees of agency within the three broad structures.

RETURNEE PROFILE

The sample consists of 29 men and 13 women (69 per cent and 31 per cent, respectively). Whereas the male-female ratio among returnees in the national census is usually more evenly balanced, the larger number of men sampled is explicable in part by access to a respondent who met the criteria for being an emigrant. In addition, more than one-third of the men were employed in the construction sector which responds well to economic recovery and to which emigrants are known to return.[41] Some women who left a rural area returned to a town or city and are therefore omitted here. Respondents' names were not sought, specific locations are not named and numerical identifiers are used in the text to ensure anonymity.

Table 2. Rural returned emigrants: age, reported conjugal status, education and employment at time of migration by gender

	Male	Female	Total
*Age group	**Number (%)**	**Number (%)**	**Number (%)**
<20	10 (34.6)	4 (30.8)	14 (33.3)
20–24	13 (44.8)	8 (61.5)	21 (50.0)
25–29	5 (17.2)	1 (7.7)	6 (14.3)
35+	1 (3.4)	0 (0.0)	1 (2.4)
Marital status			
Single	21 (72.4)	10 (76.9)	31 (73.8)
Married/in a relationship	8 (27.6)	3 (23.1)	11 (26.2)
Education			
Primary	3 (10.3)	2 (15.4)	5 (11.9)
Secondary	12 (41.4)	8 (61.5)	20 (47.6)
Third level	10 (34.5)	3 (23.1)	13 (31.0)
Postgraduate	2 (6.9)	0 (0.0)	2 (4.8)
Other	2(6.9)	0 (0.0)	
*Employment			
Employed	9 (31.0)	4 (30.8)	13 (31.0)
Unemployed	18 (62.1)	6 (46.1)	24 (57.1)
Student	2 (6.9)	3 (23.1)	5 (11.9)
Total	**29 (100.0)**	**13 (100.0)**	**42 (100.0)**

Source: survey data
*There were no respondents aged 30–34 years or homemakers.

Most emigrants moved overseas in their late teens and early twenties when there is greater freedom to migrate (see Table 2).[42] They emigrated within support networks that included a sibling, a friend or friends or a spouse or partner. Eight (28 per cent) of the men and three (23 per cent) of the women reported being married or in a relationship; two of whom emigrated with a spouse or partner and a child or children. Seven (24 per cent) of the men and three (23 per cent) of the women, who migrated alone, were joining a relative or friend, pursuing an educational course, or training as a nurse. The secondary and higher levels of education reported point to relatively high levels of 'human capital' among respondents (see Table 2). Holders of a primary education only emigrated before access to free second level education became available in 1967.[43] Although there were some long-term emigrants who were absent for several decades, the average period of absence of 6.4 years (6.3 and 6.5 years for men and women, respectively) reflects the presence of one-year visa holders in the sample. The timing of emigration and return reflects responses to the state of the national economy, as evident from Table 1. Emigration was highest during the recessionary years of 1981–1990 and 2008–2012, and return was especially common in the 2001–2006 and 2011–2016 periods as the economy recovered.

Migration between countries is subject to regulation, although compliance is not universal. The regulatory structures providing respondents with access to labour markets at different junctures include the common travel area with the UK, membership of the EU and visa-based recruitment to such countries as the USA, Australia and Canada in line with labour market demands. Twenty different locations were involved in all, with London followed by Boston, Melbourne and Sydney being of greatest importance. The main destinations suggest path-dependent emigration to major cities in Britain and the USA with which long-established associations exist based on diasporic networks of family and friends;[44] and to Australian cities with which links were re-established during the most recent recession. These transnational links provided information about employment opportunities and were a source of support on arrival, notably for skilled and semi-skilled emigrants in Britain.[45] Longer-distance emigrants to Australia and the professionally-qualified were more likely to use formal recruitment agencies and advertisements. Migration for educational and training purposes took place to Britain, through special reciprocal arrangements and recruitment programmes for nurses in the past, and to the EU through the Erasmus-Socrates programme.[46]

FROM EMIGRATION TO RETURN

Emigration took place both from employment and unemployment,[47] but 18 (62 per cent) of the men and six (46 per cent) of the women reported being unemployed at the time of migration, notably during the recession of the 1980s and between 2008 and 2012 (see Table 2). Employed people worked primarily in retail and wholesale activities, hospitality (bar tenders) and included one woman teacher. A depressed economy operated as a severe constraint on income and career prospects, as illustrated by the reasons given for emigrating – being unemployed and seeking work, seeking employment more suited to a qualification and gaining work experience. References to work experience were underpinned by the benefits that were anticipated to arise on returning at some stage in the future. Being overqualified for the position held and feeling undervalued also disposed employed individuals to emigrate and, following the onset of recession in 2008, there were references to being 'fed up with the gloom and doom'. Emigration was further influenced by family obligations as well as by personal needs and desires – supporting a parental family in the case of a young man who emigrated to California in 1983 (2013R#42) – and supporting a wife and children in the case of a 41-year-old man who moved alone to Canada in 2011 on a one-year visa (2013R#34).

Men and women, who emigrated in different decades, expressed a sense of agency in accounting for their emigration as a means of securing employment, or more appropriate employment, and of travelling abroad and learning about other cultures.[48] As conveyed by a 24-year-old unemployed woman who emigrated from County Longford to work in a bar in London in 2005 (and later trained as a nurse), the prospect of escape from rural, and perhaps family strictures, was present in a desire for 'independence'. This woman had friends and a place to stay and wished 'to become more independent, travel yet be close to family and wanted change and a faster paced life' (2013R#08). When students sought access to a particular university course or training in Britain or applied to participate in the EU Erasmus-Socrates programme, opportunities for personal advancement were at play.

The transnational social milieux emigrants lived within while overseas were sources of psychological and practical support. Interaction with Irish people at work and in pubs and Irish clubs and playing sports was the norm in all time periods for both men and women.[49] Except when precluded by long distances and one-year visas, regular visits home took place: 11 (86 per cent) of the women and 16 (55 per cent) of the men visited at least once annually.[50] Social contact was maintained with family and friends through media that changed over time from letters and telephone calls to texting, social media and video calls. Information received through these channels, about economic conditions in Ireland and employment opportunities conferred agency around the decision to return.

Apart from students who gained qualifications, training and experience, the respondents (all of whom were employed while overseas) described the economic security of being in employment – or employment commensurate with qualifications and a regular income that improved their standard of living – in terms that conveyed empowering agency. The occupational positions of respondents mostly depended on having professional qualifications or skills (such as in engineering, quantity surveying, computer operating, hotel management, marketing, teaching and craft skills). Unskilled labourers tended to move to unskilled work, while non-graduate women migrants predominantly found employment at various levels in the hospitality sector in restaurants, hotels and bars. Career advancement was reported in several instances through the acquisition of degrees, specialist training and qualifications. By contrast, there was some evidence of emigration being disempowering for some – through homesickness, as reported by two young men, and through difficulties experienced in 'making ends meet' in London in 2011, as reported by a labourer (2013R#10).

Access to city-based consumer and transport services and recreational opportunities were described positively as conferring new forms of agency in the emigrants' daily lives. More clement weather conditions in Australia were appreciated for the associated lifestyle. There was, however, also some nostalgia expressed for the tranquillity of the Irish countryside and a sense of loss in frequent references to city life being 'busier' and 'noisier' than the countryside. Nevertheless, some emigrants like the 24-year-old woman, referred to above, enjoyed a 'completely different pace of life, [a] huge contrast to rural life, [and] great facilities in comparison to the countryside' (2013#R08).

Even though economic and lifestyle benefits were reported, a sense of dislocation and anomie – indicative of somewhat more restricted agency than found in familiar community settings at home – emerged in references to large city anonymity and to missing family, friends and a familiar community where one was known.[51] A 19-year-old construction worker, who emigrated to Coventry from County Mayo in 1969, observed how 'the people were not as friendly' (2013R#11). Almost 40 years later a 26-year-old man from County Galway who emigrated to Sydney and knew 'a lot of people from home', reported a similar sense of anomie in 2008: 'Everyone knows you in rural Ireland' (2013R#29). This man also reported having to adjust to 'a different social and cultural context' in pubs and nightclubs. By contrast, a married woman with a family referred to being 'very happy' living in an Irish community in London, which 'made you feel as if you were at home at times' (2013R#30). More generally, the ethnic diversity of a large city represented a major social and cultural change for many emigrants from rural Ireland until the 1990s.

In a reversal of motivations for emigrating, most respondents accounted for their decision to return primarily in the context of social aspirations, commitments and obligations and, secondly, and consistent with previous studies, to the existence of economic opportunities. For most men and women in their late twenties, thirties and forties, the decision to return was framed with reference to stage in the life cycle and the nuclear family. Key events here included expecting the birth of a child, marriage, planning a family or having young children whom it was desired to raise in Ireland. Social and environmental considerations were also found combined in references to 'settling down' and to getting 'away from the hustle and bustle of city life' (2013R#08), sentiments suggesting a transition from the city as a place of youth and freedom to a rural environment as a place of responsibility and permanence. Six (21 per cent) of the men and four (31 per cent) of the women returned with a spouse or partner and seven (24 per cent) and three (23 per cent), respectively, with a spouse or partner and a child or children. Aspirations were expressed to have children grow up in proximity to the extended family, as the emigrants had themselves experienced. Care of family members influenced return in two instances: a young female shop assistant returned from London for one year in 1980 to care for an ill relative (2013R#24) and a mechanic, who migrated to London in 1972, returned in 1981 with his wife to care for his parents (2013R#35).[52]

Although often mentioned after family and societal factors, clearly periods of employment-creating economic growth in Ireland facilitated return for the majority. Some respondents referred explicitly to having an offer of employment as the economy recovered – establishing a business in two cases and taking over a family accommodation business in another. An electrician, who spent two years in Sydney, explained his return with his girlfriend in 2010 as being due to the 'financial security' of 'inheriting property and taking over a farm' (2013R#04). Similarly, two other men referred to returning to 'take over the family farm', one (a middle-aged man) returning with his family from London in 1992 (2013#R36) and the other (a young man) returning in 2012 having worked on an Australian farm for a year (2013#R32). There was only one retiree in the sample; this man retired to a farm with his wife. Young people in their twenties who returned to unemployment on the expiry of a work visa usually lived in the parental home, to save on accommodation costs, while seeking employment or emigrating again later.

The desire to live again in the countryside as a motivation for returning was usually listed after social and economic factors. Sentiments of escape from the pressures of urban life to a more tranquil countryside were present in phrases like 'tired of hectic city life', although some returnees reported difficulty in readapting to a slower pace of life. The countryside as a positive environment for children was present in the motivations of respondents with families.[53] Comparisons were made also between the remembered benefits of education in a small school with the experience overseas. The emigrant to California, encountered earlier, emigrated and returned twice in response to employment opportunities. On the second occasion, when he and his family returned in 2008, he cited as one of his reasons a belief that 'the Irish education system outweighed that of its American counterpart for our children' (2013R#42). A desire for their children to be educated through Irish was of concern to a family from a Gaeltacht area, who returned from London when employment became available in 1993 (2013R#37).

The decision of those in their twenties and early thirties to return was usually influenced by factors such as the completion of a period of study or training and the termination of a work visa. These individuals reported looking forward to reconnecting with family and friends and to having feelings of isolation if friends had emigrated. They included returnees who, for lack of employment and a desire to travel and live overseas, emigrated a second time to Australia, Canada, Britain and the USA. One 20-year-old man returned from the USA in 2011, on the termination of a one-year visa, lived with his parents for a year before applying for a visa to emigrate to Perth where he had friends and knew there was work available.[54] The knowledge and experience gained through emigration emerges as conferring agency and confidence among repeat emigrants. Such increased mobility was facilitated by cheaper airfares, the use of communication technologies in maintaining contact with family in Ireland and social contacts overseas. Six of the 42 respondents returned a second time for employment and social reasons. Whether repeat emigrants will return permanently is likely to depend on their longer-term employment prospects in Ireland and overseas and the personal relationships they form.

Both men and women reported family and community life as the features most enjoyed on return, thus pointing to the continuing relevance of this aspect of the rural idyll as a motivating force. A newly-qualified nurse who returned to County Wicklow in 2012 spoke of 'The feeling of familiarity and belonging somewhere. Everyone knew who you were' (2013R#39). Yet this woman also experienced a loss of privacy and independence on moving back to live with her parents while seeking work. Other tensions between the imagined idyllic features of living in the countryside – in proximity to family and community – and other aspects of everyday life were also recorded. During a period of economic growth, between 1998 and 2007, visible signs of wealth in new dwellings and new cars were viewed as signs of advancement but were associated as well with a lack of time for others. A loss of friendliness was associated with the settlement of non-locals in new housing developments in villages and towns. Friends left overseas were missed. A woman who returned from London to employment in the hospitality sector in County Longford in 2001– so as to have a 'strong social environment in which to raise my child' – observed extensive changes after 18 years' absence: 'The people in Ireland were less friendly upon return', she observed, 'there was a lot more money around, there were more job opportunities…Ireland was more multicultural…different types of cuisine were available' (2013R#01).

Change in the built environment further challenged remembered images of rural life, especially housing estate developments in villages and towns during the early 2000s and their unoccupied state a decade later. A woman who returned from London in 2002 to start a hospitality business described her County Galway village as having 'become more like a town' (2013R#20). Poor levels of service provision by comparison with a city – including public transport and recreational facilities and higher food costs – occasioned a loss of agency among returnees where living standards were concerned. Respondents with families and employment proved to be better able to adapt to these realities.

CONCLUSION

Our in-depth thematic analysis of the text of interviews with 42 returned rural emigrants has revealed underlying interrelated economic, sociocultural and environmental structures within which decisions to emigrate and return have taken place over four decades. Many respondents experienced enhanced agency on moving to employment commensurate with their qualifications in a city environment where they enjoyed access to improved services. Some also gained qualifications and experience that were used on returning to rural Ireland. A loss of social agency – arising from living at a distance from family, friends and a familiar social field – was reported also, although this was sometimes alleviated by contact with Irish people in the destination area, with family and friends at home, and through visiting home. The tranquillity and slower pace of life of a rural environment were missed. Some aspects of the desired rural idyll were recaptured on return but a loss of agency was also conveyed, associated with the changing social composition of the community and with reduced levels of services. Certain policy implications therefore arise from the findings for attracting emigrants back to the countryside.

Even if respondents prioritised social over economic factors in explaining their decision to return to live in their area of origin, it was nonetheless the economy – and the access to employment it provided – that facilitated return of those of working age, except where inheritance or care of a farm, investment to start a business or the termination of a visa or educational course were involved. The national economy emerged as being of particular importance for those seeking employment in construction, public, retail and hospitality services, all areas closely linked to general economic conditions. Broadly speaking, investment and supports for productive activities at regional and local levels are clearly relevant in facilitating rural return migration. A deep attachment to family and community in a familiar social milieu was highly influential in the decision to return and remain. Yet some of the expectations relating to the familiarity and friendliness of the local community were not fulfilled upon returning. A willingness to adapt to change was required of returnees, but what can also be concluded is that local communities would need to incorporate new immigrants and returnees in a more proactive way than hitherto has been the case. Returnees may have recaptured some of the peace and quiet of a rural environment that most of them desired, but large-scale housing estates in small villages and continuing poor service infrastructure were sources of disappointment. Clearly, local communities and planning authorities have roles to play in protecting the character of small villages and towns so that they are attractive to returnees whose presence will, in turn, contribute to improved service demand and supply.

The Survival of Rural Ireland

Mary E. Daly

The death of rural Ireland has been foretold on countless occasions over the past century. Yet in 2022, according to the World Bank, 36 per cent of the Irish population was resident in rural areas, which was by far the highest percentage in the EU.[1] Between 2016 and 2022 the population of rural Ireland increased by 2 per cent,[2] which was lower than the total population increase of 8.5 per cent but continuing evidence of rural vitality. The rural population is now back to the 1951 figure – reversing the losses inflicted by mid-century emigration. In 2022, for the first time since the Famine of the 1840s, every Irish county recorded a rise in population, and fewer District Electoral Districts recorded a decline.[3] There were over half a million more people living in the Irish countryside in 2016 than in 1966; over the same period the population of rural France fell by over four million and similar declines were common in other European countries.

In 1961 the official discourse around the census was that we were turning the corner, the rate of population decline and emigration rate were falling! But, in an indication of changing expectations, the commentary on the 2011 census noted that while the urban population increased by 10.6 per cent the rural population *only* grew by 4.6 per cent! That is not to say that all is rosy in the Irish countryside. There are potential threats on the horizon, but it is important to draw a contrast between the past 50 years and the previous century. Rural Ireland is not frozen in time; it is not, nor should it be regarded as a heritage zone. It is home to living people, and like any living entity it is subject to change, and it must evolve in order to survive. Some of these changes are desirable, others present difficulties. Survival strategies in the past among family farmers centred almost exclusively on emigration – sending non-inheriting children away, so that one son could inherit the farm and marry. An alternative survival strategy, favoured by various political movements recommended land redistribution and the creation of small holdings that could never guarantee an adequate livelihood. Modern survival strategies are different, because the links between rural Ireland and farming, while still extremely important, are weaker.

In the late-eighteenth and early-nineteenth century much of Irish manufacturing was carried out in the countryside, especially in the northern half of the island – an area that included most of Connacht and parts of North Leinster plus Ulster. Before the Famine domestic textiles employed hundreds of thousands of women and men in the countryside. Many smallholders survived on a combination of cash income from spinning – which was earned by the women or from migratory labour, and food and fuel that derived from the smallholding and a nearby bog. Most of these rural industries vanished in the mid-nineteenth century, and efforts by the Congested Districts Board to revive them had only a marginal impact. By the beginning of the twentieth century rural Ireland had come to be identified with agriculture, as if agriculture and rural Ireland was the same thing.

On the eve of the Famine rural Ireland was dominated numerically by landless labourers and those with farm holdings of less than five acres; political and economic power rested with the landed gentry. Farmers who had a middling standard of living and could survive wholly on the output of their farms, were in the minority. Cormac Ó Gráda estimated that in 1841 there were approximately 50,000 'rich' farmers, 100,000 comfortable farmers and 250,000 'family' farmers. All categories of farmer were significantly outnumbered by the one million plus labourers and 300,000 poor peasants.[4] By the 1920s the proportion of the population who were landless labourers or holding plots of less than five acres, had fallen sharply; landlords no longer owned most of the land and they had lost their social and political influence. The family farm – owned and farmed by a farmer – usually male, with the assistance of family members and an occasional young farm servant or labourer – dominated rural economy and society.

Much of the literature written about rural Ireland in the early and mid-twentieth century presents a picture of continuity, almost timelessness, and/or decay and decline. Conrad Arensberg's description of the family farm in 1930s Clare, with its 'west room' to which he accords a quasi-spiritual status, a domestic shrine – suggests that this type of house and its artefacts had existed for many generations, yet the three-room house that he describes and the bric-a-brac collected in the 'west room' only became common in the later nineteenth century.[5] Representations of rural Ireland from the 1950s onwards are increasingly of a society and culture in crisis, because of the 'flight of the girls' and the rural bachelors who were incapable of summoning up the courage to marry. Some accounts suggest that these bachelors were sexually frustrated and suffering from mental illness.[6] Pathological images were dominant, and they continued to predominate in a number of studies published in the late 1960s and 1970s, by which time the population decline was slowing, even reversing.[7]

It was also commonly suggested by many social commentators and politicians that if rural Ireland declined, if small farmers disappeared then Irish society was in peril, and the solutions to this malaise were to privilege rural society over urban life, keep women from emigrating so that they might marry some of those ageing bachelors. There were also repeated prophecies that large swathes of land, owned by the ageing bachelors or by emigrants, would come on the market – with what consequences it is unclear. Rural decline was not a uniquely Irish phenomenon. In the mid and late-twentieth century nostalgia for rural life was common, as was the mass exodus of younger people.[8] *Irish Times* journalist John Healy's description of the market in Charlestown where farmers sold cabbage plants and turnips and 'fat women waddled in with wicker baskets of eggs and rolls of butter',[9] is an example of such nostalgia; he does not reflect on how little the men or women would have earned from this weekly market, or the physical effort involved for the 'fat women' walking some distance while carrying these heavy baskets.

If rural Ireland was in terminal decline by the 1960s, why has the population increased substantially over the past 50 years? Part of the answer of course, is that the population of Ireland has increased, and I would argue that the health and well-being of rural Ireland is *inextricably* linked with that of the overall economy and society – so it is important to try and avoid simplistic urban/rural contestation. In the remainder of this chapter I want to look at the following issues: demography; education, land ownership and farming, social conditions and gender, before moving on to some reflections on current threats and opportunities.

DEMOGRAPHY AND EMPLOYMENT

Some of the issues highlighted in the studies that were carried out in the mid-twentieth century still apply – the rural population is older, there are more people, especially more women living alone. The dependency rate is higher in the countryside, with more young and old people, and fewer in the active age groups, but the disparity is not massive: 35.7 per cent dependency in rural areas in 2011, against 31.4 per cent in urban areas. The gender imbalance has also moderated; while young women are more likely to leave rural Ireland in their 'twenties, many return and settle there – presumably marrying in their 'thirties. The Central Statistics Office has described this as 'nesting'. In 1966 – there were 892 women per 1000 men in rural Ireland; in 2016 the figure was 983.[10] Again the image of rural Ireland as populated by elderly, never-married men and fewer women does not apply. The highest proportions of single people aged over 40 live in the cities. In all the Irish cities more than one-third of adults over 40 years of age are single, but there are only three counties – Sligo, Mayo and Kerry – where more than one-quarter of adults over 40 are single. So a lot has changed – and I would argue for the better.

Membership of the EEC/EU has been critical. The lowest recorded population for rural Ireland was in 1971, on the eve of Ireland joining the EEC. Ireland joined the EEC for a very clear reason – to gain a secure market and good prices for farm produce, as opposed to being subject to the uncertainties of depending on Britain, where the rules could change at short notice, and rarely for the better. Such a world may be re-emerging, in a new but happily attenuated form under Brexit. During the 1960s as Irish living standards rose, a growing share of taxes went to support farm prices and farm incomes; by 1970 the agricultural estimate, which included price supports, was the largest item in the Irish Budget.[11] EEC membership lifted that burden from Irish taxpayers. But in 1973 EEC membership appeared to carry some real dangers for rural Ireland, because the recently adopted Mansholt Plan (named after the EEC Agriculture Commissioner) envisaged a major culling of small farms across the EEC, with assistance being directed towards farms that were deemed capable of development.

The Mansholt Plan identified three types of farm – those that were commercially viable; development farms with the potential to become viable, which would be given substantial assistance, and 'others', whose days were numbered. The majority of Irish farms, and the overwhelming majority of western farms, fell into the third category. So perhaps it is not surprising that when Mansholt visited Ireland before Irish accession to the EEC he was greeted with posters saying 'Go Home Cromwell'.[12] For the same reason it is not surprising that the western seaboard was the area that recorded the highest vote against EEC membership in the 1972 referendum on membership. Between 1974 and 1982 only 23 per cent of participating Irish farms were classified as 'development farms', and only 4 per cent as commercial farms; more than 70 per cent were classified as 'others' a description that included farms on low incomes with little or no capacity to raise them.[13] In the event the

Mansholt Plan was scaled back and greater sensitivity was shown to smaller farms and the wider environment – with the Rural Environment Protection Scheme (REPS) introduced in 1994 being of major social benefit to rural Ireland. The EU's Common Agricultural Policy (CAP) created 'an agricultural welfare state';[14] and despite many predictions that expenditure under the CAP would be seriously reduced or even discontinued, it has continued to play this role. The accession of eastern European countries, where agriculture continues to account for a significant share of employment and national income, has helped to ensure its continuation into the twenty-first century.

The Irish welfare system has also supported the survival of smaller farms, because it has enabled small farmers to earn an income, while also collecting benefits. This meant that there was less of a distinction than in cities and towns, between those who were employed and those unemployed. This is a matter with considerable contemporary relevance, given the debates in many countries about the merits of a Universal Basic Income that would provide every person with a basic income, irrespective of whether they are in work or not in order to reduce the segregation and stereotyping associated with welfare dependency.[15] Rural Ireland may offer some relevant medium and long-term evidence for this debate.

Throughout the 1970s and 1980s the removal of protective tariffs and quotas, because of EEC membership, resulted in the collapse in many of Ireland's established industries, which had developed from the 1930s under protection. Car assembly plants, textile plants, shoe factories and many other traditional industries disappeared, and most of the job losses were in the cities, especially Cork and Dublin. By contrast IDA policy at that time was designed to encourage foreign direct investment to set up plants in areas outside Dublin, with consequent benefits to rural areas. The potential beneficial links between industry and rural Ireland, including farming, were first identified in the 1960s in Lucey and Kaldor's study of Tubbercurry and Scariff. They noted the benefits of the additional earnings in the adjacent rural communities. A sizeable share of the additional earnings was invested in farm equipment and fertiliser, and 'generally [that] their farms are better managed'; household spending and living standards rose; most of the money was spent locally, and the population increased.[16]

The 1972 IDA plan set industrial job targets for 172 towns and villages (excluding the mid-west region, which was associated with Shannon) which while not fully achieved, brought substantial numbers of industrial jobs to provincial Ireland.[17] This new wave of industry, often in foreign-owned firms, required farmers to rethink their attitudes towards factory jobs, which they had traditionally regarded as low-status occupations. In the early sixties farmers living near the Shannon industrial estate continued to have ambitions for their children to work as Gardaí or in the civil service, despite the fact that nearby factories were recruiting workers.[18] But Hannan discovered that by the late sixties, the hostility that farmers in Cavan had previously shown towards a son working in a factory was dwindling, though they remained reluctant to have their daughters take factory jobs, apparently because it might damage their marriage prospects.[19] The changing nature of industrial work helped make female jobs more acceptable; requirements to wear lab coats or protective headgear, which were common in pharmaceutical plants, and in factories that assembled computers and other advanced technological equipment, changed the image of factories in a positive manner. However, in the late twentieth and the twenty-first centuries the major expansion in employment has been in the services sector, especially IT and financial services, which has resulted in a major concentration of new employment in large cities. This has been a global phenomenon, not confined to Ireland.[20] Nevertheless between 1991 and 2011, when the Irish population rose by 30 per cent, the population living in rural areas increased by 44 per cent.[21]

The global financial crisis, beginning in 2008, resulted in a 10 per cent decline in Ireland's real GNP. Almost one-quarter of the labour force were either underemployed or unemployed. The impact was most acute on the construction sector, which accounted for 25 per cent of GNP in 2006, and only 6 per cent in 2012. Construction provided substantial off-farm employment for men in rural Ireland, especially those without third-level qualifications. Between 2009 and 2015, net emigration among Irish citizens reached 143,000. While many emigrants came from remote rural areas, a survey showed that 62 per cent of Irish emigrants aged between 25 and 34 had a third-level qualification, compared with 47 per cent of the overall population in that age bracket. Glynn et al. suggest that those who they describe as 'living in marginal situations' may lack the skills necessary to migrate in the modern world.[22] So for many without qualifications, some living in remote rural areas, the primary impact of the global crisis was experienced through unemployment, rather than emigration.[23]

EDUCATION AND LIFE CHANCES

Improved access to education, including a widespread expectation that rural children would participate in higher education has been one of the most significant changes in rural life over the past 50 years. In the early 1960s most children in rural Ireland attended one-teacher schools that lacked running water, sanitation and occasionally even electricity.[24] There was no entitlement to free post-primary education until 1968. Although county councils offered scholarships to secondary schools they were limited in number and highly competitive, and the syllabus for these scholarships meant that rural children attending a one–or two-teacher school were at a serious disadvantage. Geography was as important as family income and social class in determining who could participate in secondary schooling. Families who lived at a longer distance than a bicycle ride from a middling or larger town with a convent secondary school or a Christian Brothers school – where school fees were low – were effectively denied secondary schooling, unless they could afford boarding school fees. Secondary schools were not randomly scattered throughout provincial towns. There were 237 secondary schools for girls but only 175 for boys. Smaller towns with a population of less than 1,500 were less likely to have a secondary school for boys: there were 140 schools for girls in small towns and rural areas, but only 85 that accepted boys. Households living in counties Cavan, Monaghan and Donegal had the least opportunities for secondary education: the prospect of a Donegal Catholic teenager attending secondary school was one-third that of children in Cork, Kerry and Clare.[25]

Secondary schools were more plentiful south of a line from Dublin to Galway. The northern bishops were reluctant to admit schools run by male religious orders, including the Christian Brothers into their dioceses, lest they reduce the number of future seminarians,[26] but there were also fewer convent schools – perhaps reflecting a weaker Catholic middle-class/strong farmer class. Access to vocational schools that were owned and controlled by the local authority was also uneven; some counties, notably Longford, developed a network of vocational schools that offered continuing education and training in skills; other counties were less active. Lack of access to post-primary education for rural children only appears to have become a political issue in the early 1960s with communities campaigning for a secondary or vocational school. In 1962 the Inter-Departmental Committee on the Problems of Small Western Farms recommended that comprehensive schools – offering a combination of academic and practical education (including agriculture and rural science) – should be established in remote rural areas as part of a wider plan to save small western farms. The proposal gained the support of Minister for Education, Patrick Hillery and Taoiseach Seán Lemass, who suggested that it could be the blueprint for national post-primary education. These plans for comprehensive schools were superseded by Donogh O'Malley's 1966 announcement of free secondary-schooling within 12 months, to be delivered by the existing schools, both secondary and vocational.[27]

The introduction of free secondary education was of greatest benefit to rural households because it included a comprehensive school transport scheme. The bicycle sheds attached to many secondary schools emptied in 1967. The proportion of farming children aged 14–19 that was in full-time schooling more than doubled between 1961 and 1971; by the 1990s over 90 per cent were completing the Leaving Certificate a figure that is comparable to professional families. The coming of Regional Technical Colleges, now Institutes of Technology or Technological Universities, was also transformative because they demystified higher education for many families by bringing it to a familiar nearby town. There are pockets of rural Ireland with below-average retention rates in second-level schooling, but this is not a rural/urban issue – indeed the greatest problems in terms of participation in education are found in the cities, not in the countryside.

In 2012 the county with the highest proportion of 18–20-years-olds in third-level education was Leitrim, with 61 per cent, closely followed by Mayo, Galway, Clare, Monaghan and Sligo – all these counties except Galway are predominantly rural. This high participation rate is not the norm in rural communities elsewhere. Sweden for example regards the task of persuading young people in rural communities to participate in higher education as a major challenge.[28] The high participation rate presents a different challenge for Ireland: how to ensure third-level education does not mean mass migration away from rural Ireland.

CHANGING GENDER ROLES

Gender is crucial not just to the survival, but the success of the family farm, and of rural Ireland more widely. Conservative commentators such as Aodh de Blacam or the playwright M. J. Molloy, who claimed in the 1950s that the 'flight of the girls' threatened the survival of rural Ireland were correct, though their wish to keep 'girls' in domestic settings, away from urban life was not the appropriate way to achieve their goal. Rural Ireland was traditionally dominated by men, though within the home women were extremely powerful, and some of the social tensions relating to the 'flight of the girls' reflected the fact that rural women were more likely to remain in school, and to secure off-farm jobs than rural men. Despite the rhetoric condemning emigration and urban life, Irish rural families realised that departing the land offered their daughters a better future than life as an unmarried, spinster on a small farm, caring for elderly parents, bachelor brothers or a married brother's children.

Women who had lived and worked in London, Dublin or Galway city, might be reluctant to marry and settle back on the farm – cohabiting with a mother-in-law, in a home that lacked running water and other modern amenities. Caitriona Clear reported that one rural wife mentioned '"no modern conveniences"…as a discomfort on a par with living with in-laws and constant child-bearing with hard work'.[29]

The 1960s and the 1970s were the decades when many of the disadvantages of rural life were alleviated. By 1971, 90 per cent of rural homes had electricity; by the end of the decade even the outlying areas of the Black Valley in Kerry and Ballycroy in Mayo, were connected to the national grid.[30] Caitriona Clear quotes one Roscommon farmer's wife, who explained, 'When Rural Electrification came it became much easier'.[31] In 1961 only 12 per cent of rural homes had running water on tap in the house, and fewer still had a bathroom. The lack of running water meant no washing machines, and more onerous cleaning and cooking. Government measures to extend piped water supplies in rural areas were strongly opposed by the National Farmers' Association, and by the Minister for Agriculture, Patrick Smith, because of the additional charges on local rates. Some farmers suggested that their needs could be met by a tap in the yard. In this instance however the Irish Countrywomen's Association led a strong campaign, promoting the benefits of having water on tap – a campaign that was strongly endorsed by Seán Lemass. Yet in 1971, 42 per cent of rural homes were without a water supply – even an outdoor tap – and fewer than one-third had a fixed bath.[32] A pilot study conducted in county Galway and published in 1969 showed that areas with piped water and sewerage were less subject to population decline; the survey revealed that people viewed access to shops, doctors and social amenities as less important.[33]

Having a fixed bath and running water was a strong indication of overall living conditions in a home. A survey of farm homes in the west of Ireland in the 1970s by Damian Hannan and Louise Katsiouni showed that homes with piped water generally had a bathroom, a gas or electric cooker and a television; homes with a washing machine tended to have a separate sitting room. Farm houses with modern amenities were generally home to younger couples, where the wife might have worked outside farming and lived in cities or towns before marriage.[34] By the 1970s de Valera's dream of a second home on the farm was becoming the reality, as young farming couples were building their own house, supported by a local authority grant and/or mortgage, and often using the plans in *Bungalow Bliss*.[35] The emergence of homes with modern kitchens, bathrooms, central heating and a modern living room – houses that looked similar to those found in suburbia – except that they had larger gardens, were generally one-storey and had larger kitchens – or a back kitchen/utility room, was critical in persuading women to stay in rural Ireland, or more precisely move to rural Ireland, or return there to marry and raise a family.

Social life, or rather its absence was also important, though less important than running water. Accounts of rural life in the 1950s and 1960s, including the Rosemary Harris wonderful *Prejudice and Tolerance in Ulster* – a study of an area near Aughnacloy (Tyrone) showed that until the 1960s many farm wives rarely went out, other than to mass or occasional shopping trips.[36] In 1969 Dorine Rohan claimed that for rural women 'the only outing perhaps [was] an excursion to Knock or a day trip to Kerry or Donegal. Many women with whom I chatted had never been further than the nearest town and some not even further than the nearest village'.[37] When they went to Dublin or another city for the day, she suggested that they were easily identified:

> Country folk in a large town – unmistakably dressed – the poorer ones with a rough mackintosh and a headscarf, or a skirt, almost ankle-length, with the jacket of an old suit, whose skirt has been turned into dusters. Their more well-to-do neighbours in suits, and the inevitable hat. It is not only their attire which distinguishes them – they have an air of determination, a set gait, as they stride along the street, balanced by bulging string bags on either side, or Roche's Stores plastic bags which they have saved form their last visit.[38]

Rohan was probably exaggerating the urban/rural comparison in 1969, but if she was correct such descriptions are long out of date. It would be impossible today to distinguish a woman from the country from her sister/cousin in the city by her dress or lifestyle, including foreign travel. While the spread of chain stores and regional shopping centres throughout Ireland has damaged traditional businesses and the main streets of provincial towns, it has removed an urban/rural divide in terms of access to fashion and other consumer items. Increased car ownership, the falling cost in real terms of cars, and the fact that most women hold a driving licence, and have done so for decades, has helped to reduce, if not eliminate the impact of distance. There appear to be no statistics about driving licences by gender and how the numbers changed over the decades, though this is a vital social indicator. Several farm wives who were interviewed by Pat O'Hara emphasised that: 'Driving is very important. It would drive me mad not to have a car, you would have no comfort'. One-third of the women on western farms in her survey did not have a driving licence, though there was only one home without a car. The ability to drive was vital to giving farm women some independence.[39] The impact of the road improvements that finally came during the 1990s and 2000s cannot be underestimated; this has enabled men and women to work at a distance from their homes, while continuing to live in the countryside. The appalling Irish telephone service – which was not confined to rural Ireland – also enhanced the isolation. This ended with the near-universal access to mobile phones.

The removal of the bar on married women in state employment in 1973, and an end to the convention that women employed in the private sector gave up paid work on marriage (unless they worked in a family business) had a dramatic impact throughout Irish society. John Jackson's study of West Cork at the end of the 1960s reported the shock experienced by several women who had emigrated and returned to Ireland with their husband and family, when they discovered that they could not work as married nurses or teachers.[40] According to Willie Smyth, who carried out a detailed study of his home area in South Tipperary, the end of the marriage bar, brought an end to dowries; a woman's teaching or nursing qualification, the fact that she held an administrative job in the health board or some secure form of employment was seen as equalling, or surpassing the value of a dowry.[41] In 1990 an estimated 16 per cent of farm spouses had an off-farm income.[42] The figures are much higher today.

The 2018 National Farm Survey showed that 52 per cent of households had off-farm employment; in the west 40 per cent of farmers combined farming with off-farm employment. This figure was lower, 25 per cent in the south, where dairy farming as the major activity demands a full-time commitment. The diversification of employment among those living in rural Ireland is not confined to women, and it has created new household patterns. Women now constitute one-quarter of farm workers, but only one-quarter of those working in agriculture do so full-time. When a growing number of farmers began to work in outside employment women had to take a greater role in running the farm and the traditional gendered divisions within the family farm began to erode.[43] There are households where the resident farmer is a woman and the man is responsible for earning the off-farm income. In other households these roles are reversed. Both the state and the agricultural/farming community were slow to catch up with these developments. It was only in 1991 that agricultural statistics began to take account of women's involvement in farming and in a farm household with a husband and wife, official statistics continue to record the man as the farmer, even where he has a full-time off-farm job. Farm organisations have been even slower to acknowledge the role of women in twenty-first-century agriculture. The National Ploughing Championship, despite being run for many years by a woman, has used the term 'farmerette' to describe such women, and throughout its history the Irish Farmers' Association has been led by men and dominated by men, though there is now a female vice president.

LAND OWNERSHIP AND FARMING

Surveys conducted in the 1960s and especially those carried out in western areas, predicted the disappearance of many family farms because of a lack of heirs (heiresses were given scant consideration), but that did not happen. Contrary to predictions, the momentous changes that were underway did not result in large numbers of farms coming on the open market for lack of an heir. Few Irish farms, even those without an apparent direct heir came on the market; most remained in family ownership. A 1992 paper by Damian Hannan and Patrick Commins showed that rural Ireland did not conform to the patterns elsewhere – it retained a substantial landholding sector. By the 1990s, while the proportion of the population in agriculture had fallen sharply, there was very little consolidation of farms. In the 1970s and 1980s the decline in the number of farms was only 0.5 per cent annually. Things have speeded up since that time. In the year 2000 there were 140,000 farms – half the figure for 1970. A report titled *Agri-Food 2010* suggested in 2000 that there would be under 100,000 farms by 2010 and only 20,000 full-time farmers, yet 2010 figures show that there were 140,000 farms.[44] Hannan and Commins summarised the position as follows: 'Having battled so long for their land, the Irish smallholders have been very loath to give it up'.[45]

Changes however are underway, and the benign pattern identified by Hannan and Commins may not survive. There are serious concerns about the limited entry pathways to farming for younger farmers; most land continues to be transferred through inheritance.[46] Highly educated farm sons and daughters have alternative, more lucrative career options. The economically viable size of farms is rising. The 2018 National Farm Survey classified 34 per cent of farms as vulnerable, 34 per cent as sustainable and 32 per cent as viable. However, while these statistics may give rise for concern they should be compared with the statistics, cited above for the 1970s, where only 23 per cent of farms were classified as 'development farms', 4 per cent as 'commercial farms' and 70 per cent were classified as farms that had no hope of surviving.

One significant change in recent years has been the re-emergence of tenant farming, which had almost disappeared by the 1920s, with the exception of conacre (short-term rentals for eleven months). In 2010, 18 per cent of agricultural land was rented and 30 per cent of farms included some rented land; all the land was rented on 3.4 per cent of farms.[47] This growing rental market reflects the changing economies of farming, and decisions made by farmers or their heirs to retain ownership, but not to farm the land themselves. To date it had not yet resulted in the re-emergence of an identifiable landlord class. Another, related phenomenon is the emergence of part-time farming, 'hobby farming', small farms where the household often enjoys a good standard of living, because of an off-farm income. This is first evidenced in the 1960s – in Lucey's and Kaldor's study of Scariff and Tubbercurry, but it has become much more widespread.

Perhaps the most significant change is the declining significance of agriculture as the occupation of those living in rural Ireland. In 2016 farming accounted for the largest number of those in work, but that amounted to only 11.3 per cent of the occupied population. Human health and social work activities employed just 1 per cent fewer people at 10.3 per cent, the overwhelming majority being women. This was closely followed by the 9.9 per cent who were engaged in manufacturing and the 8.6 per cent who were engaged in education. It seems possible that by the next population census, agriculture will no longer be the largest rural occupation, though it will continue to be the largest occupation for men.

CONCLUSION: TRENDS AND PROSPECTS

In thinking about twenty-first century Ireland it is important to abandon the old stereotypes about rural Ireland. There is a need to question the existence or extent of the rural-urban divide. There are urban/rural differences – such as access to public transport, but historic divisions in terms of amenities, education, occupation, have been significantly reduced. Over one-quarter of those aged 35–44 who are living in rural Ireland have a third-level degree. Although this is lower than in urban areas 31.7 per cent versus 26 per cent, it is far cry from the days when the priest was the only graduate in a rural parish. The proportion of residents with a third-level qualification is higher than the proportion of graduates in some areas in Dublin, Limerick and Cork cities. In the 1980s and the 1990s, referendums on questions such as contraception, divorce or 'pro-life' revealed a clear urban-rural divide; this, however, was no longer significant in the referendums on marriage equality and the repeal of the Eighth Amendment. On the other hand, whereas 50 years ago, most Irish people had a close personal link with rural life – visiting grandparents or other close relatives who lived on farms, that is much reduced. So while on the one hand the gulf between city and country has narrowed – in terms of life style, education and so on, it may be growing in personal terms.

There are a number of serious issues facing rural Ireland. Climate change presents a potentially existential challenge. In 2021 the EU set Ireland a target of reducing greenhouse gas emissions by 30 per cent by 2030 compared with 2005 levels; in 2023 that target was raised to 42 per cent. Agriculture is the largest contributor to Irish greenhouse gas emissions, accounting for 38.4 per cent of emissions in 2022, the highest sectoral contribution among EU member states. This is primarily due to methane emissions from

Irish grass-fed livestock, and the extensive use of nitrogenous fertilisers to promote grass growth, plus the absence of traditional heavy industries.[48] Farming and agribusinesses are also exercising 'the largest pressure on water quality',[49] and this is another environmental hazard that must be addressed. Reducing livestock numbers poses a serious threat to farm incomes, especially for dairy farmers. Increased afforestation to mitigate climate change does not provide comparable incomes. Environmental policies also threaten the long-term future of one-off housing in rural Ireland, which has enabled many people working in non-agricultural jobs to live in the community where they grew up. These houses have been widely criticised by planners, and environmental commentators, yet they have played a critical role in sustaining the rural population and rural communities.[50]

Until recently, economic and social trends appeared to be favouring the expansion of cities, and indeed super cities, with jobs and people congregating in ever larger conurbations. However, the recent Covid-19 pandemic has raised serious questions about the future of cities and massive office complexes. In the mid-nineteenth century the families who could afford to do so, fled from city centres to the suburbs, to avoid infectious diseases; in the process they transformed the spatial geography of urban life, assisted by the development of trains and tramways. The Covid pandemic has the potential to be equally transformative; the highest incidences of the disease have occurred in crowded urban settings. Women and men who can work remotely are doing so, and many will not revert full-time to city offices, moving instead to some combination of time spent in offices and working from home. Such changes in work patterns afford opportunities to rural and small town communities provided that there is access to high-speed broadband. In the *Financial Times* issue for 15 May 2020 one columnist wrote of 'The rise and fall of the office', another wrote of how the office could be missed if it died. It is possible that rural Ireland will not only survive but thrive in a world where large city-centre office complexes have become redundant – but that survival will rely on access to technology and road networks, and a looser relationship between farming and rural life. However we should note that the 2022 Population Census figures show no evidence of a flight from Irish cities.

In 1943 Éamon de Valera made a much-cited speech about his ideal Ireland. If we omit the reference to 'comely maidens' and 'frugal comfort' it could be argued that his dream has been realised in twenty-first century rural Ireland with many cosy (centrally-heated) homesteads, athletic youth and sturdy children romping around – and they can be found in larger numbers than during his lifetime.

Notes

INSIDE AND OUTSIDE RURAL IRELAND: THE POLITICS OF CHANGE SINCE 1922

1. Rev. J. Newman, 'Changing Functions of the Rural Community', *Christus Rex*, XX1:1 (1967), p. 69.
2. Mary E. Daly, 'The survival of Rural Ireland', above, p. 153.
3. Mary E. Daly, *The Slow Failure: Population Decline and Independent Ireland, 1922–1973* (Madison: The University of Wisconsin Press, 2006), Chap. 2.
4. Mary E. Daly, *Sixties Ireland: Reshaping the Economy, State and Society, 1957–73* (Cambridge: Cambridge University Press, 2016), pp 152–65.
5. Barrington Moore, Jr., *Social Origins of Dictatorship and Democracy: Lord and Peasant in the Making of the Modern World* (Harmondsworth: Penguin Books, 1977 [1966]), p. x. Under the terms of the Anglo-Irish Treaty of 1921 the form political independence assumed initially in southern Ireland was that of a self-governing dominion within the British Empire.
6. Colonialism in Ireland was to have pronounced cultural as well as political and economic dimensions. 'The legacy of cultural colonialism', Peadar Kirby observed in the 1980s,'is an aspect of our national life that is largely overlooked or even denied' (Peadar Kirby, *Has Ireland a Future?* (Cork: Mercier Press, 1988), p. 98). See also J. J. Lee, *Ireland 1912–1985: Politics and Society* (Cambridge: Cambridge University Press, 1989), pp 658–7.
7. M. A. G. Ó Tuathaigh, 'The Land Question, Politics and Irish Society, 1922–1960', in P. J. Drudy (ed.), *Ireland: Land, Politics and People* (Cambridge: Cambridge University Press, 1982), p. 187.
8. Jim Mac Laughlin, *Ireland: The Emigrant Nursery and the World Economy* (Cork: Cork University Press, 1994). This is not to say that for years many Irish workers abroad (and especially perhaps those employed as labourers) didn't draw heavily on a wide range of agricultural skills.
9. John Kurt Jacobsen, *Chasing Progress in the Irish Republic: Ideology, Democracy and Dependent Development* (Cambridge: Cambridge University Press, 1994), pp 9–14, 23–4. We find Raymond Crotty depicting Ireland's changing economy and society in the 1960s as '…a socio-economic order that was inequitable and inefficient in the extreme, and was bound to fail sooner rather than later' (*A Radical's Response* (Swords, Co. Dublin: Poolbeg Press, 1988), p. 34). And writing in 2014 Denis O'Hearn characterised the 'Irish growth model…as both unsustainable and unique. It created a toxic mix of dependence on FDI [Foreign Direct Investment] and rapidly rising inequality, while failing to provide for basic social welfare' ('Just Another Bubble Economy?', in Tom Inglis (ed.), *Are the Irish Different?* (Manchester: Manchester University Press, 2014), p, 41.
10. Hilary Tovey, Trutz Haase, and Chris Curtin, 'Understanding Rural Poverty', in Chris Curtin, Trutz Haase and Hilary Tovey (eds.), *Poverty in Rural Ireland: A Political Economy Approach* (Dublin: Oak Tree Press in association with the Combat Poverty Agency, 1996), p. 3.
11. Damian F. Hannan, *Displacement and Development: Class, Kinship and Social Change in Irish Rural Communities* (Dublin: The Economic and Social Research Institute, 1979), p. 17; Patrick Commins, 'Agricultural Production and the Future of Small-Scale Farming', in Chris Curtin, Trutz Haase and Hilary Tovey (eds.), *Poverty in Rural Ireland: A Political Economy Approach* (Dublin: Oak Tree Press, 1996), pp 92–105; Ethel Crowley, *Land Matters: Power Struggles in Rural Ireland* (Dublin: The Lilliput Press, 2006), pp 32–5, 62–3. Edel Kelly, Karen Keaveney and Anne Markey, *Challenges and Opportunities for Rural Ireland and the Agricultural Sector* (Dublin: National Economic and Social Council, 2021), pp 19–35. For an account of the continuing marginalisation of small-scale fishermen in nationalist Ireland, see Jim Mac Laughlin, *Troubled Waters: A Social and Cultural History of Ireland's Sea Fisheries* (Dublin: Four Courts Press, 2010), pp 331–54. Of course, class marginalisation and class displacement on the land were nothing new in the second half of the twentieth century. Along with the ultimate demise of the landed gentry, the steep ongoing decline of the farm labourer class from the time of the Famine did much to reshape the structure of rural society and to consolidate the farmers' economic power (Gearóid Ó Tuathaigh, 'Irish Land Questions in the State of the

Union', in Fergus Campbell and Tony Varley (eds.), *Land Questions in Modern Ireland* (Manchester: Manchester University Press, 2013), pp 12–15.

12. Commins, 'Agricultural Production and the Future of Small-Scale Farming', pp 105–21; Crowley, *Land Matters*, pp 69, 95.

13. For a still useful overview of the different paths taken by modernisation and alternative approaches to the study of 'social change and development', see Alvin Y. So, *Social Change and Development: Modernization, Dependency, and World-Systems Theories* (London: Sage Publications, 1990).

14. We only need to recall here how in the region of 20 per of the country's total agricultural acreage changed hands *via* redistributive land reform during the twentieth century (Terence Dooley, *'The Land for the People': The Land Question in Independent Ireland* (Dublin: University College Dublin Press, 2004), p. 20).

15. See Ciara Breathnach, *The Congested Districts Board of Ireland, 1891–1923: Poverty and Development in the West of Ireland* (Dublin: Four Courts Press, 2005).

16. See also Éamon Ó Ciosáin, 'Bord don Ghaeltacht: Réamhstair Údarás na Gaeltachta ó 1922 go 1957', in Gearóid Ó Tuathaigh agus Breandán Mac Suibhne (eag.), *Ag cur chun fónaimh* (An Spidéal: Cló Iar-Chonnacht, 2023), lgh. 17–40.

17. K. Theodore Hoppen, *Elections, Politics, and Society in Ireland 1832–1885* (Oxford: Clarendon Press, Oxford, 1984), pp 171–4.

18. Eugene Hynes, 'The Great Hunger and Irish Catholicism', *Societas*, 8 (1978), p. 147; Tom Inglis, *Moral Monopoly: The Rise and Fall of the Catholic Church in Modern Ireland* (2nd ed.) (Dublin: University College Dublin Press, 1998), pp 192–200.

19. Hynes, 'The Great Hunger', pp 137–56.

20. James O'Shea, *Priests, Politics and Society in Post-famine Ireland: A Study of County Tipperary 1850–1891* (Dublin: Wolfhound Press, 1983), Chaps. 3, 4 and 5; Chris Eipper, *The Ruling Trinity: A Community Study of Church, State and Business in Ireland* (Aldershot: Gower, 1986), p. 104; Tom Inglis, *Global Ireland: Same Difference* (New York and London: Routledge, 2008), pp 148, 235; Diarmaid Ferriter, *On the Edge: Ireland's Off-Shore Islands: A Modern History* (London: Profile Books, 2020), Chap 4.

21. See Gerard Moran, *Fleeing from Famine in Connemara: James Hack Tuke and his Assisted Emigration Scheme in the 1880s* (Dublin: Four Courts Press, 2018).

22. See Breandán Mac Suibhne, *The End of Outrage: Post-Famine Adjustment in Rural Ireland* (Oxford: Oxford University Press, 2017); Fergus Campbell, *Land and Revolution: Nationalist Politics in the West of Ireland 1891–1921* (Oxford: Oxford University Press, 2005).

23. Gearóid Ó Tuathaigh, 'Cultural Visions and the New State: Embedding and Embalming', in Gabriel Doherty and Dermot Keogh (eds.), *De Valera's Irelands* (Cork: Mercier Press, 2003), p. 177.

24. R. V. Comerford, *Charles J. Kickham: A Study in Irish Nationalism and Literature* (Dublin: Wolfhound Press, 1979), pp 210, 243.

25. See Maurice Goldring, *Faith of our Fathers: The Formation of Irish Nationalist Ideology 1890–1920* (Dublin: Repsol, [1982] 1987), chap. 3; *Pleasant the Scholar's Life: Irish Intellectuals and the Construction of the Nation State* (London: Serif, 1993), chap. 3; Liam O'Dowd, "Town and Country in Irish Ideology', *Canadian Journal of Irish Studies*, 13 (2), 1987, pp 43–53; 'Intellectuals in 20th Century Ireland: The Case of George Russell (AE)', *The Crane Bag*, 9:1 (1985), pp 6–25; Gearóid Ó Tuathaigh, 'Ireland's Land Questions: A Historical Perspective', in John Davis (ed.), *Rural Change in Ireland* (Belfast: The Institute of Irish Studies, Queen's University Belfast, 1999), p. 26; Luke Gibbons, *Transformations in Irish Culture* (Cork: Cork University Press in association with Field Day, 1995), pp 84–5; Declan Kiberd, *Inventing Ireland: The Literature of the Modern Nation* (London: Vintage, 1996), pp 481–96; Patrick Doyle, *Civilising Rural Ireland: The Co-operative Movement, Development and the Nation-state, 1889–1939* (Manchester: Manchester University Press, 2019), pp 62–5.

26. See O'Dowd, 'Town and Country in Irish Ideology', pp 43–53.

27. Peter Gibbon, 'Arensberg and Kimball Revisited', *Economy and Society*, 2 (4), 1973, p. 486.

28. Gibbon, 'Arensberg and Kimball Revisited', pp 479–98.

29. Quoted in Diarmaid Ferriter, *Mothers, Maidens and Myths: A History of the Irish Countrywomen's Association* (Dublin: FÁS, 1995), p. 3.

30. Among the authors considered are Elizabeth Brennan, Patrick Kavanagh, Temple Lane, Maura Laverty, Sheila Pim, Mary Purcell, Patrick Purcell, John D. Sheridan, and M. L. Stewart.

31. Tony Varley, 'Learning to Make Irish Agriculture Modern: Civil Society Elites, the State and Coping with the Challenges of Globalisation in the 1890s', in Joe Regan and Cathal Smith (eds.), *Agrarian Reform and Resistance in an Age of Globalisation: The Euro-American World and Beyond, 1780–1914* (London: Routledge, 2019), pp 185–201.

32. Patrick Doyle, 'Horace Plunkett, Co-operation, and an Irish Solution to the Transnational Problem of Rural Life, 1891–1921', in Joe Regan and Cathal Smith (eds.), *Agrarian Reform and Resistance in an Age of Globalisation: The Euro-American World and Beyond, 1780–1914* (London: Routledge, 2019), pp 202–16; Daniel T. Rodgers, *Atlantic Crossings: Social Politics in a Progressive Age* (Cambridge, Mass.: Cambridge: Harvard University Press, 1998), pp 267, 322, 328, 331–5, 337–8, 366, 448–9; Barry Sheppard, 'Muintir na Tíre's Fr John Hayes – "Ireland's Rural Apostle" in America', *History Ireland*, 32 (1), 2024, pp 42–4.

33. Robert. E. Kennedy, *The Irish, Emigration, Marriage and Fertility* (Los Angeles: University of California Press, 1973), pp 95–8.

34. Ralph Miliband, 'Class Analysis', in Anthony Giddens and Jonathan Turner (eds.), *Social Theory Today* (Cambridge: Polity Press, 1987), p. 343.

35. Liam O'Dowd, 'Church, State and Women: The Aftermath of Partition', in Chris Curtin, Pauline Jackson and Barbara O'Connor (eds.), *Gender in Irish Society* (Galway: Galway University Press, 1987). pp 24–7; Maryann Gialanella Valiulis, *The Making of Inequality: Women, Power and Gender Ideology in the Irish Free State, 1922–1937* (Dublin: Four Courts Press, 2019), Chap. 4.

36. See Declan Kiberd, *Inventing Ireland* (London: Jonathan Cape, 1995), pp 403–7.

37. Mary Clancy, 'Shaping the Nation: Women in the Free State Parliament, 1923–1937', in Yvonne Galligan, Eilís Ward and Rick Wilford (eds.), *Contesting Politics: Women in Ireland, North and South* (Boulder, Colorado: Westview Press, 1999), p. 209; Caitriona Clear, 'Women in Ireland in the 1930s and 1940s', in Alan Hayes (ed.), *Hilda Tweedy and the Irish Housewives Association: Links in the Chain…* (Dublin: Arlen House, 2012), pp 59–61.

38. Caitriona Clear, *Women of the House: Women's Household Work in Ireland 1922–1261* (Dublin: Irish Academic Press, 2000), p. 15; Peter Moser, 'Rural Economy and Female Emigration in the West of Ireland 1936–1956', *U.C.G. Women's Studies Centre Review*, 2 (1993), pp 41–51.

39. Conrad M. Arensberg and Solon T. Kimball, *Family and Community in Ireland*, 3rd edn ([1940]; Ennis: CLASP Press, 2001), pp 47–8; Mícheál Ó Fathartaigh and Anne Cassidy, 'Challenging Patriarchal Power? Women Advisors as Change Agents in Twentieth-Century Irish Agriculture', above, pp 130-39.

40. Symbolising their subordination in public was apparently the still intact customary practice in 'remote districts' in 1930s Clare of the farm woman keeping 'several paces behind her man' when walking the roads (ibid., p. 196).

41. ibid., p. 47.

42. See Michel Peillon, *Contemporary Irish Society: An Introduction* (Dublin: Gill and Macmillan, 1982), p. 13.

43. Patricia O'Hara, *Partners in Production? Women, Farm and Family in Ireland* (Oxford: Berghahn Books, 1998); Sally Shortall, *Women and Farming: Property and Power* (Houndsmills, Basingstoke: Macmillan, 1999). Patriarchal domination has been flagged as a prominent theme in John McGahern's rural fiction which Tom Inglis reads as offering 'much assistance' in understanding 'how men surreptitiously dominate their wives and children in the home' (see Tom Inglis, 'John McGahern: The Sociology of Honor, Status and Shame', *Éire-Ireland*, 57 (3&4) (2022), p. 26). Compared to Patricia O'Hara's pathbreaking research which explores how patriarchal domination works – and is sometime resisted – in everyday Irish farm life, the novels reviewed by Caitriona Clear in Chapter 7 very much favour 'female self-determination'; 'happily single women populate' many of the novels she discusses. And Clear observes of Irish women how 'many married happily onto farms, relishing the skills and challenges involved in companionate agricultural partnerships' (See Caitriona Clear, 'Contemporary Rural Life in Irish Fiction of the 1940s', above, pp 103, 104. Writing recently of certain European peasant societies, Patrick Joyce observes how '…male domination was (and is) very often more formal than real' (Patrick Joyce, *Remembering Peasants: A Personal History of a Vanished World* (London: Allen Lane, 2024), p. 91).

44. Others have stressed how debt bondage was rife among the poorest smallholders early in the last century and how the practice of produce (such as eggs) being bartered for shop goods – or to clear shop debts at highly exploitative exchange rates – guaranteed their continued subordination and

impoverishment (see Peter Gibbon and M. D. Higgins, 'Patronage, Tradition and Modernization: The Case of the Irish "Gombeenman"', *Economic and Social Review*, 6:1 (1974), pp 32–3).

45. Mary E. Daly, 'The Survival of Rural Ireland', above, p. 163. For some of the ways the current physical planninng regulations are now having severe negative implications for the survival of the Irish language in the Gaeltacht regions, see Donncha Ó hEallaithe, 'Bíodh Plean Againn...Tá Gá le Cur Chuige Straitéiseach maidir le Cúrsaí Pleanála sa Ghaeltacht, *Comhar*, 81:3 (2021), lgh. 10–13; and 'Baisteadh 'BÁNÚ'...Tá Gluaiseacht Nua Ghaeltachta ar an bhFód – Feachtas faoi Chúrsaí Tithíocht', *Comhar*, 84:3 (2024), lgh. 11–13).

46. Seán Ó Ríain, 'Where is Ireland in the Worlds of Capitalism?', in Tom Inglis (ed.), *Are the Irish Different?* (Manchester: Manchester University Press, 2014), p. 23.

47. Almost two-thirds of the tenant-farmers had purchased by 1916 (Elizabeth R. Hooker, *Readjustments of Agricultural Tenure in Ireland* (Chapel Hill: The University of North Carolina Press, 1938), p. 222).

48. Paul Bew, *Ireland: The Politics of Enmity 1789–2006* (Oxford, 2007), p. 568.

49. Fergus Campbell, *Land and Revolution*, pp 303–4.

50. Terence Brown, *Ireland: A Social and Cultural History 1922–79* (London, Fontana, 1981), pp 26, 23.

51. Michael Gallagher, *Electoral Support for Irish Political Parties 1927–1973* London: Sage Publications, 1976), pp 9, 19, 30–2; Warner Moss, *Political Parties in the Irish Free State* (New York: Columbia University Press, 1933), pp 186, 193; Michael Gallagher, *Political Parties in the Republic of Ireland* (Dublin: Gill and Macmillan, 1985), p. 103; Fearghal McGarry, *Eoin O'Duffy: A Self-Made Hero* (Oxford: Oxford University Press, 2005), p. 203.

52. The main examples were the Irish Farmers' Union/The Farmers' Party, Muintir na Tíre, the National Farmers' and Ratepayers' League/National Centre Party, the Irish Farmers' Federation, and Clann na Talmhan.

53. Tony Varley, 'On the Road to Extinction: Agrarian Parties in Twentieth-Century Ireland', *Irish Political Studies*, 25:4 (2010), pp 581–601.

54. Louis P. F. Smith and Seán Healy, *Farm Organisations in Ireland: A Century of Progress* (Dublin: Four Courts Press, 1996), pp 165–6.

55. Gary Murphy, 'The Irish Government, the National Farmers Association, and the European Economic Community, 1955–1964', *New Hibernia Review*, 6:4 (2002), p. 83.

56. Maura Adshead, 'Beyond Clientelism: Agricultural Networks in Ireland and the EU', *West European Politics*, 19:3 (1996), pp 583–608.

57. Richard Breen, Damian F. Hannan, David B. Rottman and Christopher T. Whelan, *Understanding Contemporary Ireland: State, Class and Development in the Republic of Ireland* (Dublin: Gill and Macmillan, 1990), pp 190–1; Christopher T. Whelan and Richard Layte, 'Opportunities for all in the New Ireland?', in Tony Fahey, Helen Russell, Christopher T. Whelan, (eds.), *Best of Times? The Social Impact of the Celtic Tiger* (Dublin: Institute of Public Administration, 2007), pp 72–4.

58. Ethel Crowley, *Land Matters*, pp 32–5; Hilary Tovey, Trutz Haase, and Chris Curtin, 'Understanding Rural Poverty', pp 34–5.

59. Crowley, *Land Matters*, pp 62-3.

60. ibid., pp 69, 95.

61. Pat O'Toole, 'Three in Four Farmers would Vote for a New Farmers' Party', *Irish Farmers Journal*, 12 August 2023.

62. Daithí Ó Corráin, 'Catholicism in Ireland, 1880–2015: Rise, Ascendancy and Retreat', in Thomas Bartlett (ed.), *The Cambridge History of Ireland: Volume IV, 1880 to the Present* (Cambridge: Cambridge University Press, 2018), p. 729.

63. ibid., pp 733, 731.

64. ibid., p. 735. K. Theodore Hoppen, *Ireland Since 1800: Conflict and Conformity* (London: Longman, 1999), pp 264–72.

65. John H. Whyte, *Church and State in Modern Ireland 1923–1979*, 2nd edn ([1980]; Dublin: Gill and Macmillan, 1984), pp 24–5.

66. Ó Corráin, *Catholicism in Ireland*, p. 736.

67. Patsy McGarry, 'More than a Third of Catholic Priests are Aged over 60, Survey Finds', *The Irish Times*, 2 November 2022. (https://www.irishtimes.com/ireland/social-affairs/2022/11/02/more-than-a-third-of-irish-catholic-priests-are-over-60-and-just-25-are-under-40-survey-finds/).

68. Mark Tierney, *The Story of Muintir na Tíre 1931–2001 – The First Seventy Years* (Tipperary: Muintir na Tíre, 2004), pp 199–202. Margaret O'Doherty was the first woman to hold the presidency (between 2004 and 2007).

69. Chris Eipper, *The Holy Trinity*, p. 104.

70. O'Hara, *Partners in Production?*, p. 163.

71. Earlier Damian Hannon had drawn attention to the 'cumulating differences' emerging over time 'between large and small, traditional and non-traditional farmers in income, life chances and in their rates of reproduction. Class differentiation escalates with capital substitution and technical innovation' ('Peasant Models and the Understanding of Social and Cultural Change in Rural Ireland', in P. J. Drudy (ed.), *Ireland: Land, Politics and People* (Cambridge: Cambridge University Press, 1982), p. 154).

72. Shortall, *Women and Farming*, p. 96.

73. See, for instance, Linda Connolly and Tina O'Toole, *Documenting Irish Feminisms: The Second Wave* (Dublin: The Woodfield Press, 2005), pp 214–5; Evelyn Mahon, 'From Democracy to Femocracy: The Women's Movement in the Republic of Ireland', in Patrick Clancy, Sheelagh Drudy, Kathleen Lynch and Liam O'Dowd (eds.), *Irish Society: Sociological Perspectives* (Dublin: Institute of Public Administration, 1995), p. 681.

74. Connolly and O'Toole, *Documenting Irish Feminisms*, p. 215.

75. Caitriona Clear, 'Women in de Valera's Ireland 1922–48: A Reappraisal', in Gabriel Doherty and Dermot Keogh (eds.), *De Valera's Irelands* (Cork: Mercier Press, 2003), p. 106.

76. Diarmaid Ferriter, *Mothers, Maidens and Myths: A History of the Irish Countrywomen's Association* (Dublin: FÁS, 1995), p. 9. Ferriter was advising in the mid-1990s that rural women's understandings of 'modernisation at various stages this century' needed further elucidation (ibid., p. 62).

77. ibid., p. 10.

78. Patrick McNabb, 'Social Structure', in Jeremiah Newman (ed.), *The Limerick Rural Survey 1958–1964* (Tipperary: Muintir na Tíre Publications, 1964), p. 246.

79. ibid., p. 208.

80. O'Hara, *Partners in Production?*, p. 107–8.

81. Crowley, *Land Matters*, p. 61. See also Aileen Heverin, *The Irish Countrywomen's Association: A History 1910 – 2000* (Dublin: Wolfhound Press, 2000), pp 173–6.

82. Bernie Commins, 'Census: Percentage of Female Farm Holders up by 1% in a Decade', *Agriland*, 12 December 2021 (https://www.agriland.ie/farming-news/census-percentage-of-female-farm-holders-up-by-1-in-a-decade/).

83. Department of Agriculture, Food and the Marine, *National Dialogue on Women in Agriculture: Report* (Dublin: Department of Agriculture, Food and the Marine, 2024), p. 23.

84. Áine Macken-Walsh, Peter Cush and Anne Byrne, 'Strategies of Resilience: Cooperation in Irish Family Farming', *Irish Geography*, 53:1 (2020), pp 23–42; Peter Cush, Áine Macken-Walsh and Anne Byrne, 'Joint Farming Ventures: Gender Identities of the Self and the Social', *Journal of Rural Studies*, 57 (2018), pp 55–64.

SHIFTING THE GOALPOSTS: CHANGING NARRATIVES OF WESTERN REGENERATION IN THE 1920S

1. Established in 1931, as a vehicle for largely farmer-led cooperative initiatives, its relaunch in 1937 as a parish-centred popular organisation constituted a new beginning. See Mark Tierney, *The Story of Muintir na Tire 1931–2001: The First Seventy Years* (Tipperary. 2004); Stephen Rynne, *Father John Hayes* (Dublin, 1960); and Diarmaid Ferriter, 'John Martin Hayes 1887–1957', in James McGuire and James Quinn (eds.), *Dictionary of Irish Biography* (Cambridge: Cambridge University Press, 2009), pp 537–9.

2. J. H. Whyte, *Church and State in Modern Ireland, 1923–1979* (Dublin: Gill and Macmillan, 1980; Michael P. Fogarty, *Christian Democracy in Western Europe, 1820–1953* (London: Routledge & Kegan Paul, 1957); Susannah Riordan, 'The Unpopular Front: Catholic Revival and Irish Cultural Identity, 1932–48', in Mike Cronin and John M. Regan (eds.), *The Politics of Independent Ireland, 1922–49* (Basingstoke: Palgrave Macmillan, 2000), pp 98–120.

3. Lalor's letter of 24 June 1848 in the *Irish Felon*, '...the entire ownership of Ireland, moral and material, up to the sun, and down to the centre, is vested of right in the people of Ireland'.

4. Paul Bew, *Conflict and Conciliation in Ireland, 1890–1910* (Oxford: Clarendon Press, 1987); David Seth Jones, *Graziers, Land reform and Political Conflict in Ireland* (Washington: Catholic University of America Press, 1995); Fergus Campbell's seminal *Land and Revolution: Nationalist Politics in the West of Ireland 1891–1921* (Oxford: Oxford University Press, 2005); for new perspectives, see Fergus Campbell and Tony Varley (eds.), *Land Questions in Modern Ireland* (Manchester: Manchester University Press, 2013).

5. Pádraig G. Lane, 'Poor Crayturs. The West's Agricultural Labourers in the Nineteenth Century', in Carla King and Conor McNamara (eds.), *The West of Ireland. New Perspectives on the Nineteenth Century* (Dublin: History Press, 2011), pp 35–49; F. H. A. Aalen, 'The Rehousing of Rural Labourers in Ireland under the Labourers (Ireland) Acts, 1883–1919', *Journal of Historical Geography*, 12:3 (1986), pp 287–306.

6. Ciara Breathnach, *The Congested Districts Board of Ireland, 1891–1922: Poverty and Development in the West of Ireland* (Dublin: Four Courts Press, 2005); for a valuable digest of data on the CDB, see James Morrissey (ed.), *On the Verge of Want* (Dublin: A & A Farmar, 2001).

7. Morrissey, ibid., pp xii, 1–4, 229–40.

8. See Mary Kotsonouris, *Retreat from Revolution: the Dáil Courts, 1920–1924* (Dublin: Irish Academic Press, 1994); Tony Varley, 'Agrarian Crime and Social Control: Sinn Féin and the Land Question in the West of Ireland in 1920', in Mike Tomlinson, Tony Varley and Ciarán McCullagh (eds.), *Whose Law and Order? Aspects of Crime and Social Control in Irish Society* (Belfast: Sociological Association of Ireland, 1988), pp 54–75.

9. *Dáil Éireann Debates*, 2: 1909, 1 March 1923.

10. The standard account is Terence Dooley, *'The Land for the People': The Land Question in Independent Ireland* (Dublin: University College Dublin Press, 2004).

11. ibid., pp 132–55

12. For Moylan, see Seán Kearns, 'Seán Moylan', in James McGuire and James Quinn (eds.), *Dictionary of Irish Biography* (Cambridge: Cambridge University Press, 2009), pp 726–8.

13. Cited in E. D. Steele, 'J. S. Mill and the Irish Question: The Principles of Political Economy, 1848–1865', *The Historical Journal*, 13:2 (1970), p. 234; Timothy W. Guinnane, *The Vanishing Irish: Households, Migration and the Rural Economy in Ireland, 1850–1914* (Princeton, New Jersey: Princeton University Press, 1997).

14. Gerard Moran, *Sending out Ireland's Poor: Assisted Emigration to North America in the Nineteenth Century* (Dublin: Four Courts Press, 2013); ibid., *Fleeing from Famine in Connemara: James Hack Tuke and his Assisted Emigration Scheme in the 1880s* (Dublin: Four Courts Press, 2018).

15. F. S. L. Lyons, 'The Economic Ideas of Parnell', in Michael Roberts (ed.), *Historical Studies*, 11 (London: Bowes and Bowes, 1959), pp 60–78.

16. For Ginnell, see works cited in note 4 above; and Pauric Dempsey and Shaun Boylan, 'Lawrence Ginnell 1852–1923', in James McGuire and James Quinn (eds.), *Dictionary of Irish Biography* (Cambridge: Cambridge University Press, 2009, pp 102–3).

17. Dooley, *'The Land for the People'*, seriatim; Patrick J. Sammon, *In the Land Commission: A Memoir 1933–1978* (Dublin: Ashford Press, 1997).

18. For early comment see, James Meenan, *The Irish Economy since 1922* (Liverpool: Liverpool University Press, 1970), pp 205–12.

19. See *Commission on Emigration and Other Population Problems, 1948–54. Reports* (Dublin: Stationery Office, 1955), Pr. 2541; Mary E. Daly, *The Slow Failure: Population Decline and Independent Ireland, 1920–1973* (Madison: University of Wisconsin Press, 2006); Enda Delany, *Demography, State, and Society: Irish Migration to Britain, 1921–1971* (Liverpool: Liverpool University Press, 2000).

20. Mary E. Daly, *The First Department: A History of the Department of Agriculture* (Dublin: Institute of Public Administration, 2002), pp 1–51.

21. For perspectives on the historical and recent predicament of the Gaeltacht, see Brian Ó Cuív (ed.), *A View of the Irish Language* (Dublin: Stationery Office, 1969), and Caoilfhionn Nic Pháidín and Seán Ó Cearnaigh (eds), *A New View of the Irish Language* (Dublin: Cois Life, 2008). See also Gearóid Ó Tuathaigh, Lillis Ó Laoire, Seán Ua Suilleabháin agus Micheál Ó Conghaile (eag.), *Pobal na Gaeltachta: A Scéal agus a Dhán* (Indreabhán, Conamara: Cló Iar-Chonnachta, 2000), Éamon Ó Ciosáin, 'Bord don Ghaeltacht: Réamhstair Údarás na Gaeltachta ó 1922 go 1957' in Gearóid Ó Tuathaigh agus Breandán Mac Suibhne (eag.), *Ag cur chun fónaimh* (An Spidéal: Cló Iar-Chonnacht, 2023), lgh. 17-40.

22. *Coimisiún na Gaeltachta, Vol.1, Report*, hereinafter *Report*; *Coimisiún na Gaeltachta, Vol. 2, Evidence of Witnesses*, hereinafter *Evidence* (Dublin: Stationery Office, 1926).
23. Letter from President Cosgrave, *Coimisiún na Gaeltachta, Report*, p. 3.
24. Another member, Joseph Hanley, was a senior inspector in rural science in the Department of Education; and Patrick Baxter was a prominent Cavan Farmers' Party TD.
25. *Coimisiún na Gaeltachta, Report*, p. 133.
26. ibid., *Report*, p. 42.
27. ibid., *Evidence*, Ó Beirne on 3 June 1925.
28. ibid., *Evidence*, Mac Cába on 17 June 1925.
29. ibid., *Report*, p. 65.
30. ibid., *Report*, S. Mac Cuinneagáin, pp 66–7.
31. ibid.
32. ibid., *Report*, L. C. Moriarty, p. 68.
33. Cited in Dooley, *'The Land for the People'*, p.140; for later experiments in transplanting, see Mícheál Ó Conghaile (eag.), *Gaeltacht Ráth Cairn: Léachtaí Comórtha* (Indreabhán, Conamara: Cló Iar-Chonnachta, 1986); Matt Nolan, *Ráth Chairn: An Talamh Bán* (Mullingar: Comharchumann Rath Chairn, 2018); Martin O'Halloran, *The Lost Gaeltacht: The Land Commission Migration – Clonbur, County Galway and Allenstown, County Meath* (Allenstown: Homefarm Publishing, 2020).
34. For the de Valera address, see Maurice Moynihan (ed.), *Speeches and Statements by Éamon de Valera 1917–1973* (Dublin and New York: St. Martin's Press, 1980), p. 466.
35. Meenan, *The Irish Economy*, pp 88–130; Kieran A. Kennedy, Thomas Giblin and Deirdre McHugh, *The Economic Development of Ireland in the Twentieth century* (London and New York: Routledge Press, 1988), pp 202–26.
36. On the 1930s economic war, see J. J. Lee, *Ireland 1912–1985: Politics and Society* (Cambridge: Cambridge University Press, 1989), pp 175–211; Cormac Ó Gráda, *Ireland: A New Economic History 1780–1939* (Oxford: Oxford University Press, 1994), pp 406–16.
37. *Commission on Emigration and other Population Problems. 1948–1954. Reports*, Pr.2541, p. 185. The view of emigration as a 'safety valve' for potential social discontent was very much an outlier from the consensus view: see Reservation No. 2 by Alexis Fitzgerald, pp 222–5.

THE RURAL DIMENSION OF STATE PLANNING: IRELAND IN THE 1960S

1. Brian Girvin, 'Stability, Crisis and Change in Post-War Ireland', in Thomas Bartlett (ed.), *The Cambridge History of Ireland, Volume IV, 1880 to the Present* (Cambridge: Cambridge University Press, 2018), pp 381–406.
2. National Archives of Ireland (NAI), Department of Foreign Affairs (DFA), 305/57/343 F Part 2 F.T.A. – WP23 Financial Experts attached to Working Party 23 (including visit to Dublin, May 1958), Report of Meeting, European Free Trade Area: Visit of Financial Experts of Working Party, No. 23, 8 May 1958.
3. T. K. Whitaker, 'Economic Planning in Ireland', in Basil Chubb and Patrick Lynch (eds.), *Economic Development and Planning* (Dublin: Institute of Public Administration, 1969), p. 300.
4. Peter Murray and Maria Feeney, *Church, State and Social Science in Ireland: Knowledge, Institutions and the Rebalancing of Power, 1937–73* (Manchester: Manchester University Press, 2017), pp 203–4.
5. Garret FitzGerald, *All in a Life: An Autobiography* (Dublin: Gill and Macmillan, 1991), p. 59.
6. NAI, Department of the Taoiseach (DT), S17032 A/61, Seán Lemass, Taoiseach to James Ryan, Minister for Finance, 6 March 1961.
7. ibid., copy of T. K. Whitaker, Finance to J. J. Nagle, Agriculture 27 October 1960, copy of Nagle to Whitaker 17 February 1961, copy to Whitaker to Nagle 22 February 1961.
8. ibid., James Ryan, Minister for Finance to Seán Lemass, Taoiseach 9 March 1961, Lemass to Ryan, 11 March 1961.
9. See correspondence, memoranda etc. in the succession of files NAI DT S17032 A/61 to NAI DT S17032 F/63.
10. Eoin O'Malley, *Industry and Economic Development: The Challenge for the Latecomer* (Dublin: Gill and Macmillan, 1989), pp 95–6.

11. Damian F. Hannan and Patrick Commins, 'The Significance of Small-Scale Landholders in Ireland's Socio-Economic Transformation', in J. H. Goldthorpe and C. T. Whelan (eds.), *The Development of Industrial Society in Ireland* (Oxford: Oxford University Press, 1992), p. 82.

12. Interdepartmental Committee on the Problems of Small Western Farms *Report* (Dublin: Stationery Office, 1962), pp 26–7.

13. Peter Murray, *Facilitating the Future? US Aid, European Integration and Irish Industrial Viability, 1948–73* (Dublin: UCD Press, 2009) and John Walsh, *The Politics of Expansion: The Transformation of Educational Policy in the Republic of Ireland, 1957–72* (Manchester: Manchester University Press, 2009).

14. NAI, DT, S12891 D/1/62, 'Forecast of Developments in Education Services During the Five Year Period 1963–68'.

15. Marie Clarke, 'Educational Reform in the 1960s: The Introduction of Comprehensive Schools in the Republic of Ireland', *History of Education*, 39:3 (2010), pp 383–99.

16. Vincent Tucker, 'State and Community: A Case Study of Glencolumbkille', in Chris Curtin and Thomas M. Wilson (eds.), *Ireland From Below: Social Change and Local Communities* (Galway: Galway University Press, 1989), pp 283–300 and Vincent Tucker, 'Images of Development and Under-Development in Glencolumbkille, Co. Donegal, 1830–1970', in John Davis (ed.), *Rural Change in Ireland* (Belfast: Institute of Irish Studies Queen's University Belfast, 1999), pp 84–115.

17. NAI, DT, S17032 I/95, 'Committee in Defence of the West', *Western People*, 5 December 1965 (clipping), James Ryan, Minister for Finance to Lemass, Taoiseach, 9 March 1961.

18. ibid., especially Paddy Smith, Minister for Agriculture to Lemass, Taoiseach, 25 June 1964 and J. Ryan, Minister for Finance to Lemass, 1 July 1964.

19. NAI, DT, S17032 I/95, Fr James McDyer, Glencolumbkille to Lemass, Taoiseach, 15 May 1964.

20. ibid., 'Government Rebuffs Small Farmer Deputation', *Irish Independent*, 21 May 1964; 'Charlestown Committee Will Go It Alone', *Western People*, 23 May 1964.

21. Murray and Feeney, *Church, State and Social Science*, p. 196.

22. NAI, Department of Enterprise, Trade and Employment, 2002/67/48, Penny Broadsheet No. 1, sheet with handwritten comments by Whitaker and Charles Murray 29 October 1964; Tadhg Ó Cearbhaill to Whitaker, 29 October 1964; NAI DT S17474 D/95, Lemass, Taoiseach to Kevin Boland, Minister for Social Welfare, 23 October 1964, Boland to Lemass, 26 October 1964.

23. Hannan and Commins, 'The Significance of Small-scale Landholders', p. 98.

24. Interdepartmental Committee on the Problems of Small Western Farms *Report*, pp 12–13.

25. NAI, DT, S17032 G/63, Report of Meeting, Economic Development in Western Areas, 25 July 1963.

26. Department of Social Welfare, *Report 1963–66* (Dublin: Stationery Office, 1968), p. 23.

27. Mel Cousins, *The Birth of Social Welfare in Ireland, 1922–52* (Dublin: Four Courts Press, 2003) and Anthony McCashin, *Social Security in Ireland* (Dublin: Gill and Macmillan, 2004).

28. Murray and Feeney, *Church, State and Social Science*, p. 197.

29. T. K. Whitaker, Department of Finance, *Economic Development* (Dublin: Stationery Office, 1958), p. 24.

30. Peter Kaim-Caudle, *Social Security in Ireland and Western Europe* (Dublin: Economic Research Institute, 1964).

31. Murray and Feeney, *Church, State and Social Science in Ireland*, pp 179–82.

32. NAI, DT, S17032 I/95, Seán Flanagan TD to Lemass, Taoiseach, 13 June 1964.

33. James McDyer, *Father McDyer of Glencolumbkille: An Autobiography* (Dingle: Brandon Books, 1984), p. 85.

34. Murray and Feeney, *Church, State and Social Science in Ireland*, pp 181–2.

35. NAI, DT, 96/6/269, Charles Haughey, Minister for Agriculture to Lemass, Taoiseach, 16 January 1965.

36. Mary E. Daly, *The Slow Failure: Population Decline and Independent Ireland, 1920–1973* (Madison: University of Wisconsin Press, 2006), p. 241 and Murray and Feeney, *Church, State and Social Science in Ireland*, p. 198.

37. McDyer, *Father McDyer of Glencolumbkille*, p. 86 and Tony Varley and Chris Curtin, 'Defending Rural Interests against Nationalists in 20th Century Ireland', in John Davis (ed.), *Rural Change in Ireland*, p. 74.

38. *The Landmark*, 21: 8 (1964), p. 3.

39. Mary E. Daly, *The First Department: A History of the Department of Agriculture* (Dublin: Institute of Public Administration, 2002), p. 258.
40. Stephen Rynne, *Father John Hayes: Founder of Muintir na Tíre People of the Land* (Dublin: Clonmore and Reynolds, 1960), pp 195–7.
41. Daly, *The First Department*, pp 403–6.
42. Mark Tierney, *The Story of Muintir na Tíre: the First Seventy Years* (Tipperary: Muintir na Tíre, 2004), pp 101–3.
43. Jeremiah Newman, 'The Future of Rural Ireland', *Studies*, 47:188 (1958), pp 388–402.
44. Tierney, *The Story of Muintir na Tíre*, pp 129–49.
45. Murray and Feeney, *Church, State and Social Science in Ireland*, pp 143–7.
46. NAI DT S17138 B/95, 'A Plan for Community Development in Ireland Submitted to the Government as an aid to the implementation of the Second Programme for Economic Expansion', p. 3.
47. ibid., Lemass, Taoiseach to Assistant Secretary, Department of the Taoiseach, 17 August 1964.
48. ibid., Department of Agriculture 'Muintir na Tíre Plan for Community Development in Ireland'.
49. ibid., Lemass, Taoiseach to Assistant Secretary, Department of the Taoiseach, 25 September,1964.
50. Murray and Feeney, *Church, State and Social Science in Ireland*, pp 159–163.
51. George Thomason, 'Muintir na Tíre', *Reality* (September, 1967), pp 6–8 and 11 and Charles McCarthy *The Distasteful Challenge* (Dublin: Institute of Public Administration, 1968), p. 50 (quotation from McCarthy).
52. Murray and Feeney, *Church, State and Social Science in Ireland*, pp 143–7.
53. Mary E. Daly, *Sixties Ireland: Reshaping the Economy State and Society, 1957–73* (Cambridge: Cambridge University Press, 2016), pp 98–9. In terms of regional coverage Muintir was primarily a southern movement strongest in the Munster counties of Tipperary, Limerick and Cork. However, Muintir did have some Connacht grassroots presence and two figures associated with Muintir were among the Charlestown Committee's most prominent activists. These were Father Raymond Browne, a Roscommon curate who was Muintir's third President (1963–7) and Seán McEvoy, a national schoolteacher in Toomore near Swinford in Mayo. Father Browne was a moderate figure generally anxious to promote accommodation with the government. Seán McEvoy was a strident government critic who, as a Fine Gael county councillor, was later to become a leading figure in Mayo politics.
54. Whitaker, 'Economic Planning in Ireland', p. 300.
55. NAI, DT, S17032, E. F. Lyddy, Hon. Sec., Muintir na Tíre to Lemass, Taoiseach, 14 December 1962.
56. For another example of this balancing, see Terence Dooley, *'The Land For The People': The Land Question in Independent Ireland* (Dublin: UCD Press, 2004), on the replacement as Minister for Lands of Erskine Childers by Michael Moran after Lemass succeeded de Valera as Taoiseach.
57. Hannan and Patrick Commins, 'The Significance of Small-Scale Landholders', p. 101.
58. Terence Dooley, *'The Land for the People': The Land Question in Independent Ireland* (Dublin: University College Dublin Press, 2004).

COMMUNITY DEVELOPMENT VISIONARY OR SOCIAL CONSERVATIVE? CANON JOHN HAYES REASSESSED

1. See Tony Varley and Chris Curtin, 'Communitarian Populism and the Politics of Rearguard Resistance in Rural Ireland', *Community Development Journal*, 37:1 (2002), pp 20–32.
2. Margaret Ledwith, *Community Development: A Critical and Radical Approach* (Bristol: Policy Press, 2020).
3. See John Ryan, 'The Founder of Muintir na Tíre': Canon John M. Hayes 1887–1957', *Studies*, 46:183 (1957), pp 312–21; Seán Corkery, 'Father John Hayes', *The Furrow*, 8:5 (1957), pp 302–7; Stephen Rynne, *Father John Hayes: Founder of Muintir na Tíre* (Dublin: Clonmore and Reynolds, 1960); and Mark Tierney, *The Story of Muintir na Tíre 1931–2001: The First Seventy Years* (Tipperary: Muintir na Tíre Publications, 2004).
4. Eoin Devereux 'John Hayes 1887–1957, Founder of Muintir Na Tíre', *Old Limerick Journal*, 34 (1998), pp 34–6.
5. For details, see Rynne, *Father John Hayes*, p. 24. See also a detailed report on the evictions in *The Limerick Reporter and Tipperary Vindicator*, 18 April 1882.

6. Rynne, *Father John Hayes*, p. 21.

7. For a personal account, see Very Reverend J. M. Hayes 'Land League Memories', *Muintir na Tire: Official Handbook, 1946* (Tipperary: Muintir na Tire Rural Publications, 1946), pp 51–4.

8. For Muintir na Tire's recognition of the right to private property ownership, see J. M. Hayes 'The Aims of Muinntir (sic) na Tire', *The Irish School Weekly*, 24 August 1935, pp 802–4.

9. Rynne, *Father John Hayes*, p. 67.

10. Cited in Stephen Rynne's 'Living Democracy', *The Landmark*, 18:8 (1961), p. 7. See also J. M. Hayes on the theme of local patriotism in 'Neighbourliness', *Muintir na Tire Official Handbook, 1944*, pp 24–7. The Dominican priest Jerome Toner describes this local patriotism as 'practical patriotism'. 'There is something reciprocal', he writes, 'about patriotism as conceived by Muintir na Tire; the individual and family owe something to the parish for all the parish has given them' (Jerome Toner, *Rural Ireland: Some of Its Problems* (Dublin: Clonmore and Reynolds, 1955), p. 84).

11. See, for instance, his speech at the AGM of the New Inn Guild, 9 May 1952 (University of Galway Archives, Muintir na Tire Papers, P134/12/1/2/10).

12. Tierney, *The Story of Muintir na Tire*, pp 26–7; see also Fr Hayes, 'Muintir Na Tire' (Radió Éireann broadcast address, undated [possibly 1934] (University of Galway Archives, Muintir na Tire Papers, P134/12/1/2/2).

13. Rynne, *Father John Hayes*, p. 49.

14. ibid., p. 51.

15. Rynne describes Mount Carmel at the time as 'neither a slum parish, nor an exclusively Irish one' (ibid., p. 74).

16. ibid., p. 72.

17. ibid., pp 57–60.

18. ibid., pp 57–75.

19. See Eoin Devereux, 'Saving Rural Ireland: Muintir na Tire and Its Anti-Urbanism', *Canadian Journal of Irish Studies*, 17:2 (1991), pp 23–30; Liam O'Dowd, 'Town and Country in Irish Ideology', *Canadian Journal of Irish Studies*, 13:2 (1987), pp 43–54. "In the past', Hayes wrote in 1935, 'emigration drained our countryside...the lure of the city is the danger today' ('The Aims of Muintir (sic) na Tire', pp 802–3). See also his speech 'Next Stop Dublin or London' to the CYMS, February 1939 (University of Galway Archives, Muintir na Tire Papers, P134/12/1/2/2).

20. A press account notes the serious financial challenges faced by the IGGA which managed to raise less than £300 in the 1928–1933 period ('The Irish Grain Growers' Association: A New Alliance', *Nenagh Guardian*, 25 March 1933).

21. See J. M. Hayes 'Our Story', *Rural Ireland* (1941), pp 35–44.

22. 'Muintir na Tire', undated (University of Galway Archives, Muintir na Tire Papers, P134/12/1/2/2).

23. Muintir na Tire Ltd. Annual Returns, Registrar of Friendly Societies, Dublin; see also Muintir na Tire Ltd Accounts for 1933, dated 7 April 1933 (University of Galway Archives, Muintir na Tire Papers, P134/7/2).

24. A contemporary press account reports Hayes as stating that Muintir na Tire was not '...going to have any political bias. They were bringing in men on a Catholic platform to unite the people on the principles of Catholicism. Those who did not want that could get out' (*Irish Independent*, 29 June 1934; see also Rynne, *Father John Hayes*, p. 118).

25. On subsidiarity, see J. H. Whyte, *Church and State in Modern Ireland 1923–1979* (Dublin: Gill and Macmillan, 1984), pp 67, 356.

26. 'New Rural Organisation Launched', *Tipperary Star*, 16 May 1931; Eoin Devereux, 'Class, Community and Conflict; The Case of Muintir na Tire Limited', *Tipperary Historical Journal*, 8 (1995), p. 96.

27. For an insight into John Hayes's thinking at this time, see J. M. Hayes and J. J. Bergin, *An Organisation to Develop Rural Ireland* (Tipperary: Muintir na Tire Rural Publications, 1932).

28. See 'Catholic Co-Operation: The Keynote of First Rural Week-End', *Tipperary Star*, 25 November 1933.

29. ibid.

30. ibid.

31. 'A "Cell" in Each District: Muintir na Tire Drive Planned at Abbey Weekend', *Irish Press*, 20 November 1933.

32. *Muintir na Tire Constitution* (Tipperary: Muintir na Tire Publications, 1938).

33. ibid.
34. Eoin Devereux, 'Potatoes, Turf and Fireside Chats: Muintir na Tíre and "The Emergency" in Limerick', *Old Limerick Journal*, 26 (1989), pp 34–6.
35. See, for example, Fr Hayes, Radió Éireann broadcast address, 11 September 1949 (University of Galway Archives, Muintir na Tíre Papers, P134/12/1/2/2).
36. See, for instance, the anonymous 'There's No Neighbourliness In Cities', *The Landmark*, 1:4 (1944), pp 8–9. See also Devereux, 'Saving Rural Ireland', pp 23–30.
37. See 'Opening of Two Factories in Tipperary Town: Unique Occasion in Industrial Revival', *Tipperary Star*, 13 June 1936. The Bansha Jam Factory (Rural Industries Ltd.) is described in P. P. O'Reilly's Radio Éireann Broadcast, 3 November 1948 ('Rural electrification of Bansha, Co Tipperary in 1948' (*REO News* 1948 No. 12 pp 5–6, www.esbarchives.ie)).
38. Undated speech (University of Galway Archives, Muintir na Tíre Papers, P134/12/1/2/2.
39. J. M. Hayes as reported in 'Agricultural Summer School: Fifth Year at Pallaskenry, Bishop's Address', *The Landmark*, 4:8 (1947), pp 3, 8.
40. Hayes, 1955 cited in Eoin Devereux, The Theory and Practice of Community Development: Muintir Na Tíre 1931–1988 (MA Thesis, Department of Political Science and Sociology, University College Galway 1988), pp 47–8).
41. Rynne, *Father John Hayes*, pp 219–20. For an account of how Fr Hayes and Professor Alfred O'Rahilly brokered the deal, see 'Dispute Over: End of Butchers' Strike, Settlement Reached Today', *Limerick Leader*, 27 August 1949.
42. 'Bishops Say Go Back' *The Irish Democrat*, No. 25, January 1947).
43. ibid.
44. 'Muintir na Tíre Ltd.', Annual Returns to the Registrar for Friendly Societies, 1934 (University of Galway Archives, Muintir na Tíre Papers, P134/7/2).
45. 'Guild Survey 1950–1952, Muintir Na Tíre Guild Files', A total of 99 surveyed cases were discovered by the author during archival research at Muintir Na Tíre's Headquarters in Tipperary Town in 1986 (See Devereux, The Theory and Practice of Community Development, pp 102–3).
46. Devereux 'John Hayes 1887–1957', p. 36.
47. ibid.
48. Undated account of meeting Mussolini (University of Galway Archives, Muintir na Tíre Papers, P134/12/1/2/12).
49. Signor Berardis, Envoy Extraordinary and Minister Plenipotentiary to Ireland, to Fr Hayes, 24 July 1943 (ibid.).
50. 'New Rural Organisation Launched', *Tipperary Star*, 16 May 1931.
51. Enniskeen Guild, County Cork (1949–58) and Durrow Guild, County Laois (1949–59) are among the examples Lynch gives here (David P. Lynch, 'The Triumph of Failure: A Preliminary Report on The Muintir na Tíre Guild Situation between 1950 and 1962' (Unpublished Muintir na Tíre discussion document, cited in Devereux, The Theory and Practice of Community Development, pp 16–17).
52. 'Can Ireland Survive?', *The Landmark*, 10:3 (1953), p. 10.
53. Hayes to de Valera, undated (National Archives of Ireland (NAI), Muintir na Tíre General File, S10816).
54. Hayes to de Valera, undated (ibid.).
55. Hayes to de Valera, undated (ibid.). Regarding state involvement, in a speech at a rural weekend held in Lucan on 9 November 1941 de Valera said: 'At no time was there a question of the State desiring to do that…That desire has come unfortunately from people forming parish councils or groups who have been trying to bring the State in and organise them and give them statutory functions. We have resisted that and agree with Fr Hayes that it would destroy the whole movement' (Tierney, *The Story of Muintir na Tíre 1931–2001*, p. 64; see also 'Plea for Parish Councils', *Irish Times*, 18 June 1940, in which de Valera is reported as giving some tentative positive signals as to the state supporting parish councils in the context of the Emergency. From time to time de Valera communicated with Fr Hayes; see, for example, his letter to him of 14 December 1956 in which he emphasised how Muintir na Tíre's guilds could be used to revive the Irish language (De Valera to Hayes, 14 December 1956 (NAI, Muintir na Tíre General File, S10816).
56. 'Waterford and Muintir Na Tíre: Father Hayes Congratulates The Government', *Munster Express*, 11 July 1941.

57. 'Scrutator' [an *Irish Times* journalist] asked in 1942: 'Can Muintir na Tíre undertake administrative responsibility of any kind without compromising its essential principle of voluntary service and unfettered local autonomy?' (Quoted in Tierney, *The Story of Muintir na Tíre 1931–2001*, p. 61).
58. 'Founder of Muintir Na Tíre: Address in Waterford City Hall to Five Parish Council Representatives', *Munster Express*, 11 July 1941.
59. Most notably, Archbishop John Charles McQuaid clashed with Muintir na Tíre and refused the movement permission to set up guilds in the Dublin Archdiocese (John Cooney, *John Charles McQuaid: Ruler of Catholic Ireland* (Dublin: O'Brien Press, 1999), pp 157–8).
60. See Eoin Devereux, 'Muintir Versus Macra: the Parish Plan for Agriculture, 1947–1957', *Tipperary Historical Journal*, 11 (1998), pp 89–94.
61. Patrick McNabb, 'Social Structure', in Jeremiah Newman (ed.), *The Limerick Rural Survey 1958–1964* (Tipperary: Muintir na Tíre Publications, 1964), p. 237.
62. See Jeremiah Newman (ed.), *The Limerick Rural Survey 1958–1964* (Tipperary: Muintir na Tíre Publications, 1964).

Cultivating Vocational Solidarity: The Class and Gender Politics of Organising Irish Agriculture

1. University of Galway Archives, Muintir na Tíre Papers, P134/12/1/2/2 (1 of 3), Fr Hayes, 'Address in Victoria Hotel, Cork, 28 April 1932', p. 1.
2. Stephen Rynne, *Father John Hayes* (Dublin: Clonmore and Reynolds, 1960), pp 107, 127, 76.
3. For the poverty of farm labourers – particularly on big labour-employing farms – see Dan Bradley, *Farm Labourers: Irish Struggle 1900–1976* (Belfast: Athol Books, 1988), pp 96–100.
4. Rynne, *Father John Hayes*, pp 91–2.
5. University of Galway Archives, Muintir na Tíre Papers, P134/12/1/2/2 (1 of 3), Fr Hayes, 'Address in Victoria Hotel, Cork, 28 April 1932', p. 6.
6. ibid., p. 6.
7. National Library of Ireland (NLI), Commission on Vocational Organisation (CVO), Muintir na Tíre, Memorandum, Ms 941, Document 191, p. 3. Between 1939 and 1943 Fr Hayes was an active member of the CVO.
8. ibid., pp 1–2.
9. Rynne, *Father John Hayes*, p. 90.
10. ibid., pp 91–2.
11. 'For centuries', he claimed in 1932, 'it was the policy of England to exterminate the Irish' (University of Galway Archives, Muintir na Tíre Papers, P134/12/1/2/2 (1 of 3), Fr Hayes, 'Lecture delivered at University College Cork, 28 April 1932', p. 3).
12. Rynne, *Father John Hayes*, pp 89–90, 63.
13. University of Galway Archives, Muintir na Tíre Papers, P134/12/1/2/2 (1 of 3), Fr Hayes, 'Address in Victoria Hotel, Cork, 28 April 1932', p. 6.
14. Tony Varley, '"Down with the Paris Farmer!" Frank MacDermot and Class Politics in 1930s Roscommon', in Richie Farrell, Kieran O'Conor and Matthew Potter (eds.), *Roscommon: History and Society* (Dublin: Geography Publications, 2018), p. 617.
15. Tony Varley, 'Farmers Against Nationalists: The Rise and Fall of Clann na Talmhan in Galway', in Gerard Moran and Raymond Gillespie (eds.), *Galway: History & Society* (Dublin: Geography Publications, 1996), p. 591. The imagery of farmers and their families as members not of a confident new farmer-owner class but of a downtrodden slave-class was further developed by Elizabeth Bobbett, the Irish Farmers' Federation's organising secretary from its formation in 1937 and a Clann candidate in the 1943 general election. In May 1939 Bobbett was viewing young women who married farmers as facing a life of 'slavery' on the land. 'All praise and full honour to the young men of the country', she declared, 'for not asking the girls to face such slavery, such savage conditions' (*Connacht Tribune*, 20 May 1939).
16. Varley, '"Down with the Paris Farmer!"', p. 619.
17. *Dáil Éireann Debates*, 48: 2765-6, 14 July 1933.
18. ibid., 91: 64, 1 July 1943.
19. Varley, '"Down with the Paris Farmer!"', p. 619.

20. *Connaught Telegraph*, 7 November 1942. Cogan was involved in the Irish Farmers' Federation (IFF) and his prominence in electoral politics in the late 1930s can be linked to the Fianna Fáil administration's refusal to consult with the IFF in the making of agricultural policy.

21. Rev. J. M. Hayes, 'Policy or Action?', in *Muintir na Tire Offical Handbook 1943*, p. 18. Rynne observes of Hayes how his '...Liverpool days were the happiest of his life...' (*Father John Hayes*, p. 65).

22. ibid., pp 91–2.

23. ibid., p. 92.

24. ibid., p. 107.

25. ibid., p. 141. 'We had enough of skeltons and ruins to tell us what not to do', he wrote in 1941, 'but we had very little to tell us what to do' (Father Hayes, 'The Beginning', in *Muintir na Tire Offical Handbook 1941*, p. 45).

26. Rynne, *Father John Hayes*, pp 118–19.

27. ibid., p. 137; Father Hayes, 'The Beginning', p. 45.

28. Evelyn Bolster, *The Knights of Saint Columbanus* (Dublin: Gill and Macmillan, 1979), p. 64.

29. Rynne, *Father John Hayes*, p. 137.

30. ibid., p. 17.

31. University of Galway Archives, Muintir na Tíre Papers, P134/12/1/2/2 (1 of 3), Fr Hayes, ''Lecture at the Mansion House, Dublin', 22 November 1940, p. 4.

32. Rev. J. M. Hayes, 'Policy or Action?', In *Muintir na Tire Offical Handbook 1943*, p. 19.

33. Mark Tierney, *The Story of Muintir na Tire 1931–2001 – The First Seventy Years* (Tipperary: Muintir na Tire, 2004), pp 34–5.

34. A young clerical student Tom Morris (later Archbishop of Cashel) attended the first Rural Week in Ardmore in 1937 and went on to became a 'pillar' of the movement and 'a valuable counterpoise to the often-too ebullient founder' (Rynne, *Father John Hayes*, p. 145). In 1935 Fr Hayes was also viewing schoolteachers as a potential source of significant leadership (J. M. Hayes 'The Aims of Muinntir (sic) na Tíre', *The Irish School Weekly*, 24 August 1935, pp 802–4).

35. Rynne, *Father John Hayes*, p. 171.

36. Mark Tierney, *The Story of Muintir na Tire*, p. 67; Rynne, *Father John Hayes*, pp 170–1; Maurice Curtis, *The Splendid Cause: The Catholic Action Movement in Ireland in the Twentieth Century* (Dublin: Original Writing and Greenmount Publications, 2009), pp 94–7. For an account of a Protestant highly committed north Galway Muintir activist, see Diarmuid Ó Cearbhaill, 'Bobby Burke and the Tuam Parish Council of Muintir na Tíre', *Journal of the Galway Archaeological and Historical Society*, 62 (2010), pp 202–12.

37. Bradley, *Farm Labourers*, p. 43; Emmet O'Connor, *Syndicalism in Ireland* (Cork: Cork University Press, 1988).

38. E. Rumpf and A. C. Hepburn, *Nationalism and Socialism in Twentieth-Century Ireland* (Liverpool: Liverpool University Press, 1977), pp 61, 37.

39. Kieran Allen, *Fianna Fáil and Irish Labour: 1926 to the Present* (London: Pluto Press, 1997), p. 51; Fearghal McGarry, *Eoin O'Duffy: A Self-Made Hero* (Oxford: Oxford University Press, 2005), p. 203; Mike Cronin, *The Blueshirts and Irish Politics* (Dublin: Four Courts Press, 1997), p. 156.

40. Paul Bew, Ellen Hazelkorn and Henry Patterson, *The Dynamics of Irish Politics* (London: Lawrence and Wishart, 1989), pp 47, 65–7. Apparently some Munster Blueshirts were being intimidated for 'refusing to dismiss non-Blueshirt labour' in August 1934 (ibid., p. 61).

41. *Tipperary Star*, 20 January 1934; Rynne, *Father John Hayes*, pp 107, 116.

42. ibid., p. 119; see *Irish Independent*, 29 June 1934.

43. Crotty, *Irish Agricultural Production: Its Volume and Structure* (Cork: Cork University Press, 1966), p. 141; Cronin, *The Blueshirts*, p. 160. The breakthrough achieved with the Coal-Cattle pact of December 1934 has been seen as allowing Blueshirt members 'return to normal conditions as party members of Fine Gael' (ibid., p. 155).

44. Father Hayes, 'The Beginning', p. 46.

45. ibid., 'The Beginning', p. 47.

46. Rev. J. M. Hayes, 'Policy or Action?', p. 18. Listed among Muintir's local activities in 1940 was: 'Improvement in House-Keeping by arranging classes in cookery, needle-work, etc.' (NLI, CVO, Muintir na Tire, Memorandum, Ms 941, Document 191, p. 6).

47. Jerome Toner, *Rural Ireland: Some of its Problems* (Dublin: Clonmore & Reynods, 1955), p. 41.

48. Father Hayes, 'The Beginning', p. 46.

49. Rynne, *Father John Hayes*, p. 90.

50. ibid., p. 90. A parishioner remembered him as 'greatly down on the ranchers' while a curate in his first parish of Kilbeg and Staholmog in County Meath in 1913 (ibid., p, 49).

51. NLI, CVO, Muintir na Tíre, Memorandum, Ms 941, Document 191, pp 1, 5.

52. ibid., p. 1

53. Economic power differences between property owners and labourers were explicitly acknowledged in 1940. An arrangement that could vary 'from section to section' provided for farmers and business people to be asked to contribute 2/6d a year and labourers 1/- or 6d (NLI, CVO, Muintir na Tíre, Minutes of Evidence, Ms 930, Vol. 9, 8 November 1940, p. 2842).

54. To use the language of 'class' was to conjure up divisive images of strife between antagonistic classes and even the spectre of out-and-out 'class war'. Reflecting on the early days in 1941, Fr Hayes recalled how 'We were out to fight nobody, but to help everybody. Muintir na Tíre from its very name excluded class war' (Father Hayes, 'The Beginning', p. 43). The distaste for 'class' in Muintir, and in Irish Catholic social thinking more generally, is discussed by Seán L'Estrange in '"A Community of Communiites" – Catholic Communitarianism and Societal Crises in Ireland, 1890s-1950s', *Journal of Historical Sociology*, 20:4 (2007), pp 555–78. George Thomason links the consensus-seeking and unifying Fr Hayes with his move to Tipperary Town in 1934. That move he sees as bringing him '… into contact with more clearly defined class and interest group antagonisms than were apparent in Castleiny, and here he probably came to grasp more clearly than before the need for some organisation which would emphasise the whole, or the unity, and which would supplement or act as a foil for the sectional, interest-group and class organisations whose operation in isolation tended to emphasise the differences rather than the similarities' (George F. Thomason, *Giving the Lead* (Tipperary: Muintir na Tíre Publications, 1962), pp 9–10).

55. 'Sectional interests', as he once put it, 'must give way to the interests of the community as a whole' (University of Galway Archives, Muintir na Tíre Papers, P134/12/1/2/2 (1 of 3), Fr Hayes, 'More Memories', undated, p. 5).

56. At public meetings John Hayes would regularly say how the pressing challenge for Irish patriots was 'to live (rather than die) for Ireland' (Interview, Tom Fitzgerald, Canon Hayes House, Tipperary Town, 20 August 1998).

57. University of Galway Archives, Muintir na Tíre Papers, P134/12/1/2/2 (1 of 3), Fr Hayes, 'Speech delivered at Rockwell College, April 1937', p. 2.

58. Raymond Ryan, 'The National Farmers' and Ratepayers' League', *Studia Hibernica*, 34 (2006/2007), p. 177.

59. *Irish Times*, 26 November 1932.

60. Michael Gallagher, *Political Parties in the Republic of Ireland* (Dublin: Gill and Macmillan, 1985), p. 103.

61. *Irish Times*, 8 April 1961.

62. The IFF, as was true of the IFU in 1920, had officially registered itself as a trade union in 1937 (*Farmers' Gazette*, 13 March 1937).

63. *Irish Press*, 13 January, 1943; *Irish Independent*, 8 April, 1943.

64. NLI, CVO, Clann na Talmhan, Memorandum to Commission on Vocational Organisation, Ms 941, Document 185, p. 2. Michael Donnellan's early disenchantment with Irish public life wasn't confined to nationalist politicians. His suggestion in 1942 was that: 'You could take all the TDs, all the Senators, all the Ministers and members of the judiciary and all the other nice fellows and dump them off Clare Island into the broad Atlantic. Still, Ireland would succeed. But without the workers and producers the country would starve in 24 hours'. (*Irish Farmers' Paper*, 2:1, July 1942).

65. Commission on Vocational Organisation *Report* (Dublin: The Stationery Office, 1944), pp 127, 341.

66. ibid., pp 127, 341.

67. Fr Hayes had concurred with Bishop Browne's suggestion in 1940 that the 'Irish farmer is supposed to be a great individualist and to resist all organisation' (NLI, CVO, Muintir na Tíre, Evidence, Ms 930, p. 2850). See also CVO *Report*, p. 127.

68. Tony Varley, 'On the Road to Extinction: Agrarian Parties in Twentieth-Century Ireland', *Irish Political Studies*, 25:4 (2010), pp 586, 593.

69. University College Dublin Archives (UCDA), Minute Book of the National Farmers' and Ratepayers' League Standing Committee, 3 June 1933, P39/MIN/6.
70. ibid., 9 June 1933.
71. Varley, 'On the Road to Extinction', pp 586–7, 593–4.
72. NLI, CVO, Clann na Talmhan, Minutes of Evidence, Ms 931, Vol. 10, 18 April 1941, p. 3176. Donnellan excluded 'the grazing man' from the ranks of the working farmers and suggested that an over 200-acre holder was 'not, as a rule, a working farmer' (ibid., p. 3177).
73. *Connacht Tribune*, 30 March 1940.
74. Wholly exceptional here was Elizabeth F. Bobbett, the Irish Farmers' Federation's dynamic organising secretary, who as well as farming in her own right in County Wicklow stood (unsuccessfully) as a Clann candidate in Dublin County in the 1943 general election and was later elected as a member of Wicklow County Council (see Peter Moser and Tony Varley, 'Corporatism, Agricultural Modernisation and War in Ireland and Switzerland, 1935 –1955', in Paul Brassley, Yves Segers and Leen Van Molle (eds.), *War, Agriculture, and Food: Rural Europe from the 1930s to the 1950s* (London: Routledge, 2012), pp 137, 144–5, 154). Another notable exception was Kathleen Browne from County Wexford. For an account of her farming and public life as a Sinn Féin and pro-Treaty activist and Senate member, see Mary McAuliffe, *Senator Kathleen A. Browne 1876–1943: Patriot, Politician and Practical Farmer* (Roscrea: Roscrea Publications, 2008), pp 51–62 , 74–110.
75. Stephen Rynne, 'Farming, the Free-for-all', *Rural Ireland 1950*, p. 118.
76. Dermot Keogh, *Ireland and the Vatican: The Politics and Diplomacy of Church-State Relations, 1922–1960* (Cork: Cork University Press, 1995), pp 110–11.
77. See Gearóid Ó Tuathaigh, 'Cultural Visions and the New State: Embedding and Embalming', in Gabriel Doherty and Dermot Keogh (eds.), *De Valera's Irelands* (Cork: Mercier Press, 2003), pp 177–8.
78. He made a point of regularly attending the Rural Weeks (Rynne, *Father John Hayes*, pp 144–6; Frank Lyddy, 'Rural Weeks', *Rural Ireland 1960*, pp 84–5).
79. Tierney, *The Story of Muintir na Tíre*, pp 59–64.
80. Toner, *Rural Ireland*, p. 54.
81. CVO *Report*, pp 339–48.
82. Recently Patrick Joyce has reminded us how 'the townland was and is the fundamental unit of social identity in rural Ireland' (*Remembering Peasants: A Personal History of a Vanished World* (London: Allen Lane, 2024), p. 120).
83. While Muintir wasn't encouraging its parish guilds/councils to have a youth section in 1940, the CVO report's view was that '…a youth section for boys and girls, possibly on the lines of the 4-H Clubs of the U.S.A. or the Young Farmers' Clubs may be expected to develop' (CVO *Report*, p. 340).
84. ibid., p. 340.
85. ibid., pp 341–2.
86. ibid., pp 341.
87. Along the same lines Muintir had informed the CVO in 1940 that the state investing its guilds 'with administrative powers' was achievable 'without distracting from the voluntary character of the Association as a whole' (NLI, CVO, Muintir na Tíre, Memorandum, Ms 941, Document 191, p. 8).
88. CVO *Report*, p. 344.
89. ibid., pp 344. Conspicuously absent from this list of sections were farmers' wives. As to the participation of farm labourers, it was remarked vaguely that 'there may be some difficulty' (ibid. pp 344–5).
90. CVO *Report*, p. 345.
91. ibid., p. 345. For Fr Hayes's interpretation of the CVO's proposals here, and Muintir's centrality to their implementation, see Fr J. M. Hayes, 'Vocationalism and Agriculture', *The Landmark*, 1:4, November 1944, pp 2–3.
92. ibid., p. 341. Here the CVO *Report* warned that 'If government departments regard these Guilds as dangerous or as nuisances, or are unwilling to permit a certain amount of decentralisation of responsibility and administration, no scheme of local organisation can work' (CVO *Report*, p. 341).
93. ibid., p. 341.
94. ibid., p. 341, Footnote 1.

95. Don O'Leary, *Vocationalism and Social Catholicism in Twentieth-Century Ireland: The Search for a Christian Social Order* (Dublin: Irish Academic Press, 2000), p. 138.

96. While privately highly critical of the Fianna Fáil rejection of the CVO report, Fr Hayes apparently held his fire in public. See ibid., pp 137–8, 144.

97. *Irish Press*, 31 October 1944; O'Leary, *Vocationalism and Social Catholicism*, pp 111–12. Speaking at the opening of a Catholic Social Week on 30 October 1944, Minister Ryan had also 'assured Fr Hayes that there would be no opposition from the Government or the higher civil servants if [he] and his enthusiasts set out to build up a vocational organisation' (Fr J. M. Hayes, 'Vocationalism and Agriculture', p. 3).

98. J. L. McCracken, *Representative Government in Ireland: A Study of Dáil Eireann* (London: Oxford University Press, 1958), pp 115–16. McCracken's occupational analysis indicates that 25 per cent of Cumann na nGaedheal/Fine Gael TDs and 31 per cent of Fianna Fáil's up to 1948 were farmers (ibid., p. 115).

99. In like manner Fianna Fáil's main pro-Treaty rival tended to be dismissed as a party of strong farmers and ranchers (Maurice Manning, *The Blueshirts* (Dublin: Gill and Macmillan, 1970), p. 133; M. A. G. Ó Tuathaigh, 'The Land Question, Politics and Irish Society, 1922–1960', in P. J. Drudy (ed.), *Ireland: Land, Politics and People* (Cambridge: Cambridge University Press, 1982), p. 182; Emmet O'Connor, *A Labour History of Ireland 1824–2000* (Dublin: University College Dublin Press, 2011), pp 128–9).

100. *Wicklow People*, 15 January 1938.

101. Varley, '"Down with the Paris Farmer!"', pp 621, 633.

102. ibid., p. 622.

103. Interview, John Gleeson, Ballingarry, Kilchreest, 10 June 1984.

104. *Connacht Tribune*, 30 March 1940.

105. ibid., 31 May 1947.

106. O'Leary, *Vocationalism and Social Catholicism*, p. 44.

107. NLI, CVO, Muintir na Tíre, Evidence, Ms 930, p. 2844.

108. ibid., p. 2843. The parish guilds would increase in number from just 20 to 90 between 1939 and 1947 (Tierney, *The Story of Muintir na Tíre*, p. 53).

109. ibid., Chapter 7; Mícheál Ó Fathartaigh, *Developing Rural Ireland: A History of the Irish Agricultural Services* (Dublin: Wordwell, 2021), pp 244–51.

110. Robert. E. Kennedy, *The Irish, Emigration, Marriage and Fertility* (Los Angeles: University of California Press, 1973), pp 95–8.

111. Father Hayes, 'The Beginning', p. 43.

112. Mark Tierney, *The Story of Muintir na Tíre*, p. 31.

113. Grain farmers, for instance, were wont to sell dear while pig farmers desired to pruchase cheap feeding stuffs (Rynne, *Father John Hayes*, p. 107).

114. Devereux suggests that farm workers' participation was 'hampered by the often bitter conflict between farmers and their labourers' (Eoin Devereux, 'Saving Rural Ireland – Muintir na Tíre and its Anti-Urbanism, 1931–1958', *Canadian Journal of Irish Studies* 17:2 (1991), pp 25–6).

115. Patrick Bolger, *The Irish Co-operative Movement: Its History and Development* (Dublin: Institute of Public Administration, 1977), p. 118.

116. Rynne, *Father John Hayes*, pp 118–19; *Irish Independent*, 29 June 1934.

117. Patrick McNabb, 'Social Structure', in Jeremiah Newman (ed.), *The Limerick Rural Survey 1958–1964* (Tipperary: Muintir na Tíre Publications, 1964), p. 208.

118. ibid., p. 208.

119. ibid., p. 208. Farm workmen were entirely absent from the Muintir council Marilyn Silverman describes in Thomastown, County Kilkenny (*An Irish Working Class: Explorations in Political Economy and Hegemony, 1800–1950* (Toronto: University of Toronto Press, 2001), p. 495).

120. Left unexplored in McNabb's account was how much (and in what ways) the local notables' conception of the common good equated with their own economic interests. Nor does McNabb mention women's involvement in local Muintir. A list of County Limerick guild secretaries published in 1964 indicates that five of 33 of them were women ('Guilds of Muintir na Tíre in Co. Limerick', in Jeremiah Newman (ed.), *The Limerick Rural Survey 1958–1964*), pp 325–6).

121. McNabb, 'Social Structure', p. 245.

122. John J. Scully, *The Community as a Social System for Action Programmes* (Tipperary: Muintir na Tíre Publications, 1963)., pp 39–40.

123. Rynne, *Father John Hayes*, p. 145.

124. Josephine McNeill, 'Give a Hand to the Women!', *Muintir na Tíre Offical Handbook 1941* (Tipperary: Muintir na Tíre Publications, 1941), p. 52.

125. ibid., p. 53.

126. NLI, CVO, Muintir na Tíre, Evidence, Ms 930, p. 2849.

127. Rynne, *Father John Hayes*, p. 141. After it had been going for some time Fr Hayes recorded how: 'For ten years the Parish Council in Tipperary, through its women's section, has been running a restaurant for the poor' (University of Galway Archives, Muintir na Tíre Papers, P134/12/1/2/2 (1 of 3), Fr Hayes, 'More Memories', undated, p. 4).

128. NLI, CVO, Muintir na Tíre, Minutes of Evidence, Ms 930, p. 2850.

129. ibid., p. 2848.

130. ibid., p. 2850.

131. NLI, CVO, Irish Countrywomen's Association, Minutes of Evidence, Ms 930, Vol. 9, 21 November 1940, pp 2934–5. Two decades later a member of the young farmers' movement Macra na Feirme made a parallel point: 'In Muintir you have all age groups, and you cannot speak your mind when old people are present. You feel freer in Macra' (Patrick McNabb, 'Social Structure', p. 237).

132. NLI, CVO, ICA, Evidence, Ms 930, p. 2935..

133. ibid., p. 2935. Where women's involvement in Muintir was concerned Muriel Gahan further pointed out how: 'It is not possible to have women on exactly the same level as men because women, whilst being producers, are also very important consumers' (ibid. p. 2935).

134. CVO *Report*, p. 279. The CVO report could also 'well visualise the desirability' of having a specific section concerned with 'the needs and interests of the family or household', a section that 'normally...would be mainly formed by the women of the parish' (CVO *Report*. p. 340).

135. The CVO reported the IFF as having made 'ineffective efforts...to secure the co-operation of the Irish Sugar Beet Growers' Association, Muintir an Tíre and the Royal Dublin Society' (CVO *Report*, p. 134).

136. The Workers' Union of Ireland had begun to re-organise Irish agricultural labourers in 1943 and out of its efforts a new organisation, the Federation of Rural Workers, appeared in 1946 (Bradley, *Farm Labourers*, p. 74).

137. See Eoin Devereux, 'Muintir versus Macra: The Parish Plan for Agriculture, 1947–1957', *Tipperary Historical Journal*, 11 (1998), pp 92–3; *The Future of Agriculture in Ireland: Written in Plain Language by Farmers for Farmers* (Dublin: Irish Farmers' Federation, 1945).

138. The ICA women appearing before the CVO in 1940 would also argue in favour of organising Irish country women separately in the first instance. In 1964 the Department of Agriculture was accepting that Muintir was an ineffectual force for local agricultural change when compared with the mainstream farmer associations (NAI, S17138B/95, Department of Agriculture, 'Muintir na Tíre Plan for Community Development in Ireland').

139. Bradley, *Farm Labourers: Irish Struggle*, Chap. 6.

140. Michael Gallagher, *Irish Elections 1922–44: Results and Analysis, Vol. 1*, (PSAI Press, Limerick, 1993), pp 126, 136–7, 141, 158, 167–8, 172.

141. ibid., pp 260, 262–3. In the same election Clann and the Labour Party won seats at Fine Gael's and Fianna Fáil's expense in Kerry North and Tipperary (ibid., pp 255, 263).

142. Varley, '"Down With the Paris Farmer"', p. 623.

143. Likewise central to the CVO's conception of 'true vocationalism' – in Joseph Lee's view – was the subordination of sectional interests to the common good. But, as Lee points out, how the general common good '...was to emerge from a conflict in the National Vocational Assembly of sectional interests each dedicated to the primacy of its own pocket remained constantly obscure throughout the evidence and the Report' ('Aspects of Corporatist Thought in Ireland: The Commission of Vocational Organisation, 1939–43', in Art Cosgrove and Donal McCartney (eds.), *Studies in Irish History: Presented to R. Dudley Edwards* (Dublin: University College Dublin, 1979), p. 339).

144. As one of de Valera's 11 nominated members to the new Seanad Éireann, MacDermot was showing a keen interest in Catholic vocationalism in the late 1930s (Martin O'Donoghue, *The Legacy*

of the Irish Parliamentary Party in Independent Ireland, 1922–1949 (Liverpool: Liverpool University Press, 2019), pp 177–8).

145. V. Rev. M. Morrissey, 'A Long Association', *Rural Ireland 1960*, p. 31; Con Lucey, 'Community Development – How to Set About It', *Rural Ireland 1960*, pp 24–9.

POWER AND THE POLITICS OF PERSUASION: COMPARING MUINTIR NA TÍRE'S AND
TUAIRIM'S RELATIONSHIPS WITH CHURCH AND STATE IN POST-WAR IRELAND

1. Muintir na Tíre can be translated as 'People of the Countryside' and Tuairim as 'Opinion'.
2. Galway Diocesan Archives (GDA), Bishop Browne papers, B/1/3, *Irish Independent*, 14 August 1939. Bishop Browne could be critical of Muintir (at least in private) as well as a strong and active supporter. In 1952 he went so far as to reprove the organisation for its delay in 'sending a person who will explain the advantage of it to the people of this diocese' (GDA, Browne papers, B/1/3, Browne to Hayes, 17 December 1952).
3. GDA, Browne papers, B/1/3, M. Kenny to Browne, 9 July 1968 and report sent from Tomás Roseingrave to Browne.
4. Dublin Diocesan Archives (DDA), Archbishop McQuaid papers, AB8/XXI/126/4, Christus Rex, Archbishop McQuaid to Fr James Kavanagh, 2 December 1959.
5. DDA, McQuaid papers, AB8/A/VIII74/1, McQuaid 'Our Divine Lord Jesus Christ or Satan: The Real Struggle in the Modern World', 13 March, 1932, pp 19, 21.
6. ibid., McQuaid papers, McQuaid, 'Our Divine Lord Jesus Christ', p. 21.
7. ibid., McQuaid papers, IE/DDA/AB8/b/XXI/200/2, Muintir na Tíre, McQuaid to Fr MacMahon, 6 November, 1941.
8. ibid., McQuaid papers, AB8/A/VIII74/1, McQuaid, 'Our Divine Lord Jesus Christ', p. 8.
9. John Cooney, *John Charles McQuaid: Ruler of Catholic Ireland* (Dublin: O'Brien Press, 1999), p. 158; Peter Murray and Maria Feeney, *Church, State and Social Science in Ireland: Knowledge, Institutions and the Rebalancing of Power, 1937–73* (Manchester: Manchester University Press, 2017), pp 76–8; Stephen Rynne, *Father John Hayes: Founder of Muintir na Tire People of the Land* (Dublin: Clonmore and Reynolds, 1960), pp 170–1.
10. DDA, McQuaid papers, 210/121/13/5/3, P. McDonald to McQuaid, 11 February 1942. A press account reports that a Muintir Associate Guild was formed in Dublin in 1939 (*Irish Press*, 15 November 1939).
11. DDA, McQuaid papers, IE/DDA/AB8/b/XXI/200/2, Muintir na Tíre, McQuaid to Fr MacMahon, 6 November 1941.
12. Tomás Finn, *Tuairim, Intellectual Debate and Policy Formulation: Rethinking Ireland* (Manchester: Manchester University Press, 2012), pp 35–9.
13. ibid., pp 184–96.
14. ibid., pp 38–9, 24, 210–22.
15. DDA, McQuaid papers, IE/DDA/AB8/b/XXI/200/10/4, Muintir na Tíre, Letter from Rynne, 30 March 1955.
16. ibid., McQuaid papers, IE/DDA/AB8/b/XXI/200/10/2, Muintir na Tíre, McQuaid's Secretary to Rynne, 21 March 1955.
17. GDA, Browne Papers, B/1/3, Pius XII to John M. Hayes, 14 July 1954.
18. *Irish Times*, 11 August 1942, 14 August 1940 and 10 August 1954.
19. Eoin Devereux, 'Saving Rural Ireland: Muintir na Tire and its Anti-Urbanism, 1931–1958', *The Canadian Journal of Irish Studies*, 17:2 (1991), p. 27.
20. Cooney, *McQuaid*, p. 158; DDA, McQuaid Papers, IE/DDA/AB8/b/XXI/200/3, Muintir na Tíre, First National Appeal; Anonymous, 'President Opens Twenty-Second Rural Week', *The Landmark*, 16:8 (1959), pp 1–2; *Irish Press*, 7 March 1946.
21. *Irish Independent*, 1 February 1954.
22. See Don O'Leary, *Vocationalism and Social Catholicism in Twentieth-century Ireland: The Search for a Christian Social Order* (Dublin: Irish Academic Press, 2000).
23. DDA, McQuaid papers, AB8/XXI/126/4, Christus Rex, Fr J Kavanagh, UCD to McQuaid, 30 November 1959, McQuaid to Kavanagh, 2 December 1959; AB8/XV.C.194–264, Hierarchy

Correspondence (Cashel and Emly), Morris to McQuaid, 17 July 1963 [328] and 29 September 1960 [241].

24. Murray and Feeney, *Church, State and Social Science in Ireland*, pp 77–8.

25. Finn, *Tuairim*, p. 98; Tomás Roseingrave, 'Government and Voluntary Organisations', *Rural Ireland*, 30 (1970), pp 18–26.

26. Roseingrave, 'Government and Voluntary Organisations', p. 26.

27. Tomás Finn, '"Towards a Better Ireland": Donal Barrington and the Irish Constitution,' in Laura Cahillane, James Gallen and Tom Hickey (eds.), *Judges, Politics and the Irish Constitution* (Manchester: Manchester University Press, 2017), pp 217–33.

28. Finn, '"Towards a better Ireland"', p. 224.

29. DDA, McQuaid papers, IE/DDA/AB8/b/XXI/200/1/1, Muintir na Tíre, Hayes to McQuaid, 4 November 1941.

30. *Irish Times*, 22 July and 23 November 1940.

31. *Irish Times*, 10 November 1941. See also *Irish Times*, 18 June 1940 and 22 November 1941.

32. National Archives of Ireland (NAI), S10816A, Muintir na Tíre General File, Éamon de Valera to Fr Hayes, 24 October 1939.

33. *Irish Times*, 18 June 1941, 10 November 1941; *Irish Press*, 16 August 1958.

34. *Irish Times*, 3 April 1941.

35. *Irish Times*, 27 July 1940.

36. NAI, S10816A, Muintir na Tíre General file, Rev. J. M. Canon Hayes, Address to Congress, 1955.

37. DDA, McQuaid papers, IE/DDA/AB8/b/XXI/200/10/4, Muintir na Tíre. Attached to request of 30 March 1955 from Stephen Rynne asking permission to establish a Muintir group in the Naas/Prosperous district.

38. Maurice Manning, *James Dillon* (Dublin: Wolfhound Press, 1999), p. 305. Lucey criticised 'the average citizen...for his childlike, if not childish unwillingness to stand on his own feet'. (*Irish Times*, 19 August 1957).

39. *Irish Times*, 7 May 1954.

40. Mary Daly, *The First Department: A History of the Department of Agriculture*, (Dublin: Institute of Public Administration, 2002), pp 402–6 and Manning, *Dillon*, pp 302–6.

41. NAI, S10816A, Muintir na Tíre General file, Hayes to Costello, 8 September 1956. See also, *Irish Independent*, 27 August 1956.

42. Mark Tierney, *The Story of Muintir na Tire: The First Seventy Years* (Tipperary: Muintir na Tíre, 2004), pp 131–3.

43. Peter Murray and Maria Feeney, 'The Market for Sociological Ideas in Early 1960s Ireland: Civil Service Departments and the Limerick Rural Survey', *Administration*, 59:1 (2011), p. 127; Jeremiah Newman (ed.), *The Limerick Rural Survey 1958–1964* (Tipperary: Muintir na Tíre Publications, 1964).

44. NAI, S17138B/95, Community Development: Federation of Local Development Associations, General, Membership of the County Development Teams, 15 November 1964 (Copy of S17380B).

45. Liam Irwin, 'Newman, Jeremiah', *Dictionary of Irish Biography* (Cambridge; Cambridge University Press, 2009), pp 897–8.

46. NAI, DT, S17138A/61, Community Development in Ireland: Federation of Local Development Associations, 'Report on community development by the Economic Development branch of the Department of Finance', August 1961, p. 22.

47. Murray and Feeney, 'The Market for Sociological Ideas'.

48. NAI, S17138B/95, Community Development, Muintir na Tíre plan for Community Development.

49. ibid., S17138B/95, Community Development, T. Ó Cearbhaill, Memorandum, 28 Mean Fómhair 1964.

50. ibid., S17138B/95, Community Development, T. Ó Cearbhaill, Memorandum, 2 December 1964.

51. ibid., S17138B/95, Community Development, Report of Meeting, 29 October 1964, p. 2.

52. *Dáil Éireann Debates*, 176: 1577, 21 July 1959, 'Committee on Finance – vote 3, Department of Taoiseach'.

53. Finn, *Tuairim*, pp 39–46.

54. UCD Archives, John A. Costello Papers, P190/266, Memorandum, no date. [c. a. 1959]. For more on the youth political wings of Irish political parties, see Tomás Finn, 'Politics and the Praxis of Power: The Political Establishment and the Talented Young in post-WWII Ireland', in Tomás Finn

and Kieran Hoare (eds.), *Borders and Boundaries: Historical Perspectives* (Abingdon: Routledge Press, forthcoming).

55. Finn, *Tuairim*, pp 26–7.

56. Finn, The Influence of Tuairim on Intellectual Debate and Policy Formulation in Ireland, 1954–1975 (PhD thesis, National University of Ireland, Galway, 2008), pp 145–51.

57. *Irish Times*, 15, 17 April 1959.

58. Finn, *Tuairim*, p. 184.

59. NAI, S17138B/95, Community Development, Document, 1961.

60. Finn, *Tuairim*, p. 30.

CONTEMPORARY RURAL LIFE IN IRISH FICTION OF THE 1940S

1. John Feehan, *An Irish Publisher and his World* (Cork: Mercier, 1969), p. 15; Tony Farmar, *The History of Irish Book Publishing* (Stroud: The History Press, 2018), p. 217. Farmar maintains that Irish people were not great book-*buyers*; Feehan disagrees, but both agree that Irish people were great readers.

2. Elizabeth Russell, 'Holy Crosses, Guns and Roses: Themes in Popular Reading Material', in Joost Augusteijn (ed.), *Ireland in the 1930s: New Perspectives* (Dublin: Four Courts Press, 1999), pp 11–28.

3. O'Brien is a perceptive chronicler of middle-class urban life, but in the farming Costello family in *Pray For The Wanderer* (London: Heinemann 1938), a bottle of champagne is opened at (evening) dinner to celebrate a cow's recovery from illness.

4. A small selection of fiction by these authors in the 1940s and early 50s would include John D. Sheridan, *Paradise Alley* (Dublin: Talbot Press, 1945) and *The Magnificent McDarney* (Dublin: Talbot Press, 1947); Elizabeth Brennan, *Am I My Brother's Keeper?* [Hereafter: *Keeper*] (Dublin: Metropolitan Publishing Company, 1945); M. L. Stewart, *The Cliff-Dwellers* (Dublin: Talbot Press, 1943); William Hand, *Fair City* (Dublin: Clonmore & Reynolds, 1946); Annie M. P. Smithson, *Paid in Full* (Dublin: Talbot, 1946); Kate O'Brien, *Pray For The Wanderer* [Hereafter: *Wanderer*] (London: Heinemann, 1938), pp 10–11, 145 and passim. In Norah Hoult, *Selected Stories* (Dublin: Maurice Fridberg, 1946) and a collection of her stories edited by Sinéad Gleeson, *Cocktail Bar* (Dublin: New Island, 2019 [1950]), rurality is backgrounded. Mary Lavin, *Tales From Bective Bridge* [Hereafter: *Bective*] (London: Michael Joseph, 1943; Dublin: Poolbeg 1978) and *The Becker Wives* (London: Michael Joseph, 1946); Maura Laverty, *Never No More: The Story of a Lost Village* (London: Longmans Green, 1942), *Alone We Embark* (London: Longmans Green, 1943), *No More Than Human* (London; Longmans Green, 1944) and *Lift Up Your Gates* (London: Longmans Green, 1946); Olivia Robertson, *St Malachy's Court* (London: Peter Davies, 1946); *Field of the Stranger* (London: Peter Davies, 1948) and *The Golden Eye* (London: Peter Davies, 1949). Norah Hoult makes forays into rural and small-town life in *Cocktail Bar* and in the partly-comical, partly-serious *Father Hone and the Television Set* (London: Hutchinson, 1956).

5. My focus is on the 1940s more or less. The narratives of Laverty's *Alone We Embark* and Patrick Kavanagh's *Tarry Flynn* (London: The Pilot Press, 1948; Penguin 1978) commence in the 1930s, but both build towards the 1940s.

6. *Easons' Bulletin* 1945–53, for example, has profiles of and interviews with many of the authors whose works are discussed here, such as Temple Lane, *Easons' Bulletin*, 1:5 (September, 1945); Francis MacManus, ibid., 1:9 (January, 1946), and Olivia Robertson, ibid., 5:12 (April, 1950). There are many other authors who wrote about the Ireland of their time and who were reviewed in the newspapers over these years who are omitted from this analysis for reasons of time and space. Chief among second-hand bookshops for books from this era is Chapters on Parnell St. Dublin 1; Galway's Bell, Book and Candle and Bargain Books in Kilkenny's Butterslip are also very good.

7. Kathleen Joyce-Prendergast's *Windy Hill* (Cork: Mercier Press, 1945), is a bit like Annie M. P. Smithson in this regard, and therefore will be referred to only peripherally, even though it deals with rural Ireland.

8. Anne Crone, *Bridie Steen* (London: Heinemann, 1949); M. H. Campbell, *As Luck Would Have It* (Dundalk: Dundalgan Press, 1948); Kavanagh, *Flynn*, passim. References are to the Penguin reprint. Laverty's classic autobiographical novel *Never No More* (see note 4 above) although it is set in rural and

small-town Ireland (a fictionalised Rathangan, Co. Kildare,) is not included in this analysis because it is set in 1918–22 rather than in the 1940s.

9. Laverty, *Alone*, p. 6; Francis MacManus, *Flow On Lovely River* (Dublin: Talbot Press, 1940), p. 8.

10. Patrick Purcell, *A Keeper of Swans* (Dublin: Talbot Press, 1944), p. 135.

11. Kavanagh, *Flynn*, p. 89.

12. Sheila Pim, *The Flowering Shamrock* (London: Hodder & Stoughton, 1947), pp 91–2.

13. Mary Purcell, *The Pilgrim Came Late* (Dublin: Clonmore & Reynolds, 1947), pp 10–15, 25–7 and passim.

14. K. D. M. Snell, 'A Drop of Water from a Stagnant Pool? Interwar Detective Fiction and the Rural Community', *Social History*, 35:1 (2010), pp 21–50.

15. Purcell, *Swans*, p. 65.

16. Patrick Purcell, *Hanrahan's Daughter* (Dublin: Talbot Press, 1940), p. 45.

17. Francis MacManus, *Watergate* (Dublin: Talbot Press, 1942 and Dublin: Poolbeg, 1980), pp 6, 10 and passim (all references are to the Poolbeg edition); Temple Lane, *Friday's Well* (Dublin: Talbot Press, 1943); Philip Rooney, *Singing River* (Dublin: Talbot Press, 1944), p. 52.

18. MacManus, *Watergate*, p. 167 and passim and *River*, passim. See also Purcell, *Pilgrim*, pp 20–4 and passim; Pim, *Shamrock*, pp 9–61; Purcell, *Swans*, pp 36–9, 37, 72–3; Laverty, *Alone*, pp 46–50. For English anti-urban writing, see for example J. B. Priestley, *English Journey* (London: Victor Gollancz, 1934) and R. C. Sherriff, *Greengates* (London: Victor Gollancz, 1936) among many others.

19. Rooney, *Singing*, p. 60; Purcell, *Swans*, p. 44 and passim; Lane, *Well*, passim. References to bicycles are too numerous to mention in all the works, but see particularly *Swans*, p. 131. It would be impossible to list the novels in which the car forms part of a major plot device without 'spoiling' the stories.

20. MacManus, *River*, p. 26; Purcell, *Hanrahan's*, pp 108–9, 110–114; Pim, *Shamrock*, p. 110; Robertson, *Stranger*, p. 212.

21. Kavanagh, *Flynn*, pp5–6; Purcell, *Swans*, pp 135–7.

22. For example, the villages around the Shannon scheme in Ardnacrusha, Co. Clare, all had electricity from the 1930s, but they did not get a piped water supply until the early 1960s. Lane, *Well*, p. 26.

23. Robertson, *Stranger*, p. 49.

24. Kavanagh, *Flynn*, p. 122 and passim; MacManus, *Watergate*, p. 65; Purcell, *Hanrahan's*, p. 190; MacManus, *River*, p. 26; Robertson, *Stranger*, p. 48; Pim, *Shamrock*, pp 84–5; Lane, *Well*, p. 117, pp 113–14; Kavanagh, *Flynn*, p. 48; Purcell, *Hanrahan's*, p. 139, pp 129–30.

25. Purcell, *Swans*, pp 72–3 and passim; *Hanrahan's*, pp 129–40; Robertson, *Stranger*, p. 238; MacManus, *Watergate*, pp 74, 140; Joyce-Prendergast, *Windy Hill*, pp 10–11.

26. MacManus, *River*, pp 41, 43–4; Purcell, *Swans*, pp 50–4; Laverty, *Alone*, p. 31; Kavanagh, *Flynn*, pp 148–56.

27. Mary Purcell, *Pilgrim*, p. 72; Robertson, *Stranger*, p. 24; MacManus, *Watergate*, p. 79; Helen Byrne, '"Going to the Pictures": the Female Audience and the Pleasures of Cinema', in Mary J. Kelly & Barbara O'Connor (eds.), *Media Audiences in Ireland: Power and Cultural Identity* (Dublin: UCD Press, 1997), pp 88–106.

28. Russell, 'Holy Crosses', pp 13–14 and passim.

29. MacManus, *River*, p. 103, p. 105; M. Purcell, *Pilgrim*, p. 36; Purcell, *Swans*, pp 182–3, 50–4; McManus, River, pp 54, 78, 98–9; Laverty, *Alone*, p. 35.

30. Pim, *Shamrock*, p. 119; Laverty, *Alone*, p. 23.

31. MacManus, *River*, pp 41, 57, 123; Purcell, *Swans*, pp 233, 245 and passim. The two banned novels which foreground religious belief and practice (lovingly and respectfully) are Laverty, *Gates*, and Kate O'Brien, *The Land of Spices* (hereafter: *Spices*) (London: Heinemann, 1941).

32. Kavanagh, *Flynn*, pp 7, 29, 34–6, 121 and passim.

33. Laverty, *Alone*, p. 197; M. Purcell, *Pilgrim*, p. 86.

34. Lane, *Well*, p. 47 and passim; Robertson, *Stranger*, passim and pp 17–19; Pim, *Shamrock*, p. 15 and passim.

35. Kavanagh, *Flynn*, pp 5–6 and passim; the other novels, passim also; the British novels in which this theme are explored are Lettice Cooper, *The New House* (London: Victor Gollancz, 1936); Richmal Crompton, *Family Roundabout* (London: 1948, Persephone Books reprint, 2004) and *Frost At Morning* (London: Hutchinson, 1950); Monica Dickens, *Joy and Josephine* (London: 1948, Foyle's Book Club edition, 1949); E. M. Delafield, *Diary of a Provincial Lady* (London: Macmillan, 1930);

Diana Tutton, *Guard Your Daughters* (London: Reprint Society, 1954, Persephone Books, 2017). For more discussion, see Nicola Humble, *The Feminine Middlebrow Novel from the 1920s to the 1950s: Class, Domesticity and Bohemianism* (Oxford: Oxford University Press, 2001), pp 149–96 and Nicola Beauman, *A Very Great Profession: The Woman's Novel 1914–39* (London: Virago, 1983), pp 90–133.

36. Caitríona Clear, *Women of the House: Women's Household Work in Ireland 1921–1961* (Dublin: Irish Academic Press, 2000), pp 13–24; Patrick Purcell, *Fiddler's Green* (Dublin: Talbot Press, 1950), p. 19.

37. Janice Winship, 'New Disciplines for Women and the Rise of the Chain Store in the 1930s', in Maggie Andrews and Mary Talbot (eds.), *All The World and Her Husband: Women in Twentieth-Century Consumer Culture* (London: Cassell, 2000), pp 23–45; Judy Giles, *Women, Identity and Private Life in Britain 1900–50* (London: Macmillan, 1995), pp 64–95; Lavin, 'Lilacs' in *Bective* (1978 edn.), pp 13–41.

38. Purcell, *Swans*, pp 15–16, 72–3 and passim; MacManus, *River*, pp 17–18, 202 and passim; Purcell, *Swans*, pp 15, 17; Robertson, *Stranger*, p. 111.

39. MacManus, *River*, passim, & *Watergate*, pp 52, 113; Lane, *Well*; Mary Purcell, *Pilgrim*, p. 54 and passim; Clear, *Women of the House*, passim, on Irish farm women in these decades.

40. Pim, *Shamrock*; Robertson, *Stranger*. The Irish urban novels which feature contented single women are Elizabeth Brennan, *Keeper?*; M. L. Stewart, *Finishing Touch* (Dublin: Talbot Press, 1943) and *Cliff-Dwellers;* J. K. Lyons, *Before The Dawn* (Dublin: Gill, 1946); Robertson, *Court*; John D. Sheridan, *Paradise;* Annie M. P. Smithson, (to pick just three examples), *Paid*, *The Walk of a Queen* (Dublin: Talbot, 1924) and *The Light of Other Days* (Dublin: Talbot, 1943); on Kate O'Brien see Nell Mahony in *Wanderer*, the young Anna and the older Helen in *Spices*; and several characters in *The Flower of May* (London: Heinemann, 1955).

41. There are so many of these that a few examples will suffice: Dorothy Whipple, *High Wages* (London: John Murray, 1930: Persephone Books, 2009); Lettice Cooper, *National Provincial* (London: Victor Gollancz, 1938) and *Fenny* (London: Victor Gollancz, 1953); Winifred Holtby, *South Riding* (London: John Murray, 1936); Winifred Peck, *House-Bound* (London: Faber & Faber, 1942: Persephone Books reprint, 2007). For a more extensive discussion of this historical phenomenon, see Katharine Holden, *The Shadow of Marriage: Singleness in England 1914–60* (Manchester: Manchester University Press, 2007).

42. Alison Uttley, *The Country Child* (London: Faber, 1931); George Orwell, *Coming Up For Air* (London: Victor Gollancz, 1939); Flora Thompson, *Lark Rise to Candleford* (Oxford: Oxford University Press 1939) and Priestley and Sherriff cited in note 18.

43. Michael Hartnett, *Maiden Street Ballad* (Privately published: Templeglantine, 1980), p. 7; Department of Health, *National Nutrition Survey*, Parts I–VII, (1948), K.53/1-6.

44. Eric Cross, *The Tailor and Ansty* (London: Chapman & Hall, 1942). On the reception of *Never No More*, see Seamus Kelly, *The Maura Laverty Story: from Rathangan to Tolka Row* (Kildare: Seamus Kelly, 2017), pp 128–30 and passim. On its republication, see Lennie Goodings, *A Bite of the Apple: A Life with Books, Writers and Virago* (Oxford: Oxford University Press, 2020), p. 83. The present writer grew up in a milieu where there were lots of Irish-published and Irish-themed books, many of them dating from the 1930s and 40s; the only Maura Laverty book to be found in parents' or grandparents' houses was her cookery book *Full and Plenty* (Dublin: Irish Flour Millers Association, 1960).

45. Alice Taylor, *To School Through The Fields: an Irish country childhood* (Dingle: Brandon 1988). Farmar, *Irish Book Publishing.*, p.202; p.284, describes this astounding publishing phenomenon.

CATHOLIC INTELLECTUALS AND RURAL DECLINE

1. Eric Cross, *The Tailor and Ansty* (Cork: Mercier Press, 1942).
2. Seán O'Faolain, 'Attitudes', *The Bell*, 2:6 (1941), p. 7.
3. ibid., pp 9–10.
4. Seán O'Faolain, 'Silent Ireland', *The Bell*, 6:6 (1943), p. 462.
5. Damian F. Hannon and Patrick Commins, 'The Significance of Small-Scale Landholders in Ireland's Socio-Economic Transformation', in J. H. Goldthorpe and C. T. Whelan (eds.), *The Development of Industrial Society in Ireland* (Oxford: Oxford University Press, 1992), p. 101.
6. John Mitchel, *The Last Conquest of Ireland (Perhaps)* (Dublin: UCD Press, 2005), pp 213–14.

7. Conrad M. Arensberg and Solon T. Kimball, *Family and Community in Ireland* (Cambridge Mass: Harvard University Press, 1940), pp 99, 155–6.

8. ibid., pp 99, 105–6.

9. ibid., p. 155.

10. ibid., p. 207.

11. ibid., p. 206.

12. Tom Inglis, *Moral Monopoly: The Rise and Fall of the Catholic Church in Modern Ireland* (Dublin: University College Dublin Press, 1998), p. 157.

13. Caoimhín Ó Danachair, 'The Family in Irish Tradition', *Christus Rex*, XV1:3 (1962), pp 185–96.

14. Horace Plunkett, *Ireland in the New Century* (New York: Kennikat Press, 1970 [1904]), pp 101–2.

15. Max Weber, *The Protestant Ethic and the Spirit of Capitalism*, trans. Talcott Parsons (London: Allen and Unwin, 1930).

16. Fr M. O'Riordan, *Catholicity and Progress in Ireland* (London: Kegan Paul, Trench, Trübner and Co., 1906), pp 130–1, 179–80, 459–60.

17. Emile Durkheim, *The Division of Labour in Society* (Basingstoke: Macmillan, 1984).

18. Emile Durkheim, *Suicide: A Study in Sociology* (New York: The Free Press, 1951).

19. Jeremiah Newman, *Conscience Versus Law: Reflections of the Evolution of Natural* Law (Dublin: Talbot Press, 1971), p. 153.

20. Leo XIII, *Rerum Novarum: Encyclical of Pope Leo X111 On Capital and Labor*, (1891), http://www.vatican.va.

21. Bryan Fanning, *The Quest for Modern Ireland: The Battle of Ideas 1912–1986* (Dublin: Irish Academic Press, 2008), pp 223–4.

22. Brian Conway, 'Foreigners, Faith and Fatherland: The Historical Origins, Development and Present Status of Irish Sociology', *Sociological Origins*, 5:1 (2006), p. 13.

23. Peter McKevitt, *The Plan of Society* (Dublin: Catholic Truth Society of Ireland, 1944).

24. Rev. C. B. Daly, 'Christus Rex Society', *Christus Rex*, I:1 (1947), p. 27.

25. ibid., p. 30.

26. Michael J. Browne, 'Why Catholic Priests should Concern Themselves with Social and Economic Questions', *Christus Rex*, I:1 (1947), p. 8.

27. Rev. Peter McKevitt, 'The Study Circle', *Christus Rex*, I:1 (1947), pp 34–9.

28. Feirmeoir, 'Agriculture in a Vocational Order of Society', *Christus Rex*, X:1 (1956), p. 49.

29. ibid. p. 49.

30. Louis P. F. Smith, 'The National Farmers Association', *Christus* Rex, X:1 (1956), p. 19.

31. Rev. Daniel Duffy, 'The Emigration Issue', *Christus Rex*, XV:1 (1961), pp 7–15.

32. ibid., p. 15.

33. Rev. Robert Prendergast, 'Foundations of Social Justice in Ireland', *Christus Rex*, XIII:4 (1959), p. 246.

34. Jeremiah Newman, 'Documentation', *Christus Rex*, XVII:2 (1963), p. 166.

35. T. M. O'Connor, The Limerick Rural Survey', *Christus Rex*, XVIII:3 (1964), pp 187–93.

36. Peter Murray and Maria Feeney, *Church, State and Social Science in Ireland: Knowledge, Institutions and the Rebalancing of Power, 1937–73* (Manchester: Manchester University Press, 2017), p. 71.

37. E. W. Hofstee, 'Rural Sociological Research and Its Importance for the Betterment of Rural Life', *Christus Rex*, XIII:3 (1959), pp 196–9.

38. ibid., pp 199–201.

39. O'Connor, 'The Limerick Rural Survey', p. 191.

40. ibid., p. 192.

41. ibid., pp 192–5.

42. Jeremiah Newman, 'Pastoral Problems in the Rural Environment', *Christus Rex*, XVI: 3 (1963), p. 227.

43. G. A. Meagher, 'The Development Plan and National Development', *Christus Rex*, XVIII: 3 (1964), p. 168.

44. Seán F. Lemass, 'Social Factors and Emigration', *Christus Rex*, XV: 1 (1961), p. 16.

45. ibid., p. 18.

46. John XXIII, *Mater et Magistra: Encyclical of Pope John XXIII On Christianity and Social Progress*, (1961), www.vatican.va.

47. Monsignor Pietro Pavan, 'The Agricultural and Rural Section of *Mater et Magistra*', *Christus Rex*, XVI: 3 (1963), p. 192.
48. ibid., p. 193.
49. ibid., pp 193, 194.
50. ibid., pp 195–8.
51. Murray and Feeney, *Church, State and Social Science in Ireland*, p. 70.
52. Fr. Harry Bohan, 'The Social and Religious Aspects of Industrialisation', *Christus Rex*, XXIV:4 (1970), p. 251.
53. *The Mind of Canon Hayes* (Muintir na Tire, 1961) cited in Robert A. B. Leaper, 'Christian Witness in Community Development', *Christus Rex*, XVI:3 (1962), p. 170.
54. George F. Thomason, 'Leadership', *Christus Rex*, XVI: 3 (1962), pp 172–7.
55. George F. Thomason, *Community Development in Ireland* (Tipperary: Muintir na Tire Publications, 1961).
56. Bryan Fanning, *Histories of the Irish Future* (London: Bloomsbury, 2015), pp 176–86.
57. Jeremiah Newman, *Race, Migration and Integration* (London: Burns and Oates, 1968).
58. Jeremiah Newman, 'Vocations in Ireland – 1966', *Christus Rex*, XXI: 2 (1967), pp 105–12.
59. Newman, *Conscience Versus Law*, pp 152–3.
60. ibid., pp 182–3.
61. Jeremiah Newman, *The State of Ireland* (Dublin: Four Courts, 1977), p. 25.
62. Michel Peillon, *Contemporary Irish Society: An Introduction* (Dublin: Gill and Macmillan, 1982), p. 94.
63. Rev. Liam Ryan, 'Social Dynamite: A Study of Early School-Leavers', *Christus Rex*, XXI: 1 (1967), pp 11–12.
64. ibid., pp 12, 25.
65. ibid., pp 28–9.
66. Liam Irwin, 'Newman, Jeremiah', *Dictionary of Irish Biography* (Cambridge: Cambridge University Press, 2009), p. 897.
67. Olivia O'Leary, 'The Mullah of Limerick', *Magill*, 21 March 1985, pp 24–33.

WOMEN AND PATRIARCHAL POWER IN RURAL IRELAND

1. Tanya Watson acknowledges with gratitude a Teagasc Walsh Scholarship (2008–2012) to fund doctoral research on farm women's land ownership; and Anne Byrne gratefully acknowledges participation in the 'Joint Ventures to Enhance the Demographic Profile and Socio-Economic Sustainability of Irish Farming (Join-to-Farm)' project (2013–2015), funded by Ireland's Department of Agriculture, Food and the Marine's (DAFM) Research Stimulus Fund (RSF), DAFM Project Reference Number: 11/S/151. This chapter is dedicated to the generations of women living and working on Irish family farms, particularly to Ethna Viney (1929-2024), whose feminist consciousness and reporting first raised our awareness of the working and living conditions of rural women in the 1960s and to Nora C. Byrne (1894–1986), single woman farmer, influential poultry instructor, lifelong member of the Irish Country Women's Association and mentor.
2. Sylvia Walby, 'Theorising Patriarchy', *Sociology*, 23:2 (1989), p. 214.
3. See, for instance, Anne Byrne and Madeleine Leonard (eds.), *Women and Irish Society: A Sociological Reader* (Belfast: Beyond the Pale Publications, 1997); John Baker, Kathleen Lynch, Sara Cantillon and Judy Walsh, *Equality from Theory to Action* (Basingstoke: Palgrave, 2004); Linda Connolly and Tina O'Toole, *Documenting Irish Feminisms* (Dublin: The Woodfield Press, 2005); Ursula Barry (ed.), *Where Are We Now: New Feminist Perspectives on Women in Contemporary Ireland* (Dublin: New Island, 2008).
4. For a discussion of the linkages between gender and sustainability in rural Ireland, see Sally Shortall and Anne Byrne, 'Gender and Sustainability in Rural Ireland', in John McDonagh, Tony Varley, and Sally Shortall (eds.), *A Living Countryside? The Politics of Sustainable Development in Rural Ireland* (Farnham: Ashgate: 2009), pp 287–302.
5. Conrad M. Arensberg and Solon T. Kimball, *Family and Community in Ireland* (3rd ed.) (Ennis: CLASP Press, 2001).
6. ibid., p. 77.

7. ibid., p. 133.
8. ibid., p. 61.
9. ibid., p. 50.
10. ibid., p. 58.
11. ibid. p. 56.
12. ibid., p. 58.
13. ibid., p. 65.
14. ibid., p. 49.
15. A growing number of Irish women rejected the term and identity of 'housewife' in the 1930s and 1940s. See Caitriona Clear, 'Women in Ireland in the 1930s and 1940s', in Alan Hayes (ed.), *Hilda Tweedy and the Irish Housewives Association: Links in the Chain...* (Dublin: Arlen House, 2012), pp 59–68.
16. Arensberg and Kimball, *Family and Community in Ireland*, pp 48–9.
17. ibid., pp 48–9.
18. ibid., p. 49.
19. ibid., p. 48.
20. ibid., p. 103.
21. ibid., p. 223.
22. ibid., p. 213. For a discussion of single women and rural life from the 1950s to the 1980s, see Anne Byrne. 'Single Women in Ireland: A Re-examination of the Sociological Evidence', in Anne Byrne and Madeleine Leonard (eds.), *Women and Irish Society: A Sociological Reader* (Belfast: Beyond the Pale Publications, 1997), pp 415–30.
23. Patrick McNabb, 'Social Structure', in Jeremiah Newman (ed.), *The Limerick Rural Survey 1958–1964* (Tipperary: Muintir na Tíre Publications, 1964), pp 193–247.
24. ibid., p. 243.
25. ibid., p. 195.
26. ibid., p. 228.
27. ibid., p. 229.
28. ibid., p. 228.
29. ibid., p. 229.
30. ibid., p. 230.
31. ibid., p. 244.
32. ibid., p. 221.
33. Patrick McNabb, 'Demography', in Jeremiah Newman (ed.), *The Limerick Rural Survey 1958–1964* (Tipperary: Muintir na Tíre Publications, 1964), p. 188.
34. ibid., p. 188.
35. Patrick McNabb, 'Social Structure', p. 221.
36. ibid., p. 221.
37. ibid., p. 199.
38. ibid., p. 246. For a study of the ICA, see Aileen Heverin's *The Irish Countrywomen's Association: A History 1910–2000* (Dublin: The Wolfhound Press, 2000).
39. Patrick McNabb, 'Social Structure', p. 246.
40. Ethna Viney, 'Women in Rural Ireland', *Christus Rex*, XXII: 4 (1968), p. 338.
41. John C. Messenger, *Inis Beag: Isle of Ireland* (New York: Holt, Rinehart and Winston, 1969).
42. ibid., pp 77, 125.
43. Hugh Brody, *Inishkillane: Change and Decline in the West of Ireland* (London: Allen Lane, 1973), p. 98.
44. ibid., p. 129.
45. ibid., pp 99–100.
46. Damian F. Hannan and Louise A. Katsiaouni, *Traditional Families? From Culturally Prescribed to Negotiated Roles in Farm Families* (Dublin: The Economic and Social Research Institute, 1977).
47. ibid. p. 26.
48. ibid., p. 27.
49. ibid., p. 27.
50. ibid., p. 16.
51. ibid., p. 24.

52. Patricia O'Hara, *Partners in Production? Women, Farm and Family in Ireland* (Oxford: Berghahn, 1998), p. 53.
53. ibid., p. 11.
54. ibid., p. 111.
55. ibid., p. 10.
56. ibid., p. 103–10.
57. ibid., p. 106.
58. ibid., p. 106.
59. ibid., p. 106.
60. ibid., p. 107.
61. ibid., p. 108.
62. ibid., p. 109.
63. ibid., p. 105.
64. ibid., pp 100–1.
65. ibid., p. 150.
66. ibid., p. 103.
67. ibid., p. 151.
68. ibid., p. 151.
69. Sally Shortall, *Women and Farming: Property and Power* (Houndsmill, Basingstoke: Macmillan Palgrave, 1999), p. 67. See also Hilary Tovey, 'Rural Sociology in Ireland', *Irish Journal of Sociology*, 2:1 (1992), pp 96–121.
70. Shortall, *Women and Farming*, pp 155–6.
71. ibid., p. 36.
72. ibid., p. 69.
73. ibid., p. 133.
74. ibid., p. 156.
75. ibid., p. 156.
76. Department of Agriculture, Food and Rural Development, *Report of the Advisory Committee on the Role of Women in Agriculture* (Dublin: Department of Agriculture, Food and Rural Development, 2000), p. 36.
77. See Nata Duvvury, Áine Ní Léime, and Tanya Watson, 'Rural Women, Ageing and Retirement', in Mark Skinner, Rachel Winterton, Kieran Walsh (eds.), *Rural Gerontology: Towards Critical Perspectives on Rural Ageing* (London: Routledge, 2020), p. 101.
78. See Gender Equality Unit, *Assessment of the Main Gaps in Existing Information on Women in Agriculture* (Dublin: Department of Justice, Equality and Law Reform, 2003), p. 22.
79. See Gender Equality Unit, *Women and Men on Farms in Ireland: Their Activities, Attitudes and Experiences* (Dublin: Department of Justice, Equality, and Law Reform, 2004), p. 17.
80. Whether this increase is a consequence of changes in succession practices remains unclear (Central Statistics Office, 'Census of Agriculture 2020 – Preliminary Results: Demographic Profile of Farm Holders', https://www.cso.ie/en/releasesandpublications/ep/p-coa/censusofagriculture2020-preliminaryresults/demographicprofileoffarmholders/).
81. Gender Equality Unit, *Assessment of the Main Gaps in Existing Information on Women in Agriculture*, p. 22.
82. Pat Bogue, *Land Mobility and Succession in Ireland* (Dublin: Macra na Feirme, 2013), p. 11.
83. Anne Cassidy, 'Female Successors in Irish Family Farming: Four Pathways to Farm Transfer', *Canadian Journal of Development Studies / Revue Canadienne D'études du Développement*, 40:2 (2019), pp 250–1.
84. See Anne Byrne, Nata Duvvury, Áine Macken-Walsh and Tanya Watson, 'Finding Room to Manoeuvre: Gender, Agency and the Family Farm', in Barbara Pini, Berit Brandth and Jo Little (eds.), *Feminisms and Ruralities* (Lexington: Lexington University Press, 2015), pp 119–30; Sally Shortall, 'Changing Gender Roles in Irish Farm Households: Continuity and Change', *Irish Geography*, 50:2 (2017), pp 175–91.
85. Áine Macken-Walsh, Peter Cush and Anne Byrne, 'Strategies of Resilience: Cooperation in Irish Family Farming', *Irish Geography*, 53:1 (2020), p. 38. See also Áine Macken-Walsh and Ben Roche, *Facilitating Farmers' Establishment of Farm Partnerships: A Participatory Template* (Carlow: Teagasc, 2012).

86. Áine Macken-Walsh, Peter Cush and Anne Byrne, 'Strategies of Resilience', pp 23–42; Peter Cush, Áine Macken-Walsh and Anne Byrne, 'Joint Farming Ventures: Gender Identities of the Self and the Social', *Journal of Rural Studies*, 57 (2018), p. 62.

87. Áine Macken-Walsh, Peter Cush and Anne Byrne, 'Strategies of Resilience', p. 38.

88. Anne Byrne, Nata Duvvury, Áine Macken-Walsh and Tanya Watson, 'Finding Room to Manoeuvre', pp 119–30. See also Peter Cush and Áine Macken-Walsh, 'Reconstituting Male Identities through Joint Farming Ventures in Ireland', *Sociologia Ruralis*, 58:4 (2018), pp 726–44.

89. Sally Shortall and Anne Byrne, 'Gender and Sustainability in Rural Ireland', p. 298.

90. Department of the Environment, Climate and Communications, *Equality, Diversity and Inclusion: Strategy and Action Plan 2023-2025* (Dublin: Department of the Environment, Climate and Communications, 2023).

91. This 'Action Plan' follows on from the Department of Agriculture, Food and the Marine's *National Dialogue on Women in Agriculture: Report* (Dublin: Department of Agriculture, Food and the Marine, 2024).

CHALLENGING PATRIARCHAL POWER? WOMEN ADVISORS AS CHANGE AGENTS IN TWENTIETH-CENTURY IRISH AGRICULTURE

1. Mícheál Ó Fathartaigh, *Developing Rural Ireland: A History of the Irish Agricultural Advisory Services* (Dublin: Wordwell, 2021), pp 15–19.

2. Mícheál Ó Fathartaigh, 'More than a Century of Female Pioneers: Women in the Advisory Service', in *Today's Farm*, 30:5 (2019), p. 8; Peter Moser, 'Rural Economy and Female Emigration in the West of Ireland 1936–1956', *U.C.G. Women's Studies Centre Review*, 2 (1993), p. 42.

3. Liam Downey and Maura McLoughlin, 'Agricultural Education in the 19th and 20th Centuries with Particular Regard to the Munster Institute', *Times Past: Journal of Muskerry Local History Society*, 9 (2010–11), p. 32.

4. Daniel Hoctor, *The Department's Story – A History of the Department of Agriculture* (Dublin: Institute of Public Administration, 1971), pp 58–9; Joanna Bourke, 'Women and Poultry in Ireland, 1891–1914', *Irish Historical Studies*, 25:99 (1987), p. 300.

5. It must be noted that the full-time female poultry-keeping and butter-making instructresses were paid £150 annually, a salary that was £50 less than the full-time male agricultural instructors but £50 more than the salaries of the part-time male horticultural instructors (Ó Fathartaigh, *Developing Rural Ireland*, p. 39).

6. Ó Fathartaigh, *Developing Rural Ireland*, pp 28–31, 35.

7. Galway County Council (GCC), *Second Annual Report of the County of Galway Committee for Agriculture*, (1902–3), pp 4–5; ibid., *Third Annual Report of the County of Galway Committee for Agriculture* (1903–4), p. 17.

8. Susanne E. Friedberg, 'The Triumph of the Egg', *Comparative Studies in Science and History*, 50:2 (2008), p. 400.

9. Teagasc: Agriculture and Food Development Authority, Mellows Campus, Athenry, County Galway, library and archives, Galway County Committee of Agriculture: minutes, 1, 12 January 1905; *Census of Ireland*, 1901, 1911. Brigid Hogan's son, Patrick, was the big farmer and solicitor who became independent Ireland's first Minister for Agriculture in 1922.

10. GCC, *Second Annual Report of the County of Galway Committee of Agriculture*, pp 14–16.

11. Moser, 'Rural Economy', p. 43.

12. Caitriona Clear, *Social Change and Everyday Life in Ireland: 1850–1922* (Manchester: Manchester University Press, 2007), Chap 1.

13. GCC, *Third Annual Report of the County of Galway Committee of Agriculture*, p. 17.

14. Making due allowance for the belated appearance of the male agricultural instructors, the official statistics record the number of cattle in Ireland increasing by only four per cent, and the area under wheat on Irish farms actually decreasing by seven per cent in the 1903–13 period (*Farming Since the Famine: Irish Farm Statistics 1847–1996* (Dublin: Central Statistics Office, 1997). Pn 4175, pp 280, 282–3, tables 10, 11).

15. *Dáil Éireann Debates*, 8: 960, 10 July 1924.

16. Ó Fathartaigh, *Developing Rural Ireland*, p. 149.

17. Department of Agriculture, *Fourth Annual Report of the Minister for Agriculture 1934–35*, P 1943, p. 9.

18. Ó Fathartaigh, *Developing Rural Ireland*, p. 187.

19. Irene Alwenyi, Josephine Sepeku, Celia Sheridan and Mícheál Ó Fathartaigh, 'Women in Irish Agricultural History', *TResearch*, 14:2 (2019), p. 32; Moser, 'Rural Economy', p. 45.

20. Department of Agriculture, *First Annual Report of the Minister for Agriculture 1931–32*, P 802, p. 47.

21. Mícheál Ó Fathartaigh, *Irish Agriculture Nationalised: The Dairy Disposal Company and the Making of the Modern Irish Dairy Industry* (Dublin: Institute of Public Administration, 2014), pp 12–15.

22. GCC, *Second Annual Report of the County of Galway Committee of Agriculture*, pp 4–5, 14–16; ibid., *Eighth Annual Report of the County of Galway Committee of Agriculture*, (1910), p. 10.

23. GCC, *Eleventh Annual Report of the County of Galway Committee of Agriculture*, (1911–12), pp 14–15.

24. *Nenagh Guardian*, 6 August 1966.

25. Ó Fathartaigh, 'Female Pioneers', p. 8.

26. Department of Agriculture, *Thirty-Third Annual Report of the Minister for Agriculture 1963–64*, Pr 7836, p. 51.

27. Maura E. Fennelly, *Do Not Forget to Remember* (Victoria, British Columbia: Trafford Publishing, 2004), p. 48.

28. The ratio of FHM advisors to poultry-keeping and butter-making advisors was nearly 3:1 in 1979 when there were 83 of the former and 28 of the latter (Department of Agriculture, *Annual Report of the Minister for Agriculture: 1979*, Prl 8881, p. 89).

29. Department of Agriculture, *Thirty-Second Annual Report of the Minister for Agriculture 1962–63*, Pr 7222, pp 52–3; ibid., *Annual Report of the Minister for Agriculture and Fisheries 1968–69*, Prl 880, p. 109; ibid., *Annual Report of the Minister for Agriculture and Fisheries 1972–73*, Prl 3343, p. 113; ibid., *Annual Report of the Minister for Agriculture 1964–65*, Prl 8747, p. 127; ibid., *Annual Report for the Minister of Agriculture and Fisheries 1971–72*, Pr 2626, p. 109.

30. Joanne Banks, 'Policy, Practice and Performance: The Changing Role of the Irish Agricultural Advisory Service, 1945–88' (unpublished PhD thesis, University College Dublin, 2007), p. 224.

31. ibid.

32. Even if then justified not by climate change concerns but by those of financial and personal wellbeing, the diagrams the FHM advisors used to illustrate improved home insulation look remarkably contemporary (Ó Fathartaigh, *Developing Rural Ireland*, pp 329–30).

33. An Chomhairle Oiliúna Talmhaíochta (ACOT), *Agriculture in County Limerick: Annual Report for 1984*, p. 38.

34. Banks, 'Policy, Practice and Performance', p. 225.

35. ibid.

36. ibid.

37. The first female advisor had been appointed to a senior management position in the advisory service in the 1970s (Ó Fathartaigh, 'Female Pioneers', p. 9).

38. Teagasc, 'International day of rural women', http://www.teagasc.ie, 10 November 2022.

39. Carla King, 'Co-operation and Rural Development: Plunkett's Approach', in John Davis (ed.), *Rural Change in Ireland* (Belfast: Institute of Irish Studies, Queen's University Belfast, 1999), pp 50–2.

40. Such 'masculinisation' became worldwide in rural society in this period. In 1930s Minnesota, for example, a gendered transformation in wild rice harvesting took place among the native American Ojibwe nation when – under government-funded assimilation schemes – responsibility for harvesting passed from women to men (see Brenda J. Child, *My Grandfather's Knocking Sticks: Ojibwe Family Life and Labor on the Reservation* (St Paul: Minnesota Historical Society Press, 2014)).

41. Account-keeping continues to be viewed as women's work in a range of comparable contexts today. For instance, 'women outweigh men as economic actors and as agents of change' in contemporary global microfinance activities (Lamia Karim, 'Analyzing Women's Empowerment: Microfinance and Garment Labor in Bangladesh', *Fletcher Forum of World Affairs*, 38:2 (2014), p. 153).

EMIGRATION AND RETURN: LIMITATIONS AND ATTRACTIONS OF THE IRISH COUNTRYSIDE

1. The editors and Dr Caitríona Clear are thanked for inviting my contribution to the conference and the publication. Dr Tony Varley is thanked, in particular, for his helpful comments on the chapter.

2. *Commission on Emigration and Other Population Problems, 1948–1954, Reports* (Dublin: Stationery Office, 1954); Mary E. Daly, *The Slow Failure: Population Decline and Independent Ireland, 1920–1973* (Madison: University of Wisconsin Press, 2006), discusses the work of the Commission in detail; Damian F. Hannan, *Rural Exodus: A Study of the Forces Influencing Large-Scale Migration of Irish Rural Youth* (London: G. Chapman, 1970); David Meredith and Mary Gilmartin, 'Changing Rural Ireland', in Cathal O'Donoghue, Ricky Conneely, Kevin Heanue, Deirdre Frost, Brian Leonard and David Meredith, *Rural Economic Development in Ireland* (Athenry: Teagasc, 2014), pp 34–47.

3. Gerry (J. J.) Sexton, Brendan M. Walsh, Damian F. Hannan and Doreen McMahon, *The Economic and Social Implications of Emigration, NESC Report No. 90* (Dublin: National Economic and Social Council, 1991), pp 142–4. This comprehensive report is based on a representative sample of 1981–1982 school-leavers, who were interviewed in 1983, 1984 and 1987.

4. ibid.

5. Hannan, *Rural Exodus*, pp 244–8.

6. Jeremiah Newman, 'The Future of Rural Ireland', *Studies* 47:188 (1958), p. 397.

7. Meredith and Gilmartin, 'Changing Rural Ireland', in O'Donoghue et al., *Rural Economic Development in Ireland*, pp 34–47.

8. Christian Dustmann, Itzik Fadlon and Yoram Weiss, 'Return Migration, Human Capital Accumulation and the Brain Drain', *Journal of Development Economics*, 95:1 (2011), pp 58–68.

9. For a list of studies, see Alan Fernihough and Cormac Ó Gráda, *Across the Sea to Ireland: Return Atlantic Migration Before the First World War, SSRN on-line papers* (Social Science Research Network: Rochester, New York, 2020), http://dx.doi.org/10.2139/ssrn.3491676, accessed 15 July 2020; for the years 1921–1971, see Enda Delaney, *Demography, State and Society: Irish Migration to Britain, 1921–1971'* (Liverpool: Liverpool University Press, 2000), pp 226–88; for census-based analysis, see Adrian Punch and Catherine Finneran, 'The Demographic and Socio-economic Characteristics of Migrants, 1986–1996', *Journal of the Statistical and Social Inquiry Society of Ireland*, XXV111: 1 (1999), pp 213–63.

10. The student interviewees are acknowledged, as is Dr Stephen Galvin who collated their data entries.

11. Defined in *Census of Population 2016 – Profile 2 Population Distribution and Movements*, Background Notes, Appendix 1, unpaginated, https://www.cso.ie/en/releasesandpublications/ep/p-cp2tc/cp2pdm/bgn/, accessed 20 December 2018.

12. Greg Guest, Kathleen M. McQueen and Emily E. Narney, *Applied Thematic Analysis* (Thousand Oaks, Calif.: Sage, on-line edition, 2014), p. 6; Allan M. Findlay and F. L. N. Li, 'Methodological Issues in Researching Migration', *The Professional Geographer*, 51:1 (1999), p. 53.

13. Anthony Giddens, *The Constitution of Society* (Cambridge: Polity Press, 1984), pp 374–5.

14. Findlay and Li, 'Methodological Issues in Researching Migration', p. 53, citing Keith H. Halfacree and Paul Boyle, 'The Challenge Facing Migration Research: The Case for a Biographical Approach', *Progress in Human Geography*, 17 (1993), pp 333–48.

15. Halfacree and Boyle, 'The Challenge Facing Migration Research', pp 338–9.

16. Hannan, *Rural Exodus*, pp 14–28; Ní Laoire, 'The "Green Green Grass of Home"? Return Migration to Rural Ireland', *Journal of Rural Studies*, 23:3 (2007), pp 338–42; Enda Delaney refers to individual agency as being 'far more important in the process of leaving home' than has been acknowledged, in *The Irish in Post-War Britain* (Oxford: Oxford University Press, 2007), p. 25.

17. Punch and Finneran used this source in 'The Demographic and Socio-economic Characteristics of Migrants, 1986–1996', pp 213–63.

18. The unemployment rate was 17.1 per cent in 1986 and 15 per cent in 2012 –https://www.cso.ie/en/releasesandpublications/ep/psdii/sustainabledevelopmentindicatorsireland2017/soc/, accessed 15 July 2020; see Sexton et al., *The Economic and Social Implications of Emigration*, pp 43–4, for the 1980s and earlier and *Indecon Economic Report on Addressing the Challenges Faced by Returning Irish Emigrants* (Dublin: Indecon International Economic Consultants, 2018), p. 9, for more recent decades.

19. *Indecon Economic Report*, p. 9.

20. Irial Glynn, Tomás Kelly and Piaras MacÉinrí, *The Re-Emergence of Emigration from Ireland* (Washington DC: Migration Policy Institute, 2015), pp 9–10.
21. Ciara Kenny, 'Illegal Workers in Australia Face a Perilous Existence', *The Irish Times*, 29 August 2016.
22. Glynn et al., *The Re-Emergence of Emigration from Ireland*, pp 9–10.
23. Russell King and Ian Shuttleworth, 'The Emigration and Employment of Irish Graduates', *European Urban and Regional Studies*, 2:1 (1995), p. 27.
24. Daly, *The Slow Failure*, p. 141.
25. Official estimates suggest that there were about 50,000 undocumented Irish emigrants in the USA during the 1980s and early 1990s, although lobby groups suggested up to 150,000; see Linda Dowling Almeida, *Irish Immigrants in New York City, 1945–1995* (Bloomington: University of Indiana Press, 2001), p. 63.
26. ibid. One of the sample may have obtained a visa under one of the programmes whilst in the USA; non-return on holiday during an extended stay suggests undocumented status.
27. Irial Glynn, Tomás Kelly and Piaras MacÉinrí, *Irish Emigration in an Age of Austerity* (Cork: Emigré, University College Cork, 2013), p. 59.
28. George Gmelch, 'Who Returns and Why: Return Migration Behaviour in Two North Atlantic Societies', *Human Organisation*, 42:1 (1983), p. 46.
29. Fiona McGrath, 'The Economic, Social and Cultural Implications of Return Migration to Achill Island', in Russell King (ed.), *Contemporary Irish Migration, Geographical Society of Ireland Special Publications No. 6* (Dublin: Trinity College Dublin, 1991), p. 55.
30. Richard C. Jones, 'Multinational Investment and Return Migration in Ireland in the 1990s: County-level Analysis', *Irish Geography*, 36:2 (2003), p. 153.
31. Ní Laoire, 'The "Green Green Grass of Home"?', p. 332.
32. Maura Farrell, Marie Mahon and John McDonagh, 'The Rural as a Return Migration Destination', *European Countryside*, 4:1 (2012), p. 33.
33. Mary Cawley and Stephen Galvin, 'Irish Migration and Return: Continuities and Changes over Time', *Irish Geography*, 49:1 (2016), p. 11. The earlier paper deals with a different sample to that discussed here.
34. Protocols were designed for the conduct of the interview and the entry of the information to an Excel database. Incomplete interviews were not included in the reported analysis.
35. EUROSTAT, *Migration Statistics Explained* (Brussels: European Commission, 2018), https://ec.europa.eu/eurostat/statistics-explained/index.php/Glossary: Migration, accessed 10 December 2019.
36. The author checked the size of place from the addresses given, against the population numbers registered at the relevant censuses of population.
37. See Peggy Levitt, Josh De Wind, and Steven Vertovec, 'International Perspectives on Transnational Migration: An Introduction', *International Migration Review*, 37:3 (2003), pp 565–75.
38. Eleven returnees emigrated a second time (eight men and three women), six of whom returned again. They are not discussed in detail for reasons of space.
39. Guest et al., *Applied Thematic Analysis*, p. 6.
40. Per Gustafson, 'Meanings of Place: Everyday Experience and Theoretical Conceptualisations', *Journal of Environmental Psychology*, 21:1 (2001), pp 10–11.
41. Punch and Finneran, 'The Demographic and Socio-economic Characteristics of Migrants, 1986–1996', p. 225.
42. Larry A. Sjaastad, 'The Costs and Returns of Human Migration', *The Journal of Political Economy*, 70: 5ii (1962), pp 80–93.
43. J. J. Lee, *Ireland 1912–1985: Politics and Society* (Cambridge: Cambridge University Press, 1989), p. 362.
44. See Everett S. Lee, 'A Theory of Migration', *Demography* 3, (1966), pp 54–5.
45. The role of networks in providing emigrants with access to employment is discussed by John A. Jackson, *The Irish in London* (London: Routledge and Kegan Paul, 1963), pp 18, 159, and by Mary P. Corcoran, 'Informalisation of Metropolitan Labour Forces: The Case of Irish Immigrants in the New York Construction Sector', *Irish Journal of Sociology*, 1:1 (1991), pp 35–8.

46. Russell King and Ian Shuttleworth, 'Ireland's New Wave of Emigration in the 1980s', *Irish Geography*, 21:2 (1988), pp 104–8; Donal A. Dinneen, 'The Europeanisation of Irish Universities', *Higher Education*, 24 (1992), pp 396–8.

47. See Sexton et al. *The Economic and Social Implications of Emigration*, pp 142–4 for the 1980s.

48. ibid., p. 142.

49. See Bronwyn Walter for Luton in the 1970s, 'Tradition and Ethnic Interaction: Second Wave Settlement in Luton and Bolton', in Colin Clarke, David Ley and Ceri Peach (eds.), *Geography and Ethnic Pluralism* (London: Allen and Unwin, 1984), p. 270; Jackson, *The Irish in Britain*, pp 130–1, discusses social and county differentiation in clubs and sports.

50. Jackson, *The Irish in Britain*, p. 159, discusses the role of visits home in maintaining kinship ties.

51. Bronwyn Walter, *Outsiders Inside: Whiteness, Place and Irish Women* (London: Routledge, 2001), pp 197–8, discusses a sense of displacement among Irish women in England in the 1970s.

52. The mechanic may have inherited a farm also, though this was not made explicit.

53. Ní Laoire, 'The "Green, Green Grass of Home"?', p. 337, suggests that the construct of the benefits of the countryside for children may incorporate the parents' own desire to return there.

54. This man was interviewed (remotely) in 2013, whilst resident in Perth (2013#R07).

THE SURVIVAL OF RURAL IRELAND

1. 'Rural population (Percentage of total population)' https://data.worldbank.org/indicator/SP.RUR. TOTL.ZS?locations, accessed on 31 August 2023. Detailed comparisons between the 2016 and 2022 Irish Population Census relating to rural Ireland is difficult because the Central Statistics Office has made some changes to its methodology for defining urban areas.

2. Josh O'Driscoll, Frank Crowley, Justin Doran, Mary O'Shaughnessy, David Meredith and Jesko Zimmermann, 'Is Rural Ireland Really Dying? What the Facts and Figures Really Tell Us', RTÉ Brainstorm, 23 January 2023, https://www.rte.ie/brainstorm/2022/0720/1311198-rural-ireland-population-cso-census-2022, accessed on 31 August 2023.

3. Mary E. Daly, *The Slow Failure: Population Decline and Independence Ireland 1920–1971* (Madison: University of Wisconsin Press, 2006), pp 21–74.

4. Cormac Ó Gráda, 'Poverty, Population and Agriculture, 1801–45', in W. E. Vaughan (ed.), *A New History of Ireland Vol. V: Ireland under the Union, Part I* (Oxford: Oxford University Press, 1989), p. 114.

5. Conrad Arensberg, *The Irish Countryman* (Gloucester, Mass.: P. Smith, 1937), pp 38–42.

6. Mary E. Daly, *The Slow Failure*, pp 21–74.

7. John C. Messenger, *Inis Beag: Isle of Ireland* (New York: Holt, Rinehart and Winston, 1969); Nancy Scheper-Hughes, *Saints, Scholars and Schizophrenics: Mental Illness in Rural Ireland* (Berkeley: University of California Press, 1979).

8. Anna-Christina Lauring Knudsen, 'Romanticising Europe? Rural Images in the European Union Policies', *Kontur – Tidsskrift for Kulturstudier*, 12 (2005), pp 49–58.

9. John Healy, *The Death of an Irish Town* (Cork: Mercier Press, 1968), p. 17.

10. Comparable figures for 2022 are not yet available.

11. Mary E. Daly, *The First Department: A History of the Department of Agriculture* (Dublin: Institute of Public Administration, 2002), p. 498.

12. Jerome aan de Wiel, 'The Commission, the Council and the Irish Application for the EEC', in Mervyn O'Driscoll, Dermot Keogh and Jerome aan de Wiel (eds.), *Ireland through European Eyes: Western Europe, the EEC and Ireland, 1945–1973* (Cork: Cork University Press, 2013), pp 374–5.

13. Daly, *The First Department*, p. 516.

14. Ann-Christina Knudsen, *Farmers on Welfare: The Making of Europe's Common Agricultural Policy* (Ithaca: Cornell University Press, 2009).

15. Annie Lowrey, *Give People Money: How a Universal Basic Income Would End Poverty, Revolutionise Work, and Remake the World* (New York: Crown, 2018).

16. Michael Fogarty, 'Introduction' to Denis I. F. Lucey and Donald R. Kaldor, *Rural Industrialization: The impact of Industrialization on Two Rural Communities in Western Ireland* (London: Geoffrey Chapman, 1969), pp 9–11.

17. Industrial Development Authority, *Regional Industrial Plans 1973–77* (Dublin: Industrial Development Authority, 1972).

18. Brian Callanan, *Ireland's Shannon Story: Leaders, Visions and Networks – A Case Study of Local and Regional Development* (Dublin: Irish Academic Press, 2000), p. 97.

19. Damian Hannan, *Rural Exodus: A Study of the Forces Influencing Large-Scale Migration of Irish Rural Youth* (London: G. Chapman, 1970), p. 253.

20. Richard Florida, *Cities and the Creative Class* (London: Routledge Press, 2005).

21. David Meredith, *Rural Ireland: Decades of Change, TResearch*, 8 no. 4, (December 2013), p. 30.

22. Irial Glynn with Tomás Kelly and Piaras Mac Énrí, *The Reemergence of emigration from Ireland: New trends in an old story* (Washington DC: Transatlantic Council on Migration. Migration Policy Institute, December 2015), pp 2–10.

23. Meredith, *Rural Ireland*, pp 30–1.

24. Department of Education, *Investment in Education. Report of the Survey Team Appointed by the Minister for Education in October 1962* (Dublin: Stationery Office, 1966).

25. Tim Pat Coogan, *Ireland since the Rising* (Dublin: Pall Mall Press, 1966), p. 218.

26. Garret FitzGerald, *Reflections on the Irish State* (Dublin: Irish Academic Press, 2003), p. 140.

27. Mary E. Daly, *Sixties Ireland: Reshaping the Economy, State and Society, 1957–73* (Cambridge: Cambridge University Press, 2016), pp 222–7.

28. Dennis Beach, Tuuli From, Monica Johannson and Elisabet Öhrn, 'Educational and Spatial Justice in Rural and Urban Areas in Three Nordic Countries: A Meta-Ethnograpic Analysis', *Education Inquiry*, 9:2 (2018), pp 1–18.

29. Caitriona Clear, *Women of the House: Women's Household Work in Ireland 1921–1961* (Dublin: Irish Academic Press, 2000), p. 163.

30. Michael Shiel, *The Quiet Revolution: The Electrification of Rural Ireland* (Dublin: O'Brien Press, 1984), pp 154–5.

31. Clear, *Women of the House*, p. 163.

32. Mary E. Daly, '"Turn on the Tap": The State, Irish Women and Running Water', in Maryann Gianella Valiulis and Mary O'Dowd (eds.), *Women and Irish History* (Dublin: Wolfhound Press, 1997), p. 218.

33. Colin Buchanan and Partners, *Regional Studies in Ireland* (Dublin: An Foras Forbartha, 1969), p. 35.

34. Damian F. Hannan and Louise A. Katsiaouni, *Traditional Families? From Culturally Prescribed to Negotiated Roles in Farm Families* (Dublin: Economic and Social Research Institute, 1977), pp 63, 185.

35. Jack Fitzsimons, *Bungalow Bliss* (Kells: Kells Arts Studios, 1972); Jack Fitzsimons, *Bungalow Bashing* (Kells: Kells Arts Studios, 1990).

36. Clear, *Women of the House*, pp 207–10.

37. Dorine Rohan, *Marriage Irish Style* (Cork: Mercier Press, 1969), p. 30.

38. ibid., p. 30.

39. Patricia O'Hara, *Partners in Production? Women, Farm and Family in Ireland* (Oxford: Berghahn, 1998), pp 128–9.

40. John Jackson, *Report on the Skibbereen Social Survey* (Dublin: Human Sciences Committee, 1967), pp 44–6.

41. Paper presented at Teagasc conference on Family Farming, June 2014.

42. M. Power and R. Roche, *National Farm Survey 1990* (Dublin: Rural Economy Teagasc, 1992).

43. O'Hara, *Partners in Production?*, pp 103–12, discusses this at length.

44. Department of Agriculture, *Agri Food 2010* (Dublin: Department of Agriculture, 2000).

45. Damian F. Hannon and Patrick Commins, 'The Significance of Small-Scale Landholders in Ireland's Socio-Economic Transformation', in J. H. Goldthorpe and C. T. Whelan (eds.), *The Development of Industrial Society in Ireland* (Oxford: Oxford University Press, 1992), p. 90.

46. Alan Matthews, 'The Agri-Food Sector', in John O'Hagan and Carol Newman (eds.), *The Economy of Ireland: National and Sectoral Policy Issues* (Dublin: Gill and Macmillan, 2014), pp 287–311.

47. Central Statistics Office, *Life in Ireland in 1916: Stories from Statistics* (Dublin: Central Statistics Office, 2016).

48. EPA, Latest Emission Data: Environmental Protection Agency (https://www.epa.ie/our-services/monitoring--assessment/climate-change/ghg/latest-emissions-data/) accessed on 3 April 2024.

49. Teagasc, Agriculture and Water Quality, (https://www.teagasc.ie/environment/water-quality/agriculture-and-water-quality) accessed on 3 April 2024.
50. Donal Buckley, 'A Right or a Blight – Where now for One-off Rural Housing?', *Irish Independent*, 5 July 2022.

Bibliography

Primary sources

Government Papers

Department of Enterprise, Trade and Employment, National Archives of Ireland.
Department of Foreign Affairs, National Archives of Ireland.
Department of Taoiseach, National Archives of Ireland.

Institutional and Private Papers

Dublin Diocesan Archives, Archbishop John Charles McQuaid Papers.
Galway Diocesan Archives, Bishop Michael Browne Papers.
National Library of Ireland, Commission on Vocational Organisation Papers.
University of Galway Archives, Muintir na Tíre Papers.
University College Dublin Archives, Fine Gael Papers.
University College Dublin Archives, John A. Costello Papers.

Parliamentary and other Official Publications

An Chomhairle Oiliúna Talmhaíochta (ACOT), *Agriculture in County Limerick: Annual Report for 1984.*
Buchanan, Colin and Partners, *Regional Studies in Ireland,* (Dublin: An Foras Forbartha, 1969).
Central Statistics Office, *Census of Population 2016 – Profile 2 Population Distribution and Movements,* Background Notes, Appendix 1, unpaginated, https://www.cso.ie/en/releasesandpublications/ep/p-cp2tc/cp2pdm/bgn/, accessed 20 December 2018.
Central Statistics Office, 'Census of Agriculture 2020–Preliminary Results: Demographic Profile of Farm Holders', https://www.cso.ie/en/releasesandpublications/ep/p-coa/censusofagriculture2020-preliminaryresults/demographicprofileoffarmholders/, accessed on 31 August 2023.
Central Statistics Office, *Life in Ireland in 1916: Stories from Statistics* (Dublin: Central Statistics Office, 2016).
Census of Ireland, 1901, 1911.
Coimisiún na Gaeltachta, Vol.1, Report (Dublin: Stationery Office, 1926).
Coimisiún na Gaeltachta, Vol. 2, Evidence of Witnesses (Dublin: Stationery Office, 1926).
Commission on Vocational Organisation 1943: Report (Dublin: Stationery Office, 1944).
Commission on Emigration and Other Population Problems, 1948-1954: Reports (Dublin: Stationery Office, 1955).
Dáil Éireann Debates
Department of Agriculture, *First Annual Report of the Minister for Agriculture 1931-32,* p. 802.
Department of Agriculture, *Fourth Annual Report of the Minister for Agriculture 1934-35,* p. 1943.
Department of Agriculture, *Thirty-Second Annual Report of the Minister for Agriculture 1962-63,* Pr 7222.
Department of Agriculture, *Thirty-Third Annual Report of the Minister for Agriculture 1963-64,* Pr 7836.
Department of Agriculture, *Annual Report of the Minister for Agriculture 1964-65,* Pr 8747.

Department of Agriculture, *Annual Report of the Minister for Agriculture and Fisheries 1968-69*, Prl 880.

Department of Agriculture, *Annual Report for the Minister of Agriculture and Fisheries 1971-72*, Prl 2626.

Department of Agriculture, *Annual Report of the Minister for Agriculture and Fisheries 1972-73*, Prl 3343.

Department of Agriculture, *Annual Report of the Minister for Agriculture: 1979*, Prl 8881.

Department of Agriculture, *Agri Food 2010* (Dublin: Department of Agriculture, 2000).

Department of Agriculture, Food and Rural Development, *Report of the Advisory Committee on the Role of Women in Agriculture* (Dublin: Department of Agriculture, Food and Rural Development, 2000).

Department of Agriculture, Food and the Marine, *National Dialogue on Women in Agriculture: Report* (Dublin: Department of Agriculture, Food and the Marine, 2024).

Department of Education, *Investment in Education. Report of the Survey Team Appointed by the Minister for Education in October 1962* (Dublin: Stationery Office, 1966).

Department of the Environment, Climate and Communications, *Equality, Diversity and Inclusion: Strategy and Action Plan 2023-2025* (Dublin: Department of the Environment, Climate and Communications, 2023).

Department of Health, *National Nutrition Survey*, Parts I-VII, (1948), K.53/1-6.

Department of Social Welfare, *Report 1963-66* (Dublin: Stationery Office, 1968).

Environmental Protection Agency, Latest Emission Data: Environmental Protection Agency, (https://www.epa.ie/our-services/monitoring—assessment/climate-change/ghg/latest-emissions-data/).

Farming Since the Famine: Irish Farm Statistics 1847-1996 (Dublin: Central Statistics Office, 1997).

Galway County Council (GCC), *Second Annual Report of the County of Galway Committee for Agriculture*, (1902–3).

Galway County Council (GCC), *Third Annual Report of the County of Galway Committee for Agriculture*, (1903–4).

Galway County Council (GCC), *Eight Annual Report of the County of Galway Committee of Agriculture*, (1910).

Galway County Council (GCC), *Eleventh Annual Report of the County of Galway Committee of Agriculture*, (1911–12).

Gender Equality Unit, *Assessment of the Main Gaps in Existing Information on Women in Agriculture* (Dublin: National Development Plan, Gender Equality Unit, 2003).

Gender Equality Unit, *Women and Men on Farms in Ireland: their Activities, Attitudes and Experiences* (Dublin: Department of Justice, Equality, and Law Reform, 2004).

Industrial Development Authority, *Regional Industrial Plans 1973-77* (Dublin: Irish Industrial Development Authority, 1972).

Interdepartmental Committee on the Problems of Small Western Farms Report (Dublin: Stationery Office, 1962).

'Rural population (% of total population)' https://data.worldbank.org/indicator/SP.RUR.TOTL.ZS?locations accessed on 31 August 2023.

Second Programme for Economic Expansion (Dublin: Stationery Office, 1964), Pr 7670.

Teagasc: Agriculture and Food Development Authority, Mellows Campus, Athenry, County Galway, library and archives, Galway County Committee of Agriculture: minutes, 1, 12 January 1905.

Teagasc, *International day of rural women*, http://www.teagasc.ie, 10 Nov. 2022.

Teagasc, *Agriculture and Water Quality*, (https://www.teagasc.ie/environment/water-quality/agriculture-and-water-quality).

Whitaker, T. K., Department of Finance, *Economic Development* (Dublin: Stationery Office, 1958).

Newspapers, Periodicals and Journals

Christus Rex
Irish Farmers' Paper
Irish Felon
Irish Independent

Irish Press
Irish School Weekly
Irish Times
Landmark
Limerick Leader
Limerick Reporter and Tipperary Vindicator
Muintir na Tíre Official *Handbook*
Munster Express
Nenagh Guardian
Rural Ireland
The Irish Democrat
Tipperary Historical Journal
Tipperary Star

Contemporary Publications

Anonymous, 'There's No Neighbourliness In Cities', *The Landmark*, 1:4 (1944), pp 8–9.

Anonymous, 'President Opens Twenty-Second Rural Week', *The Landmark*, 16:8 (1959), pp 1–2.

Bohan, Harry, 'The Social and Religious Aspects of Industrialisation', *Christus Rex*, XXIV:4 (1970), pp 243–252.

Browne, M. J., 'Why Catholic Priests should Concern Themselves with Social and Economic Questions', *Christus Rex*, I: 1 (1947), pp 3–9.

Daly, C. B., 'Christus Rex Society', *Christus Rex*, I: 1 (1947), pp 27–33.

Duffy, Daniel, 'The Emigration Issue', *Christus Rex*, XV: 1 (1961), pp 7–15.

Feirmeoir, 'Agriculture in a Vocational Order of Society', *Christus Rex*, X: 1 (1956), pp 46–62.

Hayes, J. M., 'Our Story', *Rural Ireland* (Tipperary: Muintir na Tíre Rural Publications, 1941), pp 35–44.

Hayes, Father, 'The Beginning', *Muintir na Tíre Offical Handbook 1941* (Tipperary: Muintir na Tíre Rural Publications, 1941), pp 43–47.

Hayes, Rev. J. M., 'Policy or Action?', *Muintir na Tíre Offical Handbook 1943* (Tipperary: Muintir na Tíre Rural Publications, 1943), pp 17–19.

Hayes, J. M., 'Neighbourliness', *Muintir na Tíre Official Handbook 1944* (Tipperary: Muintir na Tíre Rural Publications, 1944), pp 24–27.

Hayes, Fr J. M., 'Vocationalism and Agriculture', *The Landmark*, 1:4, November 1944 (Tipperary: Muintir na Tíre Rural Publications, 1944), pp 2–3.

Hayes, Very Reverend J. M., 'Land League Memories', *Muintir na* Tíre: Official *Handbook 1946* (Tipperary: Muintir na Tíre Rural Publications, 1946), pp 51–4.

Hayes, J. M. and J. J. Bergin, *An Organisation to Develop Rural Ireland* (Tipperary: Muintir na Tíre Rural Publications, 1932).

Hofstee, E. W., 'Rural Sociological Research and Its Importance for the Betterment of Rural Life', *Christus Rex*, XIII: 3 (1959), pp 189–202.

Irish Farmers' Federation, *The Future of Agriculture in Ireland: Written in Plain Language by Farmers for Farmers* (Dublin: Irish Farmers' Federation, 1945).

Jackson, John, *Report on the Skibbereen Social Survey* (Dublin: Human Sciences Committee, 1967).

John XXIII, *Mater et Magistra: Encyclical of Pope John XXIII On Christianity and Social Progress* (1961), www.vatican.va.

Leaper, Robert A. B., 'Christian Witness in Community Development', *Christus Rex*, XVI: 3 (1962), pp161–71.

Lemass, Seán F., 'Social Factors and Emigration', *Christus Rex*, XV: 1 (1961), pp 16–20.

Leo XIII, *Rerum Novarum: Encyclical of Pope Leo X111 On Capital and Labor,* (1891), http://www.vatican.va.

Lucey, Con, 'Community Development – How to Set About It', *Rural Ireland 1960*, pp 24–9.

Lyddy, Frank, 'Rural Weeks', *Rural Ireland 1960* ((Tipperary: Muintir na Tíre Publications, 1960), pp 84 – 92.

McKevitt, Peter, *The Plan of Society* (Dublin: Catholic Truth Society of Ireland, 1944).

McKevitt, Peter, 'The Study Circle', *Christus Rex*, I: 1 (1947), pp 34–9.

McNabb, Patrick, 'Demography', in Jeremiah Newman (ed.), *The Limerick Rural Survey 1958-1964* (Tipperary: Muintir na Tíre Publications, 1964), pp 158–92.

McNabb, Patrick, 'Social Structure', in Jeremiah Newman (ed.), *The Limerick Rural Survey 1958-1964* (Tipperary: Muintir na Tíre Publications, 1964), pp 193–247.

McNeill, Josephine, 'Give a Hand to the Women!', In *Muintir na Tíre Offical Handbook 1941* (Tipperary: Muintir na Tíre Rural Publications, 1941), pp 51 – 3.

Meagher, G. A., 'The Development Plan and National Development', *Christus Rex*, XVIII: 3 (1964), pp 157–74.

Morrissey, V. Rev. M., 'A Long Association', *Rural Ireland 1960*, pp 30 – 2.

Muintir na Tíre Constitution (Tipperary: Muintir na Tíre Publications, 1938).

Newman, Jeremiah, 'The Future of Rural Ireland', *Studies*, 47:188 (1958), pp 388–402.

Newman, Jeremiah, *Studies in Political Morality* (Dublin: Scepter, 1962).

Newman, Jeremiah, 'Documentation', *Christus Rex*, XVII:2 (1963), pp 161–84.

Newman, Jeremiah, 'Pastoral Problems in the Rural Environment', *Christus Rex*, XVI: 3 (1963), pp 223–30.

Newman, Jeremiah, (ed.), *The Limerick Rural Survey 1958-1964* (Tipperary: Muintir na Tíre Publications, 1964).

Newman, Rev. J., 'Changing Functions of the Rural Community', *Christus Rex*, XX1:1 (1967), pp 60–9.

Newman, Jeremiah, 'Vocations in Ireland–1966', *Christus Rex*, XXI: 2 (1967), pp 105–12.

Newman, Jeremiah, *Race, Migration and Integration* (London: Burns and Oates, 1968).

Newman, Jeremiah, *Conscience Versus Law: Reflections of the Evolution of Natural Law* (Dublin: Talbot Press, 1971).

Newman, Jeremiah, *The State of Ireland* (Dublin: Four Courts, 1977).

Newman, Jeremiah, *The Postmodern Church* (Dublin: Four Courts, 1990).

O'Connor, T. M., 'The Limerick Rural Survey', *Christus Rex*, XVIII: 3 (1964), pp 187–97.

Ó Danachair, Caoimhín., 'The Family in Irish Tradition', *Christus Rex*, XVI: 3 (1962), pp 185–96.

O'Faolain, Sean, 'Attitudes', *The Bell*, 2:6 (1941), pp 5–12.

O'Faolain, Sean, 'Silent Ireland', *The Bell*, 6:6 (1943), pp 457–66.

O'Leary, Olivia, 'The Mullah of Limerick', *Magill*, 21 March 1985, pp 24–33.

O'Reilly, P. P., Radio Éireann Broadcast 3 November, 1948 ('Rural electrification of Bansha, Co Tipperary in 1948' *REO News* 1948 No. 12, pp 5–6, www.esbarchives.ie.

O'Riordan, M., *Catholicity and Progress in Ireland* (London: Kegan Paul, Trench, Trübner and Co., 1906).

Pius XI, *Quadragesimo Anno: Encyclical of Pope Pius XI on Reconstruction of the Social Order*, (1931), http://www.vatican.va.

Pavan, Monsignor Pietro, 'The Agricultural and Rural Section of *Mater et Magistra*', *Christus Rex*, XVI: 3 (1963), pp 191–200.

Plunkett, Horace, *Ireland in the New Century* (New York: Kennikat Press, 1970 [1904]).

Prendergast, Robert, 'Foundations of Social Justice in Ireland', *Christus Rex*, XIII: 4 (1959), pp 244–58.

Roseingrave, Tomás, 'Government and Voluntary Organisations', *Rural Ireland*, 30 (1970), pp 18–26.

Ryan, John, 'The Founder of Muintir na Tíre: Canon John M. Hayes 1887-1957', *Studies*, 46:183 (1957), pp 312–21.

Ryan, Liam, 'Social Dynamite: A Study of Early School-Leavers', *Christus Rex*, XXI: 1 (1967), pp 7–44.

Rynne, Stephen, 'Farming, the Free-for-all', *Rural Ireland 1950*, pp 116–9.

Rynne, Stephen, *Father John Hayes: Founder of Muintir na Tire People of the Land* (Dublin: Clonmore and Reynolds, 1960).

Rynne, Stephen, 'Living Democracy', *The Landmark*, 18:8 (1961), pp 7–9.

Scully, John J., *The Community as a Social System for Action Programmes* (Tipperary: Muintir na Tíre Publications, 1963).

Smith, Louis P. F., 'The National Farmers Association', *Christus Rex*, X:1 (1956), pp 14–19.

Smith, Louis P. F. & Seán Healy, *Farm Organisations in Ireland: A Century of Progress* (Dublin: Four Courts Press, 1996).
Thomason, George F., *Community Development in Ireland* (Tipperary: Muintir na Tíre Publications, 1961).
Thomason, George F., 'Leadership', *Christus Rex*, XVI: 3 (1962), pp 172–7.
Thomason, George F., *Giving the Lead* (Muintir na Tíre Publications: Tipperary, 1962).
Thomason, George, 'Muintir na Tire', *Reality* (September, 1967), pp 6–11.
Toner, Jerome, *Rural Ireland: Some of Its Problems* (Dublin: Clonmore and Reynolds, 1955).

Memoirs, Novels and Short Stories

Brennan, Elizabeth, *Am I My Brother's Keeper?* (Dublin: Metropolitan Publishing Company, 1945).
Campbell, M. H., *As Luck Would Have It* (Dundalk: Dundalgan Press, 1948).
Cooper, Richmal Crompton, *The New House* (London: Victor Gollancz, 1936).
Cooper, Lettice, *National Provincial* (London: Victor Gollancz, 1938).
Cooper, Lettice, *Fenny* (London: Victor Gollancz, 1953).
Crompton, Richmal, *Family Roundabout* (London: 1948, Persephone Books reprint, 2004).
Crompton, Richmal, *Frost at Morning* (London: Hutchinson, 1950).
Crone, Anne, *Bridie Steen* (London: Heinemann, 1949).
Cross, Eric, *The Tailor and Ansty* (London: Chapman & Hall, 1942).
Delafield, E. M., *Diary of a Provincial Lady* (London: Macmillan, 1930).
Dickens, Monica, *Joy and Josephine* (London: 1948, Foyle's Book Club edn., 1949).
Hand, William, *Fair City* (Dublin: Clonmore & Reynolds, 1946).
Holtby, Winifred, *South Riding* (London: John Murray, 1936).
Hoult, Norah, *Father Hone and the Television Set* (London: Hutchinson, 1956).
Hoult, Norah, *Selected Stories* (Dublin: Maurice Fridberg, 1946).
Hoult, Norah, *Cocktail Bar* (Sinéad Gleeson, ed.) (Dublin: New Island, 2019 [1950]).
Joyce-Prendergast, Kathleen, *Windy Hill* (Cork: Mercier Press, 1945).
Kavanagh, Patrick, *Tarry Flynn* (London: The Pilot Press, 1948; Penguin 1978).
Lane, Temple, *Friday's Well* (Dublin: Talbot Press, 1943).
Laverty, Maura, *Never No More: The Story of a Lost Village* (London: Longmans Green, 1942).
Laverty, Maura, *Alone We Embark* (London: Longmans Green, 1943).
Laverty, Maura, *No More than Human* (London: Longmans Green, 1944).
Laverty, Maura, *Lift Up Your Gates* (London: Longmans Green, 1946).
Laverty, Maura, *Full and Plenty* (Dublin: Irish Flour Millers Association, 1960).
Lavin, Mary, *Tales From Bective Bridge* (London: Michael Joseph, 1943; Dublin: Poolbeg, 1978).
Lavin, Mary, *The Becker Wives* (London: Michael Joseph, 1946).
Lyons, J. K., *Before the Dawn* (Dublin: Gill, 1946).
MacManus, Francis, *Flow on Lovely River* (Dublin: Talbot Press, 1940).
MacManus, Francis, *Watergate* (Dublin: Talbot Press, 1942 and Dublin: Poolbeg, 1980).
O'Brien, Kate, *Pray for the Wanderer* (London: Heinemann, 1938).
O'Brien, Kate, *The Land of Spices* (London: Heinemann, 1941).
O'Brien, Kate, *The Flower of May* (London: Heinemann, 1955).
Orwell, George, *Coming Up For Air* (London: Victor Gollancz, 1939).
Peck, Winifred, *House-Bound* (London: Faber & Faber, 1942, Persephone Books reprint, 2007).
Pim, Sheila, *The Flowering Shamrock* (London: Hodder & Stoughton, 1947).
Priestley, J. B., *English Journey* (London: Victor Gollancz, 1934).
Purcell, Mary, *The Pilgrim Came Late* (Dublin: Clonmore & Reynolds, 1947).
Purcell, Patrick, *Fiddler's Green* (Dublin: Talbot Press, 1950).
Purcell, Patrick, *A Keeper of Swans* (Dublin: Talbot Press, 1944).
Purcell, Patrick, *Hanrahan's Daughter* (Dublin: Talbot Press, 1940).
Robertson, Olivia, *St Malachy's Court* (London: Peter Davies, 1946).
Robertson, Olivia, *Field of the Stranger* (London: Peter Davies, 1948).
Robertson, Olivia, *The Golden Eye* (London: Peter Davies, 1949).
Rooney, Philip, *Singing River* (Dublin: Talbot Press, 1944).

Sheridan, John D., *Paradise Alley* (Dublin: Talbot Press, 1945).
Sheridan, John D., *The Magnificent McDarney* (Dublin: Talbot Press, 1947).
Sherriff, R. C., *Greengates* (London: Victor Gollancz, 1936).
Smithson, Annie M. P., *The Walk of a Queen* (Dublin: Talbot, 1924).
Smithson, Annie M. P., *The Light of Other Days* (Dublin: Talbot, 1943).
Smithson, Annie M. P., *Paid in Full* (Dublin: Talbot, 1946).
Stewart, M. L., *Finishing Touch* (Dublin: Talbot Press, 1943).
Stewart, M. L., *The Cliff-Dwellers* (Dublin: Talbot Press, 1943).
Taylor, Alice, *To School Through the Fields: An Irish Country Childhood* (Dingle: Brandon, 1988).
Thompson, Flora, *Lark Rise to Candleford* (Oxford: Oxford University Press, 1939).
Tutton, Diana, *Guard Your Daughters* (London: Reprint Society, 1954; Persephone Books, 2017).
Uttley, Alison, *The Country Child* (London: Faber, 1931).
Whipple, Dorothy, *High Wages* (London: John Murray, 1930, Persephone Books, 2009).

Secondary Sources

Aalen, F. H. A., 'The Rehousing of Rural Labourers in Ireland under the Labourers (Ireland) Acts, 1883-1919', *Journal of Historical Geography*, 12:3 (1986), pp 287–306.
Adshead, Maura, 'Beyond Clientelism: Agricultural Networks in Ireland and the EU', *West European Politics*, 19:3 (1996), pp 583–608.
Allen, Kieran, *Fianna Fáil and Irish Labour: 1926 to the Present* (London: Pluto Press, 1997).
Almeida, Linda Dowling, *Irish Immigration to New York City, 1945-1995* (Bloomington: Indiana University Press, 2001).
Alwenyi, Irene, Josephine Sepeku, Celia Sheridan and Mícheál Ó Fathartaigh, 'Women in Irish Agricultural History', *TResearch*, 14:2 (2019), pp 32–3.
Arensberg, Conrad M., *The Irish Countryman* (Gloucester, Mass.: P. Smith, 1937).
Arensberg, Conrad M. & Solon T. Kimball, *Family and Community in Ireland* (Cambridge Mass.: Harvard University Press, 1940).
Arensberg, Conrad M. & Solon T. Kimball, *Family and Community in Ireland*, 3rd edn. ([1940]; Ennis: CLASP Press, 2001).
Baker, John, Kathleen Lynch, Sara Cantillon & Judy Walsh, *Equality from Theory to Action* (Basingstoke: Palgrave, 2004).
Balaine, Lorriane. 'Gender and the Preservation of Family Farming in Ireland', *EuroChoices*, 18:3 (2019), pp 33–7.
Banks, Joanne, 'Policy, Practice and Performance: The Changing Role of the Irish Agricultural Advisory Service, 1945-88' (unpublished PhD thesis, University College Dublin, 2007).
Barry, Ursula, (ed.), *Where Are We Now: New Feminist Perspectives on Women in Contemporary Ireland* (Dublin: New Island, 2008).
Bartlett, Thomas, (ed.), *The Cambridge History of Ireland: Volume IV 1880 to the Present* (Cambridge: Cambridge University Press, 2018).
Beach, Dennis, Tuuli From, Monica Johannson and Elisabet Öhrn, 'Educational and Spatial Justice in Rural and Urban Areas in Three Nordic Countries: A Meta-Ethnograpic Analysis', *Education Inquiry*, 9:2 (2018), pp 1–18.
Beauman, Nicola, *A Very Great Profession: The Woman's Novel 1914-39* (London: Virago, 1983).
Bew, Paul, *Conflict and Conciliation in Ireland, 1890-1910* (Oxford: Clarendon Press, 1987).
Bew, Paul, *Ireland: The Politics of Enmity 1789-2006* (Oxford: Oxford University Press, 2007).
Bew, Paul, Ellen Hazelkorn and Henry Patterson, *The Dynamics of Irish Politics* (London: Lawrence and Wishart, 1989).
Bogue, Pat, *Land Mobility and Succession in Ireland* (Dublin: Macra na Feirme, 2013).
Bolger, Patrick, *The Irish Co-operative Movement: Its History and Development* (Dublin: Institute of Public Administration, 1977).
Bolster, Evelyn, *The Knights of Saint Columbanus* (Dublin: Gill and Macmillan, 1979).
Bourke, Joanna, 'Women and Poultry in Ireland, 1891-1914', *Irish Historical Studies*, 25:99 (1987), pp 293–310.
Bradley, Dan, *Farm Labourers: Irish Struggle 1900-1976* (Belfast: Athol Books, 1988).

Breathnach, Ciara, *The Congested Districts Board of Ireland, 1891-1922: Poverty and Development in the West of Ireland* (Dublin: Four Courts Press, 2005).

Breen, Richard, Damian F. Hannan, David B. Rottman & Christopher T. Whelan, *Understanding Contemporary Ireland: State, Class and Development in the Republic of Ireland* (Dublin: Gill and Macmillan, 1990).

Brody, Hugh, *Inishkillane: Change and Decline in the West of Ireland* (London: Allen Lane, 1973).

Brown, Terence, *Ireland: A Social and Cultural History 1922-79* (London, Fontana, 1981).

Buckley, Donal, 'A Right or a Blight – Where Now for One-off Rural Housing?', *Irish Independent*, 5 July 2022.

Byrne, Anne, 'Single Women in Ireland: A Re-examination of the Sociological Evidence', in Anne Byrne & Madeleine Leonard (eds.), Women *and Irish Society: A Sociological Reader* (Belfast: Beyond the Pale Publications, 1997), pp 415–30.

Byrne, Anne & Madeleine Leonard (eds.), *Women and Irish Society: A Sociological Reader* (Belfast: Beyond the Pale Publications, 1997).

Byrne, Anne, Nata Duvvury, Áine Macken-Walsh & Tanya Watson, 'Finding Room to Manoeuvre: Gender, Agency and the Family Farm', in Barbara Pini, Berit Brandth & Jo Little (eds.), *Feminisms and Ruralities* (Lexington: Lexington University Press, 2015), pp 119–30.

Byrne, Helen, '"Going to the Pictures": the Female Audience and the Pleasures of Cinema', in Mary J. Kelly & Barbara O'Connor (edss.), *Media Audiences in Ireland: Power and Cultural Identity* (Dublin: UCD Press, 1997), pp 88–106.

Callanan, Brian, *Ireland's Shannon Story: Leaders, Visions and Networks – A Case Study of Local and Regional Development* (Dublin: Irish Academic Press, 2000).

Campbell, Fergus, *Land and Revolution: Nationalist Politics in the West of Ireland 1891-1921* (Oxford: Oxford University Press, 2005).

Campbell, Fergus and Tony Varley (eds.), *Land Questions in Modern Ireland* (Manchester: Manchester University Press, 2013).

Cassidy, Anne, 'Female Successors in Irish Family Farming: Four Pathways to Farm Transfer', *Canadian Journal of Development Studies/Revue Canadienne d'études du développeme*nt, 40:2 (2019), pp 238–53.

Cawley, Mary and Stephen Galvin, 'Irish Migration and Return: Continuities and Changes over Time', *Irish Geography*, 49:1 (2016), pp 11–27.

Child, Brenda J., *My Grandfather's Knocking Sticks: Ojibwe Family Life and Labor on the Reservation* (St Paul: Minnesota Historical Society Press, 2014).

Chubb, Basil, *The Government and Politics of Ireland* (London: Longman, 1982).

Clancy, Mary, 'Shaping the Nation: Women in the Free State Parliament, 1923-1937', in Yvonne Galligan, Eilís Ward and Rick Wilford (eds.), *Contesting Politics: Women in Ireland, North and South* (Boulder, Colorado: Westview Press, 1999), pp 201–18.

Clancy, Patrick, Sheelagh Drudy, Kathleen Lynch & Liam O'Dowd (eds.), *Irish Society: Sociological Perspectives* (Dublin: Institute of Public Administration, 1995).

Clarke, Marie, 'Educational Reform in the 1960s: The Introduction of Comprehensive Schools in the Republic of Ireland', *History of Education*, 39:3 (2010), pp 383–99.

Clear, Caitriona, *Women of the House: Women's Household Work in Ireland 1921-1961* (Dublin: Irish Academic Press, 2000).

Clear, Caitriona, 'Women in de Valera's Ireland 1922-48: A Reappraisal', in Doherty, Gabriel and Keogh, Dermot (eds.), *De Valera's Irelands* (Cork: Mercier Press, 2003), pp 104–14.

Clear, Caitriona, *Social Change and Everyday Life in Ireland: 1850-1922* (Manchester: Manchester University Press, 2007).

Clear, Caitriona, 'Women in Ireland in the 1930s and 1940s', in Alan Hayes (ed.), *Hilda Tweedy and the Irish Housewives Association: Links in the Chain...* (Dublin: Arlen House, 2012), pp 59–68.

Comerford, R. V. *Charles J. Kickham: A Study in Irish Nationalism and Literature* (Dublin: Wolfhound Press, 1979).

Commins, Bernie, 'Census: Percentage of Female Farm Holders up by 1% in a Decade', *Agriland*, 12 December 2021 (https://www.agriland.ie/farming-news/census-percentage-of-female-farm-holders-up-by-1-in-a-decade/) accessed on 1 September 2023.

Commins, Patrick, 'Agricultural Production and the Future of Small-Scale Farming', in Chris Curtin, Trutz Haase and Hilary Tovey (eds.), *Poverty in Rural Ireland: A Political Economy Approach* (Dublin: Oak Tree Press, 1996), pp 87–125.

Connolly, Linda and Tina O'Toole, *Documenting Irish Feminisms* (Dublin: The Woodfield Press, 2005).

Conway, Brian, 'Foreigners, Faith and Fatherland: The Historical Origins, Development and Present Status of Irish Sociology', *Sociological Origins*, 5:1 (2006), pp 5–36.

Coogan, T. P., *Ireland Since the Rising* (Dublin: Pall Mall Press, 1966).

Cooney, John, *John Charles McQuaid: Ruler of Catholic Ireland* (Dublin: O'Brien Press, 1999).

Corcoran, M. P., 'Informalisation of Metropolitan Labour Forces: The Case of Irish Immigrants in the New York Construction Sector', *Irish Journal of Sociology*, 1:1 (1991), pp 31–51.

Corkery, Seán, 'Father John Hayes', *The Furrow*, 8:5 (1957), pp 302–7.

Cousins, Mel, *The Birth of Social Welfare in Ireland, 1922-52* (Dublin: Four Courts Press, 2003).

Cronin, Mike, *The Blueshirts and Irish Politics* (Dublin: Four Courts Press, 1997).

Crotty, Raymond, *Irish Agricultural Production: Its Volume and Structure* (Cork: Cork University Press, 1966).

Crotty, Raymond, *Ireland in Crisis: a Study in Capitalist Colonial Undevelopment* (Dingle: Brandon Press, 1986).

Crotty, Raymond, *A Radical's Response* (Swords, Co. Dublin: Poolbeg Press, 1988).

Crotty, Raymond, *When Histories Collide: The Development and Impact of Individualistic Capitalism* (Walnut Creek, CA: AltaMira Press, 2001).

Crowley, Ethel, *Land Matters: Power Struggles in Rural Ireland* (Dublin: The Lilliput Press, 2006).

Curtin, Chris, Trutz Haase & Hilary Tovey (eds.), *Poverty in Rural Ireland: A Political Economy Approach* (Dublin: Oak Tree Press, 1996).

Curtis, Maurice, *The Splendid Cause: The Catholic Action Movement in Ireland in the Twentieth Century* (Dublin: Original Writing and Greenmount Publications, 2009).

Cush, Peter & Áine Macken-Walsh, 'Reconstituting Male Identities through Joint Farming Ventures in Ireland', *Sociologia Ruralis*, 58:4 (2018), pp 726–44.

Cush, Peter, Áine Macken-Walsh & Anne Byrne, 'Joint Farming Ventures: Gender Identities of the Self and the Social', *Journal of Rural Studies*, 57 (2018), pp 55–64.

Daly, Mary E., '"Turn on the Tap": The State, Irish Women and Running Water', in Maryann Gianella Valiulis and Mary O'Dowd (eds.), *Women and Irish History* (Dublin: Wolfhound Press, 1997), pp 206–19.

Daly, Mary E., *The First Department: A History of the Department of Agriculture* (Dublin: Institute of Public Administration, 2002).

Daly, Mary E., *The Slow Failure: Population Decline and Independent Ireland, 1920-1973* (Madison: University of Wisconsin Press, 2006).

Daly, Mary E., *Sixties Ireland: Reshaping the Economy, State and Society, 1957-73* (Cambridge: Cambridge University Press, 2016).

Davis, John, (ed.), *Rural Change in Ireland* (Belfast: Institute of Irish Studies Queen's University Belfast, 1999).

Delany, Enda, *Demography, State, and Society: Irish Migration to Britain, 1921-1971* (Liverpool: Liverpool University Press, 2000).

Delany, Enda, *The Irish in Post-War Britain* (Oxford: Oxford University Press, 2007).

Dempsey, Pauric and Shaun Boylan, 'Lawrence Ginnell 1852-1923', in James McGuire and James Quinn (eds.), *Dictionary of Irish Biography* (Cambridge: Cambridge University Press, 2009), pp 102–3.

Devereux, Eoin, The Theory and Practice of Community Development: Muintir Na Tíre 1931-1988 (MA Thesis, Department of Political Science and Sociology, University College Galway, 1988).

Devereux, Eoin, 'Potatoes, Turf and Fireside Chats: Muintir na Tíre and "The Emergency" in Limerick', *Old Limerick Journal*, 26 (1989), pp 34–6.

Devereux, Eoin, 'Saving Rural Ireland: Muintir na Tíre and its Anti-Urbanism, 1931-1958', *The Canadian Journal of Irish Studies*, 17:2 (1991), pp 23–30.

Devereux, Eoin, 'Class, Community and Conflict; The Case of Muintir na Tíre Limited', *Tipperary Historical Journal*, 8 (1995), pp 94–102.

Devereux, Eoin, 'Muintir Versus Macra: the Parish Plan for Agriculture, 1947-1957', *Tipperary Historical Journal*, 11 (1998), pp 89–94.

Devereux Eoin, 'John Hayes 1887-1957, Founder of Muintir Na Tíre', *Old Limerick Journal*, 34 (1998), pp 34–6.

Dinneen, Donal A., 'The Europeanisation of Irish Universities', in *Higher Education*, 24 (1992), pp 391–411.

Doherty, Gabriel and Dermot Keogh (eds.), *De Valera's Irelands* (Cork: Mercier Press, 2003).

Dooley, Terence, *'The Land for the People': The Land Question in Independent Ireland* (Dublin: University College Dublin Press, 2004).

Downey, Liam & Maura McLoughlin, 'Agricultural Education in the 19th and 20th Centuries with Particular Regard to the Munster Institute', *Times Past: Journal of Muskerry Local History Society*, 9 (2010–11), pp 25–36.

Doyle, Patrick, *Civilising Rural Ireland: The Co-operative Movement, Development and the Nation-State, 1889-1939* (Manchester: Manchester University Press, 2019).

Doyle, Patrick, 'Horace Plunkett, Co-operation, and an Irish Solution to the Transnational Problem of Rural Life, 1891-1921', in Joe Regan and Cathal Smith (eds.), *Agrarian Reform and Resistance in an Age of Globalisation: The Euro-American World and Beyond, 1780-1914* (London: Routledge, 2019), pp 202–16.

Dustmann, Christian, Itzik Fadlon & Yoram Weiss, 'Return Migration, Human Capital Accumulation and the Brain Drain', *Journal of Development Economics*, 95:1 (2011), pp 58–68.

Durkheim, Emile, *Suicide: A Study in Sociology* (New York: The Free Press, 1951).

Durkheim, Emile, *The Division of Labour in Society* (Basingstoke: Macmillan, 1984).

Duvvury, Nata, Áine Ní Léime, &Tanya Watson, 'Rural Women, Ageing and Retirement', in Mark Skinner, Rachel Winterton and Kieran Walsh (eds.), *Rural Gerontology: Towards Critical Perspectives on Rural Ageing* (London: Routledge, 2020), pp 93–104.

Eipper, Chris, *The Ruling Trinity: A Community Study of Church, State and Business in Ireland* (Aldershot: Gower, 1986).

EUROSTAT, *Migration Statistics Explained* (Brussels: European Commission, 2018), https://ec.europa.eu/eurostat/statistics-explained/index.php/Glossary:Migration, accessed 10 December 2019.

Fanning, Bryan, *The Quest for Modern Ireland: The Battle of Ideas 1912-1986* (Dublin: Irish Academic Press, 2008).

Fanning, Bryan, *Histories of the Irish Future* (London: Bloomsbury, 2015).

Farmar, Tony, *The History of Irish Book Publishing* (Stroud: The History Press, 2018).

Farrell, Maura, Marie Mahon and John McDonagh, 'The Rural as a Return Migration Destination', *European Countryside*, 4:1 (2012), pp 31–44.

Feehan, John, *An Irish Publisher and his World* (Cork: Mercier, 1969).

Fennelly, Maura E., *Do Not Forget to Remember* (Victoria, British Columbia: Trafford Publishing, 2004).

Fernihough, Alan & Cormac Ó Gráda, *Across the Sea to Ireland: Return Atlantic Migration Before the First World War*, SSRN on-line papers (2020), http://dx.doi.org/10.2139/ssrn.3491676, accessed 15 July 2020

Ferriter, Diarmaid, *Mothers, Maidens and Myths: A History of the Irish Countrywomen's Association* (Dublin: FÁS, 1995).

Ferriter, Diarmaid, 'John Martin Hayes', in James McGuire and James Quinn (eds.), *Dictionary of Irish Biography* (Cambridge: Cambridge University Press, 2009), pp 537–9.

Ferriter, Diarmaid, *On the Edge: Ireland's Off-Shore Islands: A Modern History* (London: Profile Books, 2020).

Findlay, Allan M. and F. L. N. Li, 'Methodological Issues in Researching Migration', *The Professional Geographer*, 51:1 (1999), pp 50–9.

Finn, Tomás, *The Influence of Tuairim on Intellectual Debate and Policy Formulation in Ireland, 1954-1975* (PhD Thesis, National University of Ireland, Galway, 2008).

Finn, Tomás, *Tuairim, Intellectual Debate and Policy Formulation: Rethinking Ireland* (Manchester: Manchester University Press, 2012).

Finn, Tomás, '"Towards a Better Ireland": Donal Barrington and the Irish Constitution', in Laura Cahillane, James Gallen & Tom Hickey (eds.), *Judges, Politics and the Irish Constitution* (Manchester: Manchester University Press, 2017), pp 217–33.

Finn, Tomás, 'Politics and the Praxis of Power: The Political Establishment and the Talented Young in post-WWII Ireland', in Tomás Finn & Kieran Hoare (eds.), *Borders and Boundaries: Historical Perspectives* (Abingdon: Routledge Press, forthcoming).

FitzGerald, Garret, *All in a life: An Autobiography* (Dublin: Gill and Macmillan, 1991).

FitzGerald, Garret, *Reflections on the Irish State* (Dublin: Irish Academic Press, 2003).

Fitzsimons, Jack, *Bungalow Bliss* (Kells: Kells Arts Studios, 1972).

Fitzsimons, Jack, *Bungalow Bashing* (Kells: Kells Arts Studios, 1990).

Florida, Richard, *Cities and the Creative Class* (London: Routledge, 2005).

Fogarty, Michael P., *Christian Democracy in Western Europe, 1820-1953* (London: Routledge & Kegan Paul, 1957).

Fogarty, Michael, 'Introduction' to Denis I. F. Lucey & Donald R. Kaldor, *Rural Industrialization: The Impact of Industrialization on Two Rural Communities in Western Ireland* (London: Geoffrey Chapman, 1969), pp 9–11.

Friedberg, Susanne E., 'The Triumph of the Egg', *Comparative Studies in Science and History*, 50:2 (2008), pp 400–23.

Gallagher, Michael, *Electoral Support for Irish Political Parties 1927-1973* (London: Sage, 1976).

Gallagher, Michael, *Political Parties in the Republic of Ireland* (Dublin: Gill and Macmillan, 1985).

Gallagher, Michael, *Irish Elections 1922-44: Results and Analysis, Vol. 1*, (PSAI Press, Limerick, 1993).

Gibbons, Luke, *Transformations in Irish Culture* (Cork: Cork University Press in association with Field Day, 1995).

Gibbon, Peter, 'Arensberg and Kimball Revisited', *Economy and Society*, 2:4 (1973), pp 479–98.

Gibbon, Peter and M. D. Higgins,, 'Patronage, Tradition and Modernization: The Case of the Irish "Gombeenman"', *Economic and Social Review*, 6:1 (1974), pp 27–44.

Giddens, Anthony, *The Constitution of Society* (Cambridge: Polity Press, 1984).

Giles, Judy, *Women, Identity and Private Life in Britain 1900-50* (London: Macmillan, 1995).

Girvin, Brian, 'Stability, Crisis and Change in Post-War Ireland', in Thomas Bartlett (ed.), *The Cambridge History of Ireland, Volume IV, 1880 to the Present* (Cambridge: Cambridge University Press, 2018), pp 381–406.

Glynn, Irial, Tomás Kelly & Piaras MacÉinrí, *Irish Emigration in an Age of Austerity* (Cork: Cork University Press, 2013).

Glynn, Irial, Tomás Kelly & Piaras MacÉinrí, *The Re-Emergence of Emigration from Ireland* (Washington DC: Migration Policy Institute, 2015).

Gmelch, George, 'Who Returns and Why: Return Migration Behaviour in Two North Atlantic Societies', *Human Organisation*, 42:1 (1983), pp 46–54.

Goldring, Maurice, *Faith of our Fathers: The Formation of Irish Nationalist Ideology 1890-1920* (Dublin: Repsol, [1982] 1987).

Goldring, Maurice, *Pleasant the Scholar's Life: Irish Intellectuals and the Construction of the Nation State* (London: Serif, 1993).

Goldthorpe, J. H. & C. T. Whelan (eds.), *The Development of Industrial Society in Ireland* (Oxford: Oxford University Press, 1992).

Goodings, Lennie, *A Bite of the Apple: A Life with Books, Writers and Virago* (Oxford: Oxford University Press, 2020).

Guest, Greg, Kathleen M. McQueen & Emily E. Narney, *Applied Thematic Analysis* (Thousand Oaks, Calif.: Sage, on-line edition, 2014),

Guinnane, Timothy W., *The Vanishing Irish: Households, Migration and the Rural Economy in Ireland, 1850-1914* (Princeton, New Jersey: Princeton University Press, 1997).

Gustafson, Per, 'Meanings of Place: Everyday Experience and Theoretical Conceptualisations', *Journal of Environmental Psychology*, 21:1 (2001), pp 5–16.

Halfacree, Keith H. & Paul Boyle, 'The Challenge Facing Migration Research: The Case for a Biographical Approach', *Progress in Human Geography*, 17 (1993), pp 333–48.

Hannan, Damian F., *Rural Exodus: A Study of the Forces Influencing Large-Scale Migration of Irish Rural Youth* (London: G. Chapman, 1970).

Hannan, Damian F. & Louise A. Katsiaouni, *Traditional Families? From Culturally Prescribed to Negotiated Roles in Farm Families* (Dublin: Economic and Social Research Institute, 1977).

Hannan, Damian F., *Displacement and Development: Class, Kinship and Social Change in Irish Rural Communities* (Dublin: The Economic and Social Research Institute, 1979),

Hannon, Damian F., 'Peasant Models and the Understanding of Social and Cultural Change in Rural Ireland', in P. J. Drudy (ed.), *Ireland: Land, Politics and People* (Cambridge: Cambridge University Press, 1982), pp 141–65.

Hannon, Damian F. and Patrick Commins, 'The Significance of Small-Scale Landholders in Ireland's Socio-Economic Transformation', in J. H. Goldthorpe and C. T. Whelan (eds.), *The Development of Industrial Society in Ireland* (Oxford: Oxford University Press, 1992), pp 79–104.

Hartnett, Michael, *Maiden Street Ballad* (Privately published: Templeglantine, 1980).

Healy, John, *The Death of an Irish Town* (Cork: Mercier Press, 1968).

Heverin, Aileen, *The Irish Countrywomen's Association: A History 1910-2000* (Dublin: The Wolfhound Press, 2000).

Hoctor, Daniel, *The Department's Story – A History of the Department of Agriculture* (Dublin: Institute of Public Administration, 1971).

Holden, Katharine, *The Shadow of Marriage: Singleness in England 1914-60* (Manchester: Manchester University Press, 2007).

Hooker, Elizabeth R., *Readjustments of Agricultural Tenure in Ireland* (Chapel Hill: The University of North Carolina Press, 1938).

Hoppen, K. Theodore, *Elections, Politics, and Society in Ireland 1832-1885* (Oxford: Clarendon Press, Oxford, 1984).

Hoppen, K. Theodore, *Ireland Since 1800: Conflict and Conformity* (London: Longman, 1999).

Humble, Nicola, *The Feminine Middlebrow Novel from the 1920s to the 1950s: Class, Domesticity and Bohemianism* (Oxford: Oxford University Press, 2001).

Hynes, Eugene, 'The Great Hunger and Irish Catholicism', *Societas*, 8 (1978), pp 137–56.

Indecon International Economic Consultants, *Indecon Economic Report on Addressing the Challenges Faced by Returning Irish Emigrants* (Dublin: Indecon, 2018).

Inglis, Tom, *Moral Monopoly: The Rise and Fall of the Catholic Church in Modern Ireland* (Dublin: University College Dublin Press, 1998).

Inglis, Tom, *Global Ireland: Same Difference* (New York and London: Routledge, 2008).

Inglis, Tom, 'John McGahern: The Sociology of Honor, Status and Shame', *Éire-Ireland*, 57:3&4 (2022), pp 6–32.

Irwin, Liam, 'Newman, Jeremiah', *Dictionary of Irish Biography* (Cambridge: Cambridge University Press, 2009), pp 897–8.

Jackson, John A., *The Irish in London* (London: Routledge, 1963).

Jacobsen, John K., *Chasing Progress in the Irish Republic: Ideology, Democracy and Dependent Development* (Cambridge: Cambridge University Press, 1994).

Jones, David S., *Graziers, Land Reform and Political Conflict in Ireland* (Washington: Catholic University of America Press, 1995).

Jones, Richard C., 'Multinational Investment and Return Migration in Ireland in the 1990s: County-level Analysis', *Irish Geography*, 36:2 (2003), pp 153–69.

Joyce, Patrick, *Remembering Peasants: A Personal History of a Vanished World* (London: Allen Lane, 2024).

Kaim-Caudle, Peter, *Social Security in Ireland and Western Europe* (Dublin: Economic Research Institute, 1964).

Karim, Lamia, 'Analyzing Women's Empowerment: Microfinance and Garment Labor in Bangladesh', *Fletcher Forum of World Affairs*, 38:2 (2014), pp 153–66.

Kearns, Seán, 'Seán Moylan', in James McGuire and James Quinn (eds.), *Dictionary of Irish Biography* (Cambridge: Cambridge University Press, 2009), pp 726–8.

Kelly, Seamus, *The Maura Laverty Story: from Rathangan to Tolka Row* (Kildare: Seamus Kelly, 2017).

Kelly, Edel, Karen Keaveney and Anne Markey, *Challenges and Opportunities for Rural Ireland and the Agricultural Sector* (Dublin: National Economic and Social Council, 2021).

Kennedy, Kieran A., Thomas Giblin & Deirdre McHugh, *The Economic Development of Ireland in the Twentieth century* (London & New York: Routledge Press, 1988).

Kennedy, Robert. E., *The Irish, Emigration, Marriage and Fertility* (Los Angeles: University of California Press, 1973).

Kenny, Ciara, 'Illegal Workers in Australia Face a Perilous Existence', *The Irish Times*, 29 August 2016.

Keogh, Dermot, *Ireland and the Vatican: The Politics and Diplomacy of Church-State Relations, 1922-1960* (Cork: Cork University Press, 1995).

Kiberd, Declan, *Inventing Ireland: The Literature of the Modern Nation* (London: Jonathan Cape, 1995).

King, Carla, 'Co-operation and Rural Development: Plunkett's Approach', in John Davis (ed.), *Rural Change in Ireland* (Belfast: Institute of Irish Studies, Queen's University Belfast, 1999), pp 45–57.

King, Russell and Ian Shuttleworth, 'Ireland's New Wave of Emigration in the 1980s', *Irish Geography*, 21:2 (1988), pp 104–8

King, Russell and Ian Shuttleworth, 'The Emigration and Employment of Irish Graduates', *European Urban and Regional Studies*, 2:1 (1995), pp 21–40.

Kirby, Peadar, *Has Ireland a Future?* (Cork: Mercier Press, 1988).

Knudsen, Ann-Christina Lauring, *Farmers on Welfare: The Making of Europe's Common Agricultural Policy* (Ithaca: Cornell University Press, 2009).

Knudsen, Anna-Chritsina Lauring, 'Romanticising Europe Rural Images in European Union Policies', *Kontur- Tidsskrift for Kulturstudier*, 12 (2005), pp 49–58.

Kotsonouris, Mary, *Retreat from Revolution: the Dáil Courts, 1920-1924* (Dublin: Irish Academic Press, 1994).

Lane, Pádraig G., 'Poor Crayturs. The West's Agricultural Labourers in the Nineteenth Century', in Carla King and Conor McNamara (eds.), *The West of Ireland. New Perspectives on the Nineteenth Century* (Dublin: History Press, 2011), pp 35–49.

Ledwith, Margaret, *Community Development: A Critical and Radical Approach* (Bristol: Policy Press, 2020).

Lee, Joseph, 'Aspects of Corporatist Thought in Ireland: The Commission of Vocational Organisation, 1939-43', in Art Cosgrove and Donal McCartney (eds.), *Studies in Irish History: Presented to R. Dudley Edwards* (Dublin: University College Dublin, 1979), pp 324–46.

Lee, J. J., *Ireland 1912-1985: Politics and Society* (Cambridge: Cambridge University Press, 1989).

Lee, Everett S., 'A Theory of Migration', *Demography* 3, (1966), pp 47–57.

L'Estrange, Seán, '"A Community of Communiites" – Catholic Communitarianism and Societal Crises in Ireland, 1890s-1950s', *Journal of Historical Sociology*, 20:4 (2007), pp 555–78.

Levitt, Peggy, Josh De Wind, and Steven Vertovec, 'International Perspectives on Transnational Migration: An Introduction', *International Migration Review*, 37:3 (2003), pp 565–75.

Lowrey, Annie, *Give People Money: How a Universal Basic Income Would End Poverty, Revolutionise Work, and Remake the World* (New York: Crown, 2018).

Lucey, Denis I. F. and Donald R. Kaldor, *Rural Industrialization: The Impact of Industrialization on Two Rural Communities in Western Ireland* (London: G. Chapman, 1969).

Lyons, F. S. L., 'The Economic Ideas of Parnell', in Michael Roberts (ed.), *Historical Studies*, 11 (London: Bowes and Bowes, 1959), pp 60–78.

Macken-Walsh, Áine and Ben Roche, *Facilitating Farmers' Establishment of Farm Partnerships: A Participatory Template* (Carlow: Teagasc, 2012).

Macken-Walsh, Áine, Peter Cush and Anne Byrne, 'Strategies of Resilience: Cooperation in Irish Family Farming', *Irish Geography*, 53: 1 (2020), pp 23–42.

Mac Laughlin, Jim, *Ireland: The Emigrant Nursery and the World Economy* (Cork: Cork University Press, 1994).

MacLaughlin, Jim, *Troubled Waters: A Social and Cultgural History of Ireland's Sea Fisheries* (Dublin: Four Courts Press, 2010).

Mac Suibhne, Breandán, *The End of Outrage: Post-Famine Adjustment in Rural Ireland* (Oxford: Oxford University Press, 2017).

Mahon, Evelyn, 'From Democracy to Femocracy: The Women's Movement in the Republic of Ireland', in Patrick Clancy, Sheelagh Drudy, Kathleen Lynch & Liam O'Dowd (eds.), *Irish Society: Sociological Perspectives* (Dublin: Institute of Public Administration, 1995), pp 675–708.

Manning, Maurice, *The Blueshirts* (Dublin: Gill and Macmillan, 1970).

Manning, Maurice, *James Dillon* (Dublin: Wolfhound Press, 1999).

Matthews, Alan, 'The Agri-Food Sector', in John O'Hagan and Carol Newman (eds.), *The Economy of Ireland: National and Sectoral Policy Issues* (Dublin: Gill and Macmillan, 2014), pp 287–311.

McAuliffe, Mary, *Senator Kathleen A. Browne 1876-1943: Patriot, Politician and Practical Farmer* (Roscrea: Roscrea Publications, 2008).

McCarthy, Charles, *The Distasteful Challenge* (Dublin: Institute of Public Administration, 1968).

McCashin, Anthony, *Social Security in Ireland* (Dublin: Gill and Macmillan, 2004).

McCracken, J. L., *Representative Government in Ireland: A Study of Dáil Éireann* (London: Oxford University Press, 1958).

McDyer, James, *Father McDyer of Glencolumbkille: An Autobiography* (Dingle: Brandon Books, 1984).

McGarry, Fearghal, *Eoin O'Duffy: A Self-Made Hero* (Oxford: Oxford University Press, 2005).

McGrath, Fiona, 'The Economic, Social and Cultural Implications of Return Migration to Achill Island', in Russell King, (ed.), *Contemporary Irish Migration, GSI Special Publications No. 6* (Dublin: Geographical Society of Ireland, 1991), pp 55–69.

McGuire, James and James Quinn (eds.), *Dictionary of Irish Biography* (Cambridge: Cambridge University Press, 2009).

Meenan, James, *The Irish Economy since 1922* (Liverpool: Liverpool University Press, 1970).

Meredith, David & Mary Gilmartin, 'Changing Rural Ireland', in Cathal O'Donoghue, Ricky Conneely, Kevin Heanue, Deirdre Frost, Brian Leonard & David Meredith, *Rural Economic Development in Ireland* (Athenry: Teagasc, 2014), pp 34–47.

Messenger, John C., *Inish Beag: Isle of Ireland* (New York: Holt, Rinehart and Winston, 1969).

Miliband, Ralph 'Class Analysis', in Anthony Giddens and Jonathan Turner (eds.), *Social Theory Today* (Cambridge: Polity Press, 1987), pp 325–46.

Mitchel, John, *The Last Conquest of Ireland (Perhaps)* (Dublin: UCD Press, 2005).

Moore, Jr., Barrington, *Social Origins of Dictatorship and Democracy: Lord and Peasant in the Making of the Modern World* (Harmondsworth: Penguin Books, 1977 [1966]).

Moran, Gerard, *Sending out Ireland's Poor: Assisted Emigration to North America in the Nineteenth Century* (Dublin: Four Courts Press, 2013).

Moran, Gerard, *Fleeing from Famine in Connemara: James Hack Tuke and his Assisted Emigration Scheme in the 1880s* (Dublin: Four Courts Press, 2018).

Morrissey, James, (ed.), *On the Verge of Want* (Dublin: A & A Farmar, 2001).

Moser, Peter, 'Rural Economy and Female Emigration in the West of Ireland 1936-1956', *U.C.G. Women's Studies Centre Review*, 2 (1993), pp 41–51.

Moser, Peter and Tony Varley, 'Corporatism, Agricultural Modernisation and War in Ireland and Switzerland, 1935 -1955', in Paul Brassley, Yves Segers and Leen Van Molle (eds.), *War, Agriculture, and Food: Rural Europe from the 1930s to the 1950s* (London: Routledge, 2012), pp 137–55.

Moss, Warner, *Political Parties in the Irish Free State* (New York: Columbia University Press, 1933).

Moynihan, Maurice, (ed.), *Speeches and Statements by Éamon de Valera 1917-1973* (Dublin and New York: St. Martin's Press, 1980).

Murphy, Gary, 'The Irish Government, the National Farmers Association, and the European Economic Community, 1955-1964', *New Hibernia Review*, 6:4 (2002), pp 68–84.

Murray, Peter, *Facilitating the Future? US Aid, European Integration and Irish Industrial Viability, 1948-73* (Dublin: UCD Press, 2009).

Murray, Peter and Maria Feeney, *Church, State and Social Science in Ireland: Knowledge, Institutions and the Rebalancing of Power, 1937-73* (Manchester: Manchester University Press, 2017).

Murray, Peter and Maria Feeney, 'The Market for Sociological Ideas in Early 1960s Ireland: Civil Service Departments and the Limerick Rural Survey', *Administration*, 59:1 (2011), pp 111–31.

Ní Laoire, Caitríona, 'The "Green Green Grass of Home"? Return Migration to Rural Ireland', *Journal of Rural Studies*, 23:3 (2007), pp 338–42.

Nic Pháidín, Caoilfhionn & Seán Ó Cearnaigh (eds.), *A New View of the Irish Language* (Dublin: Cois Life, 2008).

Nolan, Matt, *Ráth Chairn: An Talamh Bán* (Mullingar: Comharchumann Rath Chairn, 2018).

Ó Cearbhaill, Diarmuid, 'Bobby Burke and the Tuam Parish Council of Muintir na Tíre', *Journal of the Galway Archaeological and Historical Society*, 62 (2010), pp 202–12.

Ó Ciosáin, Éamon 'Bord don Ghaeltacht: Réamhstair Údarás na Gaeltachta ó 1922 go 1957', in Gearóid Ó Tuathaigh agus Breandán Mac Suibhne (eag.), *Ag cur chun fónaimh* (An Spidéal: Cló Iar-Chonnacht, 2023), lgh. 17–40.

Ó Conghaile, Mícheál (eag.), *Gaeltacht Ráth Cairn: Léachtaí Comórtha* (Indreabhán, Conamara: Cló Iar-Chonnachta, 1986).

O'Connor, Emmet, *Syndicalism in Ireland* (Cork: Cork University Press, 1988).

O'Connor, Emmet, *A Labour History of Ireland 1824-2000* (Dublin: University College Dublin Press, 2011).

Ó Corráin, Daithí, 'Catholicism in Ireland, 1880-2015: Rise, Ascendancy and Retreat', in Thomas Bartlett (ed.), *The Cambridge History of Ireland: Volume IV, 1880 to the Present* (Cambridge: Cambridge University Press, 2018), pp 726–64.

Ó Cuív, Brian, (ed.), *A View of the Irish Language* (Dublin: Stationery Office, 1969).

O'Donoghue, Martin, *The Legacy of the Irish Parliamentary Party in Independent Ireland, 1922-1949* (Liverpool: Liverpool University Press, 2019).

O'Dowd, Liam, 'Intellectuals in 20th Century Ireland: The Case of George Russell (AE)', *The Crane Bag*, 9:1 (1985), pp 6–25.

O'Dowd, Liam, 'Town and Country in Irish Ideology', *Canadian Journal of Irish Studies*, 13:2 (1987), pp 43–54.

O'Dowd, Liam, 'Church, State and Women: The Aftermath of Partition', in Chris Curtin, Pauline Jackson and Barbara O'Connor (eds.), *Gender in Irish Society* (Galway: Galway University Press, 1987), pp 3–36.

O'Driscoll, Josh, Frank Crowley, Justin Doran, Mary O'Shaughnessy, David Meredith & Jesko Zimmermann, 'Is Rural Ireland Really Dying? 'What the Facts and Figures Really Tell Us', RTÉ Brainstorm, https://www.rte.ie/brainstorm/2022/0720/1311198-rural-ireland-population-cso-census-2022, accessed on 23 January 2023.

Ó Fathartaigh, Mícheál, *Irish Agriculture Nationalised: The Dairy Disposal Company and the Making of the Modern Irish Dairy Industry* (Dublin: Institute of Public Administration, 2014).

Ó Fathartaigh, Mícheál, 'More than a Century of Female Pioneers: Women in the Advisory Service', *Today's Farm*, 30:5 (2019), pp 8–9.

Ó Fathartaigh, Mícheál, *Developing Rural Ireland: A History of the Irish Agricultural Services* (Dublin: Wordwell, 2021).

Ó Gráda, Cormac, 'Poverty, Population and Agriculture, 1801-45', in W. E. Vaughan (ed.), *A New History of Ireland Vol. V: Ireland under the Union, Part I* (Oxford: Oxford University Press, 1989), pp 108–36.

Ó Gráda, Cormac, *Ireland: A New Economic History 1780-1939* (Oxford: Oxford University Press, 1994).

Ó Gráda, Cormac, *Across the Sea to Ireland: Return Atlantic Migration Before the First World War, SSRN on-line papers* (Social Science Research Network: Rochester, New York, 2020), http://dx.doi.org/10.2139/ssrn.3491676, accessed 15 July 2020.

O'Hagan, John and Carol Newman (eds.), *The Economy of Ireland* (Dublin: Gill and Macmillan, 2014).

O'Halloran, Martin, *The Lost Gaeltacht: The Land Commission Migration – Clonbur, County Galway and Allenstown, County Meath* (Allenstown: Homefarm Publishing, 2020).

O'Hara, Patricia, *Partners in Production? Women, Farm and Family in Ireland* (Oxford: Berghahn, 1998).

Ó hEallaithe, Donncha, 'Biodh Plean Againn...Tá Gá le Cur Chuige Stratéiseach maidir le Cúrsaí Pleanála sa Ghaeltacht, *Comhar*, 81:3 (2021), lgh. 10–13.

Ó hEallaithe, Donncha, 'Baisteadh "BÁNÚ"...Tá Gluaiseacht Nua Ghaeltachta ar an bhFód – Feachtas faoi Chúrsaí Tithíocht', *Comhar*, 84:3 (2024), lgh. 11–13.

O'Hearn, Denis, 'Just Another Bubble Economy?', in Tom Inglis (ed.), *Are the Irish Different?* (Manchester: Manchester University Press, 2014), pp 34–43.

O'Leary, Don, *Vocationalism and Social Catholicism in Twentieth-Century Ireland: The Search for a Christian Social Order* (Dublin: Irish Academic Press, 2000).

O'Malley, Eoin, *Industry and Economic Development: The Challenge for the Latecomer* (Dublin: Gill and Macmillan, 1989).

Ó Ríain, Seán, 'Where is Ireland in the Worlds of Capitalism?', in Tom Inglis (ed.), *Are the Irish Different?* (Manchester: Manchester University Press, 2014), pp 22–33.

O'Shea, James, *Priests, Politics and Society in Post-famine Ireland: A Study of County Tipperary 1850-1891* (Dublin: Wolfhound Press, 1983).

O'Toole, Pat, 'Three in Four Farmers would Vote for a New Farmers' Party', *Irish Farmers Journal*, 12 August 2023

Ó Tuathaigh, M. A. G., 'The Land Question, Politics and Irish Society, 1922-1960', in P. J. Drudy (ed.), *Ireland: Land, Politics and People* (Cambridge: Cambridge University Press, 1982), pp 167–89.

Ó Tuathaigh, Gearóid, 'Ireland's Land Questions: A Historical Perspective', in John Davis (ed.), *Rural Change in Ireland* (Belfast: The Institute of Irish Studies, Queen's University Belfast, 1999), pp 16–31.

Ó Tuathaigh, Gearóid, 'Cultural Visions and the New State: Embedding and Embalming', in Gabriel Doherty and Dermot Keogh (eds.), *De Valera's Irelands* (Cork: Mercier Press, 2003), pp 166–84.

Ó Tuathaigh, Gearóid, 'Irish Land Questions in the State of the Union', in Fergus Campbell and Tony Varley (eds.), *Land Questions in Modern Ireland* (Manchester: Manchester University Press, 2013), pp 3–24.

Ó Tuathaigh, Gearóid, Lillis Ó Laoire, Seán Ua Suilleabháin agus Micheál Ó Conghaile (eag.), *Pobal na Gaeltachta: A Scéal agus a Dhán* (Indreabhán, Conamara: Cló Iar-Chonnachta, 2000).

Ó Tuathaigh, Gearóid agus Breandán Mac Suibhne (eag.), *Ag cur chun fónaimh: Údarás na Gaeltachta ó 1980 i leith* (an Spidéal: Cló Iar-Chonnacht, 2023).

Peillon, Michel, *Contemporary Irish Society: An Introduction* (Dublin: Gill and Macmillan, 1982).

Power, M. & R. Roche, *National Farm Survey 1990* (Dublin: Rural Economy Teagasc, 1992).

Punch, Adrian and Catherine Finneran, 'The Demographic and Socio-economic Characteristics of Migrants, 1986-1996', *Journal of the Statistical and Social Inquiry Society of Ireland*, XXV111: 1 (1999), pp 213–63

Riordan, Susannah, 'The Unpopular Front: Catholic Revival and Irish Cultural Identity, 1932-48', in Mike Cronin and John M. Regan, (eds.), *The Politics of Independent Ireland, 1922-49* (Basingstoke: Palgrave Macmillan, 2000), pp 98–120.

Rodgers, Daniel T., *Atlantic Crossings: Social Politics in a Progressive Age* (Cambridge, Mass.: Cambridge: Harvard University Press, 1998).

Rohan, Dorine, *Marriage Irish Style* (Cork: Mercier Press, 1969).

Rumpf, E. and A. C. Hepburn, *Nationalism and Socialism in Twentieth-Century Ireland* (Liverpool: Liverpool University Press, 1977).

Russell, Elizabeth, 'Holy Crosses, Guns and Roses: Themes in Popular Reading Material', in Joost Augusteijn (ed.), *Ireland in the 1930s: New Perspectives* (Dublin: Four Courts Press, 1999), pp 11–28.

Ryan, Raymond, 'The National Farmers' and Ratepayers' League', *Studia Hibernica*, 34 (2006/2007), pp 173–92.

Sammon, Patrick J., *In the Land Commission: A Memoir 1933-1978* (Dublin: Ashford Press, 1997).

Scheper-Hughes, Nancy, *Saints, Scholars and Schizophrenics: Mental Illness in Rural Ireland* (Berkeley: University of California Press, 1979).

Sexton, Gerry (J. J.), Brendan M. Walsh, Damian F. Hannan & Doreen McMahon, *The Economic and Social Implications of Emigration*, NESC Report No. 90 (Dublin: The National and Economic and Social Council, 1991).

Sheppard, Barry, 'Muintir na Tíre's Fr John Hayes – "Ireland's Rural Apostle" in America', *History Ireland*, 32 (1), 2024, pp 42–44.

Shiel, Michael, *The Quiet Revolution: The Electrification of Rural Ireland* (Dublin: O'Brien Press, 1984).

Shortall, Sally, *Women and Farming, Property and Power* (Houndsmill, Basingstoke: Macmillan Palgrave, 1999).

Shortall, Sally, 'Changing Gender Roles in Irish Farm Households: Continuity and Change', *Irish Geography*, 50:2 (2017), pp 175–91.

Shortall, Sally & Anne Byrne, 'Gender and Sustainability in Rural Ireland', in John McDonagh, Tony Varley and Sally Shortall (eds.), *A Living Countryside: The Politics of Sustainable Rural Development* (Ashgate: Aldershot, 2009), pp 287–302.

Silverman, Marilyn, *An Irish Working Class: Explorations in Political Economy and Hegemony, 1800-1950* (*Toronto:* University of Toronto Press, 2001).

Sjaastad, Larry A., 'The Costs and Returns of Human Migration', *The Journal of PoliticalEconomy,* 70: 5ii (1962), pp 80–93.

Snell, K. D. M., 'A Drop of Water from a Stagnant Pool? Interwar Detective Fiction and the Rural Community', *Social History,* 35:1 (2010), pp 21–50.

So, Alvin Y., *Social Change and Development: Modernization, Dependency, and World-Systems Theories* (London: Sage Publications, 1990).

Steele, E. D., 'J. S. Mill and the Irish Question: The Principles of Political Economy, 1848-1865', *The Historical Journal,* 13:2 (1970), pp 216–36.

Tierney, Mark, *The Story of Muintir na Tire 1931-2001 – The First Seventy Years* (Tipperary: Muintir na Tire Publications, 2004).

Tovey, Hilary 'Rural Sociology in Ireland', *Irish Journal of Sociology,* 2:1 (1992), pp 96–121.

Tovey, Hilary, Trutz Haase, and Chris Curtin, 'Understanding Rural Poverty', in Chris Curtin, Trutz Haase and Hilary Tovey (eds.), *Poverty in Rural Ireland: A Political Economy Approach* (Dublin: Oak Tree Press, 1996), pp 1–58.

Tucker, Vincent, 'State and Community: A Case Study of Glencolumbkille', in Chris Curtin and Thomas M. Wilson (eds.), *Ireland From Below: Social Change and Local Communities* (Galway: Galway University Press, 1989), pp 283–300.

Tucker, Vincent, 'Images of Development and Under-Development in Glencolumbkille, Co. Donegal, 1830-1970', in John Davis (ed.), *Rural Change in Ireland* (Belfast: Institute of Irish Studies, Queen's University Belfast, 1999), pp 84–115.

Valiulis, Maryann Gianella, *The Making of Inequality: Women, Power and Gender Ideology in the Irish Free State, 1922-1937* (Dublin: Four Courts Press, 2019).

Valiulis, Maryann Gianella, and Mary O'Dowd (eds.), *Women and Irish History* (Dublin: Merlin Publishing, 1997).

Varley, Tony, 'Agrarian Crime and Social Control: Sinn Féin and the Land Question in the West of Ireland in 1920', in Mike Tomlinson, Tony Varley & Ciarán McCullagh (eds.), *Whose Law and Order? Aspects of Crime and Social Control in Irish Society* (Belfast: Sociological Association of Ireland, 1988), pp 54–75.

Varley, Tony, 'Farmers Against Nationalists: The Rise and Fall of Clann na Talmhan in Galway', in Gerard Moran & Raymond Gillespie (eds.), *Galway: History & Society* (Dublin: Geography Publications, 1996), pp 589–622.

Varley, Tony, 'On the Road to Extinction: Agrarian Parties in Twentieth-Century Ireland', *Irish Political Studies,* 25:4 (2010), pp 581–601.

Varley, Tony, '"Down with the Paris Farmer!" Frank MacDermot and Class Politics in 1930s Roscommon', in Richie Farrell, Kieran O'Conor and Matthew Potter (eds.), *Roscommon: History and Society* (Dublin: Geography Publications, 2018), pp 613–35.

Varley, Tony, 'Learning to Make Irish Agriculture Modern: Civil Society Elites, the State and Coping with the Challenges of Globalisation in the 1890s', in Joe Regan & Cathal Smith (eds.), *Agrarian Reform and Resistance in an Age of Globalisation: The Euro-American World and Beyond, 1780-1914* (London: Routledge, 2019), pp 185–201.

Varley, Tony & Chris Curtin, 'Defending Rural Interests against Nationalists in 20th Century Ireland', in John Davis (ed.), *Rural Change in Ireland* (Belfast: Institute of Irish Studies Queen's University Belfast, 1999), pp 58–83.

Varley, Tony & Chris Curtin, 'Communitarian Populism and the Politics of Rearguard Resistance in Rural Ireland', *Community Development Journal,* 37:1 (2002), pp 20–32.

Vaughan, W. E., *Landlords and Tenants in Ireland 1848-1904* (Dundalk: The Economic and Social History Society of Ireland, 1984).

Vaughan, W. E. (ed.), *New History of Ireland, V part I* (Oxford: Oxford University Press, 1989).

Viney, Ethna, 'Women in Rural Ireland', *Christus Rex,* XXII: 4 (1968), pp 333–42.

Walby, Sylvia, 'Theorising Patriarchy', *Sociology,* 23:2 (1989), pp 213–34.

Walsh, John, *The Politics of Expansion: The Transformation of Educational Policy in the Republic of Ireland, 1957-72* (Manchester: Manchester University Press, 2009).

Walter, Bronwen, 'Tradition and Ethnic Interaction: Second Wave Settlement in Luton and Bolton', in Colin Clarke, David Ley & Ceri Peach (eds.), *Geography and Ethnic Pluralism* (London: Routledge, 1984), pp 258–83.

Walter, Bronwen, *Outsiders Inside: Whiteness, Place and Irish Women* (London: Routledge, 2001).

Weber, Max, *The Protestant Ethic and the Spirit of Capitalism*, trans Talcott Parsons [1904–05] (London: Allen and Unwin, 1930).

Whelan, Christopher T. & Richard Layte, 'Opportunities for all in the New Ireland?', in Tony Fahey, Helen Russell and Christopher T. Whelan, (eds), *Best of Times? The Social Impact of the Celtic Tiger* (Dublin: Institute of Public Administration, 2007), pp 67–85.

Whitaker, T. K. 'Economic Planning in Ireland', in Basil Chubb and Patrick Lynch (eds.), *Economic Development and Planning* (Dublin: Institute of Public Administration, 1969), pp 291–301.

Whyte, J. H., *Church and State in Modern Ireland, 1923-1979*, 2nd edn. ([1980]; Dublin: Gill and Macmillan, 1984).

Wiel, Jérôme aan de, 'The Commission, the Council and the Irish Application for the EEC', in Mervyn O'Driscoll, Dermot Keogh& Jerome aan de Wiel (eds.), *Ireland through European Eyes: Western Europe, the EEC and Ireland, 1945-1973* (Cork: Cork University Press, 2013), pp 314–81.

Winship, Janice, 'New Disciplines for Women and the Rise of the Chain Store in the 1930s', Maggie Andrews and Mary Talbot (eds.), *All The World and Her Husband: Women in Twentieth-Century Consumer Culture* (London: Cassell, 2000), pp 23–45.

Index